"Manners are of
more importance than laws.
Upon them, in a great measure,
the laws depend."

—Edmund Burke,
18th-century philosopher

ALSO BY STEVEN PETROW

- *Dancing Against the Darkness:
  A Journey Through America in the Age of AIDS*

- *Ending the HIV Epidemic* (editor)

- *The HIV Drug Book* (editor)

- *When Someone You Know Has AIDS, 3rd edition*

- *The Essential Book of Gay Manners and Etiquette*

- *The Lost Hamptons* (with Richard Barons)

STEVEN PETROW'S

COMPLETE GAY & LESBIAN MANNERS

THE DEFINITIVE GUIDE TO LGBT LIFE

=

WITH SALLY CHEW

WORKMAN PUBLISHING · NEW YORK

Library of Congress Cataloging-in-Publication Data is available.

ISBN 978-0-7611-5670-3 (paperback)
ISBN 978-0-7611-6522-4 (hardcover)

Design by Lidija Tomas
Illustrations by Paul Cox
Author photo by Bryan Regan
Stock photo p175 © Galina Barskaya/Fotolia

All names appearing in this work are fictitious. Any resemblance to real persons, living or dead, is purely coincidental.

Workman books are available at special discounts when purchased in bulk for premiums and sales promotions as well as for fund-raising or educational use. Special editions or book excerpts also can be created to specification. For details, contact the Special Sales Director at the address below or send an e-mail to specialmarkets@workman.com.

WORKMAN PUBLISHING COMPANY, INC.
225 Varick Street
New York, NY 10014-4381
www.workman.com

Printed in the United States of America
First printing June 2011

10 9 8 7 6 5 4 3 2 1

For Jim

With love and gratitude

Support LGBT nonprofits—
A percentage of all author royalties are donated
to the fight for equal rights and protection for all
including the excellent work of
the Gay, Lesbian and Straight Education Network (GLSEN) and
the National Center for Lesbian Rights (NCLR)

Contents

Introduction

Every time I've mentioned over the past few years that I was writing a book on lesbian, gay, bisexual, and transgender (LGBT) manners, I got pretty much the same quizzical look. You know the one: the arched eyebrow, the piercing stare. You're probably doing it right now. It took me a while to figure out what was going on, but then it dawned on me: The whole idea of LGBT manners is new, and somewhat baffling to most everyone. It turns out that behind that look are some very provocative and meaningful questions.

Let me start with perhaps the most personal question I get asked: Where does an imperfect fellow like me get off writing a book like this? I've stumbled over introductions, asked to bring a boyfriend du jour to a formal wedding, and committed serious violations of the PDA rule (on the beach, in bars, even in the rafters of a Broadway theater). My worst transgression? I once outed a lesbian colleague who, while quite open with her friends about her sexual orientation, was not ready for me to tell our coworkers. Does all this mean that I'm a hypocrite to be writing about manners? I don't think so. Just a realist—and probably not very different from those of you who try to do the "right" thing but sometimes make gaffes or fall short.

Then there are the questions from those who find manners books to be passé or just irrelevant to their lives. How much does anybody really care where the fish fork goes or what the correct order is for a monogram on your shirt pocket or personal stationery? My answer: I don't lose sleep over such fussy details. This book takes a larger point of view: I argue that treating everyone with respect and decency makes for a better and fairer world, and that manners are among the best ways to make sure we start out—and continue—on the right foot.

That is what much of my work is about: Helping people live with greater confidence and self-esteem through simple principles of human kindness;

demonstrating how much language matters; urging recognition of LGBT families and their new or invented traditions; and documenting the customs and practices of our commitment to and love for each other.

It's up to you whether forks and monograms enter into this picture. I do feel, however, that having a contemporary version of a few key old-school manners in mind—or at least on hand for reference—gives us the freedom to focus on more pressing matters.

Here's another question I've been asked frequently: "Are gay manners any different than straight ones?" My answer: No, we don't set the table any differently than straight people. Nor do we treat houseguests in any special way. Values are values, whether you're LGBT or straight. But, yes, our weddings, our children's coming-of-age ceremonies, and many of the other rites and rituals we participate in often have a decidedly different flavor. Consider these five contemporary LGBT manners predicaments:

- If a child has two mothers and a known sperm donor, what does he or she call them?
- If you're the victim of anti-gay bullying, how do you respond and stay safe?
- If you're going through a gender transition, what and when do you tell others?
- If you're HIV-positive, when's the right time to reveal your health status—and when is it not a good idea at all?
- If you're persona non grata to your lover's parents, how do you handle the holidays and other family get-togethers?

Unfortunately, you won't get much help on the particular manners quandaries of LGBT people and families from mainstream etiquette books. We're largely invisible there. Those authors don't advise a gay or lesbian person how to make a domestic-partner or a civil-union "proposal." They don't explain the mechanics of planning a funeral or composing an obituary when a partner's family doesn't recognize your status as next-of-kin. Even in their newest editions, there's not a word about bisexual or transgender people. Sadly, what is written about gay people is—how can I phrase this in a mannerly way?—homophobic. (That is, except for the very gay-friendly Judith Martin, aka Miss Manners.) Take, as an example, the editorial decision in *The Amy Vanderbilt Complete Book of Etiquette* to talk about the rise of gay families as a result of "the breakdown of the traditional family."

In these pages, by contrast, LGBT people are front and center, out and proud—with our straight friends and families a little to stage right (but still respectfully in full view). The book deals with uniquely LGBT etiquette questions, but often in the context of more general ones. For instance, while seeking a job, there's the matter of deciding whether or not to be out on your résumé. Or when traveling, what to do if you have trouble checking in as a same-sex couple. The discussion on manners during the holidays and at other social occasions is full of advice on dealing with family members who might not accept your sexual orientation or gender identity, or who don't treat your partner (if you have one) the same as a straight sibling's spouse.

We live in a time of enormous change: Technology has transformed how LGBT people date and find sex; "Don't ask, don't tell" has been voted down; the number of gay unions from the coasts to the heartland continues to grow. With change after change, it's hard to keep up—and manners certainly have not.

Keep in mind that with turbulent times, social mores and manners always race to catch up with the new world order. It's no coincidence that the first edition of Emily Post's *Etiquette* was published soon after the bloodshed and upheaval of World War I; similarly, Amy Vanderbilt put pen to paper in the shadow of World War II, trying to make sense of the vast changes wrought by the baby boom and then the sexual revolution. Today, we find ourselves at battle on two fronts—overseas and here at home in the form of a culture war. As in previous eras, manners struggle to help us all make sense of these changes.

If you have any doubts about how quickly the world is changing, then pause with me while I recall the Sunday in 2003 when I opened the Styles section of the *New York Times* and saw that the featured wedding in the Vows column was between the playwright Tony Kushner and the writer Mark Harris. It wasn't the paper's first same-sex wedding announcement, but the prominence of the story took my breath away. A generation ago, there were no same-sex wedding announcements because there were no legal same-sex weddings in this country. Today, the vast majority of American and Canadian newspapers print such wedding and celebration announcements weekly.

This seismic shift is likewise reflected in the explosion of families with two dads or two moms or a single gay parent—even their depiction on sitcoms and in mainstream films. The experience of being out at work used to be enjoyed by a rare few, as most of us had good reason to fear harassment, discrimination, even being fired because of our sexual orientation, never mind for being transgender. Yet the majority of the largest employers now provide benefits to same-sex partners and spouses of employees, and actually *aim* to attract qualified LGBT employees in order to remain competitive. Another set of mileposts: In 1997, it shocked many when Ellen DeGeneres came out on the cover of *Time* ("Yep, I'm gay!"), losing her sitcom in the process. Then, in 2008, her wedding to Portia de Rossi graced the cover of *People*—and only enhanced her popularity as a daytime TV host.

This is not to say we have blended right in and are accepted for who we are. You can still be fired from your job for being gay or trans. Your kids may be bullied or worse because of your (or their) sexual orientation or for being too feminine or too masculine. We can't have legally sanctioned weddings in most states. No, LGBT people do not have parity with our straight brothers and sisters, parents, friends, and coworkers. That's a fact. And that's why we need smart, practical guidance for the often joyful, awkward, and, yes, sometimes painful social situations that modern LGBT life puts before us.

———————

Even with the best of intentions, language is a tricky and sticky matter that merits a central place in any manners guide. The words and phrases we use—or misuse—reveal much about our consideration of others, even our values. For example, I often hear straight people use the phrase "sexual preference" rather than "sexual orientation," failing to understand that the former implies that being gay is a choice (it's not) rather than an inherent identity. Along the same lines, the phrase "that's so gay" is regularly bandied about today to mean anything that is lame, stupid, or ugly. Even if its use isn't malevolent, such a phrase is hurtful and offensive and perpetuates negative stereotypes.

Apropos, please allow me to explain a few things about how language is used in these pages since many a firestorm has raged as a result of careless—or uninformed—usage. First, there's LGBT, which is the acronym for just about everyone who isn't straight. Likewise, "gay" by itself is an umbrella term that usually refers to all lesbian, gay, and bisexual people (though not to transmen and -women). But when I've written "lesbian," it means lesbian. Similarly, the alternating use of pronouns is intended to provide balance and gender neutrality, so when there's a "he" in one entry, usually it could just as well have been a "she" (and vice versa in the next entry). Of course, sometimes there are gender-specific entries, particularly when discussing sex, two brides and two grooms, and birthing children. Nevertheless, it's hard not to trip up in the "he/she" and "him/her" distinctions in any comprehensive discussion of the LGBT world, especially when discussing trans people.

Another potential minefield within the LGBT community is the use of terms like "queer" and "homosexual." Historically, "queer" was highly pejorative slang for "gay," but many have now reclaimed it as a self-affirming umbrella term for all LGBT people. In recent years, it has also gained greater currency because of TV programs like *Queer Eye for the*

QUEERY

"My brother outed me."

Q I recently told my older brother that I think I'm gay. I'm thirteen and he's eighteen. Even though he promised me he wouldn't tell Mom and Dad, he did. Our mom is not one bit happy about me right now, and I'm mad at my brother. What can I do now?

A Good for you for coming out; it's great that you were able to have this insight about yourself at such a young age. It's too bad that your brother didn't keep your confidence, but you'll find that most people whom you tell will honor a request to keep this news private. Over time, you'll probably find less and less need for secrecy.

Even though your brother hijacked your coming out, that doesn't mean you need to talk about it with anyone if you're not ready. It's perfectly fine to say kindly—these are your parents, after all—"I'm not ready" or "I'm not comfortable talking with you about my sexuality now." Maybe you'd rather talk to someone your own age? If you don't have peers who know you're gay or whom you could now tell, find out if your school has an LGBT youth group or a Gay-Straight Alliance. Finding others who are in the process of coming out or who have their own experiences to share with you can be really helpful.

Straight Guy and the Showtime series *Queer as Folk,* as well as in academia, where "queer studies" is often the appellation of choice for LGBT scholarship. In the end, much depends on who is using the term and in what context (see also Straight Talk this page and The Essentials on the acronym LGBTQ on page 19).

The word "homosexual" has gone through hard times as well. Before the LGBT rights movement began during the Stonewall Riots in 1969, "homosexual" was standard usage among both gays and straights, often pronounced "HO-mo-sexual"; at the time, homosexuality was still classified as a mental disorder by the American Psychiatric Association (APA) and other similar groups. But in the mid-1970s, the APA dropped its designation, and "gay" and "lesbian" soon started to curry favor within our community. But it wasn't until late in the last century that gay men and lesbians were finally successful in getting mainstream publications like the *Times* and dictionaries to use "gay" and "lesbian" instead of the clinical-sounding "homosexual." (It's noteworthy that the *Times* still doesn't allow "LGBT" in its pages.) Ironically, the word "gay," so excitedly embraced after Stonewall, has now further evolved—or devolved?—so that some people today reject it as too narrow or dated.

⸻

As I did the research for this book, talked with dozens of experts, and then started writing, I worried about the perception that, as a good friend put it to me, "by creating a set of rules for the LGBT community, you're repressing our rebelliousness and individuality." So, let me be as clear here as I was with my friend: I'm opposed to the idea that there is a correct face for us to present to the world—as some continue to maintain—in hopes of gaining an edge in the battle for LGBT rights and acceptance. I can't condone those in our community who pay only lip service to diversity, preferring to marginalize others—whether people of color, leather dykes, transmen and -women, drag queens, or bears. I hope you'll find that I've been helpful without judgment—and specific without creating another set of rules or pretending to provide one-size-fits-all answers.

STRAIGHT TALK

Is it ever okay for straight people to use slang terms like "faggot," "dyke," or "queer"?

No: Even straight people with LGBT-friendly sensibilities are better off avoiding those terms. You're probably asking this question because you've heard LGBT people say them. Lesbians frequently use "dyke" to refer to one another, in a warm, family sort of way. Gay men will sometimes do the same with the term "faggot." These phrases, however, are still extremely offensive when used as epithets by those outside the gay community, and, in fact, not all LGBT people are comfortable using them because of their history. Out of a straight person's mouth, they just don't work at all.

Finally, a question that every one of the eyebrow-raisers raised: For whom is this book intended? First and foremost, it's for those of us who call ourselves lesbian, gay, bisexual, transgender, queer, or questioning; you may not necessarily read it from start to finish but I hope you'll turn to it at the big milestones in life—when coming out, starting to date, initiating sexual relationships, moving in together, making a commitment, planning a ceremony, or having a family. Or maybe you'll remember to check its index when you need to send a condolence letter, make a hotel reservation, or write an obituary.

In addition to the hundreds of entries in these pages, you'll find several repeated features. Each "Queery" is a real question about a real LGBT social situation that has been asked of me through my website, www.gaymanners .com. Similarly, the "Vox Populi" displays your responses to many of the manners dilemmas raised in these pages (see Facebook.com/gay manners for all of them). "The Essentials" provide background on key topics; for instance, "7 Ways to Learn More About Gay-friendly Companies" or "How to Write the Dear Birth Mother" letter when seeking a surrogate to carry a child.

A good etiquette book is like a good travel guide, especially if you're visiting from another planet (so to speak). In that light, this book is also meant for straight people—our friends, family members, and coworkers. They will find guidance in these pages on the topography, currency, language, and native idiosyncrasies of LGBT people. Each chapter has what I've called "Straight Talk," questions from heterosexual visitors to my site about LGBT social situations: What do the mothers of two brides wear to a same-sex wedding? May I ask a friend if she's a lesbian? Is it ever okay for straight people to use slang terms like "faggot," "dyke," or "queer"? (Please see page xiii.)

It's also my aspiration that LGBT people will find *Steven Petrow's Complete Gay & Lesbian Manners* to be "as much a guide to contemporary living as it is an etiquette book," as Amy Vanderbilt once characterized her own work—but with a twist.

Steven Petrow
Chapel Hill, North Carolina
February 2011

PART I

BEING LGBT

CHAPTER 1

Coming Out

"Yep, I'm Gay"

———————————— ▬▬▬ ————————————

Let's start with a nod to history: If you're a person of a certain age, your initial attempts at coming out were most likely awkward at best and devastating at worst. First there was the long, private struggle to become comfortable enough with your own sexuality to actually talk about it with a close friend or confidante. Then there were the conversations themselves—tentative mumblings, explosions of guilt, bursts of jubilation, or stammering combinations of all three. And finally, most memorable of all, there was the stunned silence that often greeted the big "confession." All this drama made a certain sense: Back in the day, even the American Psychiatric Association considered homosexuality a mental disorder (until 1973), and newspapers sometimes referred to gay people as "perverts." The emotional baggage connected to just thinking you might be gay was very heavy stuff.

Fast-forward a generation or two (thank goodness!), and enter a changed world. LGBT people come out a lot younger than before—some are not even in their teens yet—and they come out differently. The boundaries between gay, lesbian, bi, and trans are more fluid, and many young people share a distaste for labels of *any* kind. It's not unheard of for a young person who's never even kissed someone of the same sex to be comfortable coming out as "curious," "bi," or "questioning," mentioning this to her friends and sometimes her teachers and parents along the way without great fanfare. Or as a letter writer to *Details* put it, "It's not 'Are you?' or 'Aren't you?'; it's 'Will you?' or 'Won't you?'"

A declaration may be as simple and off-the-cuff as "I'm a lesbian," which is how one ten-year-old explained things to her parents and brother one night at dinner. Or "I'm having sex with _____ ," the name of the sex partner being perhaps the only clue to anyone's sexual orientation. One young man recently posted continual status updates of the coming-out conversation he had with his family, presenting it to the entire blogosphere in real time.

Indeed, the Web has facilitated coming out, first connecting young people to information about LGBT life that they might never have gotten from their families, schools, or religious institutions, and then, perhaps more crucially, to one another. There has never been an easier time for young LGBT people to find each other, whether in chat rooms, on social networking sites, or through e-mail, texting, GPS apps, you name it.

Of course, just because coming out is easier than it used to be for some people doesn't mean it's easy for *you*. Your family may harbor prejudice. Or your particular racial, ethnic, or socioeconomic mix could present obstacles. Or you may fear being bullied or harassed if you come out. Certainly, coming out as transgender has its own challenges (please see page 14). Then there's the fact that our vocabulary falls short of reality, describing only a few sexual orientations and gender identities. With all these potential stumbling blocks, don't think you're alone to feel confused or even afraid.

All of this is to say that there's no one way to come out. You may find yourself doing so spontaneously or in a deliberate, step-by-step process. You may sit down with a parent or best friend over a Coke or a rum-and-Coke, write an actual letter by hand, or simply tweet your news to the world in a nanosecond. The essential thing is to do it on your own terms.

TAKING THE FIRST STEPS

Coming out is not about "flaunting" anything; it's about telling people something very important about who you are. For every social butterfly who comes out on Facebook by updating her status and every guy who has an in-depth coming-out conversation with his parents while wearing a T-shirt that says I'M QUEER! GET USED TO IT, there are plenty of people who prefer to make their sexual orientation or gender identity known in quieter, less assertive ways. No approach is better than another; in fact, how you come out is among the most personal decisions you'll ever make, and you may actually deploy different strategies at different times in your life or with different people.

Whom to Tell First

Most people come out first to a close friend, often someone who is LGBT. Whether you spill the beans in one huge confessional or just mention your sexuality or gender identity in passing, treat whomever you tell with the same respect and consideration you'll be expecting in return. It's important that you trust this confidante, whether he's your best friend, a teacher, a work colleague, a professional counselor, or someone in your family. A recent poll on my website showed that nearly half of the respondents first came out to an LGBT friend, while a quarter started with a straight friend. Only one in eight told a family member first.

These four steps can be helpful:

1. **Make a plan:** Ask your confidante to go out for coffee, take a quiet walk, or meet somewhere you will have privacy and feel comfortable. If there's any chance at all that the person might have a hostile or violent response, take that into consideration when you choose where to go. Explain beforehand that you have something personal you'd like to discuss, but don't make it sound too serious. Coming out is not like revealing a serious disease, an intractable problem, or a crime (by the way, you can "acknowledge" your homosexuality but don't "admit" it—"admitting" is something you do when wrongdoing is involved, and there's nothing at all the matter with your acknowledging who you really are).

2. **Consider all possible reactions:** How your friend responds isn't really up to you—although how you set up the conversation

---

VOX POPULI

To whom did you come out first?

"My sister and my best friend . . . but they knew before I did!"

"I came out as bi to my bi friend, and then a few other friends."

"I came out to my children first, because they were teenagers and it was going to affect their lives, too."

"To a friend who I knew would be supportive and would help me come out to the rest of my friends and family."

"A friend in high school who clued me in that he was also questioning his sexuality, and who I wanted to sleep with."

---

can help increase the likelihood of a favorable reaction. Usually, respect and trust beget respect and trust. Expect the best: acceptance, a warm embrace, words of support, as well as love and continued friendship. But prepare for the worst: rejection, anger, even the loss of the relationship. You may be equally surprised to find a friend had no idea, or to hear him say, "Oh really? That's no big deal" or "I knew it all along." Each time you come out, you will have a better sense of how to prepare for the next time.

3. **Do your research:** Although it's not your job to educate people about what being gay or transgender means, some people you come out to may have questions, and knowing the answers can help you feel more confident about how you respond. "No, it's not a choice," you might need to say if asked why you are gay. "When did you choose to be straight?" if further pressed, or "Mom,

I *do* hope you'll be a grandparent one day. There are lots of ways for LGBT people to have kids." If you can't find what you're looking for online, contact a group like PFLAG (Parents, Families and Friends of Lesbians and Gays) or GLSEN (Gay, Lesbian and Straight Education Network). Hold on to the phone number or URL in case you end up wanting to share it with the person you're coming out to. (For more coming-out information, visit www.gaymanners.com.)

4. **Keep it simple:** You might start off with, "We've known each other for a very long time and there's something personal about me that I'd like you to know." Or, "I want you to know that I'm a lesbian." Or even just, "I have a girlfriend." No need to spill your guts or make a tortured declaration. The more confident and together you sound, the more likely you'll get a positive response.

STRAIGHT TALK

"I'm straight, but I have some gay friends, and twice now people I'm close to have chosen me to be the one they tell first. I get tongue-tied and am not sure how to be helpful or what they want me to say. Any suggestions?"

Since friends are singling you out to be the recipient of this news, I'm going to guess that you're a trustworthy and supportive sort of person. Which is a great contrast with what happened when I told my best straight male friend in college that I was gay. He turned away and we really never spoke again. Believe me when I say I was hurt—and angry.

All of which is to make the point that the way friends and family members respond to someone's coming out really does matter. In a decent world, they'd be happy and shout "Mazel tov!" or "Congratulations!" In a dream world, it wouldn't even matter anymore. But, if words of support aren't in your vocabulary or heart right now, I'd suggest you thank the person for being honest with you and emphasize that you still feel the same way as before. Most LGBT people fear rejection more than anything when they're coming out.

For you, a concrete way to help your friends is to discuss and think through the ramifications of telling others. Are there financial considerations to coming out (say, she's still in college and being supported by Mom and Dad)? Or does your friend live in one of the many states that doesn't protect LGBT people against employment discrimination? It's not that you should try to talk your friend out of coming out—hardly—just that you can offer to help him or her get a handle on some of the potential obstacles ahead.

Telling Your Parents

After you've told your friends about your sexual orientation or gender identity, it may be time to have a talk with Mom and Dad—or whoever has played the parental role in your life. Even if your relationship with your folks has been distant or awkward, sharing this important aspect of yourself usually ends up being a relief—if not immediately, then later. "My father said he didn't 'understand,'" says one lesbian who came out to her parents when she was in her early twenties. "But eventually I realized his words didn't really matter, because he was always so supportive of me."

Having a good group of friends, backup from a counselor or an online community will be helpful at this point, too. What's key is being prepared for this conversation and able to anticipate your parents' needs and reactions the best you can. Remember that while you may have been thinking about this conversation for a very long time, it will likely take them some getting used to. As part of your homework, ask yourself these questions:

• Do you feel good, or at least clear, about being LGBT? Can you express that?

• Have you done enough research—either by talking with friends or teachers or through reading—to be prepared for the variety of questions your parents might have?

• Have you developed a support network that you can rely on if the conversation doesn't go as you hope?

• Do your parents have religious or political beliefs that will make it difficult for them to accept what you're saying? Are you prepared to engage them in a discussion about those?

• What's your reason for telling them now? Do you want them to know you better? Is this a way to reach out and be closer to them? Or do you have a boyfriend or girlfriend whom you'd like them to know about?

After you've thought through all the angles, make a date to sit down with your parents; once you're together, be direct. Definitely don't assume you know how your parents will react. Even liberal parents who

VOX POPULI

If you were coming out to your folks and had a boyfriend or girlfriend, would you introduce the person at the same time or do it separately?

"I would not introduce my girlfriend at first, and that is because they would most likely blame her and not take me seriously, thinking it was just 'that woman's fault' or a 'phase.'"

"Do it all at once and get it over with."

"There's an argument to be made for letting Mom and Dad know that you're well loved, since one of their concerns is likely to be that old nonsense about how gay people are all so lonely and sad."

"I'd tell them about myself and later tell them about her because I don't want them trying to threaten her, which I think they would since they're Evangelical Christians."

"Are you sure it's not a phase?"
"Absolutely!"

advocate for LGBT rights outside the home can have trouble with the idea of having a gay or trans child of their own, not necessarily because they're hypocrites but often out of an instinct to "protect" you from difficult experiences. Said one Berkeley mom after her daughter told her she planned to transition, "Above all, I just worry about the challenges she'll face." Likewise, factors such as religion, a parent's own experiences in life, their race, or their ethnicity can make for unexpected reactions. Regardless, most parents do come around in time.

Why Come Out

As you contemplate coming out to the straight people in your life, you may wonder why it's necessary. It's true that remaining in the closet is always an option; in previous generations many kept their sexuality private, and transgender people still often navigate a mixture of public and private identities. However, the stress and toll of maintaining a secret life can be challenging, even damaging.

Coming out, on the other hand, makes you visible to other LGBT people who can connect you with new friends and a new community. They can offer you moral support for this important step, plus avenues for finding work, leisure activities, and lovers.

Additionally, each time someone comes out, he opens the minds of his loved ones by setting a positive example of an LGBT person they now know. You can also serve as a role model—and a resource—to others on their coming-out journeys.

The story of longtime Congressman Barney Frank, who for many years lived a secret gay life that exploded in a sex scandal, is

QUEERY

"Mom, I'm a lesbian. Now, meet my new girlfriend."

Q **I always said that I would tell my parents that I'm gay when I actually had a girlfriend. Now I'm in high school and I do have one, but I'm not exactly sure how to do it. Like this? "Hi, Mom and Dad, I'm gay and I'd like to introduce my new girlfriend, Mindy."**

A First, two snaps to you for wanting to tell your parents. You're showing respect to them by revealing a core part of yourself, and let's hope they reciprocate with that same kind of respect for you. While I can understand that you might like to reveal all your "secrets" at once, I'd suggest you save the information about your girlfriend for the next stage of coming out. That gives your parents a chance to absorb first things first. Nevertheless, if they ask, "Are you seeing anyone?", use that as the door opener to say,

"As a matter of fact, yes . . ."

By the way, be patient if you don't get the response you're hoping for when you come out. When I finally told my own parents, I chose to read them a letter I had written because I felt I would have more control over the message and my emotions. Their initial reaction was a mix of "How do you know?", "We know a great therapist," and disappointment. But over time, they came to accept and even embrace my sexual orientation.

cautionary not just for public officials but for the rest of us thinking about coming out: "In my case, I found it was hard to meet people—being closeted—in a normal way," he said. "I had the occasion to use hustlers and made up for the emotional gap by being too close to them. I hooked up with guys who were predatory and saw an opportunity to exploit me."

THE ESSENTIALS

A Coming-Out Letter

The most important thing about a coming-out letter is to be honest about your feelings and respectful of others'. After that, it's all about who you are and how you choose to express yourself.

Dear Mom and Dad,

I want to share something about my life that is important, because I love you. I am gay. I have only known this about myself since I was twenty-five. In the years that have passed since then, keeping this a secret from you has become more and more of a burden. It has also placed an invisible wall between us in that I cannot share with you much of what goes on in my life, something that straight children take for granted. I could not share the excitement of dating somebody new or the pain when things didn't work out. I have spent many nights crying with a broken heart, alone, unable to call you for support.

I know that you may be feeling shocked, confused, angry, and/or sad; and perhaps you might feel that, somewhere along the way, you have failed as parents. From what I have read, these are common reactions. You have not failed as parents; you have both been wonderful. Nobody chooses to be gay, and I accept myself and am happy with who I am. My friends have known for some time, and they accept me as well. I hope that you will be happy for me. Hopefully, a few years from now, our relationship will be closer than it has been in the past. This is part

STRAIGHT TALK

"My college-age son recently came out to me. While the news came as a surprise, I'm very supportive of him. I'd like to share this with close family and friends, but I wonder if that's okay."

No, it's not okay to mention it—unless you get your son's approval. There are many degrees of outness: For instance, some teens are out to their parents, but not at school; others are out at school, to their closest friends and online, but not at home; while still others are fully out.

In this case, ask your son directly if he minds your telling family and friends: "How would you like me to handle what you've told me?" Then, follow his suggestion.

of the reason I am coming out to you: to tear down the wall between us. When we speak on the phone and you ask me what is going on in my life and I say "Nothing," I have been lying. This hasn't been to deceive you, but because I could not tell you the truth. This lying has been eating away at me for some time now, and I'm tired of it. So this was the choice I had to make: either keep lying and allow us to grow even farther apart from each other, or tell the truth and have a better relationship in the long run.

I know you have always loved me very much. It was very hard to mail this letter for fear of losing that love. I have cried several times while writing it. Although you may not understand about being gay, I hope that you still love me now. Know that I am the same person now as I was before you read this letter; you just know one more thing about me. I am still "Paul Jay." When you are ready, call me so we can talk about this more.

Love,
Paul

Divorced Parents

If your parents are divorced and they've managed to keep things friendly, consider bringing them together for your coming-out conversation. That way, they both get the same message at the same time and you'll avoid any competitiveness about who learned first. For some of us, however, putting both divorced parents in the same room is either not possible or would simply cause too many *other* problems. If that's the case, speak to them separately and let each know that you're informing the other as well.

Either way, treat them as individuals—not as a couple. And remember that if they've been living separate lives they're more likely to respond differently to your news. Perhaps one has been more privy to your personal life and delivers the classic "I already knew that," while the other is clueless and perhaps even shocked.

If One of Your Parents Is Lesbian or Gay

Let's start with the good news: If one (or both) of your parents is gay, he or she will likely have a better idea what you're going through when you decide to come out than a straight parent might. Your gay parent will also probably have an innate understanding of some of the challenges you may face out in the world. But be careful about your use of sarcasm or humor, even in jest: Comments like "Dad, I guess I really am a chip off the old block" rarely go over well in this situation, because of the social pressure many gay parents already feel to prove that they don't influence their children's sexuality or gender identity.

The bad news, if your other parent is *not* gay, is that your parents' marriage may have ended over this very issue. Clarify as much as possible to your straight parent that your sexual orientation is yours alone—that it wasn't caused or influenced by your gay parent's—and that you love them both equally. Don't be surprised if it takes your straight parent some time to adjust to the news of having another gay or lesbian member in the family.

If You're Estranged from Your Family

Coming out officially to your family may be especially difficult if you broke away from them in the past because of their reaction to your then-unacknowledged sexual orientation or gender identity. You may even decide that having this conversation just isn't worth it to you, that there's really no need to share this part of who you are, especially if these people are no longer in your life or you're not willing to endure the hostility it could involve. There's no rule that says you must come out to everyone.

Talking with Brothers and Sisters

Some of us happen to be best friends with our siblings; others have very little to say or share. If you're close, consider coming out to a brother or sister before you tell your parents. Maybe your sibling has a fresh perspective on how to approach your parents; maybe she knows that they know already or can advocate for you if the going gets tough. Even just trying out your coming-out news on someone you know well and feel loved by can boost your confidence. Maybe you'll be as fortunate as I was when I told my sister, who was sixteen at the time, that I was gay. She responded, "Me, too!"

In that light, don't be surprised if your revelation raises questions about your sibling's own sexuality. "After my older brother and younger sister came out to me, I couldn't help but wonder if I was gay, too," recalls one straight man. In fact, there are a number of highly reputable studies reporting that homosexuality has a genetic or biological basis, that it can "run" in families.

It's important not only that you talk about yourself, but that you listen to your sister or brother and encourage questions and future discussion.

THE ESSENTIALS

All About Parents, Families and Friends of Lesbians and Gays (PFLAG)

Parents, Families and Friends of Lesbians and Gays, also known as PFLAG, has been inviting moms and dads of gay kids to cry on its shoulders, find support, and become educated about their LGBT offspring for decades. The organization now has more than 200,000 members in all 50 states and Canada. "Support" is PFLAG's watchword. Call up one of its more than 500 affiliates scattered around the United States, Canada, and many other countries, or visit www.pflag.org if you're planning to come out, if your child has just come out, or if you think your child is LGBT. PFLAG families have walked the walk before and can talk you through the coming-out process or put you in touch with whatever facts or resources you need.

STRAIGHT TALK

"My sister recently came out but isn't involved with anyone. I keep wondering how she knows she's a lesbian. Will I hurt her feelings by simply asking her that?"

Before you talk to your sister about this, ask yourself, "How do I know that I'm straight?" You're likely to answer, "I've always felt this way." In other words, there probably wasn't a point when a flashing light went off and you said, "I'm a heterosexual!" The same is true for many or most LGBT people; our sexual orientation or gender identity is simply an intrinsic part of who we are.

If you still choose to ask this question, frame it in a way that helps your sister know that you have some understanding of the situation—something like "I know that for me being straight is something I've always thought to be part of my nature; was it the same for you?" This is much less abrupt than "How do you know you're gay?"

Why Tell Your Kids

There are plenty of reasons for you to come out to your children—not the least of which is that one of the most important lessons a parent can teach a child is to be open and truthful. Many LGBT parents have found that by being up-front about their sexual orientation or gender identity, their children were more likely to be trusting with them about their own inner lives and feelings.

Over time, your coming out also teaches your kids (and their friends and their friends'

QUEERY

"Newly out mom doesn't want trouble at school"

Q I have two preteen girls and have recently partnered with a woman after being married to their father all their lives. I don't want to draw attention to them in school, but I also don't want to hide my new relationship. How out can I be without causing problems for them at their suburban school?

A Tweens feel marked by any sort of difference, whether it's an accent or a haircut. Now bring on same-sex parents! So, for starters, involve your kids in any discussions about who goes to parent-teacher conferences or who cheers them on at school games, and what each of you will be called. Is it "Mom" and "Carol"? Or "Mom" and "Mama"?

At the same time, make an appointment with your daughters' teachers or guidance counselor—to explain your family situation and ask for introductions to other LGBT parents in the school. Then get involved: As one mother told me, "As soon as my daughter saw the other parents accepting me, she was fine."

Good neighborhood etiquette will also help. Invite families with kids about the same age as yours over for movie night or a summer barbecue. You can be sure word of mouth about your daughters' "two moms" will reach the school halls. Lastly, be aware that the kids of LGBT parents are sometimes bullied or harassed. Tell your girls to let you know right away if they run into any trouble (or trouble runs into them).

---

families) what LGBT family life really is like. In a sense, your fully out family become quiet emissaries for LGBT life; this can go a long way toward countering negative depictions of gay people that your child may pick up from people and groups opposed to same-sex marriage and gay adoptions.

When you are ready to tell a child that you are gay, bisexual, or transgender, give some thought to what sort of message you want to deliver beyond that particular news. Explained one gay dad who was in the process of divorcing his kids' mother: "I wanted them to know the real reason for our separation—and especially that it had nothing to do with them or their mom. It felt important for me to be honest after all those years of hiding."

Telling Young Children

There's no set age when it's best to talk about being LGBT to your child. Whenever you do, the smart thing is to tailor the message and the language to your child's age and maturity.

For young kids, that means speaking very simply and emphasizing the "love" part of your sexuality. For instance, you might explain to a five-year-old, "People love other people for many different reasons, and you can fall in love with different types of people." Likewise, if a young child asks her lesbian mother, "Why don't I have a father?" you don't need to talk to this child about "sexuality" or "sexual orientation." At this age, you'll be fine with, "Some families have two moms, some have two dads, some have one of each, and others have just one parent." This is also a great time to read your kids a book like *Heather Has Two Mommies,* by Lesléa Newman, with its message that "each family is special" and that "the most important thing about a family is that all the people in it love one another."

Kids who are growing up in gay or trans households often need no formal coming-out announcement, understanding that their family is different simply by nature, whether it's having a transgender parent, a single gay one, or two mothers or fathers. But you may find they still have questions. At the playground, for instance, other parents may ask in front of your child, "Who is the mother?" or "Where is the child's father?" or, if they know enough to make trouble, "How was your child conceived?" Do your best to talk to your children about these issues before they overhear something confusing or are asked directly themselves.

When you're ready to tell your children, here's what to do:

- Emphasize repeatedly that your news in no way affects your love for your child, and that your relationship with each other will stay the same.
- Speak plainly and to the point and in language he or she can understand, leaving it up to your child what direction your conversation will take.
- Also leave the pacing up to your child: Some children will have lots of questions right away, while others need to mull over what you're saying before they're ready to talk about it.
- Make sure to say whether or not your child should feel free to share this news with friends, cousins, etc. Remember that asking kids to keep anything private is not likely to happen, nor a good idea.
- Revisit your initial conversation soon after; most kids will have follow-up questions, especially after they've talked to friends or other family members.

Coming Out to Older Children

Coming out to tweens or teens is not inherently harder or easier than telling young children. The big difference is that they're more likely to know what you're talking about. But that also means your son or daughter may already have ideas about LGBT people, whether informed or uninformed. If you're nervous about jumping in blind, start by asking your child some leading questions, such as "Do you know any gay people?", "What have you heard about transgender people?", or "Have any of your friends mentioned that they have a parent or sister or brother who is gay or lesbian?"

Then, when you're ready, have the conversation. And remember: tweens and teens are going to have lots of questions. Get them to lean on you first for answers instead of their peers; keep the channels of communication open for follow-up. Since older kids can be uncommunicative, remain alert to signs that they want—or need—to discuss this more.

If you have a new beau or partner, you can make the conversation more concrete by explaining your relationship. However, many parents choose to explain their sexuality separately—and before—revealing any new relationships, if only because it's easier to raise one topic at a time.

The Transitioning Parent

A parent who is transitioning may have a more difficult time explaining gender identity to a child than a parent acknowledging he is gay or bisexual. In fact some trans people find that including a partner, spouse, close friend, or another family member in this conversation allows a child to grasp the information better and ask questions more easily.

Unfortunately, it's not uncommon for younger people to distance themselves during a parent's transition period, and you may just need to ride this part out. "At first my son felt he could handle the fact that his father would be transitioning to a woman," explained a blogger about coming out to her fourteen-year-old, "but once it actually started to happen all bets were off. He gradually retreated from me to the point that we completely lost touch of each other for almost a year."

The process of aligning your outer appearance with your gender identity—if that's what you're doing—can take years and seem endless for younger ones. As you continue to transition, remain open and forthcoming about any changes in your body or behavior, because your child is fairly sure to notice. It may also be helpful to introduce your children to other children with transgender parents. Finally, if the road remains bumpy, consider seeing a therapist or counselor as a family or finding a professional your child can see alone.

What they call you—either "Mom" or "Dad"—is up to the two of you to talk about. For instance, in the recent CNN documentary *Her Name Was Steven*, the main character, a male-to-female trans person, remains her son's "father"—and is called "Dad"—even though she became Susan to the rest of the world.

CHALLENGING SITUATIONS

Despite much progress and greater acceptance of LGBT people, sometimes coming out can test your mettle or, worse, become a true nightmare. It is not just a metaphoric door that may be slammed in your face. Your parents may cut off any financial assistance. You may lose a best friend. You may be outed by others, your privacy trampled on. Or your expression of trust may be met by a truly hurtful response: "Stop, I don't want to hear about your sex life" or "You were raised in a church that finds homosexuality a sin!" Coming out to almost anyone as a trans person is a challenge, as is finding that your decision to be open leads to discrimination or harassment in your workplace. The key question for LGBT people facing these difficult situations is this: When those around you are at best disrespectful and at worst hateful, what's the right way to respond?

Fight or Flight

If you sense a negative or hostile reaction from a friend, colleague, or family member, you may decide to avoid a confrontation, especially if you don't feel safe. But if you're up for it, go ahead and engage this person directly and challenge their homopobia. Just keep your temper under control—and your language, too. For instance, you might say, "I chose to come out to you because we're such close friends and I want you to understand this part of me." Or to someone who cites the Bible: "There are many interpretations of scripture as it relates to homosexuality." To someone who accuses you of oversharing about personal things, you might say, "I'm not telling you about my *sex* life. I'm talking to you about a fundamental part of who I am."

Often, however, it's what goes unsaid or undone that suggests someone is not comfortable with your coming out. You may find, for instance, that a friendship cools, or there's a different tone in your father's voice, or you're not invited to a friend's party that you would have been before. It's natural to assume that your recent news is the cause. Keep in mind, however, that not every inconsiderate act is homophobic, and you won't know for sure unless you ask. Inquiring whether your coming out is the reason for the change will give you greater clarity. Yes, it's possible you'll lose a friend because you've told him or her you're LGBT. That's sad, but could that really be a relationship worth preserving?

HANDLING A HOMOPHOBE POLITELY

If you find yourself discussing homosexuality with someone who is anti-gay or anti-trans, here are three proper and effective ways to press your case.

1. **Use concrete examples of the inequalities you face:** For example, even when gay men and lesbians can marry, they aren't eligible for any of the federal benefits bestowed on straight couples. In some states, we're not allowed to adopt kids. And in some school districts, LGBT dates are simply not allowed at the prom. A lot of straight people have never thought about these specific situations, but once you point them out, the inherent unfairness is often quite persuasive—and the result could be a positive change in their opinions.

2. **Don't hesitate to discuss acts of anti-LGBT violence:** By and large, straight people don't want to harm LGBT people or be responsible for their being hurt, but there are times when their words and actions do lead to pain and suffering. Talk about the heinous murder of Matthew Shepard, for example, and explain that it's all too common for young people to be bullied or beaten up in school, some because they are gay or transgender, and others just because someone thinks they are.

3. **Make it personal:** Talk about your own life and the challenges you've faced as an LGBT person. Perhaps you didn't get a promotion because you're gay. Or your same sex partner isn't covered under your health insurance plan. It's one thing to talk about "marriage equality" or even "honoring" and "respecting" LGBT people, but it's quite another to relay stories and examples where you yourself have faced concrete hardships or discrimination. For instance, I remember when my great-aunt wouldn't invite my partner and me to a family get-together even though she had asked straight spouses. My dad called her to explain the inherent unfairness: the next time we were invited.

STRAIGHT TALK

"My husband of many years has just dropped the bomb that he's attracted to men. I'm a mess but sort of frozen in my tracks. What should I do? What should I say?"

As hard as it is for one partner in a relationship to come out to the other as gay or bisexual, receiving this news can be just as difficult, if not more so. No doubt, your husband gave this announcement a lot of thought beforehand, but it sounds like it still caught you off guard.

If you're angry, my advice to you is to go ahead and let it out—within reason, of course. He may insist you not cry or be angry, but bottling up your feelings now is a bad idea. Then, consider taking a break from each other so that you can both mull over what's happening. You may want time alone, or you may want to reach out for the support of a friend or another family member. Next, you'll likely have some questions for him, along the lines of "Do you want to stay married?", "Do you want to get a divorce?", or "Do you want to tell other family members? (And what do you want to tell them?)" Be sure not to cede your own power and authority in making these decisions: Ask yourself what's best for you (and your kids, if you have any).

Finally, consider contacting the Straight Spouse Network (www.straightspouse.org), which provides nonjudgmental support and information to married people in your precise situation. This group has a wealth of advice; you might meet others who have gone through this very challenging situation already and eventually put it behind them.

Being Out and Safe at School

No question about it, coming out as a teenager or young adult can sometimes be scary. How will your friends react? Will you be safe from violence and slurs? Will your family reject you? At one college campus I visited recently, *every* student attending a meeting at the LGBT Center said they feared rejection from their families. High school and junior high kids worry about that, too.

Certainly, more openness and increased acceptance put many young LGBT people in a better position than earlier generations. Lots of tweens and teens go ahead and dress as they like or adopt new mannerisms without as much trepidation as their elders may have felt. Some explore their newfound liberation by becoming gay rights activists or holding hands with their partners in public. On campus or around the schoolyard, this ability to "be yourself" is an essential element of embracing your new LGBT identity.

But being out and proud also carries risks. You may find yourself the target of anti-gay or anti-trans hostility, which can take many forms, from the passive-aggressive but powerful rolling of the eyes to outright slurs, all the way to secret videotaping of your intimate life and even physical violence. A recent study by GLSEN reported that nine out of ten LGBT students had experienced harassment at school within the previous year. Three-fifths said they felt "unsafe" at school because of their sexual orientation.

So how do you balance the need to express yourself with the need to be safe? The answer is context. College campuses are filled with people experimenting with new ways of being in the world, sometimes even relishing the shock factor, but how many middle-school students will accept a boy in drag? Moreover, what's acceptable in Park Slope, Brooklyn's lesbian "gayborhood," is very different from what's okay in California's conservative Ventura County, where in February 2008 an eighth-grader was shot dead in class because he was known to be gay. To date, forty states have enacted anti-bullying statutes—but only ten of those have included specific protections for LGBT youth in the schools.

THE ESSENTIALS

All About GLSEN

Once you start to come out, it's difficult to close the door behind you. So take your time. Meanwhile, consider sharing your fears with friends who have already come out or some other trusted confidante. Or visit the Gay, Lesbian and Straight Education Network online (www .glsen.org), a nonprofit that fosters more than four thousand gay-straight alliances in schools coast to coast "that work to improve school climate for all students, regardless of sexual orientation or gender identity/expression."

Religious Conservatives

When planning to come out to someone who is unsupportive of LGBT people for religious reasons, be prepared for a difficult conversation and the possibility of not reaching any genuine resolution—other than to disagree.

If you intend to engage your family members about issues of faith, consider doing some research on your own first. No matter the specific religion, anti-LGBT attitudes are often a combination of actual teachings and traditional attitudes. For instance, there's the much-quoted Leviticus argument against homosexuality: "Thou shalt not lie with mankind, as with womankind: it is abomination," which is frequently translated by Christian fundamentalists to: "Homosexuality is absolutely forbidden, for it is an enormous sin." A good reply to this argument is to point out that Leviticus also says that shaving and eating pork are abominations and that owning slaves is fine.

Still, while standing up for yourself, you don't want to get into endless arguments, which generally produce more fire than light. You'll also want to be patient—or as patient as you can be—since your news could pose a very profound challenge, particularly to parents, whose love for you may clash with their belief system. Do your best to remain respectful (even if they are not), speak from your heart, and be prepared to walk away if necessary. Definitely don't expect to actually change your parents' views on homosexuality, at least not right away. One young man who came out to his fundamentalist parents advises against pushing too hard, because "the more you try to change your parents or make them accept you, the more they might resist changing or thinking about things differently."

Dealing with religious issues across generations can be especially frustrating. All too many parents sever ties—and financial support—over such matters. One Florida lesbian explained what happened to her: "My mother told me that the only reason I liked my girlfriend was because I was 'being tempted by the devil.' Eventually she told our church about my 'lesbian relationship,' and I was no longer welcome there. Even the youth director told me I was too close to my 'friend.'" (For more information about gay-affirming houses of worship, see www.gaymanners.com.)

"Hi, I'm Bi"

When young people come out, as often as not they use the term "bi" to explain what's going on. An eleven-year-old quoted in a recent *New York Times* article about tweens and teens coming out suggested that half the girls he knows are bisexual. Whether that term is considered a complete identity, a placeholder to describe the classic experimentation of youth, or chosen because it's less definitive than "gay" or "lesbian" depends on the person.

Others who come out as bi—when it's not a transitional stage or an umbrella term but a fully formed identity—find it more challenging than telling others that they're gay or lesbian.

Long-held confusion and stereotypes among straights, gay men, and lesbians about what exactly bisexuality means has fostered a certain hostility and mistrust. Negative assumptions and false stereotypes about bisexuals are plentiful: They are confused, deny their homosexuality, are more promiscuous than others, and are less capable of monogamy and stable relationships. Not true!

Whether straight or gay, it's important that we accept and respect others' decisions and announcements about who they are—even, or perhaps especially, when the experience is not our own.

IF SOMEONE TELLS YOU "I'M BISEXUAL"
If you're the recipient of such a personal disclosure, respond affirmatively, rather than challenging or discounting her. Even if you think the person is too young to make such a pronouncement or that he's actually gay or straight, don't respond with "That must be a phase," which is what many people often think—and say. In

QUEERY

"Coming out on Facebook"

Q I've wanted to come out for years, but I'm a senior in college now and haven't found the courage to tell anyone. Recently I've been thinking about just updating my Facebook profile before I tell my friends or family. What do you think about that?

A Coming out online has its benefits. Making your announcement to so many people at once can be liberating, and you don't have to go through the hassle of having the same conversation a dozen times. But I'm afraid using social networking sites this way is no replacement for direct, in-person conversations. In your case, I think it's especially unwise because you say you're having trouble speaking up offline about your sexuality. The first step in any successful coming out is getting comfortable enough to talk about it. Then, tell your closest friends, parents, siblings, and others you care about—in person. After that, it's fine to note on your profile that you're interested "in men" or "in women" and see where that leads you.

fact, bisexuality is considered a separate sexual orientation—just like gay or straight.

You may even come across a situation where a female friend says that she is bisexual, but is in a committed relationship with a woman. While this may seem confusing on the face of it ("But you're a lesbian!"), this is the nature of bisexuality: someone who is attracted sexually, physically, or emotionally to both men and women. Also, keep in mind that just because someone is open to dating either men or women doesn't mean he or she can't commit to one person—whether of the same gender or the other.

STRAIGHT TALK

"My middle-aged brother referred to himself recently as bisexual. I guess I've always just thought of him as a 'swinger' and referred to him that way to some friends, but he didn't like that. What's the difference?"

Wow, that's an old-school term you've dug up! If this were the 1960s or '70s, I'd say that "bisexuality" and "swinging" were pretty much the same. Both terms used to suggest easygoing and distinctly nonmonogamous attitudes about sexual behavior and relationships. These days, the term "swingers" instead brings to mind straight couples who like to swap sexual partners. Bisexuality, by contrast, is about identity rather than what kind of sex you have or even how often. No matter, it's a good rule of thumb that when someone, especially a relative, uses a particular phrase to describe himself that you follow suit. Got it, sister?

What the Letter "Q" Means

Often you will see a "Q" tacked on to the end of "LGBT." Sometimes this letter stands for "queer," an old term rescued from its history as an anti-gay pejorative and now embraced by people who eschew rigid sexuality and gender categories. For many, it's an all-inclusive term that sweeps up everyone who's not straight-identified.

Other times, however, "Q" stands for "questioning" and refers to a person's period of exploration with his or her sexual orientation or gender identity. While many are certain about one or both from an early age, others of us need time to try out a variety of relationships and perspectives before we can be sure.

Commonly, those "questioning" are younger people, just getting to know themselves as they mature. But even among adults, experimenting and asking questions about one's sexuality or gender identity without putting a name to it is a normal and healthy process—many people never put a name to it, in fact.

Coming Out for People of Color

Many LGBT people of color end up feeling like outsiders in their own racial or ethnic communities, as well as among white lesbians and gay men. It's possible you may find yourself without a reliable support system of other gay, bi, or transgender people or from the straight community of color. For African Americans, Hispanics, Asians, and others, coming out often involves extra challenges and hurdles. You may have to deal with intolerant churches, powerful family traditions that embrace only

QUEERY

"Racist, anti-gay names won't break my bones, but ..."

Q Not long after I came out I was at a predominantly white bar near my college when a brother called me a "snow queen." I wasn't even sure what he meant until I looked it up on the Web. Now I know and wish I had said something snappy right back at him. Have a suggestion?

A As you now know, a "snow queen" is a derogatory term for a gay black man who allegedly prefers white guys. (Its equally nasty cousin is a "dinge queen," a white guy who is said to prefer black partners.) Both are so unacceptable and deeply insulting that it's hard to imagine an appropriate "snappy" comeback. Instead, I'd suggest you either say something like "That offends me and degrades you" or practice the social cut: Look the offender in the eye, say, "I don't know you," and walk away. None of us should ever tolerate the intolerable.

heterosexuality, and a culture that is disapproving of LGBT life—plus racism in the larger LGBT (and straight) communities. "That's the one that's still given the pass," says one middle-aged black lesbian about her family's rejection of her sexuality. She adds: "Gay is still a disgrace, embarrassing."

More disheartening, within some LGBT organizations, the political arena, and the mainstream media, gay people of color still aren't visible enough to be role models for those coming out. Some gay people of color also find themselves being asked to choose between their identities. Which comes first: being black or a woman, or being black and gay? In her essay "Blacks and Gays: Healing the Great Divide," critic Barbara Smith wrote, "The underlying assumption is that I should prioritize one of my identities because one of them is actually more important than the rest or that I must arbitrarily choose one of them over the others for the sake of acceptance in one particular community."

When coming out, know that you may require an extra supply of the standard tools of information, support, patience, and courage. Also, seek out institutions and organizations that are supportive of LGBT people. Two gay-positive, inclusive churches are the United Fellowship of Metropolitan Community Churches and the Unity Fellowship Church Movement, which has locations coast to coast. You may also find support in PFLAG's Families of Color Network, a branch of the esteemed group that "works to break down barriers of sexual orientation and gender identity within communities of color." As LGBT people of color become more visible within all communities, it becomes easier for the next generation. Kenneth Reeves, who is both black and gay, and a former mayor of Cambridge, Massachusetts, poignantly captures the task at hand: "It is remarkable that we are still in the shadows. We are a people who must stand up and say who we are. We have to grow. You have to come out and tell this story. You cannot tell it in darkness!"

STRAIGHT TALK

"Is it okay to ask if an LGBT person's sexuality is just a 'phase'?"

Not really. This question is usually posed as a means to deny or object to someone's true orientation, and it can be perceived as either uninformed or hostile. Even those who are questioning their own identity or experimenting with it have a right to decide whether they want to embrace some particular term or identity. If someone comes out to you, keep in mind that he or she has given this matter some thought and has also put great trust in you. It's not likely to be a "phase," just as your own sexuality, when it first came into bloom, probably was not.

Coming Out When You're Older

Usually when we picture someone coming out, we see teenagers, college kids, and twentysomethings, but a lot of us don't come out until we're older, sometimes much older. If that sounds like you, you may find initiating a coming-out conversation especially difficult. Perhaps you hold on to traditional notions of privacy about sexual orientation. Or you may have faced significant discrimination in your life and simply shelved the process of coming out. "I'm not in hiding, but I guess you could say I haven't really come out," a gay man in his sixties told

The Boston Globe. "I'm from a generation where most of my contemporaries would be uncomfortable with it pushed in their faces. And I don't want anyone to feel uncomfortable."

Even more troubling is the trend of some LGBT seniors going back into the closet when moving into assisted living or residential care facilities—or just requesting home health care. This fear of discrimination often prevents those most in need from getting the care they need. Just as nonprofits like GLSEN assist teens in coming out by providing support and a safe haven, organizations like SAGE (Services and Advocacy for Gay, Lesbian, Bisexual and Transgender Elders) provide much-needed support as well as activities and groups for LGBT seniors to connect with one another. (For more information, visit www.sageusa.org.)

STRAIGHT TALK

"I read about the 'gay lifestyle' all the time on right-wing sites and it seems to connote a life involving promiscuity, child molestation, orgies, drugs, and alcohol. What do you think about that phrase?"

Truthfully, there's no such thing as the "gay lifestyle," although the phrase has been used widely and pejoratively to mean a promiscuous, anti-family way of life. There's actually a rather ironic site (www.gaylifestyle.info) that explains "the lifestyle" in this amusing way:

• Get up in the morning, moaning at the alarm clock.
• Shower, dress, eat breakfast.
• Go to work. Complain about traffic en route.
• Work. Worry about the job getting outsourced to India.

- Go home. Worry about gas prices.
- Stop for groceries on the way once or twice a week.
- Cook dinner. Realize there's no butter.
- Eat dinner. Worry about blood pressure and cholesterol.
- Do laundry. Try to figure out how to get that tomato stain out of that T-shirt.
- Clean the house. Realize that a sock didn't make it into the laundry.
- Pay bills. Worry about saving for retirement.
- Watch a little TV, spend time with any family members in the house, talk with friends on the Internet.
- Go to sleep.
- Repeat.

LGBT people are urban and rural, blue state and red, male and female, higher income and lower income, monogamous and not. Think about it: What's the "straight lifestyle"?

Changing Your Name to a Different Gender

One of the trickiest aspects of coming out as transgender is deciding how and when to begin living with your gender identity. Taking on a new name is often a crucial aspect of your official debut, both for establishing a new identity and for practical reasons, such as when applying for college, jobs, or government benefits. Most experts recommend getting a court order to change your name, since this form of documentation is universally accepted as valid proof.

For sure, plenty of trans people keep their names, whether because they opt to remain closeted, are comfortable presenting as mixed-gender, or are not interested in social norms at all. But if you're planning on changing genders in a public manner, you'll probably want to change your first name at the very least—unless you were blessed with something androgynous such as Alex, Kim, or Shannon. If you're seeking to blend in with your new identity, you may decide to choose a new first name that doesn't stand out or draw attention. Others, however, prefer to make more of a statement with their new name and to express their individuality that way. Still other trans people choose new names that are easily associated with their previous name. For instance, "Ian" becomes "Ina" or "Michaela" becomes "Michael."

Keep in mind that if you have a unique last name and don't change it, your past can still reclaim you, as this transwoman attests: "Unfortunately, in the world of the Internet, no information truly disappears. As my last name is somewhat uncommon, I've run into a few situations where people have searched my last name and were able to find out lots more info about me than I thought was available."

You'll also want to decide whether to change your family name. Again, some trans people do while others don't. Those who don't often prefer to maintain a family link to their loved ones, don't want to have to explain why they have a different surname than their spouse or kids, or judge it easier for legal reasons to keep the status quo. Reasons given for changing family names include: severing ties with the past, creating a completely new identity, and choosing a more pleasing-sounding name. It's also smart to choose a name you'll feel comfortable with for years to come and, before finalizing it, to conduct an online search for any negative associations.

"I don't have a name for my sexuality."

Q I'm a guy who's had a couple of relationships with other guys, but I've also had two girlfriends. So, I'm not sure if I'm gay, but I know I'm not straight. Everyone I know seems to care about labels— "straight," "gay," "bi"— and I don't know what to call myself. What should I be telling people?

A First of all, don't feel as though you need to tell anyone anything. How you define yourself is really your business. But as you've noticed, our culture values labels, whether they're about race (black, white, Asian), politics (red or blue state), or sexuality (gay, straight, bi). Labels tend to make *other* people more comfortable.

Things aren't always so red or blue or black and white, however, as a recent study of nonstraight young people demonstrated. The results suggested that nearly a quarter of them showed resistance to the usual sexual identity labels—in other words, they embraced fluidity in their sexual identities. So, take comfort that you're in a sizable minority— a minority that is often referred to as "postgay" and "postlabel," but in fact should probably be considered avant-garde in having rejected sexual identity labels.

Restroom Etiquette for Trans People

Standard "men's" and "women's" rooms are uncomfortable for "gender-nonconforming" individuals—people whose appearance is not conventionally male or female. Even those who identify as just one gender and dress that way wind up getting hassled because of the extra scrutiny so often in play on the way from the bathroom door to the stall (or urinal). "I never sweated so much as I did when I had to use the restroom at a mall or restaurant at the beginning of my transition," recalls one transwoman. Says a transman, "The problem was a daily one. I'd think about where I was going, what bathrooms I'd have access to, how much I drank during the day, whether I'd be with people who could help stand guard." In fact, many trans men and women believe it's safer to have a friend escort you into a public bathroom.

The bottom line: The smartest thing to do is use the restroom that matches how you present.

"Are You Gay?"

People not out often dread being asked about their sexual orientation because they think it will force them either to come out when they're not ready or to lie. Others think it's a clear violation of their privacy, regardless of their sexuality or whether they were asked by a straight person or an LGBT one. The most important thing to remember, should you be asked this question, is that you're in control of the information and the answer, and you have a number of appropriate choices in how you reply:

• If you're ready to come out, you might answer simply, "Why, yes I am." But you could also add in a friendly tone, "I don't mind, but you should know that most people think their sexuality is a private matter."

- If you're not ready or questioning, you could reply, "That's my own business" or "Who I spend my time with is really up to me."
- Under any scenario, a little soft humor works wonders, along the lines of "Thanks for the compliment" or "Only my hairdresser knows for sure."
- Sometimes it's a good strategy to answer a question with a question. Consider: "Why do you ask?"
- In a work environment or during a job interview, direct questions about your sexuality are illegal in most locales. Reveal as much as you choose, but think twice if you feel that by coming out you'll jeopardize your chances for a job.
- Finally, always consider your safety.

Under no circumstances should you feel compelled to reveal your sexuality (or gender identity) just because you were asked. Good manners always values an individual's privacy—that is, unless you're a closeted hypocritical politician.

Psychotherapy and Conversion Therapy

If someone (like a parent or a teacher) suggests you need therapy while coming out, feel free to reject the advice: The classic "thanks, but no thanks" will serve you just fine here, with no additional discussion warranted.

On the other hand, many LGBT people who are coming out find that legitimate forms of psychotherapy can help them build their self-esteem, overcome any shame or pain over being gay, and develop new social skills that can lead to stronger friendships and more intimate relationships. Gender therapists specialize in helping trans people transition while guiding them through the long process of consideration and self-discovery.

One lesbian now in her forties recalled how therapy helped her in her late teens: "Honestly, I had no one to talk to about being gay and I felt like it was the worst thing in the world that could have happened to me. When I finally came out to my parents, they suggested a therapist they knew—who turned out to be gay! Therapy was a very affirming process and really helped me come to terms with who I am."

Note: Standard psychotherapy is very different from "conversion therapy" (also known as "reparative therapy"), whose purpose is to change a person's sexual orientation from homosexual to heterosexual. Its tenets are based upon the erroneous assumption that being gay or lesbian is a mental disorder. Christian fundamentalists have generally supported this approach, while all legitimate psychiatric organizations disavow it, positing that this type of "therapy" is in fact quite destructive.

Helping Others to Come Out

Just as a close gay friend or relative may have proved to be a trusted sounding board for you when you were coming out, you, too, might be able to play that role for others. You may be a role model simply by the fact of being out, whether in your family, at work, or in school.

One automotive executive recalls, "I was the only gay person on the senior management team, and the CEO expected me to know everything about every LGBT issue and to speak for all my brothers and sisters. That was intimidating because I didn't feel that knowledgeable, and there were times when I didn't want to be known as the 'gay exec.' Still, I felt a responsibility to speak up for domestic partner benefits and to make sure that same-sex couples were covered by our health and disability plans."

On a more personal level, you may find a young man or woman asking your advice about coming out. Do your best to be open to these conversations—and to keep up on (or look up information about) local LGBT resources and organizations. Be compassionate and patient and allow your friends in the closet to determine their own pace for coming out.

STRAIGHT TALK

"I'd like to send my friend a card congratulating her for coming out as a lesbian and I noticed there's a set of Hallmark cards just for this purpose. Is it appropriate to use ready-made coming-out cards?"

Absolutely. Greeting cards are a great way to deliver a personal message, whether or not you also choose to say something face-to-face. The Hallmark cards you're referring to are, I hope, the first of many to address LGBT issues. Currently, there are four cards to choose from; of course, *any* preprinted card will do just fine. Just be sure to add in your own message of congratulations.

Even if the printed message is just what you want to say, a handwritten note from you turns it into something more personal. A few words of your own, such as "Congratulations on coming out" or "I just wanted to let you know I'm behind you" will go a long way to show you're supportive.

Many years ago, after I told a neighbor I was gay, he sent me a handwritten note saying how proud he was of me. You can be sure I kept it—it meant so much to me then, and it still does now.

Out in the World

Practice may not make quite perfect, but most of us find that coming out gets easier every time we do it. Each experience of speaking up to a new person or group of people is a natural confidence-booster, and you generally wind up learning new ways to initiate and conduct these conversations. You're also likely to find over time that you don't need to tell everyone. Family members, colleagues, and friends may just pass on the news themselves.

Still, most of us find ourselves continually coming out. It's a lifelong process, usually fraught with some anxiety, always building on past experiences. Let's say you're the parents of a new baby and someone asks, "Who's the mother?" or "Who's the father?" You'll need to come out. Or a new colleague invites you and your partner to a social event not knowing you have a same-sex partner. You'll need to come out. Or you choose a new doctor. You'll need to come out so she can fully understand your background, family life, and health history. Or you're at a dinner party with people you don't know and someone tells an anti-gay joke. You'll want to speak up and out.

STRAIGHT TALK

"I keep hearing about 'gender identity and expression,' but I'm afraid to appear foolish and ask my friends what it means. Can you help?"

These two related terms have become part of the LGBT lexicon in the past decade. Distinct from one's sexual orientation (gay, straight, bisexual), gender identity is about a person's emotional and psychological sense of being male or female and is not always the same as the sex assigned him or her at birth. For instance, a straight man may be a cross-dresser or otherwise appear feminine, as might a gay man. In either case, the person's gender identity (in this case female) is different from their sexuality (straight, gay, or bi). Gender expression goes hand in hand with gender identity and refers to how we communicate our gender—sometimes with a combination of maleness and femaleness—through our clothing, mannerisms, hairstyles, way of speaking, and first names.

CHAPTER 2

Friendship

The Family You Choose

Friendships matter to everyone, but they have a heightened significance to an LGBT person shunned by family or seeking the companionship of those who knows what it feels like to grow up "different" or to come out gay or trans. A bisexual college student notes, "My best friend knows everything about me and has been an amazing pillar of support as I've started dating. Unlike my family, his love is unconditional." A lesbian in her forties explains: "When I talk about 'the family,' I mean my five or six closest lesbian and gay friends, who have been by my side through my relationships, have taken care of me when I'm down and sick, and who I know will be there in the future." Striking a similar note, *Tales of the City* novelist Armistead Maupin described his characters as having "logical" as opposed to "biological" families.

No doubt you'll be making both LGBT and straight friendships in your life, but the focus of this chapter is on developing friendships within our community; of course, you can rely on much of this advice as you make friends in the straight world, too. Most of the time, the first step in making LGBT friends is to be out, whether that means wearing a T-shirt that reads GAY BY BIRTH. FABULOUS BY CHOICE, placing a photo of your same-sex significant other on your desk at work, or finding some other way to express your sexuality or gender identity. In some cases, the threat of anti-gay or anti-trans violence or loss of livelihood cautions against being out in the real world, but the Internet and social-media services like Facebook provide genuine alternatives now.

You may have noticed that our friendships can sometimes be a little more complex. Not only do some of the best LGBT friendships start as sexual liaisons, it's also quite true that some of the happiest gay and lesbian romances are birthed in friendship. That's why it's important to know how to make, maintain, repair, and sometimes end friendships, whether you are single or coupled, still in school or midcareer, new in town, or with kids at home.

"Did anyone bring the chardonnay?"

GETTING FRIENDLY

How shortsighted we can be about our friends, often failing to invest enough time and energy in our strongest allies, closest confidantes, and most ardent supporters. Fortunately, true friends will endure a lot, sometimes outliving our romantic partnerships by years if not decades. Finding and keeping the really valuable people in our lives may take some extra effort, but it's definitely worth it.

Finding LGBT Friends

It doesn't take a scavenger hunt to seek out LGBT friends in most big cities; we are just about everywhere. In smaller towns and in rural areas, it's trickier but entirely doable. The key is to break out of your daily routine so that you cross paths with different people. Try something new; go someplace you haven't been; be adventuresome; and take reasonable chances.

Here are some ideas:

• **Seek out a professional/ social group:** Meeting people through an association can help you find acquaintances with whom you have much in common. There are all kinds, from the Organization of

"My friend's lover is fooling around."

Q The other day my friend Stan invited me to his apartment for drinks. When I got there, Stan (married to my other friend Barry) answered the door wearing a towel. Moments later a guy I'd never seen before came out of the bedroom—also in a towel. It was really awkward, and I didn't know what to do. My friends have been together for years and often say they're monogamous. What to do? Yell at Stan? Tell Barry? Or just keep my mouth shut?

A Yikes! What's up with Stan? But, I know, that's not your question. So, the best thing that could happen would be for Stan to let you know that he's going to fess up to Barry—so that 1) you don't have to, and 2) you won't have to feel guilty about not doing it. But, if Stan doesn't reach out to you with this plan, call him and let him know what a good idea it would be for him to "do the right thing."

If Stan calls your bluff and says nothing, then I'd fold and sit it out. There's the slight possibility that your understanding of your friends' monogamous status was wrong—or that Barry prefers the bliss of ignorance.

Finally, I'd be remiss if I didn't point out that couples often do "kill the messenger" in a charged situation like this. If these two fellows get through this rough patch and back to trusting each other, there's a real possibility they will both view you as a troublemaker. If Barry does find out that you knew about his philandering partner and kept quiet, tell him the truth: That was Stan's responsibility—and you did your best.

Lesbian and Gay Architects and Designers and the West Point LGBT Alumni to your local gay hiking club or softball league.

- **Volunteer:** Helping a nonprofit or community group is one of the most valuable ways to spend your time. It also happens to be a low-risk way to make new friends. You're sure to find like-minded people as soon as you walk in the door. A twentysomething lesbian who volunteers at the San Francisco ASPCA explained: "Not only do I love being around the animals, it's been great as a way to casually meet new people from our community who also are crazy about cats and dogs." While you're at it, don't forget the many LGBT or HIV/AIDS-related organizations in our midst.

- **Attend a gay-friendly house of worship:** Whether religious or spiritual, seek out an LGBT church, synagogue, zendo, or other meditative retreat.

- **Join a (predominantly gay) health club:** Take part in classes like yoga, indoor cycling, or circuit training. Over time, you'll start to see the same people again and again, and it'll be easy to initiate a chat before or after your workout. If you want others to be sure there's no question that you're LGBT, wear a T-shirt or hat that makes it clear. In the past, I've worn my HRC (Human Rights Campaign) cap (with its iconic equal sign) or my National Lesbian & Gay Journalists Association T-shirt that says: WE'RE HERE. WE'RE QUEER. WE'RE ON DEADLINE. No mistaking that.

- **Take an extension class:** Your local university or community college is a good bet. Among the courses likely to put you alongside other LGBT students are gender studies, LGBT film history, and queer fiction.
- **Visit the LGBT center in your area:** LGBT community centers offer a range of activities year-round, day and night. For instance, the Los Angeles Gay & Lesbian Center sponsors activities from wine and food tasting events to beach volleyball to an annual AIDS/Lifecycle ride; Cleveland's LGBT Center has programs for youth, trans people, seniors, and more.
- **Go online to an LGBT friendship site:** Spend time filling out the profile, and make sure to check the box that indicates you are seeking *friends*—even if the lines between states of affection can often be happily blurred.

STRAIGHT TALK

"Do lesbians and gay men hang out together?"

Some lesbians have lots of gay male friends and vice versa; others have few or none. The HIV/AIDS crisis helped bridge the LGBT gender gap when lesbians took up the mantle for their gay brothers. (Many lesbians point out, however, that it's been a rather one-sided improvement, as gay men rarely put much time into women's causes

like breast cancer.) But this continuing shift toward mixing is also a result of changing notions of gayness; just visit a nightclub in a big city and you'll likely see a mélange of sexualities, genders, and ethnicities. Sexuality and gender identity are much more fluidly defined among people today, and the result is definitely greater mixing.

Making LGBT Friends

If you've recently started college, moved to a new city, switched jobs, or just come out, making new LGBT friends may be especially high on your priority list. Starting off with a positive attitude helps, as does your body language: People who don't make much eye contact or keep their arms barricaded across their chests don't come across as inviting or open to new friends. The more approachable you appear, the more likely it is that you will meet new people.

Not surprisingly, the basics of friendship are pretty similar whether you're gay or straight. Basic manners and friendliness can take you a long way fast. Here are some suggestions:

- **When you meet someone new, show genuine interest:** Listen to what she says and ask relevant questions. Don't just watch her lips while waiting to deliver your next quip. Some of us are all too practiced in the art of delivering biting witticisms and other good-natured but insulting trash talk. Learn to keep your wit in check, especially if it gets in the way of connecting. Be open about your own feelings, vulnerabilities, and opinions.
- **Be clear about your intent:** If you recently moved to a new city and are hanging out

at a park or a bar, mention that you're the new guy in town and "looking to make some friends." Or, if recently broken up and trying to move beyond your extended lesbian family, be clear and even try some humor: "I was with my partner for a decade. She got the friends; I got the cats."

- **Try not to make premature judgments:** Remember, it may take you some time to develop a rapport with someone you hardly know—and vice versa. Don't be "looks-ist" or make assumptions about new people based on superficial observations. When seeking new LGBT friends, remember they come in all genders, ages, and orientations. Develop patience.

- **Keep confidences:** Respect your new friends' privacy as you would your own. When in doubt, ask if it's okay to share a particular piece of information, photo, or video online or offline. And while we're on the topic, don't gossip about your friends—old or new—either.

- **Don't make friendship into a contest:** The beauty of a good friendship is that each of you imagines the other is the better friend.

Tips for Breaking the Ice

If you have even a hint of the introvert lurking within (and that's most of us), you probably find the idea of starting a conversation with a stranger makes you anxious. It's so much easier if a mutual acquaintance introduces you—or if you tag along to a tea dance or an all-women potluck and have your friend do the heavy lifting at first. But at some point, it's going to fall on you to keep things going.

There are a number of approaches you can take for breaking the ice and continuing to chip away at it, bit by bit. As a general rule, try to choose topics and questions that will go beyond yes or no and that will lead you into an actual conversation.

As you talk, take the time to listen to what's being said and be sure to answer questions put to you. Avoid boasting or getting too personal too quickly; those behaviors are off-putting to most of us. If you're not getting any engagement, simply say, "Nice chatting with you," and move on. There could be any number of explanations for someone's apparent disinterest, ranging from trouble at work or at home to plain old shyness. You may even make a connection with that person later on—so don't slam the door shut in a fit of gay pique.

STRAIGHT TALK

"Is it rude to ask my old friend to admit how long he's been gay, since I knew him for years and years before he came out to anyone?"

The essence of your question is fair enough and one that will probably help foster a useful conversation between you and your friend. To me, it implies that you're interested in knowing more and suggests clearly that you're accepting of your friend's sexual identity. But be careful about your language in asking. Many straight people inadvertently use the word "admitted" as you have, such as "So-and-so is an *admitted* homosexual," as though being gay is a crime one must confess to. Instead, ask your friend how long he's been out or *acknowledged* that he's gay.

At School

Not having LGBT friends, especially during the teen years, can lead to feelings of isolation and alienation. Indeed, gay or bisexual teenagers are more than three times as likely to attempt suicide as other youth, with young gay men especially at risk. Fortunately, whether in middle school or graduate school, Facebook, Twitter, and other social networking sites have become a tremendous boon to young LGBT people seeking friends and connections. You can expand your social circle by joining various online groups and clubs or just being virtually introduced by mutual acquaintances. (For more about the precautions to take when coming out online, see page 41.)

The other primary way of finding LGBT friends at school, along with gay-friendly straight buddies, is to join a campus LGBT organization. GLSEN (see page 383) supports more than four thousand high school gay-straight alliances, and a growing network of LGBT community centers offers support, advocacy, and social networking specifically tailored for those in school. One college-age bisexual who attended gay-straight alliance meetings while in high school explains their significance: "It was simply astounding to me to find a place where I could really be me, with others like me. I'd never had that before." Some schools and colleges also boast LGBT listservs, gay fraternities (such as Delta Lambda Phi), and LGBT alumni groups. Finally, a wide range of political and social groups exist that students organize on their own around issues like HIV prevention, marriage equality, transgender issues, and women's studies.

THE ESSENTIALS

A Special Note About LGBT Suicides

The statistics are shocking: Lesbian, gay, bisexual, transgender, and questioning kids may be four times more likely to attempt suicide than their straight counterparts, with that number climbing to *nine times* more likely if a young LGBT person has been rejected by his or her family. The pressure—whether coming from rejecting families or bullying, violent schoolmates—can be intense. (For more on bullying, see page 241.) Still, it's difficult for many of us to find the right words or actions when someone seems to be or says she's suicidal. Here's where knowing some smart tips and a few resources can help save lives:

- **Encourage your friend to seek help:** Suggest the person speak with a teacher, counselor, psychologist, or other trained professional.
- **Talk about community resources:** If the person is a teenager, mention The Trevor Project (opposite). Alternatively, put the person in touch with your local LGBT center for a social work referral or intervention.
- **Don't make their secret yours:** Even if asked to keep a suicide threat a secret, it's more important to make sure your friend gets help. If need be, talk to an expert yourself—or a trusted family member.
- **Reach out:** Let your friend know that you care and want to help. Offer to spend time together. Talk together. Don't dismiss his or her feelings, but do try to be helpful and positive (and reinforce the message that your friend needs to seek outside help).
- **Remind your friend that thoughts don't necessarily lead to actions:** And that it's not

uncommon for many of us—especially young people—to have thoughts about suicide without actually acting on them.

- **"It Gets Better":** Spread the word about this online video project (www.youtube.com/user/itgetsbetterproject). It was started by columnist Dan Savage to reach out to young LGBT people and let them know gay life does get better after high school—even if they can't imagine a future for themselves. The collection of videos includes a gay Jehovah's Witness, the New York City Gay Chorus, Chaz Bono, Sarah Silverman, President Obama, and others.

THE ESSENTIALS
All About the Trevor Project

The Trevor Project is the leading national organization focused on crisis and suicide prevention efforts among lesbian, gay, bisexual, transgender, and questioning youth. It operates the only accredited, nationwide, toll-free, around-the-clock suicide prevention helpline for LGBTQ youth (866-4-U-TREVOR). This hotline also helps those facing bullying, struggling with their sexual orientation or gender identity, or coping with other crises. In addition, programs include a range of public awareness campaigns and school anti-bullying partnerships, steering teens, parents, and teachers alike to practical resources for changing attitudes and protecting LGBT youth. For more information, go to www.thetrevorproject.org.

STRAIGHT TALK

"Do I say my friend is gay when introducing her to my straight friends?"

First of all, it's not a good idea in any situation to mention that someone is LGBT, unless you're certain they're out in that context. (For example, some of us are out to our friends, but not our colleagues.) That's what's referred to as "outing." But really, there's no need to bring up someone's sexuality when you're making a basic introduction. Present a gay friend to others just as you would a straight friend. No secret gay handshake, no winking, no nothing. If it's relevant, mention where she grew up, went to school, or works as a way to deepen the connection. If your gay friends want others to know, they know how to out themselves.

Couples Seeking Friendship

Seeking out new friends as a couple may be even more difficult for you than for your single friends because committed partners are often viewed as a self-contained unit—and it can certainly be more challenging to find compatibility among three or four individuals than between two. One lesbian recalled the dilemma she and her wife faced after moving cross-country: "We didn't have any built-in friends and found it really difficult to meet other lesbian couples—or even gay-friendly straight ones. They already had all the friends they needed." Nevertheless, making such connections is important both for becoming integrated into your community (whether you are a recent arrival or an old-timer) and because "couple" friends can provide support for your relationship in a predominantly heterosexual world.

Here's what LGBT couples can do to speed up and ease the process:

- **Go to neighborhood meetings together:** It doesn't matter if it's a crime stoppers get-together or something more fun, like a summer barbecue—go with your partner and be sure to introduce yourselves to others. After some initial conversation, you'll probably be able tell whom you feel an affinity for—and vice versa. Exchange phone numbers or e-mail addresses. Then follow up with an invitation for coffee or drinks at another time.
- **Get set up:** Ask your existing friends if they know any individuals or couples in your town or 'hood. If they do, get an introduction on e-mail and follow up. With friends in common, you automatically have something to talk about when you first meet.
- **Go online:** Maybe you thought online "match"-type sites were for dating and sex only. Not true. Many services cater to couples, organizing outings for wine lovers, scuba divers, yogis and yoginis, as well as book clubs and evening walking groups; some promote events explicitly for LGBT people in relationships. One gay man who participates in couples dating (this is not swinging, by the way) explained why it works so well: "In the past, if you and your partner were new in town, you might join a sports club or evening class to meet like-minded people. Now you can advertise yourselves online and speed up the process."

Maintaining Friendships

Friendships in the LGBT community need just as much investment of time and energy as do our romantic and family ties. Nascent friendships need attention if they're to take root and long-standing ones rest best on a foundation of trust, time spent together, and reciprocity. Explained one lesbian in her thirties: "I always knew that relationships were work, but I thought friendships operated on autopilot. Now I understand that what you get out of friendship depends on what you put in."

Here's what you can do:

- **Reciprocate:** Extend kindness in the face of kindness. If, say, you've been invited to a new friend's home for dinner, find a comparable way to show you care. If you don't cook, no need to make an elaborate meal; instead, take your friend out for a simple, nice dinner.
- **Think about your friend's interests and schedule when making plans:** Remain flexible: The art of compromise underlies most enduring friendships. For instance, wait an extra day to catch the local showing of a new film if your friend wants to see it with you but can't go on the night that's ideal for you.
- **Be loyal:** If others denigrate or make fun of a friend, you need to stand up for her even if it makes things uncomfortable. You don't need to be aggressive in what you say, but you do need to be firm in your defense.
- **Recognize that friendships have seasons or cycles:** They may wax and wane. Be patient, especially if a friend has started a new romance or job or is taking care of a sick relative or friend. Expect the same in return.

"Transman in search of some new trans friends"

Q I'm a transman without any trans guy friends, and usually that's fine because I have plenty of other friends and I'm out to most of them. But lately I've been thinking it would be great to know people who are also female-to-male. Where can I make FTM friends without having to skulk around the online personals or the bar scene?

A Online social networking is perfect for this sort of thing, and a big favorite of my trans friends is Transmen and Friends (www.transmenandfriends.com). Or look on Yahoo, which offers dozens of trans groups about "personal experience," "presenting and passing," "sex reassignment surgery," etc. Groups exist specifically for FTM and MTF (male-to-female) trans people.

You may find chatting online leads to offline friendships. If you do decide to meet an online contact, be sure to do so in a public place and to let a good friend know the name of the person and where you plan to meet. (Because violence against trans people is not infrequent, I'd even suggest checking in with your friend, to say you're okay.)

If you're ready to spend some time in a roomful of transmen, check out an in-person trans support group or trans event. Peer-led discussions may cover topics like the effects of hormone treatments, the emotional aspects of coming out, and the experience of being transgender in the workplace. Scout out something that sounds even remotely interesting and voilà: multiple FTMs to strike up a conversation with when the event is over.

- **Don't flirt (or worse) with a friend's beau:** Don't even think about going after that cute lesbian working behind the counter at your favorite coffee place if your friend is going out with her.
- **Be careful about dating a friend's ex:** No matter how they broke up or when, let your friend know your plans before you go out with his old boyfriend. You don't need to ask for his approval, but you don't want him to learn this news from the ex, some other person, or via a status update on a social network.

FRIENDLY COMPLICATIONS

When conflicts arise between friends over complicated issues such as money and sex, your relationship may get tense, even explosive. How do you handle loaning money to a best friend? What about the friend who flirts nonstop with your girlfriend? What is the etiquette of being a friend with benefits? And, if you have to end a friendship, can you do it—in a nice way?

Money, Money, Money

As much as we all like to pretend it's not true, dollars and cents can wreak havoc on even the most steadfast of friendships. Splitting dinner checks sometimes requires higher math skills; managing the bills for a summer share can challenge a diplomat; and making a loan may cost you a relationship.

The best advice: Be aware of the potential consequences of introducing a financial element into your friendship. And be fair with each other. Whatever the situation, try to establish your financial relationship clearly beforehand—and certainly before you're pent up with anger or resentment. If you're going to a restaurant and you don't want to just split the tab in two, simply say, "Let's have separate checks. It'll be easier." In more capital-intensive situations, it's a smart idea to write down your mutual understanding. Roommates often have written agreements, and anyone who makes a loan to a friend (or family member) should take the time to put the terms in writing.

It's also wise to avoid what are commonly referred to as "dual relationships," such as choosing your best friend to be your financial advisor or a good friend to be your business partner.

Friends with Children

It's been said that in the past decade kids have become the latest gay accessory. And it's true that parenting by choice is more and more common in the LGBT community: There are millions of kids living in households with at least one gay parent.

This situation is generally one for rejoicing, except that it makes for a wide gap in the LGBT community between the "haves" (those with children) and the "have-nots" (those who don't).

HAVE-NOTS

If you're among this group, then you know folks with kids eat around 6:00 P.M. You don't. They show pictures of their little ones all the time; you show photos of your pets or your exotic vacations. They're saving money for the kids' education; you want to go on a Caribbean adventure. Suddenly, it seems that there's no time left for the kinds of activities you once shared with your now parenting friend, not to mention that you're second fiddle to the little ones. These changes can be especially hard for those who have turned their friends into their de facto families.

If you find yourself in this situation, do your best to accommodate your friends' new lifestyle:

• Avoid getting in any kind of competition with the children, because you'll lose.
• Try not to flaunt any especially fun, child-free adventures in your life, such as nightclubbing or faraway sojourns. Showing off like that is not likely to endear you to your overwhelmed lesbian mom best friend.
• Do your best to embrace the changes and find ways to support the new moms and dads in your life. If you want to keep the friendship and you have a choice between attending a Dykes on Bikes picnic or a child's baptism, choose the baptism.
• Find mutually convenient times to visit. Make adjustments, such as staying in for

dinner, doing takeout, or even agreeing to pay for half the babysitting so that you can actually go out *sans enfants.*

- Learn how to change a diaper so that you can volunteer to babysit yourself.

HAVES

If you're the new parent, be aware that your old friends are no doubt happy for you, but also experiencing a certain loss. Acknowledge the change and tell them how much you appreciate their friendship. Then find ways to integrate them into your expanded home life:

- Include your old friends in your new family's traditions and rites; invite them for the holidays, special celebrations, and even as houseguests if that was part of your past history.
- Try to find "friend time" where you can get away from all your home distractions and catch up with each other.

- If it's part of your spiritual or religious beliefs, invite a special friend to become a godparent—which may entail religious instruction or just taking an interest in the child's well-being.

Sometimes friendships don't survive the addition of a little one. If this happens, try not to take it personally and consider the possibility that it may just be a temporary lull. Said one gay dad on the prospect of losing a lifelong friend: "I told him we'd continue our conversation when my son is eighteen."

Up, Up & Away!

Traveling together, whether as a romantic couple or just good friends, can be a wonderful adventure—or a never-to-be-forgotten nightmare. Several years ago, two friends of mine who had known each other for more than five years set off on a grand French vacation with

QUEERY

"I loaned money to my friend and he spent it on a cruise!"

Q **I've become really good friends with a tenor in the gay chorus. After he showed me his plan to expand his handcrafted gourmet Popsicle business, I loaned him $10,000. So you can imagine the pit in my stomach when I learned that he and his partner are going on one of those over-the-top gay cruises. I lent him that money for business!**

A You probably want me to say, "Call in the loan. Cancel the cruise." But I won't. Loans are delicate between friends, especially if you don't write up an agreement that lays out the repayment terms very specifically. My advice is to review the terms of your loan and see whether they need adjusting; if you never signed an agreement, then do so now.

As for the cruise, while I understand your chagrin, I'd leave that alone. Since you haven't heard about it from your friend directly, it may just be gossip. Even if the happy couple is setting sail, don't assume your friend is paying. Maybe the partner is bankrolling this vacation, or perhaps it was a raffle prize. Don't accuse your chorale mate of anything—and make sure that any future loans to friends involve extra consideration and precise paperwork.

high hopes. The only problem was that their hopes were so *different*. One was looking forward to spending time with his traveling companion while visiting historical sites and dining in local bistros, while the other was interested in clubbing and tricking—and using his travel partner to defray expenses and entertain him during the daylight hours. Not surprisingly, the trip ended in a broken friendship.

If you're contemplating a vacation with a friend, talk in some detail at the outset so that you're reasonably sure that you're compatible. Here are some questions to bring up ahead of time:

- **What's the budget?** If you can afford only one star and she's hoping for a luxury experience, you have a disconnect. Make a budget beforehand and compromise as necessary.
- **How will you divide expenses?** You can keep separate expenses or you can establish a joint pool that you both contribute to and spend from.
- **How will you handle sexual or romantic liaisons?** Sure it's cheaper to take one room when you travel, but that may preclude an important part of your adventure. Make sure you have an understanding: No overnight guests? Separate rooms some of the time? Hang the DO NOT DISTURB sign on the door as your secret code?
- **What kind of schedule will work best?** Early risers may have difficulty with night owls and vice versa. Be up-front about your habits, even those like snoring, smoking, and bathroom tidiness.
- **What kind of activities are most appealing?** One of you may like architectural ruins but the other nonstop shopping. You needn't like all the same activities; in fact, doing things

separately can be fun and a way to meet new people. Consider peeling off from time to time to pursue separate interests and then reconvening at a pre-established hour.

For more about LGBT travel, see Chapter 12.

Friends with Benefits

When you have a sexual liaison with a friend without any expectation of exclusivity or commitment to a romantic relationship, you are friends with benefits. (Although these are casual relationships, sometimes considered a fling, they are by definition and practice quite different from no-strings-attached sex, which is all about the hookup.) Friends-with-benefits arrangements are especially popular with young people still in school, those just coming out, and among those fifty-plus, who may be looking for something lighter rather than a serious relationship.

Good manners between such friends calls for direct communication and regular check-ins to make sure the situation meets each of your expectations. When difficulties arise, it's almost always because one friend has become romantically attached. A twentysomething gay man elaborated: "We used to grab a bite to eat before having sex, which was fine, because I did like him. Then one day he called and asked me if I wanted to go away for the weekend with some of his friends. That's when I knew we had a problem. He wanted us to become boyfriends."

Here are some suggestions for how to keep such a relationship balanced:

- **Things change (part 1):** If you're thinking of transitioning a solid friendship into one with benefits, remember: Once you've brought sex into it, it's hard to return to your previous relationship.

- **Put any jealousy aside:** Whom your friend has sex with when he's not with you isn't your concern. If you do start to feel jealous, you may be getting emotionally attached. If you're monogamous by nature, this type of arrangement is probably not for you.

- **Keep it quiet:** These relationships are really meant to be on the Q.T. Don't brag, and don't out your friend. She may actually be dating someone else who doesn't know about your after-hours liaisons. Or, if you're in the same social circle, you don't want your other buddies ragging on the pair of you.

- **Keep it light:** If you're not in the mood, otherwise engaged, or uninterested at a particular time, simply say so. No expectations means no disappointments allowed.

- **Things change (part 2):** Be prepared to accept the fact that most of these relationships have an expiration date.

STRAIGHT TALK

"What do I say if I think my lesbian friend is flirting with me?"

There's plenty of room for miscues and miscommunication in any relationship, and not surprisingly, this is a particular risk between gay people and straights. Is that possible in this case? What you interpret as flirty may in her mind be friendly. On the other hand, she may be infatuated with you, even though she knows you're straight. But I don't think there is anything that you *should* tell her, unless there's something specific that she's doing that makes you uncomfortable—too much touching, for instance. If that's the case, just explain why that makes you uncomfortable. Otherwise, take it as a compliment!

QUEERY

"Uh-oh! I had sex with my best friend."

Q Last week I ended up having sex with my best friend, Richard. At least he used to be my best friend— we haven't talked since. Did I mess up? I definitely don't want to lose our friendship, but I think I'd like to become boyfriends now.

A Slow down. Before you plan the rest of your life together or, conversely, prepare for Armageddon, you need to do some thinking and talking. Best friends sometimes make the best lovers; after all, who else knows you better? At the same time, you put something precious at risk— your friendship.

In a more perfect world, you would have discussed all this before jumping into bed, but call Richard now and tell him, "We need to talk." Ask him if knows what he wants from your relationship. Maybe he does—or maybe he's confused or embarrassed. But don't get caught up by the notion that once you've had sex you can't go back to being friends (if that's what you both want).

Friendships in Distress

"Natalia and I had been extremely close friends for years," explained a bisexual literature professor, "when she betrayed several confidences of mine. We tried to work it out, but I found I couldn't trust her again, and so I finally told her the friendship was over. She was devastated, and I lost someone I cared about. I never imagined there could be so much pain involved with losing a friend."

Indeed, friendships have ups and downs like any other close relationship; they may evolve and they may dissolve. Ending a friendship can be especially painful if it involves cutting ties with someone who's been your surrogate family. But before you get to the point of no return, here are some things you can do and say to help get back on track:

- **Talk together:** Before deciding to end a friendship or just quietly walk away from it, try to discuss the issues at hand. If you're on the outs already, call, e-mail, or text to set up a time to talk. But definitely meet face-to-face for the talking part, if you can: In-person conversations permit eye contact. They're also more difficult to cut off abruptly, as opposed to hanging up the phone or ending an e-mail thread.
- **Avoid the blame game:** One person is rarely entirely responsible for a dispute. Be open about your own shortcomings. Remember that the goal is not to be right, but to fix the friendship. If you both keep that in mind, you're more likely to succeed in mending the breach.
- **Apologize:** If you're in the wrong, say so. Then either ask how you can make amends or suggest a way.

- **Avoid involving other friends:** Your first inclination may be to reach out to your social circle for support and to share all the gory details about this conflict, but don't. It's not a good idea to ask other friends to take sides, and these conversations have a way of making their way where they don't belong—back to your friend, for instance, or to more public venues, like Facebook.
- **If you feel you need the perspective of a third party, talk to just one friend:** When you discuss this with someone else, agree that you'll both keep the conversation private. Or ask her to act as an emissary to your estranged friend.

Ways to Part

Perhaps you feel a friend down the hall in your dorm has wronged you in some unredeemable way. Or you have tried to resolve a difficult issue with a close friend and been frustrated by the quality of his response—or even exhausted trying to get him to respond. Or your life—or hers—has simply changed so much that trying to maintain your friendship feels dishonest and forced. Whatever the reason, there may come a time when you need to accept the fact that a friendship has run its course.

There are several ways to proceed. You can try to let the friendship peter out on its own by planning fewer and fewer get-togethers, calling less often, or not responding in a timely way to phone calls. Instead of saying "I'm busy" or "I'll be on vacation" when you're asked to do something, be purposefully vague: "No thanks, I'm not really interested in that" or just "Sorry, I can't." At some point, your friend will understand that the friendship is over and move on as well.

Or you can "break up" with your friend by initiating a conversation. You could say, "I know we've tried to work things out, but because of [fill in the blank] I think it's best we moved on." Or "I've heard what you said, but I don't see us staying friends." If you take this approach, don't let the breakup conversation devolve into another rancorous debate or rehash. Say what you need to say and then say good-bye.

But remember: Just because you're not friends anymore doesn't mean you're enemies. Don't talk badly about your ex-friend; if asked by others what happened, you can say simply, "Thanks for asking, but that's between us." Or, if you can handle it, you can become "frenemies," acting superficially as friends while silently holding on to your resentments and injuries. Not for the faint of heart.

ONLINE FRIENDS

The lightning pace of new technology is changing the way we make and maintain friendships. It's even morphing our definition of what it means to be a friend. As early adopters, LGBT people have been in the forefront of these changes. While the etiquette of online friendships is still in flux—day by day, post by post—there are some guidelines that can help.

Privacy Matters

For LGBT people, there are special considerations to keep in mind when using social networking sites—especially concerning how much you reveal about your sexual orientation or gender identity. When considering which

safeguards to use for protecting your privacy, remember that whatever information, photos, or videos you post on a social networking site may be accessible to others for years to come. That might not seem important right now, but a college admissions officer or a potential employer down the road could see what you've posted and downgrade your prospects—if not reject you.

If you're in the process of coming out, avoid using the Internet as your initial vehicle for sharing the news with family and close friends. However, once out to your core group, social-media services are a welcome way to casually let others know that you're gay or dating someone of the same sex, without making a big deal out of it or having the "I am gay" talk. You may decide to use sites like Facebook, LinkedIn (which is primarily for job networking), and Twitter in many different ways and for different purposes. Some use them to stay in touch with their real friends (people you actually know and like) and extended family.

Others have turned their pages into their own LGBT "personals" dating sites, cruising others' friends for pickups, if not messaging about their dates and hookups in real time. Still others have forsaken e-mail entirely and use the services to do their most basic communications. No matter, in each case scrutinize your privacy settings with your needs in mind and be thoughtful about how you choose friends and how much private information you share.

Responding to Friend Requests

It might surprise you, but—to most—it's definitely not considered rude to ignore "friend" or "follower" requests from people you don't know.

"I'm not stalking her, but I do know everything about my Facebook friend."

Q I connected with this really nice woman on Facebook and have been perusing her profile ever since. We're actually going to meet for coffee—just as friends. So am I allowed to "know" as much as I do about her? I don't want to creep her out.

A Unless your new friend has signed up for an app that reveals who's been reading her page, ignorance is bliss. Indeed, when the two of you get together, let her tell you where she went to school, what books she reads, and so on. Avoid comments like "So, I saw you and Annie broke up . . ." or "Sorry to hear that your mother is ill."

Online friendships are just like offline ones. Peeling back the layers of someone's life and personality should happen in a gradual way, as you build up trust. It's entirely possible that your new friend would rather tell you herself about her beloved pets and what she wore for Halloween last year, as opposed to hearing you tell her.

Imagine if a stranger just called you out of the blue. Why would you start a conversation? In fact, ignoring (or "not accepting" it right now) a request is more acceptable—and less jarring—than hanging up on someone. But if you're unclear who someone is, write back like this: "I'm not sure we know each other. Could you remind me?" Depending on the reply and on how you like to use the service, you can decide whether or not to confirm. For instance, on LinkedIn, users usually exact higher standards because of the professional nature of that service and the tacit endorsement of having someone be a part of your network.

Here are some instances when it's perfectly fine not to accept a friend request:

- When that person is not a friend in so-called real life. "I couldn't believe that Karyn would try to friend me—actually twice—after maliciously gossiping about me behind my back," said one gay Facebooker.
- If your ex sends a request and you don't want him or her to see into your new life.

- If you think someone is trying to pick you up and you're not interested.
- Work colleagues are especially dicey. For instance, you'll be in hot water if you tell the office you're out sick but write on your page that you're taking a three-day weekend. Or if you post "I wish I could take this job and shove it," your boss may do just that to you. By the way, even if your supervisor isn't in your network, other workplace "friends" could inadvertently (or, worse, intentionally) repost your musings so that your boss sees them. That's why some people decide not to accept friendship requests from colleagues across the board. (Note to bosses: Don't friend your underlings.)
- If you're trying to contact someone you don't know or someone who is famous, spend a minute or two and write a personal message making your case. Wrote one young man: "When friending my favorite public people, I usually include a message to show that I am a real fan."

PART II

LOVE & SEX

CHAPTER 3

Dating

Making Romantic Connections

———

The trajectory of an LGBT romance isn't always easy to define or predict. Dating can be a time for playing around and having sex—with no particular end game in sight. Or it can be about serial monogamy—think of the fellow who sees one guy for a while, and then the next time you bump into him he's got a new boyfriend in tow. Or, it can be a tryout for a long-term relationship, which may eventually lead to a commitment.

If there are any differences between gay and straight dating, they stem from the fact that some of us grew up in the closet, awkwardly coming of age in a hostile world. If this sounds like you, your first relationships were likely clandestine affairs. Others of us started dating as straight—and may still be trying to decipher the rules and rituals of same-sex dating.

Regardless of where you start, the road to a successful dating life is knowing what you want. Once you've got that figured out (easier said than done), you're ready to brush up on the basic strategies for finding an LGBT date in the first place and then comfortably negotiate everything that follows—whether it's okay to Google a new prospect beforehand, the rules for nonmonogamous dating, as well as how to go out with others while still living with your ex. Online dating has manners of its own, of course, and issues such as creating an eye-catching or heart-stopping profile are no small matter now that the Internet has become one of our best bets for finding a date, sex—or true love.

READY, SET, DATE

As with any challenging endeavor, it's wise to get your house in order beforehand—or in other words, to be prepared. A friend of mine who has struggled in the dating department recently asked a professional matchmaker for guidance. He reports, "He explained to me the importance of everything from grooming and hygiene to the art of listening and asking and to understanding how and when to reciprocate." While there isn't a set list of requirements for successful dating, there are things you really should consider before you start (or restart) your dating career.

Prerequisites

Before you begin to date, it helps to know where you stand, so ask yourself three questions: Are you out? What kind of relationship do you want? Are you ready to date?

IF IT'S SAFE FOR YOU, COME OUT

Ideally, you'll be out of the closet when starting to date, if only to be recognized by other gay people. If you're not out yet, think about these questions:

- How will you introduce your date to others? While you can say, "Oh, she's my friend," that's hardly ideal.
- When friends, family members, or colleagues want to include you in their social lives, will you find it necessary to lie outright, awkwardly switch pronouns to cover your tracks, or leave your beloved at home alone?
- If you vacation together, how will you deal with the question "One bed or two?" Some couples, when put in a room with two twins, would rather not say anything to the hotel staff for fear of outing themselves. Not a very sexy option.
- If you have children from an earlier heterosexual relationship, what will you be teaching them about honesty and trust if you lie about your "friend"?

WHAT KIND OF RELATIONSHIP

Do you want a boyfriend or girlfriend? A long-term relationship? A friend with benefits? A sexual liaison? It's also okay if you don't know; just be sure to acknowledge that, both to yourself and to those you encounter. Also figure out what qualities you find attractive in others. A certain body type or gender identity? Fashion sense? Kindness? Hipness? Lefty politics? Having a job? Shared interests? This will help you focus your search. However, be wary of putting too many "must-haves" on your wish list. Try to stay open to what you might not know that you like.

BEING EMOTIONALLY AVAILABLE

How much "baggage" are you carrying? Are you sufficiently disentangled from a previous relationship? If necessary, have you gone the distance in therapy or dealt with any major demons, like alcohol or drug abuse or childhood sexual abuse?

Self-esteem makes a difference in determining success in the dating arena. Are you confident and generally happy? Do you see yourself as someone worth knowing? If you don't recognize the qualities you have that make you attractive, it's generally harder to project them and to accept others' appreciation of you.

Where to Look

While plenty of romances have started in the bedroom or backroom, there are better places to spend your time if you're seeking a compatible companion. Among them:

- **Join a group:** Consider your own likes and dislikes, idiosyncrasies and passions. If you have a particular hobby or extracurricular interest, look around for LGBT social groups in your area that cater to that. There are all kinds, from hiking, rowing, wine tasting, and movie clubs to yoga and meditation; there's Alcoholics Anonymous; groups for young people coming out and for seniors who play duplicate bridge. Depending on where you live, you may find all-gay groups (e.g., a gay book club or a lesbian bowling league) or they may be mixed—with gays and straights.

- **Get a dog:** Dogs are date magnets. If you have one, walk it on the street or go to a dog park. If you don't, borrow a friend's or foster a rescue from your local animal shelter.

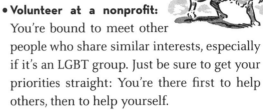

- **Volunteer at a nonprofit:** You're bound to meet other people who share similar interests, especially if it's an LGBT group. Just be sure to get your priorities straight: You're there first to help others, then to help yourself.

- **Join a social networking site or a dating site:** Choose one that is more focused on dating than sex hookups. If you've spent any time on the Internet, you know that it's easy to tell which is which. The home page of one dating site boasts, "We know you not only want to go on dates, you want to go on great dates . . . with someone you've made a connection with." Contrast that with a site that asks you, "Looking for a dom top or a boi? Power bottom or a transguy?" Need I say more?

- **Hire a matchmaker:** Real-life matchmakers do exist, and for a handsome fee they will bring together eligible gay singles. Many use lengthy personality tests, others have secret algorithms, and a few actually rely on their intuition. (For more on matchmakers, see page 53.)

- **Bars and clubs:** These can be great spots to find a boyfriend or girlfriend rather than a one-night stand, but so much depends on the bar or club. Do your homework ahead of time—or seek out recommendations.

- **Ask friends and colleagues to set you up:** Often, there's no better referral service than the people you already know. If a friend—or a sibling—happens to say, "I know this great girl . . . ," find out more! If not, don't be afraid to ask, "Do you know of anyone single who'd be a good match for me?"

"I recognize you from your online profile."

How to Know if Someone Is Flirting with You

Ask any lesbian: Gay men are generally quite good at the eye-contact game; lesbians not so much. But there are ways to tell if the person you're chatting up is simply being friendly and well-mannered or flirting. Here is what to pay attention to:

• **Eye contact:** Does he continue to gaze at you, not staring you down, but making repeated eye contact (and then averting his eyes as if caught in the act)? Someone who avoids your eyes completely, even if otherwise friendly, is probably not flirting.

• **Body language:** Does she lean toward you slightly? Does she "inadvertently" touch you, perhaps with a knee or a pat on your arm? Is she smiling? Or, are her arms crossed, in an unconsciously "closed" posture?

• **Asks questions:** Someone who asks about your life or your work—even what you're wearing—and listens to your replies (yes, even your long-winded stories) is definitely interested in you.

• **Flatters you:** Usually a dead giveaway. Be gracious in accepting compliments that come your way and don't be afraid to make them in return. Unless your prospect is swimming in the shallow end, he should get the message.

Where the Girls Are

Lesbians and bisexual women find each other pretty much the same way gay men do, whether they call themselves womyn, dykes, grrls, bois, femmes, or butches. Bars, volunteering, match-makers, pet interests, and online chatrooms have helped millions of women get dates. Not to mention queer film festivals, twelve-step groups, yoga classes, music festivals (e.g., Womenfest and the Michigan Womyn's Music Festival), and all-women cruise ship lines like Olivia. But don't forget to put women's studies classes and sports teams, two classic lesbian-date venues, on your list. Said one Brooklyn softball regular of her team, "I've never met so many lesbians in my life."

Lesbian networks—whether on the field, in a bar, or through a writing or reading group—can also be fruitful. You never know when someone new might just walk in the door at your local lesbian café or tai chi class. Also don't forget about lesbian-only social networking sites like Olivia Connect (sponsored by the cruise line Olivia). If there's a friend in your social circle who likes setting up her friends, let her know you're open to that.

THE ESSENTIALS

Gaydar for Dating

Some gay and bi people claim they have an intuitive ability, which has been dubbed "gaydar," to assess sexual orientation. Gaydar is usually based on nonverbal cues, such as eye contact, mannerisms, grooming, personal style, or even a person's line of work. Others claim to have no such sixth sense or think the whole concept is at best unscientific and at worst stereotyping.

The truth is that gaydar is elusive and often unreliable. In a poll on my site, www.gaymanners.com, only 23 percent of those who responded trusted their own gaydar. A gay man who's now in his forties blogged, "When I was first coming out, it seemed easier to recognize gay men by their facial hair, certain kinds of tattoos, even the brands they wore. Now, it's really hard to say what makes someone 'gay.'" In any case, it's a good rule of thumb (and good manners) to exercise caution when jumping to conclusions about someone you don't know. Even if you're scanning a Facebook page and see a boatload of what appear to be LGBT friends, don't extrapolate further. A lesbian noted: "I was sure this woman was gay. It turned out the girl with her in her profile photo was her sister and she was married to a man. Oops!"

Your best bet is always to get to know someone personally and allow him or her to come out to you before making assumptions.

Bisexual Dating

The term "bisexual" used to be incredibly loaded. Many didn't understand that a bi person is not a gay person hiding his or her true orientation, or a lesbian or gay man passing through a phase before coming out. Bit by bit, the message is getting out that bisexuality is a unique sexual orientation and that bi people are attracted—physically, sexually, and/or romantically—to both men and women.

If you're going out with someone who's told you that he or she is bisexual, the same questions apply as in any other dating situation: Is there mutual attraction? Are you seeing anyone else? What are your expectations? Are you in this just for the sex or might you also be open to falling in love? Are you marriage-minded? How do you feel about kids? If the answers are right, the sexuality, bi or otherwise, of the person you're dating might not matter so much.

Transgender Dating

Finding your own kind is not as much of an issue for transgender people looking to date, since few restrict themselves to other trans people. As a result, there are more and more ways for trans people to meet each other—and others—for dating and romance.

If you're a trans single who is out, consider expanding your social circle by attending trans events (often hosted by local LGBT centers) or finding them online. A number of all-inclusive transgender dating sites exists; for instance, Trans Passions (www.transpassions.com) advertises itself for "MTF and FTM transsexuals, transvestites/cross-dressers, drag queens, drag kings," and others still.

On the other hand, if you're a "stealth" trans (not out) and not interested in mentioning

"I want to ask her out but I don't know for sure if she's a lesbian."

Q Sometimes I'm not sure if the girl I want to ask out is a lesbian. Right now, I really like this woman I'm becoming friends with. I don't want to make a fool of myself: How can I ask if she's into women without embarrassing myself?

A Dating, by definition, involves taking risks and sometimes even making fools of ourselves. Determining whether someone is lesbian—or bi, or at least interested in women—can be a delicate business.

Instead of asking for a date, try getting to know her better in nonsexual ways. Are you both art lovers? Ask her to a gallery. Do you like certain kinds of books? Go to a reading together. Then, slowly weave in information about your sexuality so that she understands. You don't need

to shout, *"Hey, I'm a lesbian!"* Instead, mention that you went with some women friends to a lesbian club, or that you volunteer at an LGBT nonprofit. She'll figure out the rest—likely that *you're* interested. At that point, if she's gay, she's likely to come out to you. And if she's interested, *she'll* make that clear, too. Bingo!

Also keep in mind that even if someone hasn't dated women in the past, that doesn't mean she's out of reach. You might well be her first!

your birth gender, identify yourself on the dating scene as straight, gay, lesbian, or bi and leave it at that.

TELLING YOUR DATE "I'M TRANSGENDER"

Whether and when to disclose that you are transgender to someone you're dating is a highly personal decision, so there is no right or wrong here. It's a private fact about you that might become relevant to someone you're dating if the relationship progresses past a certain point, but you don't owe other people an explanation about being trasgender.

Some trans people prefer to be open about their transgender status in all aspects of their lives; others prefer to disclose it only under certain circumstances, and many fall somewhere in between. In the past, the standard

advice from health care providers was to keep one's trans status hidden at all costs. But now there is a growing understanding that feeling obliged to conceal such an important aspect of one's life can take a heavy emotional toll. Certainly, if you disclose your trans status upfront in a dating situation (for instance, in an online profile), you'll be filtering out those who do not accept that aspect of who you are. Yes, it can be hard to talk about something personal, like being trans, with someone new, but it can also have a pretty big payoff.

Regardless of whether or when you tell someone that you are trans, be aware of your safety. It is sad but true that violence against transwomen in the dating context is all too common, and it can be hard to know in advance whether someone is prone to violence. If there are any cues that the person might be—say, if he seems to be homophobic or controlling—be extra careful. But no matter what, make sure that you are able to get help immediately if you need it, whether from your friends and family or from local LGBT or anti-violence organizations.

Blind Dates

There are two basic varieties of blind dates: You meet a stranger via a dating service or you're set up by a mutual acquaintance. "I met this guy from a gay dating site who had misled me about everything. And from the instant he picked me up, I knew I was in trouble. He didn't have enough gas and he asked me for five dollars for that within minutes. It went downhill from there." Sadly, this story is the kind of experience that gives blind dates a bad reputation. Then there's the other kind of blind date, where you're fixed up by a friend, coworker, or relative, and you e-mail or chat on the phone with each other before moving ahead to the face-to-face. Under either scenario there are tons of things that could go wrong, and it's natural before a blind date to worry that you will be bored to death, that your date will be psychotic, or that your friends will ridicule you for being desperate.

The truth is, however, that blind dates can sometimes be great experiences and even turn into great relationships. Forget about all the horror stories you've heard. What's important is to do your homework beforehand and exercise caution.

QUEERY

"My friends want to set me up with every gay guy they know."

Q I moved to Dallas about six months ago. While I do happen to be looking for a boyfriend, I find it annoying that every straight person I've met knows *one* gay man to set me up with. You know the drill— the gay neighbor, the gay mechanic, the gay lawyer. I appreciate the good intentions, but how do I explain that being gay doesn't mean I would go out with just any gay guy?

A Hey, be thankful that you have so many friends who care enough to try to set you up. And while another man's sexual orientation is not enough to make him the match of the century, it's also true that meeting someone through a friend gives you a leg up over a chance encounter online or at a club.

Definitely don't be snarky with your matchmaker friends. Instead of giving them the "just because I'm gay" line, ask questions about the guy: How old? What line of work? Truly single? Funny? Smart? Redheaded? Why do you think we might be interested in each other? Don't make it into an inquisition, but find out a little about the potential date— besides the fact that he's gay. If you like what you hear, ask for an introduction—on e-mail, through a social media site—or let your friend know it's okay to give out your phone number. Even if you don't end up going out with a particular fellow, thank your friends for trying to help you out. And tell them to keep trying.

GETTING TO KNOW EACH OTHER

As you e-mail or chat on the phone, seek out "hard" data—what does she do for fun, where did she go to college, etc.—but also look for the intangibles. This includes topics like politics and other beliefs, what she cares about outside of her work, whether she seems to be basically content or, on the contrary, is desperate about finding a mate. Most of all, pay attention to what is said and how it's said. Does she control the conversation? Does she seem genuinely interested in you? Do you hear jealousy or contempt in the background? Is she talking about topics that feel premature to you (her addictions, exes, maybe even domestic abuse)? Trust your instincts. There's no preset timetable that says when, if ever, you need to meet.

ONLINE BLIND DATES

When starting a back-and-forth with someone new, be cautious but don't be paranoid. At first:

- Don't give out your last name, address, or personal website URL or reveal where you work.
- Continue to use the anonymous e-mail address the dating service provides you.
- If or when you decide to give out your phone number, start with your cell—instead of a landline—because it's harder for someone to track down personal information about you that way.
- After a short time, if you're still interested, don't be shy about asking to see some photos—if you haven't already. If you think they may not be current, ask when they were taken. Be sure to offer your own, too.

QUEERY

"I thought it was just dinner, but I was wrong."

Q I was out for a bite with a friend from college, who's also gay. We see each other a couple times a year, but this was the first time since each of us became single. I wasn't thinking of him romantically, but he suddenly got all Bette Davis eyes on me. When he said, "It's so great to finally be on a date with you," I panicked and told him I was dating someone. Now he's invited me and the imaginary boyfriend over for a party. What do I do?

A You actually have a lot of options, ranging from declining the invitation altogether to getting a stand-in for your imaginary boyfriend or coming solo and lying once again that the new boyfriend isn't free that night. . . . But your best bet may be to confess to your imaginary boyfriend.

My suggestion: Call your college friend and explain that his declaration made you uncomfortable because your feelings aren't reciprocal. While you're confessing, mention that you made up the new boyfriend or, as politicians say these days, that you misspoke. As long as there's no extant video, you'll live.

Professional Matchmakers

Professional matchmakers—think Dolly Levi in *Hello, Dolly!*—have been helping straights date for eons (have you seen the ads in all those airline magazines?), but it's only been in the past ten or fifteen years that LGBT-specific matchmakers have become a decent alternative to the anonymity and frequent disappointments of online dating. Explained one fortysomething San Francisco man: "The gay bar scene isn't much help to me at this age—everyone's a pup—and online dating sites have led nowhere."

Other reasons lesbians and gay men give for enrolling include:

- Wanting someone else to do the screening (as opposed to scrolling through online profiles yourself).
- Having unique requests or interests that are difficult to pair.
- Finding it difficult to meet relationship-minded people.
- Needing encouragement to get back into the dating arena, perhaps after a soured relationship or the death of a partner.
- Having just come out and not having contacts or friends within the LGBT community.
- Wanting the encouragement and practical advice of a dating coach, which most of these matchmakers are.

If you're interested in a particular matchmaker but want to make sure you get your money's worth, ask whether you can contact some clients for references. If the matchmaker agrees (some may have promised their clients confidentiality, so don't take a no to mean they have no satisfied customers), ask these clients whether the services provided matched their expectations.

Depending on the level of personal service provided, these professional matchmakers can be costly, *significantly* more than the fees you might pay to an online dating service. Just in case you need a bit of a nudge in this direction, here's one gay matchmaker's rationale: "You pay an attorney to solve your legal problems and a doctor to heal you. Why not consider paying a relationship expert to help you find a partner?"

FIRST DATES

No doubt the most fraught and yet potentially most exciting of all dates are the very first. There's so much to think about: from pickups to small talk, from who pays the check to how to say "no thanks," to how best to use texting and e-mail as you get to know each other.

The Art of the Pickup

Introducing yourself to someone who strikes your fancy is, at least in theory, fairly straightforward. Are you both walking dogs, shopping for sweaters, or waiting for a yoga class to begin? You have permission to go ahead and start a conversation about your mutual interest. Sometimes you have to take chances. "I was running in Central Park a few years ago," said a gay dentist, "and I jogged by this handsome guy walking through the park. We made eye contact, but I didn't know what to do, so I kept going. But then I circled back and stopped to say hello. After a few minutes of chatting, I asked him for his phone number. That worked."

Definitely avoid cheesy pickup lines, like "Go out with me, and you'll never regret it" or "Let me take you to dinner. It will be a night to remember." The best ones are simple and authentic, like introducing yourself or asking a relevant question such as "What's your adorable dog's name?" or "How long have you been practicing yoga?"

So how do you know if someone's interested? While gay men are known for making instant connections, lesbians joke that the way you know someone's interested is if she doesn't look at you. Of course, women do meet strangers in day-to-day life; you just may have to pretend more convincingly that your interest is purely platonic, work-related, or neighborly. Even if you both know it's not. (For more on flirting, see page 48.)

The most important step to remember is this one: Make sure you get a phone number or e-mail address, some way that will allow you to follow up. This is true if you've met at a dyke bar, a bodybuilder gym, a grocery store, an LGBT community center, or a train station. Say, "It'd be nice to have more time to talk. Can I call you?" For good reason, some people may be hesitant to give out a phone number; be sure to offer yours as well.

Whether to Text or E-mail

Texting or e-mailing to ask someone out is appropriate in some circles and not in others, depending in large measure on what LGBT generation you belong to. If text messaging is second nature to you and your intended, well

then go ahead and fire up your smartphone. An extra benefit is that texting seems to provide social insulation from the awkwardness of potential rejection. One bisexual college senior explained the prevailing norm at school: "My friends would almost never call someone to ask them out on a first date."

For many, however, picking up the phone and actually having a conversation remains the gold standard. Not only can you learn more about each other by talking and listening, there's something to be gleaned from spontaneous laughter, acerbic wit—even those pregnant pauses. (Once you've agreed to go out, it's probably easier for most to text, e-mail, or use your favorite chat function to figure out the logistics of the first date, although this too is often a generational preference.)

Making the Ask

Whatever medium you've decided to use, here are some suggestions for presenting yourself as well-mannered and worthy of a first date:

- **Be specific yet open-ended with your inquiry:** If you ask someone, "Can you have dinner with me on Thursday?" and she answers no, you don't have enough information to understand why. Is it that she's busy on Thursday? Or is it that she doesn't want to go out with you at all? It's preferable to ask, "Would you like to have dinner with me next week?" If she says yes, then you can be pretty sure she's interested; proceed to nailing down a specific day of the week that works for you both.
- **Be creative:** Make the date sound interesting and fun. Even better than saying, "Wanna have dinner with me next week?" is "I heard

there's a great new café open. Why don't we go check it out before everyone else does?" Or, if you know he likes classical music, you can ask, "I read in the paper that this great string quartet will be in town next week. Would you like to go with me?"

• **Don't shortchange yourself:** If you're asking someone out, make the offer directly and in a positive way. If you use such lead-ins as "I don't suppose you'd want to . . ." or "I'm sure you'll say no, but . . ." it hands the other person a reason to turn you down.

• **Make friends and turn them into dates:** Let's say you have a queer studies class together. Maybe you have a question about an assignment or could use a study partner for an upcoming test. Introduce yourself and jump right into talking about the class. After you've spent a couple of sessions studying, suggest going out for a drink or a bite to eat.

Bar Pickups

Sending over a cocktail is a well-utilized, low-risk, high-reward way to meet a new beau, with the only real cost being the price of the drink. After someone has caught your eye, maneuver yourself into position and either follow steps 1 and 2 or just jump to step 3:

1. **Make eye contact:** Don't frighten anyone with your stare, but cruise long enough to gauge interest, and then enlist the bartender in your cause. Ask the barkeep what your "friend" is drinking—don't rely on your own judgment here, as a gin-and-tonic with lime looks just like a

club soda with lime, a mistake you really wouldn't want to make. Have the mixologist deliver the fresh drink.

2. **Introduce yourself:** If you get a welcoming look or a smile or she waves you over, go ahead and start some small talk. If, however, the drink is refused or there's no such affirming look, I'm sorry to say you've struck out.

   Note: Don't repeat this frequently with different people during a single evening in a single venue; others may catch on.

3. **Do it yourself:** The other way to go about this pickup is to do the legwork yourself. Establish eye contact, make your way over, introduce yourself, chat for a bit, and if your new acquaintance seems friendly enough about the whole situation, then go ahead and ask if you may buy her a cocktail. Find out what she prefers and pay for it.

THE ESSENTIALS

How to Tell Whether Someone's Available

If you're dating in order to build a committed relationship, avoiding people who are partnered or otherwise unavailable sounds pretty basic. However, it's not always so easy. Certain phrases a date or potential date uses could mean trouble. For instance, if someone describes himself as "almost divorced" or "separated" or refers to the person he lives with too emphatically as "*just* a roommate," you should probably follow up with a direct question about his relationship status. A lesbian psychologist remembers a first date that went well until the woman mentioned her partner. "I asked her more about that relationship and she explained that it was an 'open' one—so 'no problem.' Well, for me it was a problem."

Here are some other signs to be on the watch for:

- **Wedding or commitment bands:** If there's a ring, ask about it: "That's a beautiful ring. Does it mean something?" It's more difficult for most people to deceive in response to a direct question.
- **Difficulty getting a home phone number or a personal e-mail address:** Does it seem like she is unreachable frequently? When you're out together, does she take calls out of your earshot? Or does she disappear completely on weekends or every night after 10:00 P.M.?
- **Excuses:** At some point, you may want to introduce your date to a friend or two. Is that sentiment reciprocated? Is there always some reason not to meet his friends? If there's a pattern, ask about it.
- **Lack of reciprocation:** Do you spend time together only at your place, never hers? Excuses like "My flat is a complete mess" or "I need to do my laundry" have a short half-life. Always meeting on your turf is a red flag that there may be a partner ensconced at home.

If you sense something is awry, don't be afraid to ask, "Are you involved with someone else?" or "Is there something you want to tell me?"

Declining a Date

What is it about "no, thanks" that many of us find so difficult to say when we're not interested? Rather than tell the truth or some close variant, we make up imaginary partners and illnesses; work obligations; phantom vacations; sometimes we avoid phone calls, delete e-mails, and even change our routines to avoid dishing out a rejection.

There can be many reasons you don't want to go out with someone—for example, you're not attracted to the person, you're currently dating someone, or your social calendar is full. Here are some strategies for saying no politely, in ways that you would probably appreciate yourself if you were on the other end of things:

- **Be true to what you're feeling, but don't be rude:** Say "I'm really not in a place to date right now." Or "I don't think we have that much in common." If pressed for more details, end the conversation; there's no reason to get into a debate about such things.
- **Try not to reply too specifically to the details of the invitation:** If you say, "I'm sorry, I'm going to be traveling for business this week," a persistent person will simply ask about the following week. Don't allude to a future date that will never happen by continuing to put off saying no; however, vagueness is okay: "I travel for my job quite a bit, and I can't really fit dating into my life now."
- **Don't disappear:** If you've gone out with the person already—even just once—it's rude to ignore an invitation. Try to tie things up, if only by e-mailing or by calling at a time when you know he's not going to pick up and you can decline by voicemail.
- **Don't lie:** Saying you have a husband (when you don't) or that your sister is having surgery (when she's not) as your excuse to decline a date will likely come back to haunt you. It's a small gay world sometimes—plus, it's bad karma.

Note: Some of your more persistent admirers will, when rejected, ask to be friends. While that has a nice ring to it, beware that they may be using that as an excuse to ask you out again—consciously or not. If you're not interested in a friendship, close the door firmly. You don't need to say, "No, we can't be friends." Something like "I'm not really looking for new friends" or "Things are really busy for me these days" will do the trick.

IF YOU ASK SOMEONE OUT AND THEY SAY NO

Don't be angry or bitter if someone declines to go out with you. Whether face-to-face or electronically, thank them for being direct with you—and not taking up more of your time. Also don't plead your case, like asking for a second chance. It's better to move on—head high.

Scheduling Dates

When asking someone out for the first time, try to give at least two or three days' notice. Anything less can make you seem a little

desperate, or your date may think that you're just trying to fill up your calendar at the last minute. A lesbian literary agent explains, "Even if I have no plans, I won't say yes to a date if it's the day before, especially if it's the weekend."

First dates are better scheduled on a weekday evening or a lazy weekend afternoon; expectations are lower and you'll both have an excuse to call it quits earlier with hardly a raised eyebrow. Say it's a Wednesday evening and you've met for a drink; you could say, "That was great, but it's a school night and I better be going." Or, if it's the weekend and you're ready to move on, "Thanks for meeting up with me. I've got a writing class that I need to get to on time."

Planning Your Date

Whether you're going on a blind date, a first in-person meeting, or for drinks when you've met the person already (say in your volleyball

---

QUEERY

"How to lose a stranger at a club"

Q I've always wondered about this: After you've been talking with a new person at a bar or a party for a while and you're ready to move on, how do you do that without seeming obvious or hurtful? I usually say I need to go outside for a cigarette—even though I don't even smoke!

A I'm going to start with two excuses I have made over the years to creep away from a creep or make a beeline toward a more attractive fellow: "I've got to use the restroom. I'll be right back" and "I need another cocktail. I'll be right back." (Notice how I didn't offer to bring one back for him.) Of course, I never came right back—and felt like a louse.

Please don't handle your escapes the way I did. Instead, try being straightforward, which

is not necessarily the same as being honest. For instance, say, "I've really enjoyed talking with you, but I'm going to walk around a bit." You may not have "really enjoyed" the conversation, but that's a nicety that offsets your departure. Or try "I don't want to take up too much of your time. It's been nice sharing a drink with you." Then, when you wind up standing in line for the restroom next to each other, you won't feel so much like a cad.

league or at a party), take some time to plan ahead and be smart about your choices.

- **Choose a place where you can actually hear each other:** A noisy bar or a club isn't conducive to easy conversation. A coffee shop or the small bar area of a quiet restaurant might be a better choice. However, don't choose a spot frequented by your friends. You want to focus on your date, without the distraction of your personal posse.

- **Don't meet for dinner:** Three courses with someone who bores you or drinks too much will ruin any appetite you may have. Make the first date short by design—30 to 45 minutes is a good target. This is one situation where telling a white lie is acceptable if you have difficulty leaving. Tell her you have an appointment to go to, a friend waiting to meet you for dinner, or an early alarm in the morning. Or you can use one of the new Web services that calls your cell at a designated time to "remind" you of your next engagement.

- **Dress comfortably but make an effort to look nice:** Remember, first dates are all about first impressions. For the same reason, be on time.

- **Rescheduling:** If you don't feel well or some other legitimate conflict arises, postpone the date, providing as much notice as you can. Be honest about what's going on, stress your sincerity about rescheduling, and then follow up in the next day or so, or as soon as you're back on your feet.

Safety Considerations

The nervous joke that underlies all discussion of first dates—but especially blind dates set up online—is that an unknown person could turn out to be a weirdo, a stalker, or even a sociopath. (Actually, the chances of someone being truly frightening are slim, so don't let this cautionary note dissuade you from dating.) While there's always a hint of risk in meeting someone for the first time, there's a lot you can do to mitigate that:

- Choose a public place—say, a coffee shop or a bar—for the rendezvous.

- Don't invite the person over to your home, even if it's just to pick you up.

- Try to have more than a mobile number and an anonymous e-mail address for your date before you decide to meet, in case you want to track your date down later.

- If you're nervous about the get-together, tell a close friend where you're going and also leave any information about your prospective date—for instance, a name and a phone number. You might also want to check in with your friend as soon as the date is over.

Last-Minute Cancellations

Unless some horrible emergency has occurred or you're stuck in a subway tunnel, the proliferation of smartphones and other devices means there's virtually no excuse for leaving someone waiting. Under most circumstances, you can send a text that reads, "I'm so sorry, but I can't make it now. Will explain later."

So let's assume you need to cancel right before your date:

- **Deliver the news as quickly as you can:** Try to phone so that she can hear the genuine consternation in your voice. Briefly explain what has happened: "I'm at the vet with my dog—she just got hit by a car" or "My boss is insisting that we all work late this evening."

- **Keep reaching out until you're certain your message has been received:** You don't want to have sent an e-mail to someone waiting for you in a café without e-mail access.
- **Apologize:** And then see when you can reschedule. If there's no time to pin down the details of your next try, make sure you're the one following up the next day, calendar in hand.
- **Next steps:** If your date follows up to ask how your dog is now or whether you completed the work project from the evening in question, make sure to have an answer—that is, that you told the truth or you remember your fib. When you do actually go out, apologize again and, as a nice gesture, start off by buying her a drink.

IF YOU'RE THE ONE COOLING YOUR HEELS

If you're the one already at the rendezvous spot waiting for your date to show up, a good rule of thumb is to wait no more than twenty minutes, erring on the generous side in bad weather or if your date could be caught in traffic. Don't jump to conclusions that you were stood up. Send a polite e-mail later on saying something like "I'm sorry I missed you this evening, but I waited at the restaurant until 6:20. I hope you're okay." If the person has a legitimate excuse, or as sometimes happens, there was a mix-up in plans, he or she will respond soon. And if not . . . next!

Googling Your Date

To Google or not to Google, how often have you wondered about that question? Your instinct may be to gobble up whatever information is available about your prospective date, and indeed it's all out there—work history, address, how much she paid for her home, criminal history, tweets, and more. Having this information may be useful on a first date, especially if you're straining for a bit of conversation.

The problem is that you will also discover things that are incorrect; information that is embarrassing; and maybe things you'd rather not know, such as court actions, even intimate details about children or previous relationships. Imagine stumbling upon the opposite-sex wedding announcement of your lesbian date, for instance. Okay, so you didn't know that she had a heterosexual past. It's not that there's anything wrong with the information; it's more that it's without context and definitely on the private side.

Using search engines also interferes with the magic of discovery. There's something to be said for learning about your date gradually and in her own words. The non-Google strategy also allows you to ask questions as you go, replying only to the information your date chooses to share.

Still, if you've gone ahead and Googled someone, don't divulge everything you've learned in the first fifteen minutes; it might seem like you've overstepped to know so many details about a near stranger. Better to let the conversation unfold at a more normal pace. If you slip up and reveal something that you learned on Google, confess that you went online and did a little "homework."

Meanwhile, don't forget to do a search on yourself from time to time to find out what kind of information is likely to be discovered by your next date.

Topics to Avoid

Are you a therapy graduate? Do you have a prison record? Are you a recovering drug user? Got any crazy exes? While there's nothing wrong with saying yes to any of these questions, timing is everything; think through how much you want to reveal about yourself to a virtual stranger and remember that dating is a process of getting to know someone. Gradual disclosure is a smart way to proceed. I still remember the poor fellow who broke down in tears after telling me the horrors of growing up in his alcoholic family—all on the first date. So, if you're meeting for the first time, do your best to stay clear of these topics:

- **Previous relationships:** Focus on your date. If asked about your exes, speak truthfully, but then turn the talk back to something you both have in common. If you end up going out again and getting closer, there will be plenty of time to share your past.
- **Therapy issues:** Everyone has baggage; it's just not a good idea to bring it on the first date. Present your best self and keep your addictions and other serious vices to yourself (for now). Of course, if you're not drinking alcohol and you're asked directly whether you're "sober," be up-front. Just don't get into the drama. If you're asked about any topic you'd rather not discuss, say in an undefensive manner, "Let's talk about that when we know each other better." With this, you also signal that you understand boundaries.
- **Negativity in general:** Don't diss your job, your friends, or your family. All that can work against you. Not that you should be a gay Stepford wife.

Under the Influence

As one veteran dater put it: "The only thing worse than getting drunk on a date is being on a date with a drunk." Since you want to get off to a good start, be especially careful not to get too sloppy. Not that you should save such excess for later in the relationship.

There are a variety of reasons that people drink too much on first dates, most notably to have a "good time" or loosen up, being nervous, or not feeling so good about themselves. A good rule of thumb is to keep your alcoholic intake to at most one drink per hour. (A drink is considered either one 5-ounce glass of wine, a 12-ounce beer, or a cocktail of 1.5 ounces of hard liquor.) If you're the kind of person who likes to have a glass in hand, alternate alcoholic beverages with soft drinks or water. Or make a spritzer, which is half wine and half sparkling water. Also, if you know you're going to be drinking, don't go out on an empty stomach. Eating a hard-boiled egg or some bread may help slow the metabolism of the alcohol, although it won't prevent you from becoming inebriated.

Bad Dates

Buck up. How long is a date anyway? In many ways, when you agree to go on a romantic outing, you've made a social contract that includes being on time, dressed for the occasion, able to pay your own way or both of yours—and ready to be pleasant. Oh, and you need to stay at least a little while. If you're on a coffee date, that's about thirty minutes or a bit more. Ditto for drinks. Still, if you find yourself with such bad company that you're ready to bolt after a dinner, when the server asks about coffee, it's fine to say to your date, "I had a long day at work, let's skip dessert." Similarly, if your disappointing companion suggests a nightcap after a concert, try, "I think I better call it a night. I'm meeting my trainer early in the morning."

If your date's behavior falls into the truly objectionable bucket—for example, he is drunk or high, physically or verbally abusive, or making unwanted sexual advances—say good-bye without making a big scene. Try this: "I'm sorry, but this really isn't what I had in mind for the evening," and then leave some cash on the table to cover your share.

If by the end of the first date you've definitely decided there won't be a second, don't think you're being kind by leading the other person on. Say good-bye in a way that doesn't give any sense of false hope, like "It was good to meet you." Even if it is the easiest thing to do at the moment, don't say, "I'll call you soon" or "I'll e-mail you next week." Because if you say it, your date—who may have had a wonderful time—may be expecting you to do just that. Not to mention that you should keep your word.

Tweet 'n' Date

Let's face it: It's rude to talk on your cell phone, text, tweet, or update your Facebook status while on a date. (Although let's also face it: People do it all the time.) The message you're giving out is that you have better things to do than pay attention to the person you're with.

QUEERY

"Speed dating intimidates me."

Q **My best friend is a champ at gay speed dating and thinks it would be great for me, too. Honestly, I'm scared by the whole game: all those guys, only a few minutes. He wants me to go with him to one that promises ten to twenty-five "dates" in an evening. Isn't this completely superficial? Can anything at all come of it?**

A Speed dating is a great way to meet guys. But it is certainly not for the faint of heart; most who make an attempt are nervous the first few times. Try not to feel intimidated, but do think of some questions you'd like to ask ahead of time because you can get tongue-tied, especially knowing you're being judged while the clock is ticking.

Steer away from questions that will result in a yes or no answer since they won't get you into the rhythm of a conversation. Ask about things that matter to you, such as "What kind of work do you do?" or "How do you spend your free time?" Try to avoid complicated questions, like "What's your relationship with your family like?" because you don't have time to do them justice. Remember, you should be asked questions, too.

Keep in mind that speed dating isn't for everyone—many find it superficial. Those who do best are gregarious and outgoing. But you won't be alone if you're more reticent or shy. Either way, all you have to lose is about twenty dollars and an evening. On the upside, you may gain a date or two with some new fellows.

"I went out with a guy last night," writes one frustrated young gay man. "All through our date he was getting text messages, so he would say 'just one sec' and then text them back. Maybe it's just me, but this made me lose interest."

It all boils down to this: When you're out with someone, the focus should be on getting to know her, not on staying connected to all your social networks. Don't think about doing this sort of thing on the down low, either, like excusing yourself to use the restroom in order to tweet. With the accessibility of social media, your date can easily find out later on what you were up to. Of course, if you're expecting an important call or need to be on call for a potential emergency, just let your companion know that beforehand so there won't be any surprises.

Check, Please

So, you asked that handsome guy out, and you've had a great conversation over dinner. Maybe you're a little flush with wine when the server puts the check down between you. This can be an awkward moment, with the potential to escalate into a tug-of-war.

Who pays for what is one of the most confusing aspects of modern dating. The basic rule for any duo on a first date is that the person who invites pays the check, but this is not a hard-and-fast one. To make things clearer ahead of time about who is hosting, either use or listen for one of these phrases: "Please be my guest"; "It will be my treat"; "I'd like to invite you to join me . . ."; or "Let me take you out to . . ."

QUEERY

"She had her hands all over me, but I wasn't interested."

Q After drinking for several hours with this leather dyke at the neighborhood gay bar, we walked back to my place, and I invited her to join me for a smoke on the front porch. Two minutes later, she was leaning in for a big, wet kiss, which I barely avoided. My reaction upset her. Is there a right way to turn down an unwelcome advance?

A It sounds as though you did a good enough job, which is to turn the other cheek, so to speak.

But I can understand why your date was confused. She's probably thinking: "How did I wind up on this girl's front porch, after an evening out drinking, sitting close, and not expect a little smooch?" That's how that story usually ends.

It would have been better for you to curb her enthusiasm earlier in the evening, by not being so flirtatious or drinking so much. Not that your leather friend should ever, under any circumstances, assume she is *entitled* to any particular ending.

Who do you think should pay on a first date?

"It gets negotiated when the bill comes."

"Sometimes one might pay in a nonmonetary way."

"Split the bill if you're not sure you want another date."

"I always offer to pay, hoping I won't be asked to."

"Don't just add up what each of you ate and then divide the bill. That's tacky."

"Who eats food on a first date?"

Nevertheless, if you're the one who was asked out, don't assume you'll be treated. It's smart to be prepared to pay your way, no matter what you think the situation is—and it's also very good manners to offer to pay for yourself or contribute toward the tip.

Of course, there are times and dates when it's not exactly clear who invited whom. In such cases, there are a couple of ways to proceed:

• Consider picking up the tab by saying, "Let me get this."

• If your date pays the check, then thank her and suggest you take care of the tip or offer to take her out for dessert down the street.

• You can always suggest splitting the bill.

• If you wind up fighting over the tab, that's okay, but don't take it too far. One of you should graciously concede and say, "I hope you'll let me take you out the next time."

One last note: Even if your date pays for you, you're under no obligation to ask him or her out to settle the score, nor to become intimate.

THE NEXT STEPS

So you've had that first date you were so nervous about. It's quite possible you're not at all interested in seeing this person again. If so, that's fine.

On the other hand, maybe you couldn't take your eyes off of her and you found each other endlessly interesting. Or your feelings could be more ambiguous or unresolved: While you're not sure yet, you're open to the idea of finding out more. If any of those situations ring true, how do you try to make sure you see this person again?

Setting Up the Second Date

It may surprise you to know that it's not necessary to hit the ball out of the park on your first date for both of you to want a second. You simply need to find enough common ground and attraction to want to learn more about each other, which is really what dating is all about.

No matter how well a first date is going, don't get ahead of yourself. For instance, don't extend the invitation for next time during that initial meeting. Finish your evening as you see fit—whether with a cigarette, a kiss, or a simple farewell—but hold back a bit.

There are two reasons to follow this route: The first is that you don't know for sure whether your date is as into you as you are into him. The second is that you don't want to appear needy. It's fine to let your date know your intentions, but leave things a little vague: "I had a great time. I hope we can see each other again" is preferable to "What a wonderful evening. Do you have plans for tomorrow?" Allow yourself to go home, debrief, fantasize, and talk with your friends if need be—hopefully, he'll be doing the same thing. Then follow up a day, two days, or even a week later with an invitation for a second date.

In a perfect world, if you asked him out on that first date, he will do the honors this time around. But don't get hamstrung by standing on form. Besides, some people are more the asking type and some people just like to be asked. If you're nervous and not sure he will say yes, send an e-mail along these lines: "I just wanted to thank you again for such a fun time on Monday. I was wondering if you wanted to go out again sometime this weekend. . . ." If he's interested, by not making the invitation too specific, you're more likely to get a "yes." Then you can narrow down the timing from there.

Terms of Endearment

After a couple of dates, weeks, or months, the woman you're dating starts referring to you as her "girlfriend." You wonder what that means and how you should handle it. The truth is that the terms "girlfriend" and "boyfriend" can mean anything and everything in the LGBT community. Some of us use them as the acknowledgment of an emotional attachment, others to a vague commitment, and still others as shorthand for exclusivity or monogamy.

That means, don't assume the word means the same thing to both of you. A gay man recounted the time the guy he was seeing asked him to be his "main squeeze." He explained, "I thought that meant his one and only, but I found out the hard way that it really meant I was number one on his short list." To avoid something like that happening to you, ask a few questions to understand better what's happening, such as "What does being boyfriends mean to you?" Or "Does being your boyfriend

QUEERY

"Looking for a second date but don't want to beg"

Q I had a wonderful evening earlier in the week with this woman I met in the neighborhood wine store. The sex was great, too. I called her a couple of days later and haven't heard back. How many times can I call back before I look like a loser?

A Give it one more shot. She may have lost your number, been out of town, or otherwise been distracted. If she still doesn't respond after a second attempt, it's more likely that this was a one-night stand and she's not interested in a second outing.

QUEERY

"The PDA rules"

Q When is it okay to hold hands in public? To kiss? Is it different for gay people and straights?

A The acceptability of public displays of affections (PDAs) is, at least in theory, more about location—that is, whether you're in a nightclub or a movie theater versus in a church, classroom, or at a family dinner—than the sexual orientation of a couple.

Here's the general rule: Hand-holding, eye-gazing, and light kissing are perfectly fine in public; groping, tongue-kissing, and touching below the waist are not. But be sure to adapt this rule as necessary. There's a world of difference between holding your boyfriend's hand in a big-city restaurant and in small-town America.

Two final thoughts:

1. No matter what the rules, if you ever feel as though any public display may result in physical harm, restrain yourself or leave the scene.

2. Some members of our community rely on edgy PDAs, such as public "kiss-ins," as a form of political theater. Like civil disobedience, there's a legitimate time and place for these actions. Just be sure to consider the context and the safety issues. (For more on such "political manners," see page 340.)

---

have anything to do with being exclusive?" Although these aren't especially romantic questions, bringing up the issue in this way may be a better route to follow than making an assumption that turns out to be false.

Paying on Subsequent Dates

If anything, the rule about who pays on the first date is comparatively easy: You invite; you pay. But when it comes to second dates—and beyond—there's a lot of confusion and sometimes clashing expectations.

A good rule of thumb is to find balance, which isn't exactly parity. If you've been treated the first time you went out, consider it good manners to reciprocate the next time, whether that's paying for brunch, a show, or making dinner at home. Over time, as you become a couple, it's smart to talk about your expectations and your finances. Some decide to go Dutch regularly, which is practical but not terribly romantic; others take turns picking up the check assuming it will come out more or less equal over time.

If one of you earns substantially more than the other (or has other assets like a trust fund), she may want to foot more of the bill more often—or you may decide together that she will pay for the big-ticket items (fancy dinners, weekends away) and that the "other" will be responsible for incidentals (cabs, bar tabs, lunches). Or you may decide to frequent less-expensive cafés and bistros.

**What do you think
are good manners when
"playing the field"?**

"Don't call someone the wrong name—
especially while being intimate!"

"Don't catch an STD."

"Don't get caught! :)"

"No secrets. Be honest."

Taking a Break

Sometimes you may need a legitimate time-out from dating: Let's say one of your parents is ill and you're the primary caregiver. Or you've lost your job and you need to put all your energies into finding a new one. Or perhaps you have an extended vacation coming up.

Assuming that you'd like to pick things up again once your schedule has cleared, be forthright and explain your circumstances. For instance: "I'm going down to Florida every weekend now to make sure that my dad is well taken care of in his new nursing home. I'd love to stay in touch and I hope we can start seeing each other again once things have passed the crisis point." Or: "I'm completely consumed by finding a job right now. Would it be okay with you if I call you again after I get a new situation?" The important thing is to be transparent, try to stay in touch during the interim, and hope that he will still be available when you are again.

However, if you have no intention of getting together again later, try not to use a challenging life circumstance as a way to avoid a breakup. And certainly don't make one up.

Talking About Kids

If you desperately want kids (or emphatically don't want them), it's best to know relatively early in a relationship if your new girlfriend (or boyfriend) has a totally different life plan. While these kinds of conversations happen more commonly in the straight community, it makes sense to approach the topic in a similar fashion: directly. If it's on your mind, ask the question: "How do you feel about kids?" Ideally the subject would come up in context, not as part of an interrogation.

If you want to know how your someone feels about the subject, here are some good opening lines to try out: "Isn't the family at that table adorable?" "The kids are so well behaved for such little ones!" Or "I spent some time with my nephew this weekend—we had so much fun together. Do you have any kids in your extended family?"

Nevertheless, please hold off planning a future family while you're still just getting to know each other.

ADVANCED DATING

LGBT dating scenarios are full of challenging twists. Whether you're dating someone still in the closet, conducting a long-distance relationship, seeing a member of the military, or trying to deal with criticisms from friends about age differences, you'll need an extra dose of patience—and ingenuity.

Dating Someone in the Closet

Seeing someone who is not out and perhaps not ever planning to be out can pose a unique set of challenges. Many a gay or bisexual lover has maneuvered those waters, but others find it too difficult to turn a dating relationship into a full-fledged affair while one person remains closeted—so much so that some LGBT people insist in their personal ads that any potential partner be out.

If you're heading into what feels like a relationship with someone closeted, what's most important is that you develop mutual expectations. Is it okay that your boyfriend is not out at work or that you won't ever be recognized by his family as his lover? Similarly, is it acceptable to him that your whole family and all your friends know you're gay? Each scenario would likely raise other issues. As you continue, you'll also want to give your beau time—say, two to three months—to see

whether he is more comfortable about coming out (or, if he's not, whether you're okay with continuing the subterfuge).

At the same time, don't try to cajole anyone into coming out. We all need to take those steps on our own timetables, although leading by example is certainly helpful for those who are trying to come out.

No matter, if you're going to be seen together, you'll need to decide together how to introduce each other to friends, family, and colleagues. Talk about this beforehand so that you're on the same page and then use the same language.

Age-Appropriate Relationships

As long as both partners are of legal age, there's really no manners question—or answer—about how wide an age span is appropriate in any relationship, much less a same-sex one. Nevertheless, it's worth pointing out there have been many successful "age-inappropriate" relationships in

QUEERY

"Playing the field"

Q **After about three dates with this guy I met online, he asked me if I was seeing anyone else. I was honest and said yes, and he had a meltdown and called me a slut. What is the etiquette of playing the field?**

A First of all, it's awfully rude to call someone a "slut"—and you did nothing wrong. But there is some basic etiquette for juggling multiple suitors. To start, be discreet. For example, pay attention to the volume on your answering machine when you have a visitor at home. You don't really want him to hear "Great sex last night! Let's get together again soon." Also, don't keep anyone else's razor

or toothbrush visible in the medicine cabinet. Second, don't flaunt it. If you're with boyfriend A, don't flirt with anyone else. And if you wind up at the same party with girlfriends A and B, good luck and plan better next time. Third rule: Until the two of you have a conversation about being monogamous (if you ever do), assume that you're not. This is important for protecting both your heart and your health.

our community. Writer Christopher Isherwood and painter Don Bachardy, whose partnership was examined in the documentary *Chris and Don: A Love Story,* had an age difference of thirty years. Playwright Terrence McNally and lawyer Tom Kirdahy have twenty-five years between them. Ellen DeGeneres and her wife, Portia, are fifteen years apart.

Where manners do get involved is in curbing the various judgments made about "daddy-boy" liaisons (and their female counterparts) by friends and others. Those who like to trounce the younger partner do so under the guise of protecting the older one with an odd cocktail of envy ("He's got a young, hot one"), caring ("As soon as she grows up, she'll leave you with a broken heart"), and dismissal of the young-un's motives or sincerity ("She's got 'gold digger' written all over her"). Those who take up on behalf of the more junior partner usually make note of how the cradle is being robbed, the young man is being used for his body and body parts, or the young woman is being exploited by a controlling elder.

Whatever half-truths may exist in these kinds of nasty allegations is irrelevant. Friends don't judge friends and don't make jokes at their expense. The bottom line is that friends should actually support their friends' choice of partners—unless they have strong reason to think someone is unsuitable. (In a situation like that, bring up your concerns gently but directly with your friend.)

Since it's hard enough to find a compatible boyfriend or girlfriend, don't shy away from pursuing someone out of your age range. Perhaps the best advice of all is encapsulated in an old song lyric: "Love is where you find it."

Long-Distance Affairs

People in long-distance relationships don't generally choose them on purpose, but tolerating the distance is certainly a choice. They are plenty common in the LGBT community, where people are forced by all kinds of circumstances to live separately. Think gay high school sweethearts who have gone off to separate colleges; transgender lovers connected by the Internet but not out in their earthbound lives; closeted gay and lesbian military separated during their deployments overseas; or those who work in different cities, or have joint custody of kids from a previous relationship and can't move hundreds of miles away to their new squeeze's hometown. While these dating relationships often pose stiff challenges, many have found success in navigating them all the way to cohabitation, if that is the goal, or at least to sharing the same town.

If you are interested in being serious with each other, make the effort to talk often (the introduction of Skype has been a godsend to long-distance couples). Make phone dates—and keep them. The best way to stay close is to check in with each other both about the mundane events of your daily life, such as the vexing thing your boss did to you today or what your gym workout consisted of, as well as the more profound ones, such as family relationships and your career path.

Also try out the other electronic tools you have at hand, such as e-mail, texting, and social media. And, while it may sound old-fashioned, consider writing postcards or even love letters. It's nice to have something concrete to cherish when you miss each other.

"Soldier on the lookout for a safe date"

Q I've been in the Air Force for just under a year now and I'm wondering how I can go about dating other guys without jeopardizing my career or standing. Any suggestions?

A Even now that "don't ask, don't tell" is, thankfully, almost history, being fully out in the military will not be easy for all soldiers or under all circumstances.

Fortunately, the Internet and social media sites have made things a lot easier for gay military personnel because you can choose to be anonymous. There are dozens of sites now catering to LGBT military men and women, whether for dating or sex hookups.

As with all dating sites, use common sense and think twice about how much personal information you share. And since you're on active duty, be *especially* cautious about revealing your identity or data such as your address or your unit. At the outset of any new liaison, be sure to use an anonymous e-mail address and if/when you do call, either block your phone number with the Caller ID feature or use a pay phone.

It's also reassuring to be able to look forward to your next visit with a long-distance lover, even if those visits aren't as frequent as either of you would like. Consider setting up a schedule of visits so that you can anticipate and plan for them. At the very least, always try to know when you'll next see each other when you say good-bye. It will make those farewells less painful.

Dating While Living with Your Ex

It used to be that when couples broke up, someone always moved out. However, that's not always possible these days. There are any number of reasons that one of you can't leave, but most have to do with the high cost of housing: For instance, a couple may own their place jointly and neither can afford to buy the other out. Or it's rent-controlled and you'll never

find such a good deal on the open market. Whatever the cause, more and more couples are finding themselves continuing to cohabitate after breaking up.

This can be tricky, not only financially, but also emotionally. Imagine: You've broken up, you're ready to date again, but your ex is still on the premises. If this happens to you, continue to do whatever you possibly can to move out (or to get your ex to do so). Ask friends or family members if you can stay with them for a predetermined period; such a window could give you enough time to get on your feet. If you absolutely cannot find another place to live, set up some basic rules for your new form of domestic living:

- **Be explicit about your financial arrangements:** While you needn't do a legal agreement, it's not a bad idea to put the terms in an e-mail so you both can refer to it if necessary.

- **Create two separate sleeping spaces:** If necessary, buy or borrow a pullout sofa so that you can establish boundaries.
- **Allow each other some privacy:** Especially if it's a small place, agree that each of you will be out at certain times so that you both have time to be alone at home, talk on the phone, or entertain.
- **Decide whether or not you can bring new dates or sex partners to your home:** The wisest answer is usually no, especially in the immediate aftermath of a breakup. There are usually too many raw feelings for most people to pull this off successfully.

ONLINE DATING

E-mail, texting, instant messaging, and social networking have many of us in a state of constant communication. And this new techno world has vastly altered the tempo of dating. It's a long way from the days of Jane Austen, when prospective lovers wrote letters and waited patiently for a reply. Sometimes even leaving a voicemail message feels too slow, especially if you don't hear back by the next day. For sure, the speed of things can make a new attraction extra-thrilling. But, to pace yourself for the long haul, remember that it's much easier to pump up the volume than it is to turn it down. Start slowly. Enjoy the prospect of hearing from your date and seeing her again. Anticipation often beats out

"I want to break up by e-mail."

Q My boyfriend and I have been dating for about three months. He told me that he and his ex-partner broke up before we met, but I just found out that they're still seeing each other. I'm really disappointed, but I'm not sure I could say everything I want to his face without getting really upset. Is it okay to break up with him in an e-mail?

A No matter how much of a jerk or liar he may be, you owe it to him and to yourself to actually have a breakup conversation, whether in person or by phone. Sure, it *seems* easier just to dash off a well-crafted e-mail or a snippy text, and yes, it may *be* easier. (Indeed, breaking up by text, IM, or even with a relationship "status update" on Facebook is more and more prevalent; one recent study found that one in seven of us has been dumped electronically.)

But the truth is that getting the last word is not as important as trying to better understand what happened. The point of a face-to-face breakup is to help you both find closure.

The only exception to this rule is if your relationship had been so casual, that is, no strings attached, and your main nonsexual communications were via text or e-mail. Then I would say go ahead and stay true to the medium. But this doesn't apply to your situation. Sorry.

VOX POPULI

When do you think it's okay to break up using text or e-mail?

"Never. Unless, of course, one is a complete and total chicken."

"When you are twelve."

"If the person is abusive or off their meds, you might have no other alternative."

"When they won't answer your calls or when their phones are off but they're online all the time."

instant gratification as an aphrodisiac. Allow yourselves the time to discover common interests and values—or if the end goal is sex itself, then do some chatting about that to make sure you're on the same page. (For more about talking about sex, please see page 82.)

Whether the current spate of online services, like Chemistry.com and Gay.com, are the future of LGBT dating and mating or an odd postmillennial phase is hard to say. But this aspect of our community is an ever more central meeting place, with etiquette of its own. Any LGBT single using the Internet to find a date would be wise to become familiar with this special set of manners.

Know What You're Seeking

Be clear about what you're looking for online, so that you don't waste other people's time— let alone your own. Is it conversation, friendship, casual sex, or a relationship? Finding out that all you're interested in is sex may be just as frustrating to a relationship-seeker

as finding out that you're straight. One lesbian explained on Nerve: "I just assumed that because I met this woman on a dating service, that's that what we were doing: dating! But after two really long amazing dates, things slowed down a little so I said, 'What's up?' She said this is how she makes *friends,* and I was really disappointed."

Screen Names

Online dating is just as much about first impressions as terrestrial dating. That's why it's important to give some considered thought to what you call yourself when you select a screen name, also known as a username or handle. Start out this process by taking a good look at the other screen names on the site you're joining and then do your best to navigate the still murky science of crafting a winning one for yourself.

Choose a screen name that says something genuine and compelling about you. Cryptic abbreviations of your real name (for instance, "wndyjnes34" for Wendy Jones) are not big attention-grabbers, for instance. Upbeat, confident screen names are considered a good bet, like "SportyNSpiritual" or "MensaDyke," and so are those that reveal something physical, such as "BlueEyes" or "muscleman." Short names are generally more effective. Using a combination of upper- and lowercase letters—not all caps, which is just irritating—can be easier to read and more noticeable to others.

Another way to go in creating a username is to focus on some especially attractive aspect of your personality or the kind of connection you're looking for. "LezzieBoater" may not

"I want to 'friend' this guy I just met but don't want to seem too eager."

Q I just met someone I really like at a party and I'd like to friend him so I can ask him out. But just like in real life, I don't want to come across as too eager or hungry. What's the right amount of time to wait before sending a friend request?

A One Mississippi, two Mississippi—even on Internet time, that's too fast. Assuming you had a pleasant enough conversation and discovered some mutual interests, follow up in the next day or so, but understand that many people don't think of Facebook as a dating service. Definitely hold back on sending a friend request right away—that suggests you have no self-control or are too eager. On the other hand, if you wait more than two or three days, this guy may have no idea who you are.

Be sure to add a personal message to your friend request and say something like "Nice chatting with you at so-and-so's the other night. I was wondering if you'd be my friend. ☺" This kind of note could pass for either a true friend request or the gateway to a date request, without much risk of rejection.

attract a lot of women, but if sitting on your boat with a fishing rod is precisely what you're hoping to do with your new girlfriend, then go right ahead. In the same vein, if it's a purely sexual connection you're looking for, consider names like "Jeff11X7" or "SexyStoner." (If you have multiple profiles on different kinds of sites, go ahead and create different screen names for each.)

Writing Your Profile

To join an LGBT online dating site, you'll need to set up a profile. This is not just so that other people can stumble on you in their searches but because your profile is your "calling card" when you reach out to someone who looks interesting. Don't take this step lightly! Put some time into it, and get outside opinions (from, for instance, your close friends). The way you present yourself on your profile is just as important as what you say and do while you begin to navigate the site yourself, with flirtatious e-mails perhaps, IM conversations, or even simply arrangements for a rendezvous.

The key is being yourself but putting all the good stuff out front. And if your intention is sex, be especially clear about that. There's no reason to hold back on how you like to have it, especially if you're on a hookup-oriented site such as Manhunt. If it's an actual relationship you're after (or at least open to), answer questions and fill in the blanks about who you are and what kind of person you're looking for with a good deal of honesty and thoroughness.

As you complete the profile, remain very attentive to how you will come across. It rarely works in your favor, for instance, to refer to a broken heart or a long single stretch. In the same vein, do your best to be upbeat and enthusiastic (but cool). Even a lesbian who likes intense, emotional women generally won't clamor to date someone who seems depressed. Stand back, if you can, and imagine stumbling on your profile as a stranger: Does it scream "desperate"? What about "raunchy"? Again, give serious consideration to asking a friend to look at your profile; it's amazing how many people play down their best strengths and give impressions they really didn't mean to give.

THE ESSENTIALS
Personals Cheat Sheet

The LGBT world is full of abbreviations and acronyms. While a lot of these terms are used in everyday slang, nowhere do you find a heavier concentration than in online profiles and chatrooms. Here's a quick guide to some of the most common shorthand.

BB	Bodybuilder or barebacking (depending on context)
BBW	Big, beautiful woman (or big-breasted woman)
BD/SM	Bondage/domination/sadomasochism
BI	Bisexual
CD	Cross-dresser
CPL	Couple
D/D FREE	Drug- and disease-free (often rendered as DDF)
DL	Down low (not out)
DOM	Male dominant
DOMME	Female dominant
FA	Fat admirer
FS	Financially secure
420	Marijuana
F2F	Face-to-face (meeting in person)

GG	Genetic girl
HWP	Height/weight proportionate
ISO	In search of
K	Kids
LDR	Long-distance relationship
LS	Legally separated
LTR	Long-term relationship
ND	Nondrinker
NK	No kids
NS	Nonsmoker
NSA	No-strings-attached sex
P	Professional
PNP	Party and play (drugs; often refers to crystal meth)
RTS	Real-time sex
S	Single
SUB	Submissive
T4M	Trans looking for men
TG	Transgender
W/E	Well-endowed
W/S	Water sports
WTR	Willing to relocate
X	Extreme

There are many more abbreviations being used online, especially about sexual proclivities. If you're stumped, search for an online guide to abbreviations or visit www.gaymanners.com for a more complete and updated list.

Posting Your Photo

Are you hesitant about posting a photo? Will you be embarrassed if friends or family members see you on a dating site? Are you afraid of outing yourself? Unfortunately, if you're not ready to show your face in your profile, you're probably not ready to use this medium. How interested would *you* be in someone who's basically invisible or too hesitant to show a face pic? Not surprisingly, studies from dating sites report that profiles with photos get both a larger response and a better one, which is to say that they attract gay men and lesbians more serious about dating.

Okay, but then, which picture? First and foremost, the photo you post should be a fair and accurate depiction of what you look like these days. What you want to avoid is having your first in-person meeting with someone you're interested in dominated by the revelation that you have misled your date about your appearance in some substantial way—age, height, weight, or body type, for instance. If you want to make sure you do the right thing, keep these suggestions in mind:

• **A recent photo:** Make sure that you have at least one picture that shows you within two to three years of your current age. If you have some great shots from your thirtieth birthday

QUEERY

"Everyone else lies in their online profiles."

Q How much leeway do I have in describing myself in my online profile? I noticed everyone else seems to stray from the truth.

"I'm a competitive bodybuilder, 6' 4", 250 pounds . . ."

A You're right about that: A Michigan State University study found that 90 percent of people lie in their dating profile. The most common fibs? Guys exaggerate their height and women lose five pounds. Needless to say, it's a bad idea to start a search for a relationship with a falsehood, if only because the time will come when you need to tell the truth.

I know many of us want to shave off a year or more, sometimes for vanity, sometimes to stay within arbitrary search parameters—really, if you're just thirty-six, it seems unfair that you're left out of results of someone looking for a guy twenty-five to thirty-five. But the fact is if you start with this deception, your date may wonder what else you've been less than honest about. (By the way, you

can always say in your profile: "Look early thirties.")

There are several ways to get around having to be completely honest about something that makes you self-conscious, such as your weight. For instance, you can say in your profile—or while messaging with others—that you're "height and weight proportionate." Some sites also allow you to choose a body type, slim, athletic, or stocky, although everyone knows anyone's choice is somewhat open to interpretation.

By the way, the rules are different if you're seeking a sex hookup—in that case, it matters less how old you really are and more how old you actually look. In addition, if you do meet up, there'll be other things on the agenda than whether you resemble your true age.

QUEERY

"Friendly online and then silence"

Q You've probably heard the story: I exchanged a few encouraging messages with this woman or that, saying things like "Your profile picture is hot" or "I went to school in Seattle, too!" and after some flirty banter, suddenly, nothing. Silence. No explanation at all. I'm left wondering, was it the way I drooled over her profile picture? Does she actually hate Seattle? Something else I said? Why do some people think they can be rude just because you meet online?

A Sad to say, this is where online dating heads off in its own direction and leaves old-school dating manners behind. You can bitch and moan about how ill-mannered it is, but people often just move on without saying a word—or good-bye—after some initial conversation. And they're not actually breaking any rules. The reason this has become so acceptable is that the online dating world, by its very nature, is intended to save time and awkward explanations as you cast the widest possible net.

I could definitely argue for sending even the briefest note, such as "Hey, thanks for chatting but I don't see us dating. Good luck!" Whether it's out of kindness, your own hope that the Internet will learn some manners, or a belief in karma, this takes so little effort that it's a good idea. But it's not de rigueur.

"... Me, too!"

party and you're now forty, it's fine to post them as long as you caption them to indicate it was some time ago.

- **Make sure your face is visible:** Don't hide behind shades or friends or in the shadows. Don't go for the shot where you can't really see your face at all but the background shows how cool your life is. Given a choice, select one that shows you smiling, or at least upbeat.
- **Consider a professional headshot:** If you can afford it and it doesn't look too staged, it's not a bad idea to hire a photographer.

- **No group shots:** You want potential admirers to know who *you* are, not that you have two best friends who summer with you in Provincetown.
- **Dress for success:** What you're wearing can say a lot about what you're seeking. If you're looking for a romance, choose a photo of yourself in casual dress. Nude or seminude shots are for sex sites.
- **Acknowledge any deviations:** If you're blonde in your photo but now pass as a brunette, mention that in your e-mail. Similarly, if you

no longer have that goatee—let him know. You never know what it is about you that attracts another.

• **A note for transmen and -women:** Photographs of trans folks raise another set of issues; while being up-front about being transgender may narrow your options, waiting to disclose the fact until later can lose you a date and lead to other issues. Make some decisions for yourself ahead of time about whether being trans is going to come up in any way in your profile. Then choose a picture that reflects that strategy. For instance, "Slender woman seeks trim older man" versus "Slender transgender woman seeks trim older man." (For more about trans people coming out, see page 14.)

CHAPTER 4

Sex Etiquette

Bedrooms & Backrooms

As a rule, manners books barely visit the bedroom. Recent editions
of Emily Post's *Etiquette* and *The Amy Vanderbilt Complete Book of
Etiquette* provide only the most cursory discussion of sex, like how to have
the "sex talk" with your teen. When it comes to safe sex, the advice in Post's
Etiquette is noteworthy for its impracticality, recommending that you bring
printouts of your HIV and STD test results with you and exchange them with
your partner before getting down to business, since "people may lie. . . ."
Others are simply judgmental; Letitia Baldrige posits in *New Manners for New
Times* that having "multiple sex partners is the worst of all worlds."

To no one's surprise, LGBT people have all kinds of questions about
sexual manners and mores that need to be answered, but reject advice that's
infeasible or woefully out-of-touch. Our concerns run the gamut from how to
initiate sex or talk about our sexual histories to the best ways to tell someone you
are HIV-positive or to turn down a potential partner because he is—or is not.

Then there are the racier questions those focused on casual sex, public sex, threesomes, open relationships, and the hiring of paid escorts.

But, those specifics aside, sex belongs in this manners book because LGBT people are pretty much responsible for inventing good sex manners in the modern age, in the form of "safer sex." HIV is a strong reminder that being honest, patient, and respectful of others should always be the norm, whether in the bedroom or any other room.

One last point: While today's sexual "fluidity"—the rejection of traditional labels like gay, lesbian, bi, or even trans—is confounding to the generation or two that fought so hard for them, it's very reassuring to others. And by nudging LGBT sex etiquette to be more inclusive and less defined, there's more support for experimentation, not just with other genders but also with some of the sexual playfulness that lesbians and gay men have always enjoyed.

THE PRELIMINARIES

Sometimes sex is just sex—a hookup, a tryst, or an orgasmic release. At other times, it becomes a language of its own, mythical and mysterious, an important element in fostering intimacy in a relationship. Consider this first section for those meet-ups and dates that you think have "potential" for a relationship—as best you can tell. (A later section in

the chapter tackles casual sex, also known as no-strings-attached sex.) Good manners and respect definitely have a place in this conversation, which focuses on etiquette for first timers (and their partners), when to say yes, how to say no, and when to reveal you have an STD or HIV/AIDS. You might be surprised to learn that sex etiquette isn't always the same in the backroom as it is in the bedroom.

When to Have Sex

If you want to signal that you're ready to become intimate, nonverbal cues are a great place to start. Sitting closely, touching lightly, or making sustained eye contact can deliver the message clearly enough. But there's nothing wrong with using words (for instance, "Do you mind if I kiss you?"), especially if you're recently out of the closet or not confident yet about interpreting more subtle signs.

Keep in mind that just because one of you is ready, that doesn't necessarily mean the other is. If you know you want to head toward the bedroom and aren't quite sure of your friend's feelings, try asking a question like "Think we should fool around?" That should prompt an answer—or a first move. Or strike up a conversation about your sexual history, thereby making it clear what's on your mind. Plus you'll need to have that discussion anyway. (For more on talking about your sexual health, including STDs and HIV, see page 82.)

Before moving ahead, however, consider these questions:

- **Do you know how to protect yourself from STDs?** If you don't, you must take the time to learn how sexually transmitted diseases are passed on and the variety of steps you can take to protect yourself (and your partner)—starting with getting tested for the most common STDs and HIV.

- **Do you trust each other?** Since sex is so much about trust, don't rush into it with someone you don't feel entirely comfortable with. If you're okay with your intimacy so far, then sex may be a logical next step.
- **Do you have the necessary accoutrements on hand?** These may include lube, condoms, latex gloves, and dental dams.
- **Are you and your prospective sex partner on the same page about your encounter?** Problems can arise when one of you expects to stay for breakfast while the other is expecting you gone after sex so that he can curl up to his pillow.
- **Are you both above the age of consent in your state or province?** If so, there's no legal issue. Problems arise when one of you is considered an adult—in the eyes of the law—and the other isn't. Even if there's only a couple of years' difference in age between the two of you, depending on where you live, you could face jail time if convicted of having sex with someone under the age of consent.

Waiting for Sex

Some LGBT people choose to have sex right away when they meet someone they like, while others wait days, weeks, sometimes even months, before they're ready for this kind of physical and emotional intimacy. Do what feels right for you—in each new situation. One young gay man writes, "I won't have sex before the third date—that's my rule, and I'm sticking

to it." Similarly, a Bay Area lesbian explained her decision to go slow with the woman who eventually became her wife and the other mother of her two kids: "By waiting and actually having to date, talk, and interact, rather than just jumping into bed together, I got to know her in a very different way. And when we did make love, it was the continuation of an ongoing discovery rather than the first dive in."

Taking the opposite view, a retired firefighter, now in his sixties and in a long-term relationship, describes how he preferred to "road test" his potential partners. "I think you need to get the sex-compatibility thing out of the way immediately. Without some sexual connection the relationship is not going to last, and you might as well find that out right off."

Saying No or Not Yet

You may find yourself on the receiving end of a proposition or a pucker that just doesn't interest you—at least not right now. If that happens, try to let your friend down lightly, but avoid lying if possible. Put yourself in her shoes: Wouldn't you rather hear some soft-pedaled version of the truth, whether it's a "maybe later" or "I'm just not comfortable having sex now" than a direct rejection like "You're too old [or too young] for me" or "Your tummy isn't flat enough"?

If you have a specific reason for saying "not yet"—maybe you're not feeling well or you just have an early morning—explain that. This clarifies your "not yet" sufficiently to make it clear that you're not rejecting your new friend. Delivering this explanation with a warm tone and flirtatious smile will get the message across that you do in fact want things to happen sometime soon.

If you keep postponing becoming intimate, there's a risk that you'll lose the moment—or the person's interest. Since you haven't had sex yet, your friend may get confused, wondering, "Does she find me attractive?" or "Will I be turned down if I come on to her again?" But rushing into bed can leave you with a sex hangover the next morning, wondering, "What happened?"

Saying no can be more difficult than saying "not yet." Again, be as honest as you're able, saying firmly—but kindly—something like "I don't see us having that kind of relationship" or "No, I don't want to have sex." If you're already in the midst of making out, you'll need to stop, switch gears, and start talking. Your friend may ask you why you've changed the road map. Be truthful about your feelings—and, if you're just not sure yet what they are, say so.

In all situations, trust your intuition. You don't actually need to have a reason not to have sex with someone, nor to leave any situation if it becomes uncomfortable.

THE ESSENTIALS

The Four Most Important Sexual Health Manners

There was a time not very long ago when the recommendations of public health experts were cut-and-dry when it came to preventing the transmission of HIV. The rule was simple: Practice safe sex—all the time, no matter the circumstances. These days, the message is more nuanced and realistic, as evidenced by the guidelines below from the New York–based HIV/AIDS social service agency GMHC (www.gmhc.org; the group formerly known as Gay Men's Health Crisis). It's still equally important.

- **Know your HIV status:** If you test negative, you can remain negative by educating yourself about safe-sex practices. If you test positive, there are specific steps you can take to prevent the spread of the virus to your partner(s). In addition, if you find out that you're HIV+, it's wise to seek out support to deal with the feelings that inevitably arise with such news. And remember: Infection with HIV can take up to three months to show up in blood tests.

- **Know your partner's HIV status:** Knowing your partner's HIV status, whenever possible, helps you make decisions about the level of risk you're comfortable with. If you and your partner are up-front with each other about this, you can more easily choose an appropriate method for reducing your chances of HIV transmission. For instance, if both members of a couple are HIV-negative and intend to be monogamous, they may decide to practice safer sex in some but not all of their sexual activities. If, on the other hand, one member of a couple is HIV-positive, extra caution is required.

- **Educate yourself:** Learn about available barrier methods (male and female condoms, dental dams, gloves, etc.). The consistent and proper use of condoms has been proven to significantly reduce the risk of transmitting HIV and other STDs.

- **Get tested for STDs:** Regular testing for STDs is important for anyone who's sexually active. If you have herpes, chlamydia, gonorrhea, or syphilis, it's easier to become infected with HIV. Women also need regular gynecological exams.

- **Reduce other high-risk activities:** People are more likely to engage in risky sexual behaviors when drunk or high because substance use tends to lower inhibitions and impair judgment. If you can't or won't stop using drugs or alcohol, don't share needles, clean your works, and keep condoms or other barriers handy.

The First Time

If you're about to have sex for the first time, or it's your first same-sex encounter, you may be both anxious and excited, wondering whether to reveal your newbie status or keep it to yourself. You may also have questions about how to initiate a conversation about your sexual histories. The good news is that practice tends to make all of these situations easier.

If your first sexual experience is just a casual hookup—that is, someone you hardly know—it's your decision whether to acknowledge this is your first time. Some of us choose not to say anything because these kinds of encounters tend to be fleeting—without a lot of emotional attachment.

If your "first" is someone you already have a strong emotional bond with, mentioning your "virgin" status can be an opportunity to share any anxieties about sexual performance. It can also be part of a bigger conversation about intimacy and where your relationship is headed. One man regretted not saying anything during his college "debut": "When we got down to brass tacks, I kind of flipped out, because I really hadn't known what to expect. I wish I had had the ability to talk with him beforehand. I'm sure that would have made it more enjoyable."

Remember that being the veteran is not necessarily any easier than being the first timer; the responsibility of being someone's initial sexual encounter can be a lot to handle. Not surprisingly, some find it quite exciting, or are at least happy to rise to the occasion;

QUEERY

"The guy I'm dating has never had sex before."

Q I've been going out with a man who's never had gay sex before and is more than a little apprehensive. We're really into each other, but to tell you the truth I'm a little nervous myself at the thought of initiating a virgin. I just want to make sure to handle things right. Do you have any advice for me?

A There's a special responsibility in being someone's "first." I don't know about you, but I still remember my very first time—and let me just say I was a nervous wreck. Since you already know that your fella is anxious, see if you can tease out what's on his mind. Often a first timer's main concern is that he'll do something "wrong." If you can help your new lover realize that it's not about technical performance but rather emotional connection, you'll both benefit. Also, let him know that he can determine the pace. Still, there will likely be some teachable moments as he tries new things on for size. I wouldn't make corrections or suggestions in the heat of the moment, but instead maybe chat a bit later on if you feel the need. One last thing: Be sure to lead by example when it comes to the topic of safe sex.

others prefer their partners to be experienced. If you knowingly find yourself in this role, take it seriously, making sure to talk about STDs and HIV (see below) and thinking about other ways to be helpful.

Talking About Sex

For some of us, conversations about sex are, umm, uncomfortable. You may find yourself mumbling or just embarrassed. Others, however, are born to run their mouths when it comes to intimate matters. No matter which description best characterizes you, a little talk goes a long way to facilitate mutual understanding—and mutual pleasure.

One way to talk about sex is casually, as the thought or feeling arises, and in the moment. Keep it simple: "That feels great" or "I love this" makes your message clear, even if it's just to confirm what your body has already announced on its own. Of course, these conversations don't always need to take place in the heat of passion or in the bedroom—before or after may suit the situation just as well. And a favorite postmortem moment of many is the next morning over coffee. If that's when you chat, make your point about what turns you on or works for you, but don't make it into a big deal. With luck, the information will find its way back into the bedroom.

Speaking up is even more important if there's something that you actually don't like or that makes you uncomfortable. Do your best to explain to your partner what's not working while focusing on the positives. Don't say, for instance, "I really don't like you touching me there." Do say, "Please touch me here." Or if you

want more foreplay or nipple work, don't say "Hey, can you spend a little more time warming me up?" Instead, try "Wouldn't it be hot if we could spend ten minutes just kissing each other?" or "Harder!" Positive encouragement also goes a long way. And don't forget to reciprocate, asking in turn, "Do *you* like this?" and "Anything *you* want to try in bed?"

When to Talk About STDs and HIV

Everyone who is sexually active needs to be responsible for considering the risks of spreading sexually transmitted diseases, as well as for taking steps to protect themselves and others. Regardless of your health status, you owe it to yourself and any new partner to talk about your sexual health before having sex. If you can, have this chat before taking off your clothes or otherwise getting too carried away by desire. That way, the heat of the moment doesn't seduce you into skipping the conversation—or taking risks you might not take otherwise. It needn't be an involved conversation—and admittedly it can be hard to make it a romantic one—but this is no time to be reticent. Among the infectious diseases to worry about are HPV, gonorrhea, syphilis, herpes, chlamydia, and HIV/AIDS.

Getting this talk started is pretty straightforward. Be truthful and direct, saying, for instance, "I just want you to know that as far as I know I'm STD-free; are you?" or "I have the herpes virus, but I haven't had an outbreak in six months. Is there anything else I can tell you?" Of course, if humor is more your style, don't feel as though you must sound like a public health educator.

Keep in mind that, beyond talking about STDs and HIV with your partners, good sexual manners includes knowing your health status, getting regular tests, understanding (and communicating) your sexual preferences, and using the level of protection the two of you agree on for different kinds of sexual activities. If you don't discuss STDs with your partner before sex, use a condom and don't exchange any bodily fluids.

The same rules apply for HIV as other STDs, and the most basic one bears repeating: If you feel intimate enough to have sex with someone, then you're close enough to talk about HIV status. Neither partner is more or less responsible to start this conversation.

IF YOU'RE HIV-POSITIVE

First of all, even if you have hinted about your seropositive status, don't assume the other person knows. The subtle signals of human interaction—especially sex-charged interaction—are easily misinterpreted. With the consequences in this case so potentially significant, it's up to you to be forthright and truthful.

The words you choose depend as much on your personality as on the kind of connection you have with your friend. Some come right out and say, "I'm HIV-positive." Others get there sideways, launching the conversation by asking, for example, "Have you ever dated someone who is HIV-positive?" and then steer it toward their own status.

Once your friend knows, it's a good idea to talk a little about your general health and how you define "safer sex." By the way, don't assume a partner is HIV-negative, even if he says he is. We're all fallible.

IF YOU'RE HIV-NEGATIVE

It's both smart and good manners to tell all of your partners that you're HIV-negative. This

---

QUEERY

"I've had only a couple of lovers so I couldn't have HIV."

Q I'm in college and recently started having sex with guys. There's a new fellow in my dorm that I've been going out with, but we haven't had sex yet. He says he won't have sex with me until I get an HIV test. I've only been with a couple of others and have always been safe. What should I do?

A No matter your age or sexual experience, it's important to be tested regularly for HIV/AIDS and other STDs if you're at all sexually active. Your new friend is right to ask you to take the test and share the results with him—and he's actually doing you a favor by pushing you on this.

Sure, most of us intend to have safer sex all of the time and younger people often feel especially invincible; but condoms break, people tell untruths, and drugs and alcohol can override rational thinking, leading us down the slippery slope of unsafe sex.

Here's a cautionary finding from the Centers for Disease Control and Prevention: College-age guys are among the most likely to be infected with HIV. Need I say more?

may well help HIV-positive individuals to disclose their status, or to gauge where they play on the safer sex spectrum with you (no doubt on the safe side).

Keep in mind, however, that your HIV status is only as good as your last test, with a three-month window, and that you have as much responsibility as a partner who is HIV-positive to disclose and ask questions.

THE ESSENTIALS

Safe-Sex Practices for Women

Woman-to-woman transmission of HIV is so rare that many lesbians think of safer sex as being more about other STDs and the importance of talking about your sexual history than it is about rolling out the latex. Nonetheless, there are factors that could mean HIV should be part of the discussion: For instance, women who have had sex with men, taken drugs intravenously, or had a blood transfusion are at a higher risk for contracting HIV than those who are sexually active only with women.

Definitely don't underestimate your risks, though. Women can expose each other to STDs, including HIV, if infected menstrual blood makes contact with open cuts. Latex barriers such as gloves and dental dams do an effective job at preventing transmission of many, but not all, such infections during cunnilingus, manual penetration, and rimming. What's most important is that you discuss your sexual health history and decide together what sexual practices you will engage in and how to enjoy them in a way that prevents transmission of any infectious disease.

STRAIGHT TALK

"Since we're worried parents, can we ask our son if he and his boyfriend (they're both twenty-one) are having safe sex? We want to make sure we're not shirking our parental responsibilities, but we also want to respect his privacy."

It may sometimes seem in this Twitter-mad world that privacy doesn't matter anymore, but what consenting adults do in their bedrooms is still their own business—even when it's your own kid. In this case, I'd suggest you err on the side of privacy.

Still, parents are parents, and it may be impossible for you not to worry, which I understand. If you think your son has somehow missed the barrage of safe-sex information disseminated in bars and clubs and via the Internet, then strike up a conversation about HIV that's not personal. Try bringing up the rising rates of HIV infection or the paucity of government funding for treatment as a means to open this door with your son. With any luck, he'll realize your concerns and assuage those fears (my own mother brought the subject up in such a manner years ago, and she was relieved to hear me say I practiced safe sex). But that's really as far as you can go without overstepping.

Caveat: If you had told me your son was a teenager, I would have answered, "Go ahead, ask away." When it comes to younger LGBT people (anyone under eighteen), I do want to emphasize that it is well within a parent's rights to talk about safer sex; indeed, it's your duty.

"Too chicken to tell my ex about my STD"

Q I need to tell my ex that I contracted a venereal disease and that I may have passed it on to her, but I can't bear the idea of talking to her. Is it rude to just e-mail her about this?

A One way or another, your ex needs to have this information and you have an obligation to get it to her. The medium isn't important, but making the effort to actually talk with your ex will give her a chance to ask questions, some of which you may be able to answer on the spot.

Nevertheless, if your animus toward your ex is really strong, then go ahead and e-mail her. Ask her to let you know that she received your news—you wouldn't want information like this to wind up in a junk folder.

If you were talking about a casual sexual hookup and not an ex, you might get away with sending one of the e-cards available through inSpot (www .inSpot.org). The site delivers messages like "I got diagnosed with an STD and you might have been exposed. Get checked out." You can either sign your e-card or send it anonymously.

BEDROOM ETIQUETTE

Manners most certainly play a role in successfully navigating the day-to-day details of LGBT sex. Whether you're the host or the guest, mutual respect and civility are crucial and can take you a long way in handling such things as condom use (and breakage), strap-ons, the imminent spill from a session of oral sex between men, or simply making sure your partner is sexually satisfied.

When You Are the Host

Entertaining is entertaining no matter what room you do it in: Being prepared for sex at your own home means making your guest feel welcome and comfortable. Take the time beforehand to tidy up, put new sheets on the bed, hang clean towels in the bathroom, and, if necessary, hide any photos or mementos of anyone else you're currently seeing.

"I'm glad we chose your place."

Mood-setting gestures are good, too: Light some candles, have some fresh flowers in the house, and turn the lights down low. If you live with others, either in a college dorm or with a roommate, make sure you'll have enough privacy—most important, a door to close behind you.

Finally, be prepared with the basic necessities, which include not only condoms/dental dams, water-based lubricant, and any sex toys that may be of interest, but tea and coffee (in case there's a morning after) as well as a spare toothbrush and razor. Said one man: "It was so thoughtful when my date handed me a toothbrush after we had been to bed."

When You Are the Guest

Ironic as it may sound, the first rule of being a good guest in this context is knowing when to leave. No one wants to overstay his or her welcome when sex is involved, whether it's a brief interlude, an overnight visit, or a weekend affair. Follow the lead of your host, which is to say, let her invite you to stay on—for breakfast or until the end of a fun-filled weekend. For instance, if after sex there's no invitation to spend the night, it's time to get dressed, say thank you, make sure (if appropriate) that you've exchanged numbers or e-mail addresses, and leave. (For more about the etiquette of one-night stands, see page 97.)

By the way, no matter how curious you may be when you're visiting, don't go snooping in the office, on the computer, or in the medicine cabinet. Respect your host's privacy and if you need something (say, contact lens solution or some toothpaste), ask for it. Finally, while hosts are responsible for providing the necessities for safer sex, bring your own as well. It never hurts to have extras in this category.

Satisfying Your Partner

There's more to sexual satisfaction than your enjoying a great orgasm. Reciprocity defines good manners. It's vital that you make an effort to understand each other's needs and do your best to take care of them. No matter what the situation, be sure to focus on your partner's desires, even if—perhaps especially if—you've been satisfied already. Or if one of you enjoys foreplay or kissing more than the other, talk with each other about how to find the right balance to meet each of your desires.

Here are some ways to bring consideration into the bedroom:

- **Don't be shy:** Speak up about your desires and your worries. Not only is learning to talk about sex likely to make things more pleasurable; these kinds of conversations also feed the trust and communication that build intimacy. And for some, sex talk can be a turn-on!
- **Pay attention:** Listen to the moans and groans of your partner to understand what is pleasing and what is not. If he redirects you from "here" to "there," remember that in the future. Or if the gentle directive is "Not so hard," do your best to follow the advice the next time— or ask her if you're doing okay.
- **Pace yourself:** If you tend to orgasm early in the game, keep a slower pace and pay attention to your partner for clues that it's time to go there. Or if it's typically "lights out" for you

after orgasm, playfully mention that early on, so that you can work together to be sure neither of you is left disappointed.

- **Understand your partner:** Sometimes you may encounter people with somewhat specific tastes or predilections, say a lesbian whose entire interest in sex is giving pleasure to her partner or someone who enjoys SM practices. You're not expected to know this on your own, or necessarily to explore it the very first time you have sex together. But once again, good communication is very helpful.

What Not to Say in the Heat of the Moment

Some people treat a sexual encounter like a temple where silence is expected, and others seem to talk nonstop. Wherever your position is on the talk-or-not spectrum, there are definitely times when talking isn't such a good idea during sex. In addition, there are certainly topics or clichés to avoid. Otherwise, you risk embarrassment—either yours or your partner's.

- **Don't call your new squeeze the name of your ex:** Mentioning former lovers in the bedroom is a no-no, but especially in the heat of passion. If you're the type who's inclined to get lost in the moment, try using generic terms of affection instead, like "honey," "baby," "sweetheart," or even something role-play-ish like "boi" or "daddy."
- **Be present:** Don't mention while you're still frolicking that it's getting late, that you're hungry, or that you wish you'd bought the red car instead of the blue one.
- **No judgments:** Don't comment on the sexual performance of your partner in the middle of the game. If such a conversation is needed, wait until the postcoital embrace or, better

QUEERY

"I stuttered stupidly when he asked what I like in bed."

Q Here we were in bed for the first time, wrapped around each other, when he whispered, "What do you like to do in bed?" I wasn't sure what he meant and just mumbled like an idiot. It's not the first time this has happened. What could I have said?

A Your bed partner may have been asking you this question because he wanted to please you and, perhaps, so that you would reciprocate and ask him, too.

How you might have responded depends entirely on what turns you on. It could be anything from "Talking about sex doesn't come so easily to me" to "Any kind of leather turns me on." Also speak up about being a top, bottom, or versatile—if you think providing such specifics will make for better sex or help you weed out those you're not sexually compatible with.

There are two reasons you might not always want to tell someone directly what turns you on. First, you may not actually know what will be enjoyable with a specific person. Second, sometimes doing—and not talking—allows you to discover more about each other's preferences and predilections. There's definitely something to be said for spontaneity.

yet, the next morning. However, if you're not enjoying something or it's uncomfortable, guide your partner elsewhere or speak up.

• **Don't reveal startling fetishes:** If you want your partner to dress you in diapers or slap you—anything that might shock—talk about this beforehand rather than surprising your partner in bed.

The Etiquette of Fellatio

Just what are "proper manners" for two guys when it comes to having oral sex? How do you let someone know this turns you on? And how do you figure out whether it's okay to ejaculate in his mouth? Obviously, good hygiene and grooming are great places to start. Even if you feel a little hesitant talking about sex

(whether it's with a new partner or your "old" boyfriend), it's considerate to discuss these kind of preferences beforehand—rather than resorting to the traditional head push. Let your partner know what you're thinking and ask him whether it's okay. You could say, "I love it when. . . ." but don't *pressure* anyone to accept your "invitation." If he says no or his actions belie a lack of interest, respect the decision.

Once you're both on the same page, the next rule of oral sex etiquette comes into play. Give him a head's-up before you come, by saying something like "Now!" or "I'm going to come" (you know, it's bad manners to surprise people). Finally, don't forget to say thank you, which may come in the form of words or reciprocal actions.

While we're on the subject, a word about oral sex vis-à-vis HIV and other STDs.

QUEERY

"She pulled out a strap-on."

Q I met a woman—really butch, and a lot younger than me—recently through friends and was really into her. That is, until we went back to her apartment and started to get busy. Suddenly, she pulled out a harness and a dildo and it kind of ruined things for me. Isn't that something you introduce later on—if you're both into it? Am I being old-fashioned?

A You're not old-fashioned, but there does seem to be a generational shift in the lesbian community about using dildos, also known as strap-ons.

Testing the waters is usually the best approach with a new sex partner. In your case, it might have made for a smoother introduction if your date had said something about her "equipment" or her "strap-on" (or even casually taken it out) and then gauged your reaction. In that case, you might have said anything from "Sorry, I'm just not into that" to just plain "Cool . . ."

Whatever your response, the gentle approach might have allowed you to explore the idea of letting her teach you about using these toys, as it sounds like you don't have experience with strap-ons.

Indeed, it's her job to notice your desires and reactions just as much as it's yours to notice hers. Bottom line: If the way a casual date wants sex or the way she communicates about it rubs you the wrong way, you may decide there's no reason for you to continue to see each other.

Although the risk of contracting HIV/AIDS from oral sex is considered to be extremely low, you can contract other sexually transmitted infections that way.

"Is it okay to ask a lesbian friend, 'Who's the man in bed?'"

The idea of lesbian and gay sex is fascinating to some straights, as is the notion that there are only two starring roles in the bedroom: catcher and pitcher, or top and bottom.

Actually, "the gays" are quite a varied group in terms of income, intellect, politics, design sense—and sexual tastes. So, before you ask your question, know that your friend's answer may disappoint, especially because these days there's more and more fluidity of sex roles among LGBT people.

Nevertheless, if you and your friend are in the habit of talking about your mutual sexual likes and dislikes, boyfriends and girlfriends, go ahead and ask away. Don't be surprised if you're asked in turn: "Who's the man in *your* bed?"

Body Image

Sex is an extremely intimate and revealing act. And it's very common to feel vulnerable or insecure about being naked in front of another person. Nearly everyone worries about something, whether it is a little extra weight around the midsection, a receding hairline, penis or breast size, or the signs of aging.

One lesbian who's had a complete hysterectomy posted this on her blog: "There's a huge scar on my belly that is quite noticeable, so that's more of a vanity thing, but it's always on my mind when I get naked for the first time with a new girlfriend." A gay man worries about getting old: "By the time I turned forty I felt like I had become invisible in the gay community. It's all about youth and beauty out there."

If body image problems are getting in the way of your sex life, becoming intimate with someone, or just how you feel about yourself, there are a number of things you can do and say that can make things more comfortable:

- **Make adjustments to the setting:** Some people choose to have sex in the dark when they're anxious. After all, turning down the lights or firing up some candles not only are romantic gestures but also provide privacy. Lights or no lights, keep in mind that most of us become more comfortable with each other and our bodies once we've had sex a few times together.

- **Don't feel that you must be naked:** Perhaps you'd be more comfortable wearing a tank top as a cover-up or some other article of clothing that just makes you feel more comfortable being undressed. Or, if you're having chemo and are self-conscious about any hair loss, wear your wig to bed (although you'll want to make sure it's secure).

- **Don't forget your funny bone:** Look at the lighter side of it, as this gay man does: "At five foot two, I decided a long time ago to accentuate my 'shortcoming' by only dating men over six feet tall!" he jokes. "But seriously, being horizontal evens the playing field, so to speak."

- **Acknowledge your concerns:** Before you get into the bedroom, talk with your partner about any fears so that he or she may be both more attentive and not so surprised. If the conversation isn't comfortable, maybe it's not the right time—or the right person.

Sexual/Medical Conditions

"My partner can't keep it hard very long anymore, and I'm really not sure what to say or do that is polite and comforting," writes a young man about his older lover. "Should I just get a prescription for Viagra from the Internet and leave it for him?" he asks. Probably not; that's a bit too harsh of a message. Still, sexual issues ranging from premature ejaculation to erectile difficulty are very common among men, especially those of a certain age and on certain medications. Meanwhile, women can suffer loss of libido or have trouble achieving orgasm. And trans men and women taking hormones in order to transition very often experience big changes in sexual desire or performance. Also keep in mind that even when there's a physiological cause—such as a medication side effect, a hormonal change, or an underlying disease such as diabetes or HIV—being embarrassed, fearful, or otherwise obsessed can make the situation worse: Sexual arousal and orgasm are so closely tied to your state of mind.

If you have a condition that greatly affects your ability to have sex, talk about it with your sex partners beforehand. You don't need to go into a lot of detail—"I've got a medical issue" may be sufficient—but saying a few words will help reduce your own anxiety and clear up any curiosities your partner may have.

If things go well, your partner will take any revelations in stride. But be prepared for his questions.

QUEERY

"Breast cancer makes me uncomfortable about my body."

Q **I'm a lesbian who's had several cancers, including breast cancer. I've been dating a little but am uncomfortable about my body and not sure when to discuss the various health issues and the marks they've left. What should I say and when? I don't want to scare anyone away.**

A Having sex with someone new raises enough issues without also feeling self-conscious about scars. That's why many people who have lost breasts or otherwise been physically changed by surgery choose to wait to have sex until they're comfortable enough with a new partner to discuss their feelings ahead of time.

In a sense, your question is similar to the very common one about dating: When do you talk about the skeletons in your closet? And here again, the answer is "in time." As the relationship becomes more trusting, offer up the basic facts and be open to any questions. Each of us is the composite of our experiences (surgery included), and these make our beauty unique.

However, prepare yourself for the possibility of rejection. Once, after I told a new boyfriend that I had had testicular cancer, he thanked me for being honest and then sent me on my way, saying "I just buried my partner of ten years. I can't go down that path again." Difficult to hear, but better to have it all out in the open.

Are there good and bad manners when it comes to sex?

"Hygiene makes or breaks it."

"No begging! The art of seduction = good manners."

"Bad manners is leaving before it's finished."

"Don't do stuff your partner doesn't want to do."

"If they're trying hard at sex but they're not very good, it's still nice to tell them, 'You're great!'"

If the shoe is on the other foot, and you are the recipient of such news, be gentle in your response. If, for whatever reason, this information is a deal breaker, it's best to express yourself clearly but kindly. For instance, if you have decided not to date HIV-positive people, and someone tells you he's poz, you might say, "I'm so sorry. It's best for me to tell you now that this won't work for me."

If He Won't Wear a Condom

Condoms are one of the best tools men (gay and otherwise) have to prevent the spread of STDs, including HIV. Used properly, with a water-based lubricant, latex or plastic condoms provide a high degree of protection to both partners. Despite these facts, you may find yourself with a partner who doesn't want to use one. Here are some of the more common reasons given to subvert condom use, each followed by a helpful response:

He says: "I'm HIV-negative."

THE TRUTH: How can you be sure? You must wait at least three months since your last risk of exposure to HIV to consider yourself HIV-negative. And don't forget that there are many other STDs to be concerned about, too.

He says: "I'm too big."

THE TRUTH: Condoms come in all sizes and shapes. Among the available jumbo-sized options are Trojan Magnum XL Lubricated, Durex XXL, and Kimono MAXX.

He says: "I can't stay erect when I wear one."

THE TRUTH: This does happen a fair amount to many men. First, check to make sure that the condom isn't too tight or too thick. More often that not, though, it's primarily a psychological response, one that unfortunately becomes a self-fulfilling prophecy. To counter that, try making the unveiling and capture playfully sexy. Another technique—don't proceed directly to insertion the moment the condom is on; you can return to foreplay for a while and then, when he's happily erect (and covered), go from there.

He says: "I'm allergic to latex."

THE TRUTH: Some men are, but there are condoms made out of other materials—including plastic (polyurethane)—that provide protection against HIV and all other STDs. Keep in mind, though, that lamb's skin condoms don't protect against HIV and that you must use a water-based lubricant with latex or plastic condoms for full protection.

91

He says: *"It ruins the mood."*

THE TRUTH: If you plan ahead, a condom can be whipped out without losing your focus for a second. Keep them in a nightstand along with your lubricant. What's more fun, however, is incorporating it into the sex itself. Use your imagination.

If the Condom Breaks

When choosing a condom, make sure that it's not past its expiration date, it's latex or plastic, you use a water-based lubricant, and you put it on correctly. All these actions will reduce the likelihood of the condom tearing (or falling off). If the condom fails after ejaculation, most physicians would likely counsel both of you to get tested for HIV and other STDs immediately, and then at three- and six-month intervals. However, if you know (or believe) one of you has HIV, call your doctor or a clinic right away to discuss your potential risk; you may need postexposure prophylaxis, a "morning after" treatment for HIV that can prevent infection. (If the condom breaks before orgasm, be sure to replace the torn one with a new one and double-check the criteria listed above.)

Postcoital Etiquette

What do you and your lover like to do after sex? Sleep? Talk? Eat? Light up a smoke? It's great if you have the same habits, but if your natural inclination is to do one thing (perhaps cuddle) and your partner, another (rush to shower), you could miss out on one of the most bonding and lovely portions of an intimate encounter.

The key is to check in with your partner before taking off on your usual path and to compromise as necessary. Take the cuddler/dasher divide, for instance: If you're the dasher, instead of "forcing" yourself to stay in bed for another fifteen or twenty minutes, stay for five or ten. When you're ready to get up, touch your partner gently to make it clear that you're not trying to sneak away and announce your intention to clean up or go to the kitchen.

Same-sex similarities may be an advantage in this area because, whatever your other differences, at least you can count on a similar physiological reaction to having an orgasm. After coming, the heart rate of a man drops precipitously (which often leads to instant sleep); by contrast, women can get right back on the *horse,* again and again. (Note to lesbians, bi women, and straight transmen: Just because she is able to have multiple orgasms doesn't necessarily mean she *wants* to. Check in with your partner before proceeding to round 2.)

CLEANING UP AFTERWARD

Be prepared. Keep a box of Kleenex, some baby wipes, a glass of water, and a trash basket nearby. If your only extra towels are in the downstairs linen closet, make sure you bring some upstairs beforehand.

For Everyone

Refrain from showering with anything stronger than soap after you have sex. Douches and other chemical cleaners can be abrasive to your skin and even encourage infections and skin rashes. Make sure to clean sex toys with hot water and soap between uses.

For Men

If you're the condom wearer, it's your responsibility to dispose of it by taking it off soon after ejaculation—certainly while you're still erect—so there is no spillage. Then, tie off the end, wrap it in toilet paper, and put it in the wastebasket—not the toilet.

For Women

Towels are great for sopping up female ejaculate (men's, too, but women's is more watery, so towels absorb it better). Or try putting a plastic or rubber sheet underneath your regular linens.

WHAT OUR PARENTS NEVER TAUGHT US

When sex is just sex, the basic negotiations involved in an individual encounter are different—not necessarily easier or harder—than with sex that's part of a dating relationship. Casual sex, whether anonymous or simply a one-time thing, can be very liberating when both parties are able to shelve the emotional element; you just need to send the right cues. Indeed, the word "casual" is sort of a misnomer, because in the LGBT community there are carefully defined rituals for these kinds of hookups (whether picking each other up online, through a GPS match service, on the street, or in a dark backroom). Likewise, "rough sex" may sound spontaneous, but there are well-established codes for so-called BD/SM, as well as for bringing pornography or "kinky" practices into the bedroom. No matter, it pays to know what's expected—so that you can make sure things stay safe and enjoyable. This section also takes on the manners for one-night stands and sex at bathhouses and backrooms, as well as the etiquette for open relationships and three-ways.

No-Strings-Attached Sex

No-strings-attached (or NSA) sex has long been a common practice among some gay and bisexual men (as well as straight folks), in recent years made even easier due to the Internet, GPS-location services, and social media sites. But other LGBT people like to play around, too, whether for experimentation, between relationships, or even when in a loving partnership. Nor is this kind of sex limited by generation. Explained one now middle-aged lesbian: "I had loads of casual sex as a teenager, but then I moved on to a more serious relationship for years. After we broke up, I was happy to go back to the casual affairs for the time being."

If you're planning to have casual sex, be sure you're both on the same page about its casualness. Obviously, if you met through an online profile using "NSA," "play," or a similar phrase, you're set. (By the way, hooking up via the Internet or phone and proceeding to have sex at your home or his is known as "ordering out.") However, if the other person is making plans for later or getting too personal, it's okay to say something direct like "I hope you realize this is a purely sex thing for me."

Regardless of how you meet your sex partner, here are some rules for safety, sexual and otherwise:

- Don't feel the need to use your real name or your full name. First names and nicknames are fine.
- Resist the urge to ask the kinds of personal questions you might ask a date. You are *not* on a date.
- If he is coming to your place, tuck away your valuables, including any personal information such as bank statements, physician appointments, etc.
- Conduct yourself as if your partner is HIV-positive. Period. NSA sex is inherently risky.
- Don't allow any photographs or videos of you to be taken without your consent.
- While just about any location will do, abide by all ordinances about public sex.

IF YOU'VE MET ONLINE

There are a few additional guidelines if you hook up via the Internet and are meeting for the first time just for a romp in the hay.

- Make sure to get a phone number to call and confirm the hookup. If the partner isn't willing to provide one, something's not right. You may never have sex together again, but later—in case you forgot your cell phone or some other valuable item, or need to be in touch to explain you have a STD—you may need to have it.
- Leave your trick's name and phone number with a trusted friend or roommate prior to the hookup.
- Don't give out your address unless you have received and confirmed the phone number of your trick first.

If you run into each other again later, it's fine not to acknowledge each other—or, if you're so inclined, just nod your head in recognition (especially if one of you is with someone else). Neither of you is likely to want to answer the question: "How do you know each other?"

Public Sex Etiquette

Okay, so you've located the tearooms (aka public bathrooms), sex parties, or backroom bars in your town or holiday destination, and you want to play without insulting anyone or getting arrested. While gay men are the most common practitioners of public sex, folks of all sexual orientations participate. Lesbian sex parties, such as New York City's famous Submit events, are simply a more underground affair, often with a BD/SM (bondage/discipline and sadomasochism) theme and a special welcome to trans people. (For other sex-related abbreviations in common use, see page 73.)

Regardless of the mix of people and the venue, here are a few points to keep in mind if participating in public sex:

- **Do your research:** This could involve talking to friends or going online to pick up some information about particular locations, like beaches and public parks. Find out what you can before you get there, not just to avoid getting arrested but because regulars can tell you what to expect.
- **Follow the rules at sex parties:** Guidelines are generally posted at parties and bathhouses about safe sex, drinking, dress code, joining in, etc. Once you're inside, words may open

doors, but a nod of the head that says "yes" or "no" is the best. Direct eye contact works, too. Watching is also encouraged.

- **Safeguard valuables:** Keep your money, keys, and so on locked away, in the lockers provided or—if you've driven—hidden in your car. Losing your wallet while your jeans are around your ankles is not a good thing.
- **Follow the dress code:** In general, keep your shoes on, take your clothes off (or some of them), and stay upright.

THE ESSENTIALS

The Hanky Code

What's old is new again. While the hanky code, the 1970s phenomenon of flagging (where gay men wore colored bandanas in their back pockets to indicate particular sexual preferences) seemed destined for the dustbin, a new generation of young gay men is embracing it with vigor and a twist. Not surprisingly, an iPhone app exists that creates a virtual hanky that the developers claim is the ultimate "gay decoder ring," turning your iPhone into a digital handkerchief. As in the "old days," stick it in your right pocket if you're a catcher and in your left if you're a pitcher!

A sampling of a long and extensive list of colors and patterns follows. Take note that color codes vary by region and that while there's widespread agreement on the colors for the more common sexual practices (for example, black for SM, yellow for water sports), you'll want to double-check with your sex partner before you dive into anything esoteric. (For a more comprehensive list, see www.gaymanners.com.)

PURPLE	*Piercing*
HUNTER GREEN	*Daddy play*
MINT GREEN	*Mommy play*
KELLY GREEN	*Hustling*
GOLD LAMÉ	*Muscle boys*
BLACK	*Heavy SM*
RED	*Fisting*
FUCHSIA	*Spanking*
LIGHT PINK	*Dildos*
DARK PINK	*Nipple play*
YELLOW	*Water sports*
OLIVE	*Military scenes*
BEIGE	*Rimming*
ORANGE	*Anything goes*

Dildos and Vibrators

No longer do you need to go into a sex toy store to buy accoutrements like dildos and vibrators. Online retailers like Adam Male allow for anonymity for those who worry about being caught buying a favorite item—and make it much easier for those in nonurban areas to do any necessary shopping.

When purchasing dildos, be sure to buy silicone ones; make sure they're phthalate-free either by reading the item's description, asking a customer rep, or—if you're in a brick-and-mortar store—avoiding those that smell like chemicals or perfume. Phthalates are believed to be bad for your long-term health and also can irritate your skin. When using dildos, clean with soap and hot water between uses (sterilize them in boiling water every once in a while as well).

Vibrators come in an even wider array of styles than dildos, ranging from motorized phalluses to tiny "bullets" you can insert (anywhere, not just vaginas). You'll eventually figure out what works for you, but some people like to have a number on hand in case a visiting sex partner has a particular preference. Follow the same guidelines as with dildos for keeping them clean and hygienic (except don't boil them).

Bathhouse Etiquette

There are basic guidelines prevailing at gay bathhouses—if you can still find one of these once-beloved and much-maligned institutions—or what are more commonly called sex clubs today. Many clubs require memberships, which can be bought for the day and entail bringing some form of identification as well as cash or a credit card. (If you're on the down low, either pay in cash or ask how the charge will be listed on your card, to make sure there are no surprises when you receive your monthly statement.)

Most venues dispense free condoms and lube, with a prohibition against unprotected anal sex. But enforcement is usually spotty, even with "monitors."

You'll generally find that bathhouses feature some combination of saunas, showers, pools, a television screen for watching porn, and open areas to play. If patrons pay extra for a private room, instead of using a locker, they generally leave the door completely open if they're looking for visitors to come in and have sex, or just ajar if others are welcome to watch what's going on or possibly join in—on the occupant's invitation, that is.

If you're interested in someone at a bathhouse, make eye contact. A nod or a sustained look means yes. A shake of the head or a look away means no. Definitely don't touch someone unless you get an indication that it's okay. If he shakes his head or moves away, stop what you're doing and move on.

Sex and Drugs Make Strange Bedfellows

The quest for better or longer-lasting sex leads some gay and bisexual men to a variety of substances like ecstasy, cocaine, crystal meth, and recreational Viagra. For too many, use of these drugs leads to poor decision-making and, by extension, the spread of various STDs and HIV—not to mention the additional side effects for those who become addicted to these drugs.

Of course, gay and bi men are not the only ones mixing drugs and sex with disastrous outcomes. And it's not just party drugs. "I started a relationship high on our first date and continued through the relationship thinking I had it under control," says one lesbian who was a heroin user. "In the end I lost everything and barely walked away alive."

If you want to avoid hooking up with sex partners who use drugs, look for profiles that say "no party and play" (which means no use of PNP, or crystal meth) or "420 ok" (only marijuana but nothing heavier). If you find yourself in a situation being asked to smoke, swallow, or inhale a substance that you're not comfortable with—especially by someone you don't know very well—say or indicate "no" and consider leaving.

Open Relationships

Open relationships have long been a part of lesbian and gay culture and can be as healthy or viable as monogamous ones. What's important in making them successful is your commitment to each other (as primary partners) and mutual respect for each other's needs and the boundaries you establish.

Here are some questions to consider in having this discussion with a partner:

- Do you both agree to practice safer sex with others? Are there sexual practices, like anal intercourse, that aren't okay? If you slip (have risky sex), do you agree to tell the other?

- Will you discuss each encounter or not? Some couples may find it a turn-on to hear of each other's trysts; others choose to turn a blind eye or just prefer the bare-bones facts to a blow-by-blow description.

- Is it okay to make rules involving geography? For instance, maybe it's not okay to trick when you're in your hometown, but it's fine if you're away on a business trip.

- Are friends, mutual acquaintances, exes, or any others on a "no-play" list?

- What about bringing sex partners home? Is that acceptable? Sometimes? Never? What about having sex in the bedroom you share with your partner? Or should

QUEERY

"How to handle a one-night stand"

Q **Here's the deal: While I was on vacation, I met this guy at the local bar, had a couple of drinks, went back to his place and had great sex. End of story . . . or so I thought. As I was leaving, he asked me for my number so that we could "get together again." I thought he understood this was a one-night stand. I just said, "I'll see you when I see you." I felt like I didn't handle the situation properly, but did I do anything wrong?**

A Not really, no. It just sounds like one or both of you could have been more explicit ahead of time. But it's a situation that requires some finesse. Unless you're having sex at a club or in a backroom, it's easy to misunderstand what another person's intentions are. Then, in the throes of passion, it may not feel quite right to say, "I only want to have sex with you and then you've got to go." But what might get the message across is "I'm just looking for a quickie tonight." If he's looking for more than a hookup, he'll know to look elsewhere.

Once the deed is done, it's wise to avoid getting into a lot of postcoital chitchat if you're hosting, since that could lead your guest to think you're extending his invitation. Instead, offer him a glass of water and the use of the bathroom, and then start to tidy up. If he's not taking the hint, you could say after a short while, "Hey, thanks for coming over." That's definitely a cue that it's time to exit. (If you're the guest, be sure not to overstay your welcome and, when you leave, to take all your belongings.) For a polite noncommittal goodbye, supplement by saying, "That was fun," with a parting hug.

If your guest expresses interest in getting together again (as yours did), be gentle and say "Sorry, I'm not looking to date right now."

all extracurricular encounters be anony-mous (for instance, at a gym steam room or bathhouse)?

- Do you both need to participate, which is to say, is it always a three-way? If so, do you each have veto power over the third party?
- Does there need to be a limit on the number of sexual episodes with each new person? Some couples limit the number of trysts per person as a means of keeping the connection more sexual than emotional or romantic.

If your discussion results in your agree-ing to have sex with others, make sure you're both comfortable with the ground rules you've established. Over time (and perhaps especially at the beginning), these guidelines may need to be revisited and amended as you find that some rules work while others don't.

Three-Ways

While threesomes can be exciting and sexy, they're often fraught with anxieties and insecurities. Not surprisingly, a well-defined sexual etiquette has evolved in the LGBT com-munity. The most common problem is that two members of the party will pair off in an exclusive way and the third will be given short shrift. If all three people are single, the major rule of three-ways is to pay attention to both your playmates.

If your ménage à trois consists of an estab-lished couple plus a third person, here are some additional guidelines.

FOR COUPLES

- **Don't coerce a partner into a three-way:** If your partner is not as excited about the idea as you are, at least make sure you have his or her genuine consent.
- **Discuss your "exit strategy":** Before you get started, talk together about how and when you will determine when it's time for your third to move on. This can be as simple as saying, "That was a lot of fun. Maybe you'd like to shower off." Or as direct as "We need

---

"I don't tell my anonymous sex partners I'm poz."

Q **I'm having a gnarly debate with my two best friends. I say that when I'm at a sex club I don't need to tell anyone that I'm poz. No one really talks anyway. My friends think I need to let my sex partners know my status beforehand. Who's right?**

A As you note, in these kinds of situations it's hard to imagine such a conversation taking place, since so few words about *anything* are actually exchanged. Still, you must assume there are HIV-negative men present whose judgment may have been clouded by drugs or alcohol—and for whom becoming infected with HIV is a rather high price to pay for a night out on the town. So, you're off the hook for disclosing your HIV status, but you must take all the necessary precautions to protect your sex partners.

"To tip or not to tip after massage 'with release'"

Q I went to a new masseur in the Castro last month and as we were winding down he asked me if I wanted "release." I had actually never heard that term before and so to be adventurous I said, "Yes!" Now I know what it means. What I don't know is: Should I have tipped him extra?

A It's a good practice to tip professionals for services well delivered; in general, tip masseurs as you would a haircutter, which is to say 15 to 20 percent. If you're seeking "massage with release," also known as a "happy ending," tip a little bit more—unless that service is tacked onto your bill, in which case tip normally.

In seeking a masseur who provides such services, read ads for terms like "sensuous massage," "erotic massage," "sexual release," "hand release," "prostate massage," and "light touch."

If you're seeking nonsexual bodywork, pay attention to a masseur's credentials (look for the appellation LMT, for licensed massage therapist); the ads of such masseurs use terms like "therapeutic massage," "nonsensual," and "professional."

---

to call it a night. Maybe we can do this again."

- **Postmortems are helpful:** After your guest has left, talk out any awkwardness or discuss any issues with your partner that may have come up.

- **No cheating:** Unless you've expressly agreed that it's okay for one of you to pair off with a third in the future, don't.

IF YOU'RE THE THIRD WHEEL

- **Be clear about what to expect:** When making a plan, talk with the couple about your and their expectations. If any rules are established or activities proscribed, abide by what you agree to.

- **Make sure no one is neglected:** If you want to be invited back, be sure to please both members of the couple.

- **Know when to leave:** Unless invited to spend the night or stay longer, assume it's time to go

soon after the main event. There's no need to be hasty, but follow the lead of your hosts.

Paid Escorts

The LGBT world has its own well-established traditions of hiring folks for sex. Gay and bisexual men have a particularly wide range of services at their disposal. You can find escorts, rentboys, and hustlers (to some the terms are synonymous, although hustlers are more likely to be working the streets) at bars, outside of them, online, in the LGBT newspapers, or through agencies. Another approach is to consult one of the online directories for male massage: While some of these masseurs are licensed and do only therapeutic massage, others—the ones advertising "sensual" or especially "erotic" massage—often provide services beyond the massage itself.

When you're using an agency, be prepared to specify what type of man—or woman—you're seeking (age, ethnicity, body type), what kinds of sexual activity you prefer (especially any fetishes or kinky stuff), and ask ahead of time how much the service will cost. Expect to spend $100 to $500 depending on the escort, your menu of activities, and the time involved. Generally, "out" calls—those at your home or hotel room—are more expensive than "in" calls at the escort's place.

If you're unclear about how to behave when you meet, try pretending you're on a date. Chatting a little on general topics may help you relax—or ask for a massage. Just don't ask for a lot of personal details, such as whether he has a boyfriend or what kind of sex he likes. (After all, he's being paid to like the kind of sex *you* like.) If you're paying for an hour, that's counted from the time of his arrival, by the way, not from whenever it is you started having sex. A tip of 15 to 20 percent is customary if you've been satisfied with the service provided.

Police entrapment is sometimes a risk, especially in small towns with strongly anti-vice or anti-gay police departments. Escort services aren't technically illegal, with the conceit being that you are paying simply for companionship. However, a transaction becomes prostitution through an open offer of money in exchange for sex. When in doubt,

QUEERY

"Talk dirty to me!"

Q I met this really cool professional woman at a local club recently and after a couple of drinks we went back to her apartment and started to fool around. Then, she whispered in my ear: "Talk dirty to me!" I said, "What?" So she explained: "It would turn me on if you called me _____." I thought this was hysterical and embarrassing and couldn't do it and then the whole evening fell apart.

A Your tale of woe is a perfect example of how useful social media services and hookup sites can be in helping to set expectations. If someone has a foot fetish or happens to get turned on by hearing "dirty" talk, those venues allow you to put it out there sooner rather than later. While there may not be much mystery, there's also not much likelihood of the kind of surprise you encountered. On the other hand, when you meet someone at a bar or club, it's not usually appropriate to announce you're seeking a potty mouth or "verbal pig" as a sex partner. It's best to ease into such conversations slowly, using your words carefully at first, gauging the response, and then continuing on (if given a green light).

I'd also suggest that if you find yourself in a situation like this again, try not to let on that you find it "hysterical." People who request kinky behavior with someone they barely know are making themselves vulnerable, so it's important to be considerate to that and to them. Remember that what you experience as outré might be basic boudoir banter to another. No judgments, please.

avoid actually vocalizing your money-for-sex arrangement; instead, insist that you are paying for someone's "time."

As for picking up a street hustler in a public place, keep in mind that you're a lot more vulnerable to getting ripped off or even gay-bashed. On the plus side, these services tend to be more affordable.

Kinky Sex and Porn

Because "kinky" means out of the ordinary or edgy, your idea of kinky sex may be quite different from the next person's. In general, the term "kinky" refers to the idea of exploring sexual boundaries, experimenting with something new, and/or seeing how it feels to do things a little differently than usual. That could mean any number of things, including tying each other up, watching porn, doing it in your car, or simply trying a new sex position.

Some adventurous types share their preferences up-front, before finding themselves in bed, while others first like to build up a little trust between the sheets. The trick is finding a way to bring up the subject of your fantasy or fetish in a way that doesn't scare or intimidate your partner ("You want to do *what*?"), but that, to the contrary, inspires him or her to participate. Remember, it's all about voluntary participation. It's often a good idea to bring up new ideas gently, sometimes even sort of indirectly. Try saying, for instance, "I was online the other day and saw some amazing sex toys. What do you think about buying some?" Or "Did you know that Lucy and Cyndi dress up as cops in bed? That could be fun, don't you think?"

THE ESSENTIALS

The Well-Dressed Leatherman

Gay male leather culture first showed up in the 1940s and '50s, when postwar motorcycle clubs (think Marlon Brando in a leather jacket and Muir cap in *The Wild One*) presented a masculine alternative to effeminate stereotypes. Today, the leather community has spawned all sorts of subsets, from the BD/SM community to leather bears, martial attire, cowboy, daddy/boy, and so on. But if you're going to go for the classic "old guard" look, here's what you need to shop for:

REQUIRED

Black leather boots (construction, army, Dehner's, or black cowboy boots)

Black leather belt (usually wide with prominent studs)

T-shirts (either solid white or black or with leather/BD/SM themes, wife beaters, or ribbed tank tops)

Black leather jacket (either biker or bomber style)

OPTIONAL
(all black leather except the jeans and handkerchiefs)

Vest

Black or navy Levi's

Chaps

Gloves

Cap

Handkerchiefs (see page 95)

Harness

Collar

Studs

Rough Play

The phrase "rough play" usually refers to variations of bondage and discipline (often referred to as BD) and sadomasochism (known as SM), which is the infliction of pain or humiliation on a partner or the pleasure that is enjoyed in being the object of such punishment. What's especially important if you're going to participate in BD/SM activities is strong verbal and nonverbal communication, respect for each other's limits and, above all, mutual consent. The mantra in the BD/SM community is "safe, sane, and consensual." If you don't follow the agreed-upon rules, you risk toppling the whole scenario and possibly inflicting pain that crosses the line of consent. Think of these rules as a couple's own personalized set of BD/SM manners.

In general, those who participate in rough play are considered either dominant or submissive (although plenty of LGBT people switch roles from time to time). No matter, the top or dom is expected to follow rigid rules. Often, SM partners pick a "safe word" before getting started, a word or phrase that is a password for putting a halt to the sex play. This is necessary because a submissive partner may be saying "no, no, no" and actually mean "yes, yes, yes." Many partners also use the so-called traffic light system, with "green" meaning harder or more; "yellow," slow down or too hard; and "red" meaning stop right now.

Being Pressured to Do Something Uncomfortable (or Unsafe)

It's completely appropriate to decline a request to participate in any kind of sex act involving an activity that you really don't like, that makes you uncomfortable, or is unsafe. Granted, this can be difficult in the heat of the moment. One young man in the midst of a sexual encounter with a guy he was extremely attracted to explained: "It was really hard not giving in because he was so amazingly hot. But since his idea of rough sex scared me, I had to leave."

Don't be shy about suggesting limits ahead of time or during sex—or pausing to talk about what's bothering you while in the throes of it. Raise a red flag to put an end to what you don't like. It's your right to do this, and stick to your guns—even if your partner begs you in a loving way, gets angry with you, calls you "sex-negative" (someone who is prudish), or threatens you. As the young man quoted above discovered, leaving is very often the only way to entirely shut down such a confrontation.

CHAPTER 5

Committed Relationships

Making Partner

Without sufficient role models in past generations, LGBT couples have learned to improvise as we develop and deepen our loving relationships. Often we have to figure out how we want to refer to each other ("Are you my 'lover' or 'partner'?") and then ask others to do the same. Then, when we make a commitment (legal or not), we need to have those conversations all over again ("husband," "wife," "spouse"?). Now, with more and more LGBT couples visible—among celebrities alone, Neil Patrick Harris and partner David Burtka; Jane Lynch and wife Lara Embry; and trans activist Chaz Bono and partner Jennifer Elia—we're finding ways to honor and celebrate the ones we love.

But as with all couples, sometimes things don't go right: Affairs, exes, and disagreements are just some of what we face. Add in living together, which has its own set of manners; this is about as intimate as it gets, but there are practical concerns, too, such as the extra steps that LGBT couples need to take when it comes to financial and legal security while living together—or during a breakup.

GOING PUBLIC AS A COUPLE

For some, big romances are so completely personal and disconnected from the outside world that sharing your good news with others may feel beside the point. Then there are others among us who tweet or Facebook every step of the way. Regardless of which camp you fall into, there comes the time to introduce your new sweetheart to friends or family. And this raises questions: how to come out as a couple? Whether to post your new status online? What is the right language to use to present each other to the world? Don't be surprised if this requires an extra dose of patience with each other or with the other people in your life, both LGBT and straight.

Don't Forget Your Friends

As romances heat up, it's natural for some of us to spend more and more time with the new boyfriend or girlfriend and less time with our friends. No matter how much your head is spinning, be aware of the impact this sudden shift can have on your friends. Said one lesbian: "As soon as my best friend gets caught up with a new girl, she completely forgets she has any friends." Or you may find yourself talking incessantly about your new beau to the consternation of those subjected to your love rants.

QUEERY

"We're embarrassed that we met online."

Q I met my sweetie on a dating site and now that we've gotten serious, people keep asking how we found each other. We're embarrassed! What should we say?

A Meeting people on dating sites used to have a certain stigma, signaling desperation, if not a single-minded focus on sex. But that's not true anymore. Most folks are used to the idea that dating sites can increase your chances of finding someone with the qualities that are most important to you.

These sites are great for connecting, especially considering some of the alternatives—bars, clubs, and the stray personal introduction.

In fact, by meeting online you're in good company—a recent study from the American Sociological Association reported that more than 60 percent of same-sex couples met that way.

However, if in the end you decide to rewrite the story of how you met, confer with your partner in devising a tale you're both comfortable with, and stick to it—together.

You're talking with your boyfriend or girlfriend about moving in together. What's important to discuss (and do) before making the big decision?

"Sleep over at the person's house for a week and find out who he or she really is!"

"What to keep and what to get rid of."

"Monogamy—yes or no—must be agreed upon."

"Very clear money agreements are essential."

If you see yourself in this light (perhaps a good friend exclaims, "I never see you anymore!"), acknowledge the situation, ask your friends for some temporary "forgiveness," and let them know you still care about *them*. Make the effort to include others in activities that don't just involve watching the two of you slobber over each other. Here are some tried-and-true suggestions for introducing your new sweetie to friends:

- **Schedule drinks or dinner:** This is a straightforward way for your beau and a close friend or two to have a chance to get to know one another without a lot of pressure.
- **Plan a group meet-and-greet:** If your new boyfriend or girlfriend is up for meeting the entire gang (be sure to ask first), choose a low-key venue where everyone will feel comfortable and be able to hear one another. Consider this a "coming out together" party.
- **Organize an outing:** Find a social activity you enjoy with your friends and your beau, such

as hiking, bowling, or going to a play or concert (with time to chat before or after). This kind of unstructured time allows everyone to mingle at a relaxed pace.

A final note: If you're the "third-wheel" friend who is feeling left out while a new romance burns brightly, try not to take it to heart. Be patient. Whether or not this relationship endures, both lovers will eventually need their friends again. And with any luck, you'll be granted the same amount of leeway when your turn comes.

STRAIGHT TALK

"I want to be politically correct and use the right terminology when referring to the beloveds of my gay and lesbian friends. Any advice?"

Listen to your friends as they introduce this important person. What words do they use to characterize their relationship? Is it boyfriend/girlfriend, partner/spouse, or husband/wife? Then, when it comes your turn to introduce one or both of them, use that same language.

Avoid improvising. There are no bonus points for creativity. If you're not sure of their preferred way of referring to each other, then *ask* them. After all, these are your friends! "How do the two of you like to be introduced?" should do the trick.

Meeting the Parents

The first meeting with parents can be stressful for most LGBT couples (and our families, too), especially if the folks are uncomfortable with their gay or trans offspring or closed-minded about a difference of race, ethnicity, or age. "I knew that 'Dad' was a real Southern aristocratic type, and Brett had already told me to call him 'Mr.' if not 'sir,'" recalls one gay man of encountering his in-laws. "The first time we went over there for dinner, I was petrified of everything—using the wrong fork, spilling my wine, even touching my boyfriend. But it all went pretty well and when we left that evening, he said, 'Good to meet you, son.'"

To ensure that meeting your squeeze's parents goes as well, try these steps:

- **Find out as much as you can ahead of time:** Indeed, prod your partner for information you think could help navigate the waters ahead and establish some commonalities. What kind of work do they do? Do they volunteer or have other hobbies? Is their health okay? Are there topics to steer clear of?

- **Ask your partner how they feel about gay or trans people:** Have they met your partner's other significant others? (If so, how did it go?) Do they socialize with LGBT people? What positions do they take on LGBT political issues like same-sex marriage, gay adoption, or ending workplace discrimination?

- **Bring a small gift as a token of friendship:** No matter your sexual orientation, it's always wise to bring an offering to the "parents-in-law" (whether legal or otherwise). Good choices include a bouquet of flowers or a houseplant; a favorite book or bottle of wine; or something you've baked or made.

Keep in mind that all your preparations may be for naught. The truth is that you can't predict how your partner's family will react. The most homophobic dad might just melt at the sight of your Yankees T-shirt, while the friendliest mother could happen to have had a bad day and torture you all the way through dinner with rude questions and embarrassing comments. Families are like that, as you probably know: unpredictable and idiosyncratic, especially when it comes to a new relationship among one of their near and dear.

INTRODUCING YOUR NEW PARTNER

There are things you can do to smooth the way with your family as you introduce your new partner to your parents. Here are some guidelines:

- **Don't surprise your family:** If you're not already out, come out before you throw your girlfriend at their feet.

- **Brief them:** Provide some information about your partner's background, schooling, work, or whatever else you think will give them a sense of her. Let them know a little bit about where you met and how long you've been together.

- **Stay away from politics:** If you know their political positions to be anti-gay, there's no reason to get into heated debates about LGBT issues during this meet-and-greet.

- **Make them comfortable:** Consider inviting them to your place or wherever you think they will be most at ease. Go out of your way to do it up a bit—to make it a special and memorable encounter.

- **Always make sure you will both be safe:** If you have even the slightest doubt, hold off or make sure you have a Plan B, like your own car to leave quickly.

QUEERY

"She's not out, but I am."

Q I'm very comfortable with my sexuality, but my partner's not out to her family or colleagues. When we go to her parents' house I am asked to be her "friend," which feels like a lie. When they come to visit, she moves into the guest room. This is making me very uncomfortable, and I'm not sure what to do about it.

A Life in the closet is difficult for the person choosing that life, but often just as hard or harder for a partner required to keep the nature of a closeted relationship secret.

What you can do is suggest that your partner contact PFLAG, find a therapist to discuss her coming-out issues, or agree to help her make a coming-out plan.

In the end, however, her decision whether to come out—or not—is hers. If she remains closeted and you choose to stay together, you may find it easier to limit your visits with her family and forgo the pretense of being a "friend." Or you may decide the cost of her being in the closet is simply too high for you and end things; you won't be the first couple to break up over this challenging issue.

Remember that families and new relationships need time to get used to each other. Try to have neither overly high expectations nor dire ones.

Using Social Media to Announce Your Relationship

How you use social networking sites to broadcast personal news depends a lot on your generation. Boomers and Gen-Xers are more likely to rely on more traditional means to let their friends and families know of a new love interest: phoning a few close friends, e-mailing a wider circle (not in a group e-mail), or introducing them at a small gathering.

In some networks, especially among younger people, using Facebook or Twitter to announce a new relationship makes it official in the same way that "back in the day" one might have thrown a housewarming party or brandished a ring. One young lesbian changed her online status to "in a relationship," explaining: "I wanted everyone to know at the same time. It was so gratifying to see all the responses I got back on my Facebook wall affirming us." Still, these updates can be easy to miss, so don't rely on social media as the *only* vehicle for letting everyone know about your new relationship.

In addition, don't change your relationship status without first discussing it with your significant other. When you both agree, that's what's called going "Facebook-public." It's not unheard of for one person to think he's now coupled—and the other to think, well, "It's complicated."

"When should I start including a friend's new partner in social events?"

Apply the same rules here as you would to a straight friend's new beau. In general, once a couple presents themselves as a twosome—going out together regularly, meeting the 'rents, and so on—it's time to invite them together to casual events, such as brunches, dinner parties, and theater outings. But there's a higher standard for more formal affairs, like weddings. In that case, wait until they either move in together, announce that they're a committed couple, or have a partnership ceremony (whether or not they legally marry).

YOUR PERSONAL LIFE AS A COUPLE

Early on in a relationship, you'll probably find yourself discussing how much privacy each of you needs, and even how to define your new relationship to others. Later, other questions come into play, such as how to mark anniversaries, whether to move in together, and any other day-to-day conundrums. Every romance is different, but if you proceed with mutual respect and good communication, you'll be better able to stay in step with each other.

Privacy and Boundaries

At the beginning of a relationship, your tendency may be to merge—that is, to give in to every little desire for intimacy and sharing or, on the contrary, to be extra-assertive about the fact that "I'm a separate person with a life of my own and want to keep it just that way." We all have different needs in this regard, but it's not a bad idea to err on the side of being extracourteous and respectful of boundaries until you learn more about each other in this regard. Knock on closed doors, honor any request to spend time alone, and give each other space while dressing, washing, thinking, even sleeping.

Some people may also need greater privacy in the long term, and this is where a sensitive partner needs to be alert. For example, some trans people don't get fully undressed during sex. And some people see the bathroom as sacrosanct—even if just showering. You may also discover that you have a partner who doesn't like to talk about his family or a previous divorce. Be sensitive.

Borrowing Each Other's Clothes

One of the enormous advantages of being in a same-sex relationship (assuming you are even vaguely the same size as your partner) is that suddenly you have twice the clothes to wear, right? For instance, say your favorite slim-fit evening shirt is at the cleaners: You can just borrow hers.

Not so fast. Many couples go through a "we are one" stage, especially in the early infatuation period, but not everyone wants to share his or her clothes at that point—or ever. "Even though my boyfriend and I are exactly the same size, he's been really clear with me that his identity is in his clothes and he doesn't want me borrowing that," said one gay man six months into a new relationship. "He accused me of wanting to borrow his style." Others, meanwhile, will give you the shirts off their backs and are flattered to see a partner in their best duds, or just don't care as long as the clothes come back laundered.

If you decide you want to borrow clothes from your lover, keep these pointers in mind:

- **Ask each time:** Just because she said yes once, you don't have carte blanche to make a habit of wearing her clothes.
- **Don't assume:** Even if you feel that what's yours is hers, she may not feel the same way.

- **Return it promptly, clean:** If you borrow something, return it laundered within the week. And, yes, this rule applies even if it wasn't in a pristine state when you took it.
- **You break it, you replace it:** If you damage the goods, replace them. That's why it's unwise to borrow really expensive or one-of-a-kind threads.

Sharing Your House Key

There are few things as plainly symbolic that a relationship is getting serious as when the person you're dating gives you the house keys. Indeed, this small step should be thought through with care. A gay psychoanalyst explained the significance: "Giving the key to your home says, 'You now have access to my private world.'"

QUEERY

"My girlfriend is a snoop."

Q My partner and I have been living together for a couple of months now, and I suddenly realized that she's going through my personal papers and reading my e-mail. I actually don't have anything to hide, but I feel as though she's invading my privacy and don't like that one bit. When I called her on this behavior, she said, "That's what lesbian couples do." Is it?

A No, lesbian couples don't do that. Nor do couples of other kinds—if they want their relationships to last. And you're quite right that it's irrelevant whether or not you have anything to hide. There is a fine but important distinction between "looking" and "snooping." It's just looking when there's a bank statement or personal letter on the table or a racy photo on the wall, but it becomes snooping when you take some action, like opening the letter, looking through papers, opening a photo album, or visiting an online account.

To start, I suggest changing your password, getting a file cabinet that locks, and telling your partner that her prying is not acceptable. The larger issue here may be one of trust, however; she doesn't seem to trust you, but is also apparently not trustworthy herself. But I'm only a manners expert, not a therapist, so I'll stop here.

If you decide to "key" your girlfriend, be clear about what's going on. Maybe you just need her to walk the dog or housesit once in a while—that's fine, but put it that way. If, however, giving keys to your significant other is a step toward deepening your relationship, consider planning a "moment" to present them. This is a great way to mark this rite, which for some couples can be the precursor to a ring exchange or cohabitation. Here are two creative ways to hand them over:

- On a birthday or anniversary, make a nicely wrapped key the centerpiece of your gift. Include a note explaining to your lover what the significance of the key gift is to you.

- Hide a key under your doormat with a note after you're both inside. Tell your partner that you've left a surprise for him or her out front. Be ready to celebrate with a glass of champagne.

Note: If you are the key recipient, take your time before fully exercising your "rights." Don't immediately rearrange the furniture or reorder the pantry. In fact, don't open that front door on your own at all unless that's what you've both discussed. Respect your partner's space and privacy just as much as you did before.

Giving Each Other Gifts

People come into relationships with their own very specific ideas about gift-giving. Woe to the guy who has always measured love in dollars and cents (presents!) and tries to get serious

QUEERY

"When is our anniversary, honey?"

Q **It seems that straight couples have it easy when it comes to knowing when to celebrate their anniversary; it's the day they got married. But what about for LGBT people? Is it the first date? The first time you had sex? When you made a commitment?**

A Actually, straight people have this predicament, too—lots of straight couples mark first dates, first overnight, and so on. And the right to marry brings with it even more moments to celebrate: the day the couple got engaged, for instance. It's true, however, that the word "anniversary" itself screams marriage. That leaves it to most same-sex couples to find a day or days of their own to mark as their anniversary.

How to pick that day is really up to the two of you, however. If there was a day that you made a commitment, registered as domestic partners, or had a ceremony of some kind, that's a ready-made anniversary. Some people choose the day that they met, which may also be the first time they had sex. The idea is to be romantic about it and consider the uniqueness of your relationship.

Needless to say, if you can't choose, there's no reason to stop at merely one celebration a year.

with a fellow for whom birthdays, anniversaries, and holidays are more about meals, family, terms of endearment—or perhaps no different than any other day of the year.

Such different expectations can spell disappointment, however you wrap it. If your gift-giving traditions are very different from your partner's, discuss them. "Do you like exchanging gifts for the holidays?" is a good toe-in-the-water test. But don't wait until the last minute. Popular compromises include in-kind gifts (think personal massage, making a multicourse dinner, a new deck cobbled lovingly together); smaller presents such as books or music; or just exchanging gifts once a year. One gay couple always make twin donations to community or LGBT organizations in each other's name. "When I see James's name on the list of donors at the landmark movie house downtown, I feel good about helping support his volunteer work with my gift."

Here's some more gift-giving etiquette (for couples and other gift-giving situations alike):
- Make sure it fits.
- Don't grin boastfully as you hand it over.
- Be sure to cut off the price tag.
- Don't place a gift bought at Walmart in a Neiman Marcus box.
- If you bought it on supersale, you don't need to mention that—unless it needs to be returned.
- Keep the gift receipt.

(For more about the holidays, please see page 345.)

THE ESSENTIALS
Anniversary Gift Guide

When shopping for an anniversary gift, get your partner whatever you think will make him or her happy—and that you can afford. It may be a favorite bottle of wine, a weekend away, or a houseplant—even a household appliance (for the more practical than romantic). Or she may be a nonmaterial girl; if that's the case, consider writing a poem or letter, framing a photograph of the two of you, or even making her breakfast in bed (as corny as that may sound). But sometimes a little guidance is helpful. If you're the traditional sort, here's a list of what to give a spouse or partner at each momentous year along the way.

FIRST	Clocks
SECOND	China
THIRD	Crystal or glass
FOURTH	Appliances
FIFTH	Silverware
SIXTH	Wood
SEVENTH	Desk sets
EIGHTH	Linens or lace
NINTH	Leather
TENTH	Diamond jewelry
FIFTEENTH	Watches
TWENTIETH	Platinum
TWENTY-FIFTH	Silver

MOVING IN

For some LGBT couples, the decision to live together is like getting married; for others, it's simply a natural next step after spending lots of days and nights together. Either way, it can be a big deal, financially, emotionally, or both. Joyful? Indeed. But moving in with a sweetheart is often just as stressful as breaking up with one. No matter how fraught some of your discussions may become, remember not to let technical questions get in the way of the goal of deepening your relationship. This is a great time to exercise the kind of love and respect that can set the tone for your new life together.

Deciding Whether to Move In

Cohabitation isn't for everyone. Plenty of long-term, committed couples choose never to live together at all. There's also nothing wrong with waiting. Perhaps you live in different cities, one of you has a tiny rent-controlled apartment, or a difficult career change is in the offing. Nevertheless, there are some nice benefits to living together, such as greater intimacy, dividing expenses like rent or a mortgage, spending more time together, and enjoying greater societal recognition of your relationship.

Before cosigning a lease or house mortgage, make sure you're both ready to take this step together. And do your best to put everything aboveboard about the reasons you want to move in. If they're partly financial—wanting to be closer to your boyfriend or girlfriend *and* about saving money—be clear about that. Said one recent college graduate, "I really do love Russ, but I'd be lying if I didn't admit that living together would save us both a lot of money. One rent. One utility bill. One car, in our situation." Grounding this chapter of your relationship on a solid foundation will reap benefits today and in the future.

HOME RULES

If you both feel you're ready, set aside some time before the moving van shows up to review any "rules" involving your domestic relationship. Does your girlfriend expect her parents to come to dinner every weekend? Does your boyfriend equate living together with monogamy? How will you divide expenses? Finally, start to talk about how you'll merge belongings. Although this may not be much of an issue for younger couples, for more established ones it can be a real headache.

Where to Call Home

In a perfect world, you and your partner would be able to move into a completely new home of your own. There's nothing like a fresh start for giving this new phase of your relationship the breathing room it needs.

More often than not, however, it's not so perfect. A common scenario is that one of you owns her own home and can't put it on the market. Or maybe you have such a great deal on a rent-controlled apartment that it doesn't make sense to give that up—at least economically. It's even more complicated if you've been a long-distance couple, and you're facing the issue of who moves and who stays put, with the additional pressures on the partner who pulls up stakes to leave old friends behind and find a new job in the new city.

Regardless of your exact situation, talk about any sacrifices you or your partner may be making. It behooves both of you to keep any possible resentment to a manageable level. If your partner is moving in with you, consider making a bold gesture, such as inviting him to redecorate. Alternatively, if you're the one moving in, try not to completely up-end your partner's household—at least not at first!

For any couple, the stress of turning a single person's apartment into a home for two can be hard on both parties, so keep in mind why you've chosen this option—and choose another one if it proves to be too challenging.

Are You Compatible?

As you and your partner discuss cohabitation, remember that *any* personality quirks and individual habits really start to make a difference. Spend some time considering these potential conflicts:

- **Neat vs. messy:** Look at each other's current homes. "I had my socks lined up by color, my suits by season, and my shoes by style," explained one gay man. "I never realized how this must look to someone else. He thought I was completely anal. I thought this was normal." The real issue is: Will your idiosyncrasies drive each other crazy, or can you find common ground? By the way, when it's said that you can't change a person, it generally means you can't turn a Democrat into a Republican—or vice versa. You can, however, help someone learn to put his dirty clothes in the hamper, take out the garbage, wash dishes, and keep the bathroom tidier. But only if he wants to learn.

- **Introvert vs. extrovert:** Is your partner a homebody and do you crave the nightlife? If so, will you both be okay about spending lots of your free time separately? Or, again, can you find common ground? One lesbian in a long-term relationship said that she, the more outgoing of the couple, now used a number system to let her partner know if it matters whether she comes along. "If I say 'eight,' 'nine,' or 'ten,' then she knows it's important."

- **Busy vs. needy:** How much attention and companionship do you need from each other? One lesbian, a painter who spends all day alone in her studio, can't wait for her partner to come home from her office job. As she says, "The problem is that as soon as she walks in the door, I'm all over her, since I haven't talked to anyone but our cat since breakfast. Alas, for her, she's ready to shut down after dealing with clients all day. Now, when she comes home, we kiss and say hello, but then I give her an hour to herself."

- **Monogamy vs. Non:** Sometimes it takes the discussion about cohabitation to bring this issue to the fore. Perhaps sharing a home simply doesn't suit your old "don't ask, don't tell" arrangement. Or is it okay to trick, but just not in your home or your bedroom? Or does a sexually exclusive arrangement suit one of you but not the other? (For more about monogamy, see page 120.)

- **Smoking, pets, sleep habits, and more:** It's a lot easier to tolerate what bothers us when we don't live with it 24/7. A girlfriend who smokes in her own apartment is different from one who smokes in yours. Your boyfriend's adorable Wheaten Terrier may be the perfect weekend guest, but less desirable as a live-in. Another issue to consider is whether your sleep habits are compatible (early riser vs. night owl, snorer vs. light sleeper). Chances are that you'll find a way to accommodate each other on these matters, but better to communicate about them early on.

Telling Family and Friends You Now Live Together

There are a number of ways to announce that you've moved in with your partner, depending what your budget is, how tech-minded your circle is, and how out you are.

The simplest method for letting your friends know is via your favorite social networking site—however, don't post personal data like a phone number or street address because of concerns about identity theft. Alternatively, send an e-mail message with all the pertinent information or a moving announcement like those found on various online stationers such as PaperlessPost.com. Those who are more traditional will want to consider printed change-of-address cards that can be snail-mailed. (By the way, there is no rule as to whose name comes first on either stationery or labels. It's up to you to decide; when in conflict, let the alphabet guide you.)

Some special considerations come into play if living together amounts to your coming out. Make an effort to deliver the news to close friends and family members in person or by phone. This is not the sort of news that you'd really want to text or e-mail because that can seem impersonal if not disrespectful. (For more about coming out to close friends and family members, see page 4.)

The Cohabitation Shower

Cohabitation showers (also known as nonwedding showers) are popular among some LGBT couples looking to make a wedding-style fuss about moving in together. If that sounds like you, try to get a close friend or family member to host such an event in your honor. That way, she can send invitations, deal with questions about gifts, and decide on a menu. Besides, it's tacky (read: greedy) for a couple to host their own shower.

When it comes to gifts, you might want to register at a traditional department store, a neighborhood boutique, or one of the growing range of LGBT-friendly vendors (see Resources, page 381). Not only does registering make shopping easier for friends and family, you'll also avoid having to make a large number of returns or deal with regifting presents. By the way, because showers are considered more informal than weddings, it's acceptable to note on these invitations where you're registered.

Here's an example of what a printed or electronic invitation to such an event might look like:

It's a good idea (and cost effective) for the couple or the host to enlist others' assistance with food, beverages, and decorations. In addition, designate a reliable friend to keep track of the gifts as they are opened during the event: The list of who gave what will be invaluable when you sit down to write thank-you notes, especially since signed gift cards often become separated from their corresponding packages.

THANK-YOUS

No more than a week or two after the event, be sure to do your thank-yous—with paper and pen. A good way to do this in a timely way is to do half each, signing your partner's name along with your own message of thanks that includes a mention of the specific gift.

Also, don't forget to thank your shower host with both a nice note and perhaps a floral arrangement or a dinner out.

Invitations to Couples Living Together

Once you move in together as a couple, it's good manners for invitations to be addressed to both of you and accepted (or rejected) by both together. This doesn't mean that you need to do everything together, of course, just that it's easier if you RSVP at the same time. If only one of you can attend, say something like "I'd love to come to dinner on the twelfth, but Harrison will be on a work assignment and won't be able to join me."

Sometimes, it takes a while to educate your friends (LGBT or straight) that you're a bona fide committed couple who expect to be invited together. If one of you is left off

an invitation, respond by saying something like "Marcy and I will be around that weekend, working on our new place downtown." Hopefully, that will prompt your host to tell you to bring Marcy along, too. If your hint is not successful, then it's fine to say directly, "Since Marcy and I are now a couple, I'd love for her to join us at dinner. Is that possible?"

Combining Furniture and Tastes

If you happen to have wildly different decorating tastes from your new live-in girlfriend, you'll need to practice the art of compromise while considering what you can each tolerate from the other's "collection." Can you live with the portrait of her mother in the living room, or is the hallway a good compromise? What about the midcentury Breuer knockoff you're just not willing to let go of, even though all of her furniture is eighteenth-century French?

Before actually moving in together, it's smart to eliminate duplicate items. How many outdoor grills do you need? King-sized beds? Sets of towels? If you need to decide which grill to keep, consider holding on to the newer item or the one that works better (unless one of you has a personal attachment to a particular object). Then have a yard sale, donate your superfluous items to a thrift shop, or rent a storage space.

When it comes to the actual decorating, do your best to be empathetic and, again, compromise. Believe it or not, you don't have to love every item of furniture or piece of bric-a-brac that he

carries in with him. And maybe you will come to tolerate her Chinese red nesting tables over time. A good solution is to repaint, reupholster, or refinish various household items so that they fit in better with your new "joint" decor. Over time, find ways to showcase things that are "both of yours," items you have selected together or received as housewarming gifts.

Another approach is to make a list of rooms and divide them up, with full permission to decorate "your rooms" as you see fit. "I have the living room, the study, and the den," says one lesbian who reports that this strategy worked. "She has the dining room, our bedroom, and the guest room. And we let our six-year-old decide on things in her own room."

MOVING INTO YOUR PARTNER'S HOME

Decorating issues are especially tricky when you move into your partner's well-established and cramped apartment. The original occupant needs to make room, physically and emotionally:

- Rearrange closets, dressers, and medicine cabinets so that you both have sufficient space.
- Add some hooks or even new furniture for storing clothes, books, and other possessions.
- Work together on ways to incorporate art and artifacts into a completely "new" home, one in which you both feel comfortable.

Sharing a Bathroom

So many heated arguments between couples start with bathroom issues, whether it's "You spend too much time in there," "It's your turn to clean the toilet," or "You used up all the

"No, that's my styling mousse!"

shampoo!" Maybe it's such a pressure point because space is almost always at a premium in this room. As a gay man living in a cramped New York apartment with his partner of five years explains, "If my partner could have anything, he'd wish for a second bathroom." There's also the matter of this room's personal nature, which makes it extra-important to be considerate of your partner.

Whether you're sharing your first flat together while attending grad school or living in the big house you've always dreamed of, here's the bathroom etiquette you'll need to stay in harmony:

- Make a schedule, or just decide who showers first, if your mornings are a race out of the house.
- Don't leave your damp towels on the floor, and make sure you put your dirty clothes in the hamper.

QUEERY

"Our renovation is tearing us apart."

Q I had the most peaceful relationship in the world until it came time for us to buy a kitchen counter. Seriously, moving in with my partner of eight years turned us into fighters instead of lovers as soon as the renovation started. We always appreciated how different our tastes were. Now it's a big problem, and sometimes I think we should never have decided to live together. Can you help?

A If you're asking me to share your pain about trying to establish a joint household with a bullheaded homosexual with alleged deficiencies in taste and style, the answer is: Yes I can! Been there. Done that. But now let's get practical:

- Have you ever heard the saying "It's not the destination; it's the journey"? Try discussing your differences with an eye to creating a better process for home decorating. Resolving these kinds of conflicts may help you with future ones, too.

- Give in from time to time on a wall color or a piece of furniture that you may not like but don't hate. The idea here is simply to choose your battles; if every decision becomes a tug-of-war, you both may become disillusioned—if not simply exhausted.

- Appreciate the aspects of your partner's taste that you do like, and do so out loud.

- Don't let the material world get in the way of more important things. Sometimes an ugly painting is just an ugly painting.

- Put the toothpaste cap back on.
- Replenish the toilet paper supply *before* you run out (keep stocked up—it disappears a lot more quickly when there are two of you).
- After using the sink, wipe down the basin and clean the drain. Ditto for the shower stall and tub.

If the two of you have trouble keeping the bathroom clean enough to satisfy the more finicky partner, investigate hiring a housekeeping service.

Divvying Up Household Chores

Like all live-in couples, LGBT ones face the day-to-day chores of running a house, which may go smoothly and equitably or lead to disagreements and pent-up resentment. For instance: Who takes out the garbage? Does the laundry? Walks the dog? Makes the bed? What about going to the supermarket? Raking the leaves and so on? Some people gravitate toward certain tasks naturally, but in most cases a little discussion or some sort of system is helpful. Here's one approach that, while it takes a little time to set up, has worked for many couples:

- **Create a list of daily, weekly, and monthly chores:** Sit down together and draw up a comprehensive task list. In addition to laundry, vacuuming, and so on, remember to include lawn mowing and grocery shopping. Then go back and forth between yourselves, choosing what you each prefer to do or what you're good at. If there is a chore you both detest, alternate it each week—or find another solution, such as hiring outside help (if that's an option). Once you've drawn up a division of labor, revisit it to make sure you think the time commitment is roughly equal and that the list feels fair. Then, post it on the fridge where you both can see it.

- **Schedule periodic meetings to review your list and make adjustments:** Don't ask out of the blue, "How come you didn't mow the lawn today?"; your partner may find that mean or petty. Instead, wait for a planned meeting, and then nail him with "How come you didn't mow the lawn this week? It was on your list." Keep yourself open to making changes in the task list; for instance, if there are things you like done a special way—say, the ironing of your shirts—do them yourself.

- **Fair is more important than equal:** Once the two of you settle into a routine of chores, the meetings can be less frequent. There may even come a time when you don't need to rely on the schedule. (However, don't throw it out—put it in a drawer for safekeeping, in case conflict erupts later on.) The goal is not so much to make sure everything is perfectly equal but that it feels fair to both of you. And when it doesn't, it's time to sit down again and revisit your list.

Household Money Issues

One of the most important things to work out when you're living together is how you'll operate financially. People often have such different

attitudes about saving and spending that, despite notions of domestic bliss, managing household finances can become challenging.

"Perhaps it's because my partner, Evan, is fifteen years younger than me, but he never thinks about saving a penny of what he earns," explained Geoff, a gay man with two teenagers from an earlier marriage. "As for me, I'm still paying alimony to my ex-wife and child support, so I often feel like Scrooge in this relationship—even though I earn more." Counters Evan, "We're trying to build a life together, but it irks me that Geoff has so many preset expenses that cut into the way we live, especially our vacations."

When starting a life together under one roof, here are some important first steps for managing your financial life together:

- **Talk about your income:** If you haven't done this before, it's vital to sit down with your partner and share how much you each earn. This will help you understand your overall financial picture and determine day-to-day budgeting.

- **Make a realistic budget:** Add up all the basics—housing, groceries, utilities, and so on—and then add in the extras, such as date night or your Netflix subscription, entertaining, and vacations. See if you can agree to live within certain parameters. Often couples will agree that each can spend a certain amount on household items—$50, $100, or $200, for instance—without prior "partner approval."

- **Put it down on paper:** When you make joint decisions about your finances, write it down and sign it together as a contract between yourselves. Among the items to consider: the kind of bank accounts to maintain (individual, joint, or both); how you will account for household expenses; and even how to apportion your assets if you break up. (For more on prenuptial agreements, see pages 136, 385.)

- **Think about the big picture:** Discuss your financial goals and your general aims in life. Do you want to own your home? Or a second home? Are kids in your future? Does one of you want to start a business? Is retirement fast approaching? Each of these options requires planning and saving—together.

STRAIGHT TALK

"If I'm not sure my new neighbors are a gay couple, may I ask?"

No, that's not a good idea. Feel free to invite them both over for a drink, barbecue, or weekend brunch, but don't just come out and ask them about their sexual orientation. Once you've started to get to know one another, it's fine to ask them some personal questions. And their answer to a query like "Where did you meet?" or "How long have you been together?" will usually do the trick. My guess is that they'll come out to you then—unless they're straight roommates.

THE ESSENTIALS

Leases and Mortgages

LGBT couples living together need to make more of an effort to protect their assets and their homes than straight married couples because the law generally doesn't. Taking additional legal precautions is especially important in case of breakup or death. Since laws vary widely throughout the United States and Canada (and they are constantly changing), consult a local lawyer who is well versed in the legal rights of LGBT people.

FOR RENTERS: Consider putting both your names on the lease agreement, even if that means updating an existing lease.

FOR OWNERS: Decide whether one or both of you will be on the title and how that decision affects each of your financial obligations (notably, the tax implications). While having both partners on a title offers great advantages, keep in mind that it's not always the best alternative. For example, one of you might want to take advantage of a special tax break or an income cap; one of you may have a bad credit history; or you may find that being listed together prevents one of you from being able to buy a second home later.

Finally, talk very specifically about how you will share, or not share, the rights and responsibilities of owning property together and what would happen if your relationship ended. Once you're on the same page, write up an agreement spelling out those terms in detail. Again consult either an LGBT-friendly lawyer or Denis Clifford's *A Legal Guide for Lesbian & Gay Couples*, which provides sample agreements. While this contract may or may not be enforceable—depending on where you live, among other factors—the process of committing your understanding to paper can be invaluable, especially if there's future discord.

CONFLICT AND RESOLUTION

Some arguments between lovers are easily resolved while others are more toxic and entangled. Usually couples who do best together are more practiced at being direct with each other, show respect, and understand the power of compromise; they also tend to rely on the classic rules for fair fighting. For some, it's also important to have necessary advice for initiating a conversation about couples therapy, the ins and outs of breaking up, and divorce LGBT-style.

The Art of Compromise

Whether the topic is "You don't take the trash out when the can is full," "You promised to go to my family this Christmas," or "We agreed not to take that Fire Island house share until the economy got better," compromises are often the best tools in difficult times. While good manners such as respect and consideration won't save a couple in trouble, they can be a big help. Here's how:

- **Try to see things from your partner's point of view:** When confronting an issue, do your best to put your emotions aside and look at the situation as objectively as you can. Almost every situation has at least two points of view—try to see beyond your own.

- **Talk to each other:** Discuss the pros and cons of an issue in person. Talk with your partner not just to trade points of view but also to feel the "heat" behind each other's perspective. (Don't rely on e-mail, texting, or other technologies to communicate like this unless you absolutely have no other choice.) Sometimes there's a common middle ground that will work—rather than seeing his sister and her lover weekly, you visit with them biweekly or monthly. In other situations, compromise might not be possible: You can't be monogamous some of the time.

- **Learn to let go of some things just to make your partner happy:** Every decision needn't make you happy: You can find happiness by making your partner happy.

- **Break old patterns:** Just because you've "always done it that way" or "it never bothered anyone before" doesn't make it right. Change is good, not to mention an integral part of any healthy, evolving relationship.

Being Unfaithful

If you've agreed to be monogamous, what do you do when you get caught with your pants down or your skirt up? Are good manners of any kind helpful in a situation like this? Your best bet is to pull out all the stops, try to learn from what you did—and hope that the fracture can be repaired. Consider these suggestions:

- **Apologize:** Say you're sorry in person (if that's the case). Later write your partner a letter explaining your actions and reiterate that you're sorry. In a highly charged atmosphere like this, a well-crafted letter is more tangible evidence of your effort and commitment.

- **Be as honest as your partner would like you to be:** Some partners may want a full, play-by-play accounting and confession; others already get the big picture and can live without the details. How do you know which he'll prefer? Ask "How much would you like to know?"
- **Bring or send flowers home:** Again, with a note.
- **Do the heavy lifting:** Agree to do the necessary work to regain her trust—whether via couples counseling, a separation, or more talking together.
- **No excuses:** Don't claim that you were drunk or stoned, or that the other person came on to you. Take responsibility for your actions.

- **Be a realist:** Face up to the possibility that the breach in your relationship may be irreparable.

VOX POPULI

What would you do if you found out your partner had been unfaithful to you?

"Kick 'em to the curb."

"Pray."

"Revenge sex."

"Work on the relationship."

"'Fess up, make up, and move on."

QUEERY

"We can't agree where to spend the holidays."

Q **My partner wants to spend time with his family over the holidays, and I want to spend time with our friends. Neither of us is willing to give in. How do we figure this out?**

A For starters, be grateful that you have a loving partner and good friends. I also hope you both appreciate how lucky you are to have extended family that is so welcoming. Ideally, this embarrassment of riches would make things easier when it comes to making holiday plans, but it doesn't sound like that's the case. Since I'm not a therapist, I can't get into your heads, but I can affirm that disputes about the holidays are common among couples judging from my e-mail inbox.

Still, I do have a few suggestions to offer. First of all, who says couples have to be together every holiday? Many LGBT couples spend them apart. A gay couple I know who have been together for ten years now have actually never spent Christmas together; they simply make sure to celebrate the holiday either before or on New Year's.

Others play the game of trading off: Hanukkah or Christmas this year at his family's, and next year with your friends. Or perhaps there's another solution, especially if you can't agree on his way or yours. How about finding something you both want to do? Hawaii? Stay home? Start your own family traditions and invite others to join you?

Finally, plan ahead: It's better to start having this conversation early in the fall, so that you have time to figure things out.

Rules for Fair Fighting

Unfortunately, talking and compromise don't always lead to solutions. Before you know it, you're down the rabbit hole, fuming, venting, and on the verge of a full-fledged, out-of-control screaming match.

While there's nothing wrong with arguing per se (when done properly, it can be very good for your relationship), keep in mind that its purpose is to resolve your dispute, not to be abusive or just spew venom.

Adhering to these guidelines could very well be a big help—both to you and to your partnership:

- **The point is not to win a fight or "beat" your partner:** Ask yourself whether it's more important to be right or happy.
- **Don't fight if one of you is inebriated:** If necessary, leave the room or the apartment and restart your discussion later.
- **Avoid any kind of violence or emotional abuse:** This includes the use of curse words as a form of aggression.
- **Avoid exaggeration:** Don't say, "You never . . ." and "I always . . ." No one is ever 100 percent right or wrong. Give your partner time to speak his or her mind. Don't dominate, and don't allow yourself to be dominated.
- **When you are wrong, admit it:** Even if it means having to change your mind or your position.
- **Focus on one problem at a time:** Try to avoid what therapists call "kitchen-sinking," which means throwing a whole bunch of different issues into one fight.
- **Avoid the nuclear option:** Threatening to break up during a fight keeps you from focusing on the issue at hand.

- **If you need a time-out or a break, call one:** Use this period to cool off and get some perspective, think about what your partner has said, why you might be having a strong reaction, and how you can come to terms. When you're ready to resume talking, let your partner know.

THE ESSENTIALS

Domestic Violence and Abuse

Recent studies have shown that 30 percent of LGBT couples experience domestic violence. However, partly because of stereotypes about its being only a straight issue, domestic violence and abuse can be difficult for LGBT people to recognize or acknowledge. A common misconception is that same-sex violence or abuse is "just fighting" or even sex play.

Like other victims of physical or emotional abuse at the hands of their partners, gay men and lesbians often fail to see what's going on, because of low self-esteem, denial, or because the abuse itself blinds them to it. Nevertheless, there are often common aspects of how LGBT people experience this kind of abuse. According to the New York City Mayor's Office to Combat Domestic Violence, same-sex-abusing partners often do one or more of the following:

- Threaten to out their lover to family members, friends, even fellow church members or coworkers.
- Threaten to infect the abused partner with HIV/AIDS.
- Deny the abuse by arguing that it cannot be so because it is a same-sex relationship.
- Make the abused partner feel ashamed about his or her sexual orientation or gender identity.

If you think you're at risk, pay attention to any controlling or isolating behavior, name-calling and other insults, out-of-control anger, jealousy, or threats of any nature. If your partner is physically or verbally abusive toward you, do your best to disengage, get out of the house, or talk to someone at a local hotline or the National Domestic Violence Hotline (www.ndvh.org or 1-800-799-7233).

If you have a friend who you think is in an abusive situation, try to balance her right to privacy with your willingness to help. If you jump in by saying, "I think your girlfriend is hurting you," there's a good chance you could be met with stonewalling and denial. Instead, ask questions like "How are things at home with the two of you?" or "Is there anything on your mind that you'd like to talk about?" Or just let your friend know that you're there should she need you. No doubt, you'd hope for the same.

Making Up

If there's any benefit to fighting, it's making up, which has the capacity to deepen your appreciation and understanding of each other—plus, you may have great makeup sex. Explained one bi grad student: "After we had worked our way through several difficult moments, then I knew we had the emotional capacity to make our relationship work."

To properly let bygones be bygones, try these ideas:

- **Again, apologize:** Someone needs to start by apologizing and the best way to do that is with the two words "I'm sorry." If you take that first step, more often than not (since there's usually enough blame to go around), you'll hear the same words come right back at you.

- **Make a gesture:** Buy some flowers, write a sweet note, or make a date to do something special. Let your partner know how much you care and why it's important that you're together. Say something soothing but genuine.

- **Take responsibility:** How did you contribute to the disagreement? Do your best to learn from any mistakes and tell your partner that's what you're doing.

- **Revisit your rules for fair fighting:** If necessary, take the time after you've made up to set new guidelines for the future. At this point, you may even want to write down your rules for fair fighting and keep them on hand—for the next one.

Couples Therapy

Couples therapy is often called for when talking to each other on your own feels unsafe, unproductive, or simply too stressful. It also helps when your styles of communication are so different that you don't know how to discuss difficult subjects—for example, one of you yells and the other cries; or one says hurtful things, and the other runs out of the room.

Good, professional therapists—a term that includes social workers, counselors, psychologists, and psychiatrists, among others—are by definition unbiased. They also have the training to ask questions that may not have occurred to either of you. "We see therapy as an exercise program where we get homework," says one gay Midwesterner who has been with his boyfriend for almost twenty years. "So we go and learn some stuff and then it is time to practice and see how we can apply what we learned."

If you decide to suggest such a course to your partner, be clear that the idea is to improve your relationship, not to mount an assault and blame her for all your troubles. For instance, you could say, "I've been thinking I'd like us to see whether a therapist can help us with our arguing. What do you think?" Don't be discouraged if your campaign meets resistance—some people who haven't been through therapy think it's only for those with serious mental health problems. If that's the case, lie low and then raise the topic again in a couple of weeks or months. (Nevertheless, press your case if you think getting outside help is truly urgent.)

In the end, it's best if the two of you are in agreement, both about the decision to do it and the choice of therapist.

CHOOSING A THERAPIST

When deciding on a professional counselor, you're probably better off with one who is either LGBT or LGBT-friendly and who has couples experience. (There are plenty of straight counselors who work well with LGBT couples, too.) In most major cities you can find LGBT professional organizations that provide referrals. Or ask your friends. Or go online and do a search.

BREAKING UP

There's no question that breaking up is generally a difficult and painful process to get through: Your heart may be hurting; you may need to uproot a household and move; or there may be children to worry about, too.

Perhaps you still love each other but don't think you can stay together anymore. As you work through ending a relationship, do your best to be considerate of and kind to each other. This is no time to push anything under the rug between yourselves—but do hold back when it comes to being outright mean or sharing too many details with curious friends.

Telling Your Partner You Want to Separate

Ideally, breakups evolve gradually as part of a couple's ongoing discussions about problems between them. However, the truth is that this process is usually more one-sided and less predictable than that. Perhaps you've reached the end of your willingness to work on things, or you may have come to a flash point and decided it's time to end the relationship. Even so, try not to do it on the spur of the moment; this is too important a decision to make in haste.

If you're the one initiating the breakup, make sure that you're sure. Weigh and reweigh the pros and cons. Talk to someone else about your feelings if you need to—therapists can be more objective than friends, but you may benefit from both.

Once you've made the decision, devise a plan that not only includes the words you want to use to tell your partner but covers any contingencies that you can deal with before breaking the news. For instance, if you're living in his home, where will you go? If you have a joint checking/savings account, what if he closes it? Some individuals even consult a lawyer who understands LGBT law before taking the first steps.

You need to be the one delivering the news, by the way. A lesbian in Ohio recently found out from her best friend that her lover was planning to move out that very day. She said, "I guess she couldn't tell me to my face, so she called Annie instead, who called me the moment she got off the phone. Talk about a double world of hurt."

When it comes time to talk to your partner, consider this approach:

- **Make your breakup a face-to-face conversation:** If you are in the habit of avoiding confrontations, this is not the time to give in to that predilection. You owe the truth to your partner.
- **Choose a comfortable and private location:** Your home may be the ideal locale, or you might suggest going for a walk together. Think ahead about what will be comfortable if things get emotional and how to safeguard your privacy, considering your partner's needs in particular.
- **Be deliberate about starting the conversation:** Lead into the news by using a statement like "There's something important that we need to talk about" or "I've had something on my mind for a while now, and I need to discuss it with you." Clearly and as calmly as you can, explain the reasons you want to end the relationship; if you're still on the fence or want to "negotiate," explain that, too.
- **Be fair:** Don't blame your partner for everything. By the same token, it's best not to assume all blame yourself, in order to make things go more smoothly or to avoid weightier issues.
- **Listen to what your partner has to say:** Even if you're sure you won't change your mind, it's respectful to listen to your partner. It's also

in your interest to be open to learning from what he has to say.
- **If you share a home, a car, a pet, or anything else, you both have an obligation to deal with these issues:** You don't need to get into all of that in this breakup conversation. There will be other opportunities to discuss the details of what's next.
- **Give your partner some time to process the news:** Your instinct may be to cut things short and leave. Sometimes that's exactly the right thing to do. But as much as you can (and as circumstances dictate), be kind and gentle; after all, this is someone you once loved.

Finding Out Your Partner Wants to Separate

If you're on the short end of the stick, you'll probably experience a wide range of emotions, from anger and shock to hurt. Confide in a friend or two, but try not to go on a public rampage. After she was dumped, one lesbian learned why telling the world isn't a good idea: "I wrote an e-mail to everyone we knew telling them all the horrible things Sandra had done to me. While I was expecting sympathy, my friends were appalled at what I had done. Lesson learned. Keep rage private."

If you find yourself in this unfortunate situation, here are some things you can do to help you make sense of your situation and carry on as best you can:
- Ask for an explanation.
- Enlist support from friends and family.
- Stay busy.
- Understand your rights (about your home, your kids, or any other joint possessions or

accounts), if need be by talking with a lawyer who understands LGBT family law in your state or province.

- Fantasize about revenge if you want, but don't go there.
- Make the necessary plans to move on (when the time comes).

THE ESSENTIALS

Divorce LGBT-style

As more and more same-sex couples legally marry, some inevitably face the prospect of divorce. It doesn't help that in the United States same-sex divorce is proving to be almost as complicated a legal matter as gay marriage (Canadians have it easier). In theory, all states are supposed to recognize marriages performed in other states, but the federal Defense of Marriage Act, which prohibits the recognition of same-sex marriages, provides the legal underpinning for most states not to do so.

Similarly, those states that haven't recognized gay marriages will not hear same-sex divorce cases, even from LGBT residents legally married elsewhere. For instance, a gay couple married in Massachusetts would likely find it impossible to obtain a divorce in most states.

Adding insult to injury, Massachusetts will grant divorces only to current residents, creating a legal conundrum for gay couples who have moved out of state since their weddings. One gay professional, now legally married, put it succinctly: "Be careful what you ask for. When you break up, you may have a nasty fight in a court with no rules." (For issues surrounding divorce and child custody, see page 245.)

Telling Others About Your Breakup

Breakups are best announced one-on-one to your closest friends and family members, no matter how painful and despite one's natural preference to rush through the process. Regardless of whether you were the one breaking up or the one broken up with, use discretion and tell people on a need-to-know basis. Do your best not to belittle or degrade your ex to others in any way.

If you have children together, go out of your way to make sure that they hear the news directly from you—if possible, the two of you should speak to them together. Explain what's going on and what your plans are. Stress that you both love them and reassure them that they're not at fault for the separation. (Repeat these points frequently.) Answer any questions your children have, right then or later, the best you can.

From there, move on to other family members and/or your closest friends. Usually, each partner will speak privately to her own family and to the friends that she is closer to. There's no need to go into all of the gory details. Instead, say something like "Charlotte and I are separated. I'll be staying at the apartment and she'll be living at. . . ."

For friends or family members who don't live close by, send a personal e-mail, write a note, or call them on the phone. It really all depends on how you usually communicate and how close you are.

By the way, it's considered bad form to send out "divorce" cards. And it's especially ill-mannered to tell the world *first* on a social media site by changing your relationship

126

"May I e-mail everyone about our separation?"

Q Jane and I were together for more than ten years. After lots of couples counseling and a trial separation, we've decided to call it quits. How do we tell our friends, some of whom know of our difficulties and some who, blissfully, don't? Is a mass e-mail okay for this?

A No, e-mail is not a good medium for this—it's too impersonal and too likely to be reforwarded. Also, as much as you may think you're sending an entirely unemotional announcement, sometimes hurt feelings or resentments creep into these things.

Although e-mail is efficient and egalitarian and would save you the heartbreak of having to tell and retell your story of woe, once you've told those closest to you, word will get around soon enough on its own.

Later on in this process, when you've both really begun to move on, go ahead and send a mass e-mail letting friends know of a new address, e-mail, or phone number—along with anything personal, such as perhaps that things are now going well for you.

status from "in a relationship" or "married" to "single." After you've told those closest to you, then go ahead and change your status if you'd like. However, do let your ex know this ahead of time, since there will likely be lots of questions from distant friends just finding out.

What Not to Say When Told of a Friend's Separation

Even when the breakup of a friend or family member isn't surprising, it's common enough for any of us in the moment—whether LGBT or not—to say the wrong thing and cross the line of propriety or raise unnecessarily difficult questions. Here are some things to avoid asking or saying:

• Was he cheating on you?
• Were you having an affair?
• We never liked him.
• Things happen for a reason.

• Will you have to move now?
• Are you okay financially?

Instead, thank your friend for sharing this news with you, give him a hug, and ask if there's anything you can do to help through the next several weeks or months—being specific. For instance, you might invite him to dinner or an outing with other mutual friends. Then, over the coming weeks and months, don't forget him—keep being a good friend.

PART III

TYING THE KNOT

CHAPTER 6

Weddings &
Commitment
Ceremonies

Marriage LGBT-style

I f you and your partner have decided to make a formal commitment, let me be among the first to say "Congratulations!" Whether you're planning a legally sanctioned ceremony or a private commitment celebration, you'll likely find that your first thoughts (after the romantic bits are taken care of!) center on logistics—in other words, etiquette. And that's the moment when you'll realize that you're entering unmapped territory, since many of the "rules" for same-sex weddings have yet to be figured out: Do gay men and lesbians get engaged in the formal, traditional sense? Are the roles and responsibilities of the wedding party different when you have two brides or two grooms?

What kind of engagement or wedding showers are appropriate? Do you invite unsupportive or hostile family members? What's the right way to word a same-sex wedding invitation? And finally, who pays for what?

There are plenty of LGBT couples who find that old-school wedding traditions serve them remarkably well in the ceremonies and celebrations they devise: formal invitations, engagement parties, gift registries, and frothy white dresses alongside well-tailored black tuxedos. The only major difference in those affairs may be the matter of having two brides or two grooms. For many of us, there's also a very strong spirit of invention in play as we create new roles and rites, not only for ourselves, but for everyone in attendance. The good news is that it's up to you and your sweetheart—or fiancé(e), if you prefer—to make these choices, which will no doubt become the foundation of LGBT wedding etiquette to come.

Still, there are signs by now of some basic differences. Most notably, parents and other blood family members of the brides and grooms may find that they play a lesser part than they might expect. Often, gay couples marry or partner later in life (usually after having lived together for many years), which means that they may be paying for the ceremony and the reception themselves (which certainly lessens Mom and Dad's involvement), or that they have lifelong friends to whom they would like to assign the roles traditionally played by family members in the wedding party. And then there's the reality that some parents or siblings may be uncomfortable with the very notion of gay unions; for them, a less public role may be just what they're hoping for.

The one part of your wedding that you have no control over is whether your union will be officially recognized. Regardless of individual state laws, federal recognition of same-sex marriages—which would entitle lesbian and gay couples to more than 1,100 of the most useful protections and benefits that straight married couples enjoy—is still prohibited by the 1996 Defense of Marriage Act—although President Obama recently said his administration would cease defending it. (This is not the case in Canada, where same-sex marriage has been legal for many years.) Even so, in recent years more and more LGBT couples in the United States have become legally wed, signed up for same-sex domestic partnerships or civil unions, or had a commitment ceremony.

Every time two brides or two grooms make the decision to publicly announce their relationship and affirm its strength, they're taking yet another step forward in coming out—and helping to change stereotypes of LGBT people and our families. Call your nuptials whatever you both like, regardless of their legal standing. Yours may be a "commitment ceremony," "wedding," "civil union," "love fest," or some other wording of your own design. In that spirit, when the words "wedding" and "marriage" are used in this chapter, they refer to any kind of LGBT union, regardless of its legal status. This is not to suggest that anything but full marriage equality is essential; nevertheless, the focus here is on the joys of affirming your commitment to each other publicly—and before an audience of friends, family, and other loved ones—and on the many manners situations that arise during this important and celebrated ritual.

MAKING IT LEGAL

The excitement of making a formal commitment to each other will carry you quickly enough into the tasks ahead, but first things first. Before mocking up your guest list and getting distracted by reception menu options, look at what tying the knot will mean legally. Because same-sex marriage is legal throughout Canada, it's just U.S. couples who are vulnerable to geographic marriage nuances. This section provides the basic information you need to understand about your partnership options and many other kinds of legal 411, from prenup agreements and changing your names to creating durable powers of attorney to protect your health and wealth. These legal agreements may seem businesslike and unromantic, but they are intended to cement and support your partnership—and are recommended for couples on both sides of the border. In fact, these agreements may well turn out to be the best wedding gift you could give or receive.

Your Partnership Options

LGBT couples in the United States rarely get to actually choose from the following list of legal options; you usually just take what you get, depending on whether your state allows same-sex marriage, your city affirms domestic partnerships, or your job extends benefits to same-sex partners. Before stepping into any of these arrangements, it's smart to understand the legal underpinnings of each and to discuss them with your intended so that you're both clear about what's to come. (For an up-to-date list of which states confer which partnership status, please see www.gaymanners.com.)

MARRIAGE

The word "marriage" has kicked up almost as much dust in recent years as the rights associated with it, with opponents of same-sex marriage arguing that gay people should have neither, and many LGBT people insisting nothing short of full marriage will do because of the benefits it confers—child custody and visitation; important tax advantages (especially regarding home ownership); the right of inheritance; and access to spousal benefits (such as Social Security, Veterans Administration, and health insurance, as well as family/medical/bereavement leave and more). By the way, even in states where same-sex marriage isn't legal (forty-four at the time this book went to press), many lesbian and gay couples embrace the "M" word anyway, in order to show how serious they are about the commitment they're making.

CIVIL UNIONS

Civil unions, now legal in several states, provide gay and lesbian couples with some of the rights that marriage confers, especially regarding state taxes, estate planning, and medical decisions. Note, however, that civil unions are not usually recognized if you travel to another state. And like same-sex marriages conferred by states, civil unions offer none of the aforementioned thousand-plus federal benefits. While opponents to civil unions see them as a back-door method of legalizing same-sex marriage, many

Why is same-sex marriage important?

"The institution of marriage can bestow instant credibility to gay families."

"If relationships must be recognized at the government level, then all relationships should be civil unions. Leave marriage to the churches."

"It's all about the money. Gay people pay the same taxes as straight people but are denied the same benefits."

anti-marriage groups have begun to embrace the concept in the hope of warding off rising pressure to push for full marriage equality.

DOMESTIC PARTNERSHIPS

Since the 1990s, many localities and a handful of states have allowed unmarried partners to sign domestic partner (DP) agreements in order to formally acknowledge cohabitation and commitment as a couple. At this time, California, Connecticut, New Jersey, Hawaii, and the District of Columbia have enacted DP laws. Many companies also now provide those benefits, including a majority of Fortune 500 companies. Check with your HR department on what documentation it needs to set this in motion; certain companies require employees to sign domestic partner agreements and/or live together before a same-sex partner can be eligible for health insurance and other benefits.

COMMITMENT CEREMONIES

These are marriagelike ceremonies that are a way for a couple to make a public declaration of their partnership and love for each other. Although recognized by some houses of worship, these ceremonies are not legally binding and confer no state or federal benefits. Commitment ceremonies go by many other names as well, including "unions," "affirmation ceremonies," "life partnership ceremonies," "blessings of love," or even, simply, "weddings."

STRAIGHT TALK

"I'm not sure if my gay son is having a civil union ceremony or a domestic partner one. Is there a difference?"

First of all, congratulations to you, as well as your son and his partner-to-be. Both ceremonies you mention signify a deep and loving commitment. If you're not clear what sort of commitment your son is making, I suggest asking him directly. As you may know, gay couples who partner usually avail themselves of whatever kind of union is legally possible. In Massachusetts, for instance, same-sex couples can marry, while in New Jersey, the law provides for civil unions, and there are comprehensive domestic partnership laws in other states that provide many of the same *state* rights as marriage (but none of the federal ones).

Any differences between such ceremonies are more about an LGBT couple's own tastes than they are about the law, except for the binding words spoken by the officiant. If it's a legal wedding, she'll say something to the effect of, "Who supports this couple in marriage?" and, at the conclusion of the service, "I now pronounce you married" or "I now pronounce you husband and husband."

WEDDINGS & COMMITMENT CEREMONIES

Other Couple's Agreements

Even if you decide not to take one of the formal steps described above, it's wise for LGBT couples in committed relationships to consult with an attorney versed in LGBT family law, in order to make sure you're doing everything possible to protect your interests as a couple. For instance, LGBT couples in both the United States and Canada are often advised to grant each other a durable power of attorney and a medical power of attorney; in addition, each partner should create and file a last will and testament. These documents can be vital in case one partner becomes ill or dies. Some states also recognize the value of other types of agreements that unmarried couples can execute, especially those involving property and finances, like a durable power of attorney for finances. (For more on such documents, see page 360.)

Changing Your Names

Same-sex couples enjoy a range of options these days when considering whether to change, combine, or invent names after a marriage or commitment ceremony, although the predominant custom to date is for each spouse to keep his or her name. In fact, all LGBT couples can make name changes, regardless of the type of religious or civil ceremony and regardless of the relationship's legal status. A lesbian with two young girls, who took her partner's name after marrying in Canada, explained, "It was really important to our identity as a family to all have the same last name." You needn't do it that way, but for many LGBT people, our family names have a symbolic component. Consider for a moment the way your parents might have been referred to as "the Steins" or "the Garcia-Lopezes." Using the same surname affirms a connection between all the individuals in that family. For example, a recent newspaper wedding announcement of two lesbians noted prominently, "The couple is using the surname Epstein."

Here are the four basic options:

1. **Keep your surnames:** By far the most popular choice for LGBT couples, this is also the easiest. Frank Roberts and Mack Stasio simply stay Frank Roberts and Mack Stasio. Not surprisingly, this is what most same-sex couples choose to do. The downside is that you don't have the instant family identity that sharing a surname confers.

2. **Use both your names:** A dual last name proclaims publicly that you have merged into a family unit. Giselle Ullman and Jeanne Basile become Giselle and Jeanne Ullman-Basile (or Basile-Ullman). By the way, there's no rule as to whose name goes first; most couples make the decision based on how the new name sounds to them. If one or both of you has a long or hyphenated name to start with, consider shortening them as you combine the names.

3. **Take your partner's name:** Some gay couples opt to choose between their family names. For instance, Ariel Sexton and Alicia Gomez might become Ariel and Alicia Gomez. This is an especially good option when kids are involved. "It was easier once she started school," reports one lesbian mom who picked up her partner's surname when they adopted their first daughter.

4. Choosing a brand-new name: Creating a new last name by combining family names is a viable option and not that uncommon. It generally involves more legal work for the couple—and a little extra effort from friends and family to remember. One couple who created a new name explained that their new moniker reflected "a commitment to equality and a nod to family history—with a dash of creativity."

LGBT advocates recommend that you get a court order to change your name. The court order will serve as proof of your new name—for filing your taxes, travel overseas, driver's licenses, and more. Generally, this is an easy and straightforward process for gay men and lesbians.

If Your Partner Is Not a U.S. Resident

Perhaps you've fallen in love with a gay man or lesbian while on an overseas vacation or you've met an LGBT noncitizen here at home. If the relationship progresses and you're thinking about making a life together, your partner's not being a citizen or resident alien is going to make things more complicated in the United States. (In Canada, same-sex partnerships between citizens and noncitizens are treated exactly the same as straight ones.)

Currently, a foreign-born partner can come to the United States without a visa if she is from a particular handful of countries, mostly Western European ones. Alternatively, she can apply for a tourist visa, which if granted can be used for multiple visits, up to six months each.

Straight people, of course, don't have this problem: If a foreign national marries a U.S. citizen, she is on a fast track to get a green card that entitles her to permanent residency in the country with her new husband. As a result, some foreign-born LGBT people seek out a U.S. citizen of the opposite sex to marry in what's called a "green-card marriage"—which the federal government regards as a fraudulent marriage. The partner is either a close friend or an individual whom you hire, usually for a fairly substantial fee. LGBT legal advocates caution that green-card marriages are illegal; there may be hefty fines and jail terms for anyone involved in the scheme, not to mention the likely deportation of the foreign-born partner.

Prenuptial Contracts

Prenuptial agreements are a good idea if one or both of you have significant assets (like a family-owned business or property) or if you mix assets or share expenses. By signing your names to a formal agreement instead of just making verbal promises or requests, you can be very specific about how income, property, and other assets would be divided should you break up. These agreements can also cover such topics as who will pay household bills, how credit cards are used, and whether one of you would support the other's education.

One gay man with a wealthy lover explained the value of their prenup. "At first I was appalled that he would ask me for this. But the more we talked, the more we both understood our financial fears," he said. "Now,

QUEERY

"I keep putting off asking for a prenup."

Q My lawyer is insisting that we sign a gay prenup because I make more money and have a bigger bank account than my husband-to-be. I keep trying to find the right time to do this, but now our wedding ceremony is only weeks away. Can't I just give him the agreement and say "Sign here!"?

A Alas, you can't just do that, and it's a good thing. Raising the topic of having a prenuptial agreement makes many of us uncomfortable because it means bringing up the dreaded topic of *money*. But without this discussion, you may be in for some rude surprises later on about who is responsible for which costs, and, if the relationship ends, how each of you will be protected. It's also an excellent opportunity to have a most necessary talk about your financial life together.

Waiting until the weeks before your ceremony, I'm afraid, may not have been the wisest approach. I'd suggest that you find a time, as soon as possible, when the two of you are alone and not busy, and raise the topic. Begin by saying something like "I've been thinking about our financial future together, and I think it's a good idea to talk about the benefits of a prenup." Give your lover some time to digest this news—understandably, it may come as something of a surprise—and then do some explaining. Sure, it's partly a selfish move because you'll be protecting your superior assets, but you may also be agreeing to pay more rent or bear the cost of joint vacations.

if we break up after five years, I get a pretty good payout. I wouldn't have had that before the agreement."

By the way, if you and your partner agree on the need for a prenup, it's recommended each of you hire your own lawyer rather than share a lawyer. In fact, this is sometimes required by law, but even if not, it's simply a better method to protect each of your interests.

Because this can be such a delicate matter, there's an etiquette to asking your partner for such an agreement:

- Don't pull out a prewritten agreement the first time you bring the subject up; that can be intimidating. But also don't wait until the last minute before your wedding day, which only adds an unnecessary sense of drama and urgency.
- Fully disclose all your assets. Not only is this good manners, it's the law.
- Explain that this kind of agreement is not about a lack of trust, but a business agreement about being able to put financial issues behind you.
- Don't coerce your partner. If you hit some thorny or emotional issues, consider talking with a mediator.
- Be reasonable and be prepared to make concessions.

"Even though my lesbian daughter can't marry her girlfriend, because it's not legal in our state, should I treat the girlfriend as I do my other sons- and daughters-in-law?"

It all depends on your daughter's relationship with her girlfriend. If she is a casual girlfriend, then no, she doesn't have the same status as a son- or daughter-in-law. But if they are in a committed partnership—regardless of its legal basis—then yes, do the right thing, even if state law doesn't permit them to.

YOUR ENGAGEMENT

LGBT couples get engaged all the time. Some of us even get right down on bended knee, present a diamond ring, and ask, "Will you marry me?" (That is, once we've figured out how to pop the question and fumbled our way into a jewelry store to pick up a suitable ring.) Getting engaged is both romantic and nerve-wracking (will she say yes?).

After that, it's time to reach out with the good news about your impending LGBT union, first to your circle of close friends and family— and then beyond. If proposing, you'll also want to know how to find a gay-friendly jeweler, who pays for the rings in a same-sex couple, which finger is "proper" to wear yours on, and the skinny on engagement and prewedding parties and festivities.

All About the Proposal

Who asks in an LGBT relationship? Here's the good news: Either of you can. And here's the bad news: Either of you can.

All of which means that LGBT proposals can sneak up on you. For instance, Ellen DeGeneres asked Portia de Rossi (now Portia DeGeneres) for her hand while they were taking care of some goldfish that had been rescued earlier in the day from a TV shoot. De Rossi told *People* magazine that she joked, "This is a pretty romantic moment, right?" DeGeneres responded, "Every moment with you is romantic," and then proposed with a marquis-cut diamond.

Another lesbian got engaged under similar circumstances. "I guess my partner had been struggling with the 'perfect' proposal, and then ended up blurting it out while we were watching *Jeopardy!* on a Monday night," she said, recalling her surprise.

More often than not, however, there is no actual question "popped." Many LGBT couples contemplating marriage have been together for a long time and are likely to have discussed a commitment ceremony or wedding well in advance of settling on it. "Once marriage became an option for us," says one gay man, who by then had been with his partner for twenty years, "we started chatting about it—very much like we did about taking out a second mortgage."

How to Ask

Even if you've talked about making a commitment before, be sure to test the waters before you actually ask the question. If you know your partner has doubts, a surprise proposal is not the way to go. Whether you're relying on tradition, reinventing the wheel, or finding some middle ground that suits you both, keep these four considerations in mind when asking your LGBT sweetheart to marry you:

1. **Make it personal and unique:** Tradition is great for some people, but perhaps for you it's a beachside or circus-side proposal or simply at breakfast one morning after you've poured the coffee and sat down to eat. Or you may choose to ask where you had your first date or in the middle of a European vacation.

2. **Make it about your loved one (not about you):** Give some thought to your partner's tastes and put your own aside for the moment. How would she like to be proposed to? How can you make his dream come true?

3. **Make it genuine:** Speak simply and say what you mean. No clichés. Why do you want to marry him? What do you love about her? If

spontaneity isn't your thing, write it down and then read it aloud or just pass it along and ask your sweetheart to read it. Or find a moving poem and share that with her. If you're still nervous, practice ahead of time.

4. **Keep it private:** Find a location where you can be alone together—not surrounded by friends, family, or strangers. You'll have plenty of time to broadcast your good news afterward. (Although, if you're feeling pretty certain about the answer, there's no reason not to have the scoreboard flash your proposal during the seventh-inning stretch—or fly a plane over your beach outpost with a banner that says WILL YOU MARRY ME, ERIC? LOVE, SAM.)

If You're Not Certain

Your boyfriend would probably prefer if you said yes to his commitment proposal. But what if you don't feel so sure about the idea of getting hitched? You may have grown up thinking

QUEERY

"Will you be my domestic partner?"

Q **Asking someone to become my domestic partner doesn't sound nearly as romantic to me as "Will you marry me?" Any thoughts on how to sex up this kind of proposal?**

A You're right, that phrase would not really make me swoon. But just because the government is denying you and your darling the freedom to marry, that's no reason to deny yourselves the pleasure of a proper proposal. Make it special and memorable, whether that means a candlelit dinner at your favorite restaurant or a weekend away at a bucolic

B&B. Put a little time and effort into your proposal plans. Even if you can't legally marry in your state, you can present a ring, and you can even say "I wish we could marry. But since we can't, I hope we can be together forever. Will you have me?" Remember, the government controls the laws, but not our hearts or how we express ourselves.

QUEERY

"Do gay guys propose with engagement rings?"

Q I'm ready to propose to my boyfriend (and I'm pretty darn sure he's ready to say yes), but I can't figure out if I should do it with an engagement ring. What do LGBT people do about rings now?

A What with all the creativity and invention going on in the LGBT community around different ways of symbolizing commitment, it would be impossible to say there is a right way to get engaged. Some gay couples exchange engagement rings and then, during the ceremony, wedding bands. Others wear none at all.

Sometimes only one partner wears the rings in the family. An easy and economical solution—if you both like the idea of wearing just one ring each—is to purchase rings for your engagement and then use those same rings again during your wedding ceremony. Now it's time to go shopping!

that marriage was only for straight people. Or you don't feel ready to make a lifetime commitment. Alternatively, your life could be just too up in the air right now to make big plans— say, one of you doesn't have job security or is planning to move or start school.

Be honest and explain in detail—and in person—the reasons you're saying no. Do your best to explain your hesitations. If you're not sure, or need more time as a couple, that's a sign of encouragement to your sweetheart. However, if you mean to close the door on marriage or commitment altogether, you'll be doing both of you a favor by saying so as soon as possible.

The Skinny on Rings

You certainly don't need a ring to show commitment. Although more and more gay couples are choosing to wear them as symbols of their union, maybe you prefer to buy a new bed together instead—or a puppy. If you do

decide to go for an engagement ring or wedding ring, make sure they feel comfortable, you can afford them, and that you love them.

Start your hunt for an engagement ring at a reputable jeweler. Find one who is recommended by friends or family members, has been in business for a long time, or is a member of the National Gay and Lesbian Chamber of Commerce or your local Better Business Bureau. Before committing to a piece of jewelry, understand the store's policies, including the way they handle layaways, returns, or issues such as "conflict diamonds" (those mined in specific African nations and used to fund civil wars and other atrocities against the local population). Also, be sure to discuss whether you want to purchase your rings together or separately (and surprise each other).

Browsing a store's selections (whether in person or on the Internet), you're likely to find bands designed in platinum, yellow gold, and white gold. You can also find rings that intertwine each of these metals, as well as those in rose gold, green gold, black gold, and more. You'll also need to select a finish, such as polished or matte, as well as decide on the width of the ring. Traditionalists tend to prefer rounded, brightly polished yellow gold bands, which can come in 14, 18, or 24 karat. (The higher the karat number, the more golden your ring will appear and the more expensive it will be.) More contemporary rings have a flatter surface and squared-off edges, with platinum and white gold the metals of choice.

Consider engraving some special message inside, such as first names or initials, your wedding date, or a tiny sentiment, something like "I love you" or "Always yours." (Once you've engraved a ring, however, it can't be returned, so you may want to wait until your proposal has been accepted before personalizing it.) One gay man chose the infinity symbol as his inscription on his partner's ring—a message meant to symbolize the never-ending nature of their relationship.

Adding diamonds or other precious stones will add significantly to the cost of your rings. If you can't afford these gems at the start of your relationship, consider upgrading your rings on a later anniversary.

Who Pays for the Rings

If there's one prevailing custom today, it's that most lesbian and gay couples shop together for their rings, and pay for them together; this scenario usually comes out of a conversation where one of you suggests, "Hey, let's get married" or "Want to make a commitment?" This approach makes for a romantic shopping expedition and the chance to go a little extra fancy. "We went to Tiffany because I always wanted something from there," reports a lesbian who split the bill with her fiancée. On the other hand, if it seems more loving, you could each pay for the other's.

However, if you're planning to surprise your LGBT sweetheart with an engagement ring, then it's on you.

QUEERY

"Ring finger predicament"

Q Should I wear my wedding ring on my left hand or right?

A This is another decision that's handled in widely different ways these days. True enough, the ring finger of the left hand is still the most traditional option, yet some LGBT people who don't want to mime straight marriage will wear it on their right hand or on a different finger on their left hand. The bottom line is that as long as your lover slips that ring on one finger or another, you're good. Wear it on whichever hand you like, and make sure it's comfortable. Its meaning remains the same: You're partnered.

Announcing Your Engagement

When you're ready to tell others about your pending nuptials, start with those whom you're closest to and who have been supportive of your relationship—whether your family or your friends. (One exception: If you have kids, share your decision with them first.)

How you relay the announcement is up to you, but calling or sending a personal—not mass—e-mail to those dearest to you is a great start. (If you're the recipient of such a call, suggest celebrating over a coffee or a cocktail in the near future.) A man who married his partner in California in 2008, when gay marriage was briefly legal there, recalls that it was the couple's LGBT friends whom they contacted first. "We felt part of an important moment in history that we wanted to share," he says.

Once your closest cadre is informed, go ahead and post, share, tweet, etc. One groom-to-be shared his happiness on Facebook this way: "Benjamin: is incredibly blessed to know his heart has finally found its home. I am now truly engaged, in every sense of that wonderful word."

Unfortunately, you may find that not all share your happiness—either because of their opposition to same-sex marriage or because they may not "approve" of your partner. If you encounter such a reaction, take it in stride and don't let it taint your joy. Sometimes, though, you may find yourselves happily surprised: Here's how one man explained how he and his partner remember the conversation with his parents: "I explained that after living together for three years we were now ready to make our commitment permanent and have a civil union ceremony. My dad was pretty quiet, but

QUEERY

"I need an LGBT-friendly jeweler."

Q **After my partner and I decided to make a commitment, we went to a local jewelry store to buy rings. The sales associate couldn't have been nicer until she realized we were a gay male couple. Then she got a bit icy. We did wind up buying our rings from her, but wonder if you have pointers for how to find more LGBT-friendly jewelers in the first place.**

A A similar thing happened to my partner and me when we went to buy rings. Our sales clerk didn't actually get cold (okay, maybe a little frosty), but she did leave the floor for a few minutes to recalibrate herself after she figured out the situation. Then when we were finished with the transaction, she explained that we had been her first same-sex couple. This may well have been what happened in your case, too. What you may have understood as homophobia could just have been shock or surprise.

In any case, to avoid this kind of uncertainty, ask friends to recommend a gay-friendly jeweler, consult one of the many LGBT-friendly wedding sites, or call a shop in advance and ask if they can provide advice for a same-sex couple seeking wedding bands. You'll be able to tell a lot by the way they answer your questions.

No matter what, expect to be treated professionally and, most important, with respect. If not, take your business elsewhere. And, if you think you are the victim of discrimination, talk to the manager, or call back later and make a complaint to the owner.

Mom asked a lot of questions. Her final one was 'What role do your father and I have?' I couldn't have been more surprised—or thrilled."

"Our son recently told us that he and his partner plan to get married next summer. We're very happy for them. As both our straight sons are married, we know the drill about what parents-in-law do in that situation. But we're not so sure here. Do we call our in-laws and set up a meeting? Do our sons do this? Also, we hear that our counterparts are not as thrilled as we are about this news. Where do we start?"

Gay wedding manners haven't evolved to this level of detail yet. As you know from your past experiences, traditional etiquette suggests that the families get to know each other or at least extend a welcome gesture as an expression of support for the impending union. Usually, it's been the bride's family that kicks things off, although that doesn't apply here either, of course.

I suggest you chat with your "sons" (it's great you're referring to your son's partner this way!) and get their thinking on this matter, especially since it sounds like the partner's family may have issues about the impending marriage. If given the okay, then go ahead and call, write, or e-mail your in-laws-to-be. If they live nearby, invite them over. Otherwise, just use the opportunity to open the door and say how happy you are about the news. If there's any resistance on their end, let's hope your enthusiasm rubs off.

Engagement and Prewedding Parties

In the weeks and months before your wedding, you may decide that you'd like to have one or more of the "before the big day" get-togethers, such as an engagement party or a bachelor/bachelorette outing. Or one or more of your friends may suggest just such a get-together. Then there's the last event before the wedding itself, the rehearsal dinner, where it's customary for members of the wedding party to do a walk-through, followed by a hosted evening combining close friends, supportive family members, and often (but not always) out-of-towners. LGBT people are finding innovative ways to celebrate these traditional parties, but the point remains the same: to bring loved ones together to fete the couple to be married.

ENGAGEMENT PARTIES

As more and more LGBT couples decide to partner or marry, it's becoming increasingly common for us to have what's essentially an engagement party to celebrate the good news. Such engagement celebrations generally take the form of a dinner party or small cocktail party (under twenty guests). Who hosts? It's pretty open these days: It could be someone among your friends; your parents or a sibling; or the couple themselves could do it.

Here are a few helpful hints:

- Not all guests invited to the wedding need to be invited to the engagement party. However, everyone invited to the engagement party should be invited to the wedding.
- Invitations can be printed and sent via snail mail. Alternatively, using e-mail invitations is

fine, too. The choice depends largely on how formal a party it will be.

- The party should take place soon after the announcement, which may vary from a couple of weeks to even a couple of months. The point is to keep enough distance between the engagement party and the wedding shower.
- Gifts are optional. If you (as host) are asked about this, a good reply is "Your presence is their present."
- Any friends who have voiced concerns about the relationship should understand that it's time to let go of the past, attending with as much of an open mind and heart as they can muster. Or, they should pass altogether.

COUPLES SHOWERS
(AKA WEDDING SHOWERS)

Wedding showers are another opportunity to bring together family and friends of the couple. They are meant to be fun and celebratory and, while presents are not actually required, most showers have evolved into gift-giving occasions. For same-sex couples planning to marry, these events are commonly referred to as couples showers.

Usually, couples showers are hosted and held by one or more of your closest friends, or by your best man, your maid or matron of honor, or the equivalent (see page 161). However, it's considered acceptable these days for a family member to host the shower as well. These parties are usually held anywhere from a couple of months to two weeks before the ceremony. Invitations can be mailed or sent electronically.

QUEERY

"Disinvited from my ex's engagement party"

Q **After a cooling-off period, my ex-boyfriend and I had managed to become good friends. When he and his new partner got engaged, I was glad to be invited to their engagement party. But the day before the fete, my ex sent an e-mail disinviting me, saying that his husband-to-be wasn't comfortable with our relationship, and it would be better if I didn't come. It's spilled milk now, but what could I have done?**

A Withdrawing an invitation is a serious manners offense. Most commonly, there's some sort of political context, such as when the White House rescinds an invitation to a public figure who has been suddenly disgraced or is otherwise too controversial to appear in a photo with the president.

It seems you may have fallen into the same category, albeit on a smaller scale. Unless you did or said something egregious, you've become a pawn in some drama of the new couple's own making. My best advice would be to follow the Buddhist saying "Let go or be dragged." In the meantime, don't hold your breath for a wedding invitation.

Hosts needn't pick up all the costs of a shower. The hosts may decide to ask others to provide a cake, the flowers, or some wine—or even, especially if it's at a public venue (like a restaurant, a wine bar, or beauty salon), ask guests to chip in. In those cases, be sure to say in the invitation: "Join us for a dutch brunch (entrées range from $15–$20) . . ." or "Please make your own spa appointment and bring $35 to cover the groom's mani-pedi." Nevertheless, since it's always nicest for guests if they're hosted, try to keep their contributions to a minimum.

Twenty guests is a good cap. Otherwise, it's difficult for new acquaintances to get to know one another. While showers don't need a theme, some gay and lesbian couples borrow ideas from their straight friends; others create new ones. Themes do help suggest the type of gift for the lucky couple; some of the more common shower themes and gifts are:

- **The spa shower:** Massage oils, scented candles, a gift certificate for body work, slippers.
- **The cook's shower:** Kitchen linens, knives, spices, glassware.
- **The liquor cabinet shower:** Bring a bottle of a favorite alcohol.
- **The alphabet shower:** Guests are assigned to bring a gift beginning with a designated letter as well as an attribute of marriage that begins with that letter. For instance, someone assigned the letter "c" could bring a box of candles as well as a card describing the virtues of companionship in a relationship.
- **The naughty shower:** Sex toys, leather gear, sexy underwear (hosts should provide sizes when relevant).
- **The happiness shower:** Bring a saying, note, poem, or original writing about the meaning of happiness. These are read aloud during the shower, collected, and then put into a book for the couple.

If the couple is registered, it's acceptable for the host to let guests know. This can be done in a number of ways: by including this information on the shower invitation (but not on the wedding invitation—see page 192); on a separate card enclosed with the invitation; or posted on the couple's wedding website. In addition, if asked, hosts may spread the word. At the shower itself, make sure someone is designated as the official scribe to keep a list of who gave what for the thank-you notes.

MAKING A TOAST

There's one more custom for showers: Those closest to the grooms- or brides-to-be often make a toast to the happy couple. If that's you, keep these toasting tips in mind:

- **Be prepared:** If need be, write down your thoughts so that you can deliver them eloquently or just have them on hand in case you need to refer to them.
- **Make it memorable:** Talk about the couple's relationship, perhaps how they met, any struggles they've been through, funny stories, what you've learned from them, or how each couple that marries helps all LGBT people move toward greater equality. But don't make it too memorable by embarrassing either of them with inappropriate stories or comments.
- **Keep it short:** You don't need to go into anyone's life history, nor all of his past boyfriends or her old girlfriends. Three minutes—max—is a good rule of thumb.
- **Plan the time:** Do the toast after all the guests have arrived but before they start to leave.

Prewedding Parties

Bachelor (and bachelorette) parties take place in the weeks or days before the wedding, usually symbolizing the last rites of "freedom" before getting hitched. Then there's the last party before the wedding itself, the rehearsal dinner, where it's customary for members of the wedding party to do a walk-through, followed by a hosted evening combining close friends, supportive family members, and often (but not always) out-of-towners. While most gay couples don't have these parties in the precise way that straight couples do, we do have our own variations that accomplish the same goals: bringing loved ones together and celebrating the couple—individually and together.

LGBT BACHELOR/BACHELORETTE PARTIES

Some younger LGBT people—let's call them "new traditionalists"—are embracing the idea of bachelor or bachelorette parties, even though these kinds of events aren't that common in the gay community. Usually, they're organized by a close friend, best man, or maid of honor—but not necessarily paid for by that person (each friend usually pays his or her own way, and everyone chips in to treat the guest of honor). It's worth noting that some gay couples actually have joint bachelor parties, which makes the party more of an excuse to simply have a good time than the traditional bawdy send-off.

One way to settle on the right kind of party is to look at the guest list and give some thought to what has brought this particular group of friends together over the years. One recently married groom suggested this approach in a blog post: "Most people end up doing something that is a celebration of their closest friendships. Look to what you do for fun with friends on other occasions and it will probably give you some good ideas!" If they've

"May we ask our shower guests to pay their way?"

Q **My girlfriend and I are planning what we jokingly call a "lesbian couples shower." Right now, we're up to about forty friends and family on our guest list and we can't really afford to throw such a big event. A couple of our friends suggested we ask our guests to help us cover the costs. Would that be bad lesbian manners?**

A It would be bad manners, period. The problem is not that you are short on cash but that your guest list is too long. Besides, showers need to be small enough for guests to get to know one another. I suggest that, instead of thinking of your shower as one big meet and greet, you try and consider it a cozy, intimate gathering of your nearest and dearest. (Some couples actually have more than one shower so that everyone can be included—albeit at different times.)

been members of the gay rugby team, for instance, then having a night out at the local sports bar might be just the thing. Schedule the party at least several days before the big event. You'll want to allow ample recovery time, just in case someone winds up with a killer hangover—especially a bride or groom.

THE REHEARSAL DINNER OR PARTY

For more formal weddings or those with a number of out-of-town guests, you may decide to hold a wedding rehearsal the day before the ceremony. Although a rehearsal dinner or party is technically part of the overall wedding celebration, this event also happens to mark the last night of your engagement. It's usually held in a restaurant or in someone's home, and is attended by all those at the rehearsal and, when larger, guests who've traveled a considerable distance for the wedding.

The purpose of a rehearsal party is to bring together core family and friends, to thank them for their support of your relationship, and to give small gifts to those in your wedding party (as a side "benefit," it's also often the time when the two of you become the butt of touching, funny, or risqué stories). When LGBT people have rehearsal dinners, the couple generally does the inviting as well as the hosting.

Invitations for the rehearsal party are best sent the old-fashioned way—in writing, through the postal service. Here's an example of an elegant invitation for such an event:

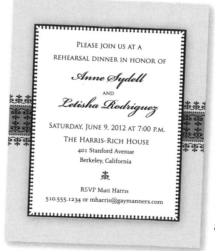

PLEASE JOIN US AT A
REHEARSAL DINNER IN HONOR OF
Anne Sydell
AND
Letisha Rodriguez

SATURDAY, JUNE 9, 2012 AT 7:00 P.M.
THE HARRIS-RICH HOUSE
401 Stanford Avenue
Berkeley, California

RSVP Matt Harris
510.555.1234 or mharris@gaymanners.com

PLANNING YOUR CEREMONY & RECEPTION

Dreaming about the big day with the one you love is the best place to start out when it's time to plan a wedding. Do your best not to let finances, family tensions (especially those about your being gay or trans), difficult caterers, or even the threat of bad weather distract you from the big picture. Even so, planning a smooth LGBT wedding ceremony and reception takes some effort: You'll want to create a budget, get organized, and make myriad decisions far enough in advance so that you can both enjoy the day itself—along with everyone else.

Whether a small event at your home, a destination wedding, or a soup-to-nuts grand affair, there are many questions to consider. How do you decide on your guest list? And how do you cut it? Is creating a wedding website appropriate? What's important when choosing an officiant? selecting a venue? picking the music? And how do you decide if you need attendants? Once you've determined those answers, the only thing left to think about is how you'll be wiping the dance floor with your beloved at the reception.

What Kind of Wedding

There's not much of a difference between planning a commitment or civil union ceremony and a legally sanctioned, honest-to-goodness wedding. In fact, most gay and lesbian couples focus less on the imprimatur of the official event and more on the size, style, and sentiments of the ceremony. Such is the price of equality that gay couples are now in on two big secrets: Weddings require putting together a jigsaw puzzle with a million little pieces—and they can be expensive: The cost of an average wedding is more than $25,000. However, there are many workarounds; for instance, luncheons, cocktail receptions, and at-home affairs can significantly bring down your costs while still providing a lifetime of four-color memories.

Most couples choose to tackle the first big questions together, as they start to plan a ceremony that reflects the tenor of their relationship. Later on, you can divide up some of the other, smaller decisions—or even parcel them out to trusted friends and family members.

Here are the initial questions to consider:

- How many guests do we invite to the ceremony and reception?
- What's our budget?
- Will it be a religious or secular ceremony?
- What time of year and what time of day will it take place?
- What kind of affair do we want? How formal will it be?
- How will the ceremony reflect our personalities?

- Who will officiate?
- How will friends and families participate?

THE ESSENTIALS
A Wedding Budget Checklist

In preparing a budget, it helps to plan for all possible expenses. Scan this list and make sure you have considered each element (whether or not you incorporate each one in the end).

- Caterer
- Musicians
- A wedding planner
- Florist
- The menu
- Cocktails, wine, and champagne (soft drinks, too)
- The cake
- Invitations
- Ceremony and reception location
- Wedding attire
- Photography/videography
- Gifts for the wedding party
- Honeymoon
- Unplanned expenses
- Bartenders and servers
- Rentals: tables, chairs, linens, and silverware

Making Decisions Together

One of the advantages gay couples find in making our wedding plans is that we're usually much freer of family directives ("You must invite your mother's bridge partner!") and family traditions ("But all the women in our family have worn *that* wedding dress"), leaving us a great deal of freedom to design our own ceremonies and in the process to create new traditions.

As might be expected, with the roles and responsibilities of two grooms or two brides ill-defined, this freedom can be as challenging as it is exciting. It's up to you as a couple to make your own decisions, compromising as necessary to each other's needs, dreams, and—naturally—your budget. If anything, couples may have different notions about the kind of wedding they envision. Perhaps one of you has dreamed of a grand event, and the other, a small, intimate get-together. Or your girlfriend wants a church ceremony, but you picture a nonreligious affair. Or you would rather save for a down payment on a house while your partner wants to put every last cent into the wedding celebration.

As you start your planning, definitely put everything on the table right away. This is the time to speak up about wedding fantasies and fears alike. Some couples even keep a journal of their discussions and decisions so that they can refer to it later. The process of sorting all this out—as two members of a team, with equal votes—may be slow, but it's a smart way to settle on a plan that works for both of you.

This isn't to say that one of you can't take the lead, especially if he has time or she has the expertise. One bride-to-be reports, "I'm doing almost all of it, but I run all decisions by my partner. She thinks it will be great 'no matter what,' and I'm a a total control freak who thinks the whole wedding will be ruined if we have the wrong color napkins."

WHAT CAN YOU AFFORD?

In many ways, everything about your ceremony and reception hinges on the budget, and one of the most challenging tasks for any couple is talking about financial matters. With any luck, by the time you get to the point of planning your wedding, you've already been through some dry runs when it comes to money issues (like paying and planning for vacations, or—if you live together—how you deal with the monthly bills, the rent, or your mortgage payment).

More often than not, gay couples foot most of the cost for their weddings and receptions. The first pair of questions to ask yourselves are: What can we afford? and What do we want to spend? (These may be two very different amounts.) Even if you are fortunate to benefit from some "financing" from your families or another source, it's likely that you'll still be carrying the lion's share of costs. "My dad and stepmom are paying about a third," says one lesbian. "They offered us a lump sum, which would have been enough, except that it costs triple to get married in New York City than it does anywhere else."

THE ESSENTIALS
Nine Ways to Cut Your Wedding Costs

1. **Reduce your guest list:** This is the number one way to curb your out-of-pocket costs.
2. **Combine the ceremony and reception sites:** If you can find one site that will work for both events, you'll likely be able to lower this line item. Often, venues have different locations within them, giving you the cost savings but maintaining the feel of two separate spaces.
3. **Find a naturally beautiful spot:** If you don't need to decorate a chapel or a reception hall,

you'll save on flowers and much more. Think about locations that include views and vistas, as well as outdoor spaces like backyards or more formal gardens.

4. **Plan your wedding for a time of the year or a day of the week that is less expensive:** For instance, winter weddings usually cost less than spring or summer ones. Similarly, choosing a weekday rather than a weekend date will help your budget.

5. **Don't make dinner the focus of your reception:** Luncheons, cocktail receptions, and at-home/potluck affairs can significantly bring down your costs while still providing a lifetime of four-color memories.

6. **Ask friends or family members to help you with costs:** Not with cash, but by providing a location, preparing some of the foods, arranging for the flowers or the music, or other out-of-pocket costs like linen and table/chair rentals. These smaller ticket items can add up and your friends can really help you out.

7. **Decide what you can live without:** Sure you need wedding photos, but do you need a video? Of course you'll want to dance, but perhaps a DJ will suffice instead of a band.

8. **Limit your bar:** Alcohol is a major cost in most receptions. Instead of a full bar, consider serving beer, wine, and soft drinks, plus just enough champagne for everyone to toast you but not enough to swill throughout the reception.

9. **Elope!** The cost of a wedding is one of the main reasons straight couples do this.

Deciding Whether You Need a Wedding Planner

Wedding planners are not just for elaborate, formal weddings and receptions. These days, planners can help you with smaller or less formal affairs, too.

Many couples are daunted by what they fear is the expense of hiring a wedding planner, even if they're tempted by the idea of having so many of the details handled by a professional. Keep in mind you're not required to hand over the whole operation. Today's wedding planners can work with you in a variety of ways—such as on an hourly basis (say, for two to three hours of advice), or for a package deal of specific tasks, like helping with seating arrangements in the church, providing sample vows, decorating the reception hall, or planning the menu along with a caterer.

Not surprisingly, there are planners who specialize in gay and lesbian weddings (there's gold in them thar hills!), and they may be especially attractive to you because of their newfound expertise in the etiquette of same-sex ceremonies. Whatever your wishes and whatever your budget, it's wise to familiarize yourself first with the pros and cons of engaging a planner:

PROS
- Generally is well-versed in the minutia of wedding ceremonies and receptions (invitations, seating, how much alcohol to have on hand), which can be helpful if you're time-constrained or not up to speed.
- Can help you determine and keep to a budget.
- Will assist in choosing caterers, florists, and other vendors, which may save you time and money. She can also screen vendors to make sure they're either gay-owned or gay-friendly, if that matters to you.
- Can supervise the last-minute details, so you can actually enjoy the ceremony and reception.

- May be able to help you realize a dream you've long held.

CONS

- Will charge between 10 and 15 percent on top of all costs. Depending on whether or not she has saved you money on some hard costs, you may consider this reasonable or excessive.
- Could be a wild card. As with any contractor, be sure to choose someone with a good reputation, and make sure that you have a detailed, signed contract before she starts work.
- May make decisions on your behalf, and you may not like these decisions.

Finding LGBT-friendly Vendors

Some LGBT couples prefer that everyone who works their ceremony and reception also be LGBT—or gay-friendly. "This is really, really important to us," says one lesbian bride-to-be. "Most of our vendors are gay but the ones who aren't *must* be active in the LGBT community. To us that means having a history of being very gay-friendly."

These days it's much easier to find LGBT-friendly vendors in cities and towns with a big lesbian and gay presence. No matter your location, it's best to start with an online search or to ask LGBT friends for any recommendations. Often the names of the companies will make things pretty clear: GayWeddings.com, Pride Bride, and Purple Unions are just three of the national sites with listings. You may also find help in your local yellow pages; some locales have gay yellow pages as well. Once you've made a list of potential vendors, follow up by e-mail or phone. If your instincts tell

you something isn't right, either ask a friend to give you a second opinion or move on to another choice.

By the way, the fact that a business hasn't previously provided services to an LGBT couple or isn't gay-owned doesn't mean you necessarily need to avoid or exclude them. If a company is enthusiastic about doing your wedding and meets your needs in every other way, why not be their "first"? "I have been really surprised how excited straight vendors have been to work with us," says one lesbian bride.

Whatever set of vendors you settle on, make sure it's quite clear that you are two men, two women, or that one or both of you is transgender. Better to overstate this fact beforehand than to find yourself in a difficult situation at the last moment.

STRAIGHT TALK

"I don't see why gay people can't use the terms 'husband' and 'wife' even when they're not married by law. Am I concerning myself too much with word choice?"

I don't think you can ever be too concerned about word choice. In fact, more and more LGBT couples are using "husband" and "wife" to refer to their partners—whether legal or not. Still, some gay couples just aren't used to the moniker. A lesbian friend of mine who married her lover in Massachusetts put it this way: "We're just of a generation that prefers to use 'partner.' I think the more we hear it from other gay couples, the more likely we'll be to start calling each other 'the wife.'"

Sound Business Practices for Wedding Vendors

Before you sign any agreement with a vendor, whether it's a caterer, florist, reception hall, or wedding planner, ask them these questions:

- How long have you been in business? Will you provide references?
- Are you a member of the Better Business Bureau or the National Gay and Lesbian Chamber of Commerce?
- What is your experience with same-sex couples and ceremonies?
- How will you ensure that everyone who works at the event is LGBT-friendly?
- Who will be managing things at my event? Can I meet the other staff beforehand as well?
- What is included in your standard fee?
- What is not included? (Make sure to get this in writing.)
- Will you commit to working within our budget?

WHERE TO HAVE YOUR CEREMONY

Before you get serious about selecting wedding ceremony and reception venues, make sure you have decided on the maximum number of guests you'll need to accommodate. Keep in mind that most guests are usually invited to both events, unless you're having a very intimate ceremony (where only your nearest and dearest attend). Don't let budgetary concerns dictate a short list of sites you're not totally happy with. Choose a location that has special meaning for the two of you and that feels like the right place to start this chapter of your life together. From there on, you're really only limited by your imagination. Here are some traditional venues to consider:

- A house of worship that is LGBT-friendly, whether a church, synagogue, or temple.
- At home.
- A hotel or inn.
- A restaurant or resort.
- City hall or another official building or site, such as a botanical garden.
- A college facility.
- On the beach, lakeside, atop a hill, or at another scenic outdoor site.

Outdoor sites have some additional considerations, beginning with weather conditions. You'll need to check if a permit is required, even for areas that may at first seem quite public. Also, visit any outdoor venue on your short list on the same day of the week and at the same time that you'll be there to see how private it is; there's nothing like a troop of anti-gay oglers to ruin an LGBT wedding.

If you decide to hold the ceremony and the reception in different locations, figure out ahead of time how people will get from Point A to Point B. Consider how much time and distance there is between the two: You want there to be enough time to get there, but not so much that people are idling. One lesbian regrets her error of judgment in allowing for a three-hour "interlude" between events: "We had wanted to have our ceremony in this particular church and then our reception at a club right on the bay at sunset. Unfortunately, the latest time we could do the ceremony was at 2:00 P.M., so we had this big gap."

THE ESSENTIALS

Location Checklist

Before finalizing your decision about the venue, you, your partner, and the planner (or whoever is assisting you) should quickly review these points:

- Make sure that all your guests can be accommodated comfortably; you don't want to have more guests than seats.

- Make sure your sexual orientation or gender identity won't pose a problem or be a surprise.
- Confirm the date and time.
- Confirm the fees.
- Find out if any other services are being held that day and if there are time constraints or extra fees if your event runs longer than planned.
- Make sure there's sufficient parking and wheelchair accessibility.
- Plan for inclement weather.
- Find out if there are any restrictions on music, flowers, or photography/videography. Determine whether the venue provides audio/visual services.
- If it's a house of worship, ask whether you may bring your own music. Is church equipment (such as an organ) off-limits?

QUEERY

"Hitting up the parents for our wedding"

Q Last year when my older sister got married, our parents paid for most of her wedding and her fiancé's folks took care of most of the rehearsal dinner and some other incidentals. (I think Sissy and her fiancé also made some contribution themselves to the wedding.) Now that my partner, Jerry, and I are planning a ceremony, we're wondering whether it's okay to approach my parents, too.

A Bad news, there's no established etiquette of who contributes to a same-sex wedding. But what do you have to lose in asking them?

I'd raise the subject gently with your parents. Although I don't suggest you launch right into a comparison with Sissy's situation, there's nothing wrong with emphasizing the fairness issue if they resist. But be prepared: They may tell you that a daughter is one thing and a son, whether straight or gay,

is another. Or that they saved money for her wedding, but not yours. Or that the economy has taken a big toll on their finances. If any of that's the case, it's time to move on to your partner's parents (good luck), plan to make a greater contribution yourselves—or downscale your plans to fit your budget. At this point, your parents become guests at the wedding instead of hosts—and there are certainly advantages to that.

Choosing a House of Worship

Every religion has its official policy on same-sex marriage, and it's obviously wise to do some research before moving forward with plans to get married somewhere that's not fully embracing of gay partnerships. However, don't forget that congregations and sects vary within religions, so be sure to carefully check out the *specific* house of worship you're interested in—especially if you're not already a member of that congregation.

Among the larger religious denominations in North America that have been supportive of same-sex marriage are the Episcopal Church, the United Church of Christ, and the Reform and Reconstructionist Jewish movements. On the opposite end of the spectrum are the Roman Catholic Church, the major Baptist churches, and Orthodox Judaism. (For a more detailed discussion of LGBT-friendly places of worship, see www.gaymanners.com.)

Destination Weddings

Perhaps there's nothing more romantic for you and your partner than making a commitment on a Caribbean beach, or with the Grand Tetons as the backdrop, or at some extraordinary venue such as Althorp House, the ancestral home of the late Princess Diana. Many LGBT couples decide to tie the knot at a so-called destination wedding, often combining ceremony, reception, and honeymoon in one. It can be exciting for the couple and guests alike to take such a trip, and the luxury of spending so much time together is a rare pleasure in our busy lives. One guest at a recent

Hawaiian ceremony reports, "In addition to the ceremony and reception, our hosts organized a kayaking and biking trip. I felt like we were all one big, extended family by the end!"

In your excitement about planning such a wedding, don't forget to consider who won't be able to join you, whether because of the travel expense or because they're unable to get the time off from work. One possible solution to include those who aren't able to travel is to have a second reception at home.

For those who do make the journey, clarify beforehand whether you'll be footing any of the travel or accommodation costs. That's generally not 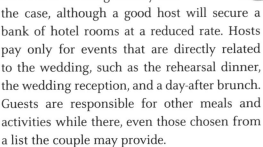 the case, although a good host will secure a bank of hotel rooms at a reduced rate. Hosts pay only for events that are directly related to the wedding, such as the rehearsal dinner, the wedding reception, and a day-after brunch. Guests are responsible for other meals and activities while there, even those chosen from a list the couple may provide.

If you're getting married outside of the country, make sure you choose a location that's gay-friendly; being gay is still illegal in many countries, and patently uncomfortable in others. Also be sure to give your friends and family members sufficient time to update their passports, if expired, and get any necessary immunizations. (For more about gay travel overseas, please see pages 326–331.)

At Home

Having your ceremony or reception at your own place is another good alternative for

LGBT celebrations, especially for couples who have already been living together for some time. Not that "at home" celebrations need to be at your own home: Perhaps a friend has a house in the country or a relative offers the use of a spacious urban loft. If you decide to have your celebration at a private home, allow sufficient time to prepare and organize—that is, to take care of any gardening, touch-ups, or light remodeling that might be necessary to make the house picture-perfect.

Other questions to keep in mind about a home wedding include:

- Will you need to rearrange furniture to make people comfortable, allow them to dance, and to create a space for you to take your vows?
- Are there any valuables that should be secured? Do you need to remove any medications from the bathroom?
- Do you have a sufficient number of restrooms? Can the sewage system handle the higher-than-normal traffic? If not, you may need to rent portable toilets.
- Is there sufficient seating and are there enough tables for your guests?
- Are there parts of the home that will be off-limits?
- If you plan to use a tent for an outdoor service or reception, can the home serve as the backup venue if the weather doesn't cooperate?
- Will the kitchen be used to prepare foods? If so, are the facilities sufficient? Would that preparation interfere with any part of the celebration?
- Do you need any outside help, such as bartenders and servers?
- Will you need to rent linens, dishes, utensils, and glassware?

- Are there pets that will require special arrangements?
- Are there any noise ordinances that you need to be aware of—especially for late-night events?

If you do "borrow" someone else's home for your wedding, arrange for a professional cleaning after the ceremony and take care of the bill for your host.

THE ESSENTIALS

Planning Your Honeymoon

First things first: Who pays for the romantic getaway that generally follows an LGBT wedding or commitment ceremony? You do. It's fine to use cash you may have received as wedding gifts, or contributions to your honeymoon registry (see page 193)—or, perhaps, you've been putting cash away for a while into a special honeymoon fund.

Among popular same-sex honeymoon destinations are the LGBT-friendly destinations mentioned below, as well as Argentina, Brazil, and Spain. Here are some tips to help you plan a memorable trip:

- **Dream (and then compromise if necessary):** When planning a honeymoon, start by chatting with your sweetheart about what this dream trip might entail. Are you looking for a quiet place or a bustling city or club scene? Is time away more important than where you go? In fact, how much time off will you have?
- **Make a realistic budget:** Can you afford to fly to Hawaii? What about a few nights at the beach on Cape Cod instead? Begin devising a budget with the basics—airfare, food, and

lodging. Don't forget to include such other items as local transportation, cocktails, snacks, tips, and the price of any tours or vacation activities you decide on.

- **Plan ahead:** If you're planning to travel during high season, it's important to get an early start and book your flight and hotel as far in advance as you can. Note that although it's traditional for a couple to honeymoon right after the wedding, there's no rule that says you have to. Go when you can and when it makes sense. For instance, you might want to avoid the Caribbean during hurricane season—or do the opposite in order to take advantage of lower, off-season rates.

- **Choose an LGBT-friendly location:** A honeymoon is definitely one trip where you'll want to express all the PDAs you're feeling, so North American locales like New Orleans, Provincetown, Palm Springs, South Beach, San Francisco, Vancouver, and Nova Scotia are especially appealing.

(See Chapter 12 for information on traveling as an LGBT couple, including how to choose an LGBT-friendly destination and tips on visiting other countries.)

THE GUEST LIST

One of the most exciting things about planning a wedding or commitment ceremony is getting to invite your loved ones as witnesses to share your joy, publicly support your same-sex relationship—and make a big fuss about you. Deciding who is in or out of the big event can be a wrenching experience because so many factors need to be considered. Chief among them are the composition of the guest list—there are those whom each of you wants to attend, those whom you feel you must invite out of obligation, and so on—and your budget, which sets a limit on how many guests you can actually afford to host.

Even after you settle on an initial number of guests, don't be surprised by what's called "guest creep." As the weeks go by, one of you will say, "Oh, we need to invite my other friend from work, because she'll feel left out" or "Josie and Lydia's kids are coming, so we have to let Gerard and Fred know they can bring theirs."

Where to Start?

There are a number of ways to begin to assemble a guest list. Often, couples like to divide their list in half—that is, you each get 50 percent of the invitations. That approach works fine if each of you has approximately the same number of friends and relatives, but it can present problems if one of you has six married siblings or happens to be on the Gay Games swim team. However, if you've been partnered a long time already, it's likely that you share a lot of the same friends, so there may be no need for separate lists at all.

Another common approach is that together you create so-called A and B lists. Then, once the invitations are mailed out to the A list and the RSVPs start to come in, you can extend invitations to people from the B list. (This is one reason why it's important for guests to reply promptly.) However, this approach requires some care: Don't invite your B-listers too close to the wedding date, because you don't want them to know they weren't among your top-tier friends. A good rule of thumb here is that no invitation should be sent within two weeks of the RSVP date.

Many LGBT couples, who have long been sustained by their friends, often start with them rather than with their families. While there are no unbreakable rules about who must be invited, consider the following groups of guests highest on your list:

- **Your closest friends:** In addition to your obvious best friends, don't forget those who may be important to you in other ways, such as people who helped you come out, advised you on your relationship (like a therapist or a teacher), or have otherwise supported you.
- **Your closest family members:** That means parents, children, siblings, grandparents who support your relationship, as well as their spouses or committed partners.
- **The officiant:** Don't forget to invite the officiant, along with his or her spouse/partner, to the reception.

STRAIGHT TALK

"I'm opposed to gay marriage. What should I do about my gay nephew's invitation to attend his wedding?"

If you think your nephew is aware of your views, then by inviting you to his wedding, it's pretty clear he feels close to you nonetheless. I often say that family trumps politics, so I'd hope you could be present for this important event in his life without having to wave the flag against gay marriage. However, if you don't feel you can keep your mouth shut or think that you'd be a hypocrite, definitely decline the invitation.

Inviting Unsupportive Family Members

What do you do about parents or other family members who aren't welcoming, don't support you as a couple, or are openly homophobic? Where do you draw the line between "good" manners and your right to make your wedding day as happy and stress-free as possible?

This is a dilemma that some LGBT couples face as they plan to tie the knot. Perhaps you haven't had much of a relationship with your family or you've actually been shunned because of your sexual orientation or gender identity. Because weddings are about new beginnings, they're often an occasion to make peace even with the most difficult relations.

One of the most effective things you can do is talk directly with any disapproving family members—together, as a couple—about your love for each other, the commitment you're making, and your ceremony plans. Take the time to explain to them why marriage matters: whether because it makes for stronger families, that you've always dreamed of affirming your relationship before your loved ones, or that you'll become eligible for various state, provincial, or local benefits.

Then, depending on how your conversation goes, make your decision as to whether to extend an invitation. In the end, if they can't find it in their hearts to support you, there's no reason to have them present at such an important moment in your lives. If it just went so-so (but not atrociously), err on the side of graciousness by inviting them. After that, your work is done.

"I want my ex-wife at my wedding."

Q My partner, James, and I are planning our commitment ceremony, and we've hit a snag. I've got two teenagers from my first marriage, and we'd like to invite their mother to the wedding. James is uncomfortable with this and said recently, "A new wedding is no place for an old wife." Is he right?

A It's not a matter of right or wrong, but of what kind of relationship James has with your ex-wife. If James and your ex-wife haven't found their way to the peace table yet, your impending ceremony is not the place to kick off that kind of rapprochement.

Instead, think about celebrating with the entire family—your ex, your kids, and James—sometime before the actual ceremony. A family dinner at home or at a comfortable restaurant can be a great way to start this new chapter in your family's life. Welcome to the world of blended families.

Two last somewhat contradictory thoughts: It might behoove James to make a gesture to his two stepchildren by inviting their mother. On the other hand, you might remind your teens, gently, that it's not their ceremony, and that their mother is no longer your partner.

Ex-Lovers and Ex-Spouses

Usually it's a healthy sign when your partner has a solid relationship with an ex—whether a former opposite-sex spouse or a previous girlfriend or boyfriend. However, inviting an ex to your wedding ceremony can be a delicate matter. If you're the partner with the ex, your current lover may not be thrilled with this idea, so make the effort to ask him or her outright. If there's any semblance of stress, worry, or jealousy about extending an invitation, it's better not to. A gay man explained, "When John and I were planning our commitment ceremony, he really wanted to have his ex-lover be there. But I had never trusted the guy and didn't see any reason to let down my guard on our special day."

Then, there's the potential distraction an ex may have on your other guests (imagine the whispering: "Can you believe that *she* dared to come?!" Or "She must still have feelings for him if *he's* here"). Your friends and family members may also be somewhat constrained in expressing their joy at your ceremony with an ex so front and center.

Still, there are some circumstances when it's appropriate to invite an ex:

- If your new partner and ex have met and have established a good, solid friendship, with no apparent anxieties or insecurities on either side.
- If you've remained good friends with your former partner and all your relationship issues are history.
- If you and your current partner were invited to and attended your ex's wedding ceremony and all went well. Reciprocation is just fine.
- If your ex is part of your larger gay family, which is to say your family of choice—

someone who has been there for you and vice versa over the years. Many of us turn lovers into friends, if not family.

- If you have had kids with an ex and everyone gets along reasonably well, take the high road. The children will appreciate having their other parent present—and you may have a built-in babysitter if they're young.

When an ex-partner attends, pay special attention to how you introduce her at the event. Avoid drawing attention to her status and your former life together. Instead of "This is my ex-wife, Samantha," for instance, you could introduce her as "a good friend of mine."

Adult-Only Weddings

An adult-only wedding may sound like an X-rated event, but it's simply one with no children present. This approach can be a fair enough way to cut the head count and cost without nixing key friends. It also gives adult parents the opportunity to enjoy themselves without the distraction of their kids, and your reception can go on into the night without friends needing to leave early to put their little ones to bed.

How to make clear to your guests ahead of time that it is an adult wedding? Simple: Don't include the children's names on the invitation—specifically, not on the inner envelope—and trust that your guests understand basic etiquette: If there's no mention of the kids, they're not invited. But don't write "No children" or "Adults only" on the invitation itself. It's just not nice to actively *disinvite* people.

As a backup, explain to close friends and family members that it's an adult-only wedding—that way, if some parents ask about bringing their children, they'll know the plan. You'll find that word of mouth is quite effective.

Finally, don't break your own rule. If in the end you allow one guest to bring his kids, then other guests who hired babysitters will rightfully be confused, and even upset.

THE ESSENTIALS

Creating a Wedding Website

More and more gay and lesbian couples, especially younger ones, are creating personal wedding sites as a way to communicate information about their ceremony, reception, and gift registry. A website is also an excellent means to share photos, provide maps and directions, make it easy for your guests to RSVP, and much more. Most of these services also provide good wedding advice (and clear setup directions, so that even most technophobic couples can create a personal site).

Premium sites, where you pay a monthly fee for hosting, offer additional benefits such as background music, splash pages, personalized domain names, and unlimited support and photo storage. One Midwesterner who married his partner in a civil ceremony in the United Kingdom explained the benefits of their site: "We started to be deluged with calls and letters as to whether guests should dress formally or wear hats. With so many logistical details, it became much simpler to design a website."

If you decide to go this route, here are some pointers to keep in mind:

- Choose a design for your site that reflects the style of your ceremony. You can often customize themes with colors and fonts.

- Be careful about publicizing events that are not open to all guests. With some of these services, you can create password-protected areas enabling an additional level of privacy for family members and members of the wedding party.
- Include any necessary information about your gift registry. If you want to encourage donations in lieu of gifts, you can also highlight your favorite nonprofit and even provide a link to the charity's site.
- Consider whether you have any unwired family members or friends (what about Grandma?) and how you will keep those people in the loop.

WHO'S IN THE CEREMONY?

Deciding who stands up—literally—for the happy couple and who sits below to watch may seem like a small detail at first, but it's important. Give careful consideration to exactly whom you want participating in your ceremony and how. One of your most important choices will be selecting your officiant and the members of your wedding party—all of whom are there to support you emotionally and practically on this particular day. They're also present to help you define your lives together, thus becoming an integral part of the "family" that loves and honors you in this commitment.

Choosing an Officiant

You'll have lots of options for who can preside at your wedding, from clergy to ship captains, judges, and tribal chiefs. You can even invite a friend or relative to get a wedding officiant license if you want someone you know well to perform the ceremony (by the way, your officiant needs a license only if you're being legally married). The criteria for these licenses vary widely in states where same-sex marriage is legal, even county by county, and from province to province in Canada, so make sure you know the locale of your ceremony far enough in advance for someone to get licensed in the interim. No matter whom you pick, don't finalize your wedding date publicly until you've selected an officiant and confirmed that he or she is available for that specific date.

Ideally, officiants are good speakers, receptive to your ideas about getting married, and familiar with and supportive of the two of you. It's also a plus if the person has enough experience officiating to be able to make suggestions about such issues as procession order or vows, or simply to guide you impartially through difficult decisions (and premarital counseling, if necessary). If you get a friend to act as the officiant, you may find that what she lacks in experience is made up for by her connection to you as a couple.

If you're having a religious ceremony and prefer to have an officiant from your place of worship, do your homework first in order to determine how LGBT-friendly both the institution and officiant are. If all seems feasible, explain to your officiant what kind of service you have in mind, especially whether you envision any differences from the heterosexual weddings he or she may have usually performed (see "Choosing a House of Worship," page 154).

By the way, you and your partner can be your own officiants, if you like. So-called self-united marriage is a fine idea, especially if you want to focus the ceremony on your joint vows or readings. Many LGBT couples like the idea of technically marrying each other, as opposed to "being married" by someone else.

THE OFFICIANT'S DUTIES AND FEES

Your officiant is the director of your ceremony, at least insofar as he or she moves it along at a certain pace and is aware of the big picture—that the ceremony is part Jewish and part pagan, or that your transgender bridesmaid will be reading a poem.

Also count on a professional officiant to answer basic questions beforehand about state and provincial requirements, should you be fortunate enough to have your LGBT marriage so sanctified, such as:

- Whether you need a blood test.
- Where to get your marriage license.
- What documents you need to bring to the ceremony.
- Whether there is a government-mandated waiting period between the day you sign your license and your actual wedding day.

Religious officiants will usually tell you what's required from their vantage point as well. If you're being married in a church or synagogue, your officiant is technically already being paid, but a $100 to $200 gift will be appreciated. Independent officiants often charge more—in fact, quite a bit more. If it's a good friend who steps in, no fee per se is necessary but it's a courteous gesture to take her out to dinner before or after the ceremony as thanks, or to give a gift, such as a framed portrait of yourselves, even a memorable bottle of wine.

The Wedding Party

Who besides the couple and the officiant will actually be in your wedding party? LGBT ceremonies often stray from traditional ideas about attendants' duties, as well as what they're called, but the basic idea is that these friends and loved ones are there to assist you in tangible ways as you plan your celebration—and beyond. Even couples who are not having an elaborate ceremony often find they need help planning various details—for instance, couples showers and bachelor parties—and for hands-on assistance on the big day itself.

Your wedding party may consist of some if not all of the following attendants: maid and/or matron of honor, best man, bridesmaids and groomsmen, a ring bearer and a flower girl, as well as ushers, and—of course—the parents of the brides or grooms. It's not surprising these days for a groom's best man to be his best female friend, or for the bridesmaids (attendants to the *brides*) to be a mix of men and women, and so on. At an LGBT ceremony, the roles, and the gender identity of those holding each position, can be as traditional or unconventional as you wish.

MAID OR MATRON OF HONOR/BEST MAN

In an LGBT wedding, the roles of maid (or matron) of honor and best man often overlap and are best described as the generals-in-charge. For instance, you may see two grooms with two best men or with just one fellow and a maid of honor; these attendants may or may not be called by the traditional monikers. Similarly, two brides may have any configuration that suits their needs and their friendships.

Regardless of what these friends are called, here are the range of tasks they are usually responsible for (especially in a big or formal ceremony):

- Organizing a couples shower and/or bachelor/bachelorette party.
- Assisting with the invitations (addressing, mailing, handling RSVPs).
- Consulting with the couple on attire for other members of the wedding party.
- Helping to coordinate the schedules of the entire wedding party (picking up out-of-town attendants at the airport, keeping all members of the party informed on when they need to be where, etc.).
- Helping the grooms or brides dress on the day of the wedding.
- Pinning the boutonnieres on the grooms.
- Helping with the train on the bridal gown(s).
- Holding the ring(s) during the ceremony.
- Witnessing the signing of the marriage certificate or any other legal papers.
- Making sure wedding-related checks are written and delivered on time.
- Doing any necessary tipping on the day of the wedding.
- Offering the first toasts to the couple at the reception.
- Handling any problems that come up during the ceremony or reception.
- Throughout the entire process, providing an ear for any needed emotional support.

BRIDESMAIDS AND GROOMSMEN

These are often simply called "honor attendants" at LGBT weddings, with a gender mix of the couple's choosing. Ideally, select attendants who are responsible, have good judgment, and are known for their communication and people skills. They should be available to you in advance and on the wedding day itself for moral support and to help with a laundry list of possible to-dos. Attendants' tasks range widely but may include:

- Acting as ushers (in some regions, ushers are distinct from groomsmen—which is also a good way to include more friends and relatives in your wedding party).
- Carrying an emergency kit that includes sewing accessories and makeup.
- Standing up with the couple during the ceremony or offering a reading.
- Participating in the bouquet toss and the receiving line.
- Decorating the car for the getaway.
- Getting guests to sign the guest book.
- Arranging for transportation between the ceremony and the reception.

Choose the number of attendants according to the size of the wedding you're planning, but, if you a need rule of thumb, have at least two attendants for every forty to fifty guests. Or make the decision based on how big—or small—of a wedding party you want.

THE RING BEARER AND FLOWER GIRL

Traditionally, a boy carried a set of rings down the aisle on a cushion. They weren't the real rings, which the best man and maid of honor had in safekeeping, but a faux set. These days, however, the bearer is just as likely to be a girl or an honor attendant—or perhaps someone's dog, with the rings tied to a Burberry scarf or nifty black bow tie looped around a studded leather collar.

The flower girl is often a young relative who precedes the brides or grooms down the aisle and scatters petals, or simply carries flowers. Many gay couples like the inclusion of children to make their ceremonies multigenerational, especially if they have children of their own or are close to nieces and nephews.

PARENTS

The role of parents varies widely at LGBT weddings, with some "giving away" their daughters and others standing up with their offspring during the ceremony or walking in with them together. It's more common, though, for parents to be considered special guests with no specific roles or duties. You can certainly recognize them without having them under the chuppah or right there next to you at the altar. Seating parents in the front row of any venue, whether it's a place of worship or a sunny hillside, is respectful and also provides good sight lines.

Throughout the day, introduce your parents to any new friends; acknowledge or toast them at the reception; put them at their own tables at the reception (or together if they wish); and ask them if they'd like to honor any friends or family members at their tables. If both members of the couple and the parents are agreeable, consider keeping with tradition and dancing with your parents.

MAKING YOUR FINAL CHOICES

Deciding who makes the cut to be an official member of your wedding party can be difficult. Start by making a list of those closest to you as a couple, whether dear friends or family members, regardless of gender or sexual orientation. Think carefully about whom you want to be part of this special group. Remember, there are specific duties to be carried out (which means choose responsible people) and there are sometimes significant costs involved as well (be aware of the expense of travel, buying a wedding outfit, or hosting a shower). You'll also want to give consideration to those who might be slighted if left out. It's often a good idea to talk through your preferences with your partner or a close family member before extending invitations. Perhaps, for example, your partner is much closer to his college roommate than you realized.

• **How to ask?** This is an important invitation you're extending, and it requires a modicum of formality. It's nicest to reach out to your prospective attendants by phone, but there are also preprinted cards for this purpose. However you do it, take the time to explain why you're asking him or her to be an attendant. For instance: "We've been friends ever since I came out in high school and you were there for me." Use e-mail to ask only when it's a done deal—for example, you've already spoken about the wedding and there has never been any doubt that this person would be in it.

• **When to ask?** Be sure to invite your attendants well in advance of the wedding—even if it's an informal affair. (If you can, ask them even before you send out your invitations.) Some people may need to take time off from work, especially if it's a destination wedding or if they have to travel to your hometown. And if there are special clothes involved (for instance, bridesmaid dresses or tuxedos), make sure everyone has enough time for measurements and fittings.

QUEERY

"I hurt my friend by not inviting her to be in our ceremony."

Q I'm told I've really hurt one of my oldest friends by not choosing her to be in our wedding party. It's going to be a small ceremony, so my partner and I decided to have very few attendants, mostly family members. Now I hear from my best friend that this other friend doesn't even want to come to the wedding. What do I do?

A I'd start by reaching out to this friend right away to try to clear things up. Forget communicating through your mutual friend, and don't rely on e-mail or a letter—this is one time when you really need to pick up the phone and have a conversation. Before calling, however, think through what you want to say and then once on the phone together (no voice-mail messages here, except perhaps just to say that you called) explain that you're having a small ceremony and that most of your attendants will be family members. Do your best to make her understand this is not a litmus test of your feelings for her. (For others in a similar situation who may be wondering: This is definitely not the time to confess that you never liked someone, prefer your other friends, or don't trust the person with an attendant's responsibilities.)

Before ending the call, let her know how much you hope she'll attend and how much you value your friendship. Then, wait until the RSVP deadline to see how persuasive you were.

If Someone Says No

There are many reasons you may be turned down by an attendant of your choice. Among the most likely is the expense of participating. Since attendants generally pay their own transportation and clothing costs, this can be a deal breaker for younger or unemployed people. Others may need to say "no thanks" due to work conflicts. Definitely don't assume that if someone declines, it's because the person doesn't approve of your sexuality or your relationship.

However, if you have reason to believe you're being turned down because you're LGBT, you may want to try to confirm your suspicions. Say something like, "We were really excited about having you as part of our wedding and are disappointed that you can't be with us. Is there anything we can do to change your mind?" This sort of open-ended inquiry is more effective than questions that might be taken as confrontational, such as "Why won't you come?" or "Is it because we're gay?"

Making the Ceremony Your Own

You can personalize a ceremony in many ways, from the choice of readings and the wording of your vows to the type of music, from the blessing offered by your officiant to how you involve your guests and even what you choose to wear. All these small decisions add texture and personality to a ceremony and make it your own. While many LGBT couples follow well-established religious or straight wedding traditions, others of us choose to be less formal, more activist, or even whimsical. In the end, you're constrained only by your creativity, your budget, and, of course, any rules that a specific venue may impose.

Weddings with an LGBT Twist

Some LGBT couples making a public commitment to each other want the fact that they're gay or transgender to speak especially loud. There are endless ways to include statements about your LGBT lives or current politics into your ceremony—beyond the sheer fact of your union. An American lawyer married his British lover in England because they would be conferred with so many more rights and benefits, which were read aloud during their ceremony. The midwesterner reports, "For my many American straight friends, it had never quite dawned on them in such a powerful way just what we as a society lose for being gay; and to hear that

in the context of a very traditional wedding—except for the fact of two grooms—politicized many of them."

Here are other ways to add LGBT touches to your ceremony:

- In your vows, talk not only about your love for each other, but the struggle for our right to marry in every state. If you can't legally marry in your state, make note of that.
- Ask the officiant to speak to some of these same issues in her remarks.
- In lieu of gifts, ask your guests to make a donation in your name to an LGBT advocacy group.
- Choose readings that have a political dimension. Two examples are provided here.

> The Supreme Court of the United States has repeatedly described the right to marriage as "one of the vital personal rights essential to the orderly pursuit of happiness by free men"; a "basic civil right"; a component of the constitutional rights to liberty, privacy, association, and intimate choice; an expression of emotional support and public commitment; the exercise of spiritual unity; and a fulfillment of one's self.
>
> In short, in the words of the highest court in the land, marriage is "the most important relation in life," and "of fundamental importance for all individuals." As the witnesses in this case will elaborate, marriage is central to life in America. It promotes mental, physical, and emotional health and the economic strength and stability of those who enter into a marital union. It is the building block of family, neighborhood and community. The California Supreme Court has declared that the right to marry is of central importance to an individual's opportunity to live a happy, meaningful, and satisfying life as a full member of society.
>
> —*Theodore Olson, January 2010*

A possible reading: an excerpt from attorney Ted Olson's opening statement at the 2010 trial on the constitutionality of California's Proposition 8

> Everyone is entitled to all the rights and freedoms set forth in this Declaration, without distinction of any kind, such as race, colour, sex, language, religion, political or other opinion, national or social origin, property, birth or other status. . . .
>
> Men and women of full age, without any limitation due to race, nationality or religion, have the right to marry and to found a family. They are entitled to equal rights as to marriage, during marriage and at its dissolution.
>
> —*Universal Declaration of Human Rights*

Another political reading: a passage from the Universal Declaration of Human Rights

THE ESSENTIALS

The Wedding Ceremony

Every LGBT wedding or commitment ceremony is different, but as you go about planning yours, here's a basic list of core elements to consider that provide an overall structure, including:

- Prelude (guests are seated during the prelude)
- Processional music and procession
- Officiant's welcoming remarks
- Vows
- Ring exchange
- The pronouncement
- The kiss
- Recessional music and recessional

You may want to add readings or songs by a friend or family member, an opening prayer, some words about the definition of marriage or the meaning of the vows you are about to take, or a symbolic action to represent your commitment, such as the lighting of a "unity" candle.

World Traditions

LGBT weddings often incorporate a mix of cultural and ethnic traditions, whether as a small part of the ceremony or as the centerpiece of the celebration. Some couples draw on their own heritages, while others borrow symbolic elements that have particular meaning for them. These may include specific rituals, like the Hindu tradition of creating a fire in the center of the wedding altar as an offering, or variations on the Jewish tradition of couples standing under a chuppah or canopy and stomping on a wineglass wrapped in cloth to symbolize the fragility of love. A beloved African American wedding tradition involves jumping over a broom to honor the families of slaves, who weren't allowed to marry, while Chinese couples often serve each other's families tea in a special ceremony.

Your wedding ceremony can be as inclusive of these and other ethnic traditions as you like, although be sure to take note that many of these rituals have gender-specific elements that need to be creatively adapted by LGBT couples.

Other world traditions to consider include:

- The signing of the *ketubah,* a marriage contract central to the Jewish faith, which is often read by the rabbi during the ceremony.
- The *gath bandham,* a Hindu ritual performed to signify the couple's new family bond. A scarf is wrapped around the couple's hands and then others place their hands on top of theirs.
- The Hispanic ritual of designating a *madrina* (godmother) and *padrino* (godfather) to accompany the bride down the aisle.

- The *yuino,* a Japanese ceremony, is an exchange of symbolic gifts between the couple's families. Some examples are a long white piece of hemp, which represents the desire for the couple to grow old together, and a folding fan, which when spread represents future wealth and growth. The primary gift is cash, placed in a special envelope called a *shugi-bukuro.*
- Sand-blending rituals based on Native American ceremonial sand-painting traditions, which symbolize the blending of both partners and their families.
- Tossing the bouquet and garter are actually old Anglo-Saxon traditions dating to the early Middle Ages, symbolizing the relinquishing of the bride's status as a virgin.

OTHER CUSTOMS TO CONSIDER

There are even some traditional rituals you may want to incorporate into your reception. Give the items below some thought, chatting together about whether or not they fit in with the rest of your celebration. If so, they take less planning than some other reception details, so it should be easy to figure out how to make them part of the celebration.

- **A receiving line:** Everyone in your wedding party stands in a row at the beginning of the reception to great each guest individually. This is usually reserved for large, formal weddings.
- **Tossing the bouquet:** This is pretty rare at LGBT weddings, but it does happen on occasion. If you decide to throw a bouquet, open it

---

QUEERY

"Raising marriage awareness at work without crossing a line"

Q **For both my partner and me, getting "married" is as much a political statement as it is one about our love. Generally, I don't bring politics into the office, but I do want to raise everyone's awareness of the marriage-equality issue, especially since we live in a state where we can't legally marry. How do you suggest I do this political consciousness-raising without crossing the line into inappropriate office behavior?**

A You're right about not bringing politics into the office, although I'd guess that most of your straight colleagues wouldn't view your impending nuptials in that light.

Still, I suggest you tread lightly in your efforts to change hearts and minds (for example, don't ask colleagues in the office to sign petitions in favor of same-sex marriage or challenge them to debates). Instead, do what your straight colleagues do when they're engaged. Talk about the love of your life, your impending ceremony, where you're going on your honeymoon, etc., just like any engaged couple would. When spouses and significant others are invited to office parties, introduce yours to your colleagues and let them get to know the two of you as a couple.

One last thing if you want to raise the political consciousness of your coworkers: Without getting angry or being too aggressive, casually mention that you can't legally marry or qualify for any of the federal benefits provided to married straight couples. Or, if asked, let them know that in lieu of gifts, you'd appreciate a donation to Freedom to Marry or one of the many other organizations fighting for same-sex marriage.

up to a mix of your single friends, regardless of gender.

- **Saying grace before the meal:** Your officiant, a close friend, or a family member may do this. If this is an important tradition for you, by all means go ahead with the understanding that not everyone present will share your faith.

Wedding Vows

Vows remain the cornerstone of any wedding ceremony. Whether that means simply answering "I will" to the preset vows of your church or spiritual home, adjusting those words to your liking, or proclaiming your love and devotion in your own words, vows highlight the spiritual, religious, or legal commitment being made by marrying or partnering. The ring exchange then comes to symbolize what you've just proclaimed to each other in front of all your guests, who support your union and celebrate it with you. No matter what words you finally decide to say, vows are a public affirmation that you will be with each other, from this day forward.

WRITING YOUR OWN

Choosing the words for your own wedding vows provides yet another opportunity to personalize your ceremony. Perhaps the most common way to approach vow-writing is for each partner to look inward and come up with language of his own to describe his experience of love, commitment, and respect. It's best if this language has some meaning to your partner as well as to your assembled friends and family members.

For many, this process doesn't come easily. How to put in words a set of feelings that perhaps you can't even describe to yourself?

QUEERY

"I can't write my own vows."

Q My partner is an actor and certainly knows how to deliver his lines. He'd like us each to write—and, as he says, "perform"—our own vows for our ceremony. I'm shy and can't imagine baring my soul in front of all our friends and family. Will it matter if I don't write mine? Or will our guests think I don't love him?

A Just as your rings or your wedding-day outfits need not match, your vows can be as different as your personalities. It's fine for your lover to write and "perform" his vows, just as it is lovely for you to deliver a passage someone else has written and read it aloud (with attribution). Find some text—a poem, a selection from an essay, some favorite lyrics—that captures your feelings about your partner. I'm sure your guests will understand that you love him, even if you don't use your own words.

Here's another option: Prepare something original to share with your partner before the big day, when you two are alone. You can read it to him aloud or he can read it himself, then raise your champagne flutes and enjoy a prewedding smooch.

Sometimes it helps to start with something standard and adapt it as you see fit. "We asked the officiant to send us different sets of vows that other [straight] couples had used," said one recently married gay man. "We gave her suggestions and then added our own statements to her more-or-less standard format." There are also a number of questionnaires found online that can help guide you through the process of creating your own vows, as well as examples of vows used by LGBT couples. Religious and professional officiants can also guide you to relevant examples.

If you're planning on writing your own vows:

- **Keep them brief:** This is not the time to recount how you met or the ups and downs of your relationship. Focus instead on the commitment you're making to each other.
- **Make them personal but not overly so:** Your vows should reflect your personalities, but keep the metaphors and generalizations in check. Don't embarrass your partner by revealing private information.
- **If you're having difficulty composing them, ask for help:** Your officiant, partner, or closest friend is a good place to start.
- **Write them down:** Even the most poised may become flustered or forgetful during the actual ceremony. Remember to bring them with you (also, give a copy to your officiant a day or so ahead of time—just in case you forget).
- **Practice ahead of time:** Some couples even do this together as a way to keep their emotions in check during the service.

THE ESSENTIALS

Two Sample Wedding Vows

Here's what one lesbian couple said to each other when they got married in rural New York recently:

Before these witnesses, I take you to be my partner in life and my one true love. I will cherish our friendship and love you today, tomorrow, and forever. I will trust, honor, and respect you. I will be tolerant, patient, and true. Through the best and worst, through the difficult and easy, I will appreciate your uniqueness. I will take responsibility for our happiness in life together.

What may come, I will always be there. As I have given you my hand to hold, so I give you my life to keep.

A gay male couple included these lines in their vows, which, they report, have since been reused by several other same-sex couples:

Bless all families, O Lord: not only the often-invoked families with neat, intact geometries, but also those which thrive in marvelous variations of the mythic family structure.

Bless the families with adopted children, whose parents journeyed to find them.

Bless the blended families as they learn to accommodate new sources of love.

Bless the families with two dads or two moms.

Bless the families of gay men and lesbians who have opened their hearts and minds to celebrate what is different from themselves.

Give courage to the families in which lesbians and gay men are afraid to be open.

Ceremony Readings

A romantic poem or other favorite text read aloud during the ceremony can complement your vows, delivering a particular message or evoking a full spectrum of emotions. A friend, a family member, or the officiant may recite these texts. There's an almost infinite range of sources to borrow from, including the Bible, a favorite children's story, poetry, prose, song lyrics, or a passage from a book that has personal, religious, or family significance.

Inviting others to read is also a gracious way to make your guests feel part of the ceremony. Ask a child to read a poem, an aunt to recite her favorite Psalm, or your best friend to read a sonnet that has meaning to you. If a member of the wedding party has a beautiful voice, perhaps she can perform the tune that you and your partner have come to regard as "your song."

THE ESSENTIALS

Some Favorite LGBT Ceremony Readings

- "We Two Boys Together Clinging," by Walt Whitman
- "If Thou Must Love Me," by Elizabeth Barrett Browning
- "The Owl and the Pussycat," by Edward Lear
- "Touched by an Angel," by Maya Angelou
- "Sun and Sand," by Arthur Rimbaud
- "The Apache Wedding Blessing" (author unknown)
- Any of Pablo Neruda's *100 Love Sonnets*
- "Tin Wedding Whistle," by Ogden Nash
- The snake's speech from Antoine de Saint-Exupéry's *The Little Prince*
- "Of Marriage" or "On Love" from Kahlil Gibran's *The Prophet*
- Select passages by Langston Hughes, Frank O'Hara, Thom Gunn, Carol Ann Duffy, Gertrude Stein, Marilyn Hacker, or May Swenson

Seating Arrangements at the Ceremony

At informal weddings, guests usually take whatever seats are available, although it's wise to mark off the front rows for your closest friends and family members. (This is easily done with a ribbon.) If yours is an old-school wedding, especially one taking place in a church, it's traditional to divide up the room by family, putting each of your parents up front on a center aisle, with other relatives alongside and behind them. This approach may not speak to your own needs and guests, especially since many of the guests are likely to be equally close to both of you (so don't let your friends get hung up on choosing sides).

Nevertheless, here are a few timeless tips and modern adaptations that are worth considering at LGBT weddings:

- Use ushers to bring guests to their seats if you can. Designating a few friends, male or female, for this task is a nice touch and will help your guests feel welcome and connected. The ushers should also be familiar with any seating plans you may have drawn up. Typically, ushers offer a crooked right arm to female guests or anyone needing extra assistance and walk them to their seats. But if you'd like equal treatment for your male guests, go ahead. If there's a program for the service, your ushers hand them out.

- Make sure the ushers are dressed appropriately, which is to say formally (if it's a formal wedding); however, unlike groomsmen they do not have to all wear similar outfits or rent special attire.
- Traditional weddings make quite a fuss over the process of seating the bride's mother, and require that once she's seated, any late-arriving guests need to watch from the back or sit out of the way. While you may not follow the same protocol, the idea is to honor those closest to you—whether beloved friends or family members. This may be as simple as seating them up front or asking them to sing or read a text during the ceremony.
- Ex or exes (if invited) can sit among your other friends, but it is preferable if they keep out of the front rows. (For more on exes, see page 158.)
- This is not an occasion to be fashionably late. In fact, it's smart to be at least fifteen minutes early.

STRAIGHT TALK

"My lesbian daughter is getting married, and I'm not clear whether I have a particular role. Can you advise?"

Frankly, it's hard to say with any accuracy what the role of the mother-of-the-bride is at *any* wedding these days. I'd suggest you sit down with your daughter and her fiancée and let them know you'll be happy to assist them in whatever ways you can afford or that they would like. Your assistance could range from helping them decide what to wear to suggesting locations for the ceremony and reception, perhaps even offering your home.

You might also ask if they want you to reach out to the other mother-of-the-bride, help with the budget and planning, suggest friends and families to be invited to the ceremony, or just act as a wise friend and source of support.

Many LGBT couples are more hands-on with wedding arrangements than their straight counterparts; so don't take it personally if you feel a little more on the sidelines than you expected to be.

INVITATIONS & ANNOUNCEMENTS

If you've ever received a wedding invitation (or one for a commitment ceremony), you know that there's always something special about them, whether the paper stock, the cursive handwriting, or just the expectation that lies within the envelope. The main purpose of the invitation is to communicate—clearly, concisely, and with a certain style—all the information your guests need to know: details on the time, date, and place of the ceremony and reception, as well as clues as to what to wear (or not wear). It helps to know the A to Z's of invitations, from casual to formal, as well as the other announcements you may consider: save-the-date cards, e-mail invitations, and newspaper announcements of your impending LGBT ceremony. In addition, there's the surprising—but important—etiquette of how to address invitations to committed gay couples.

Save-the-Date Cards

Once you've decided on a date for your ceremony and reception, consider sending or e-mailing a "save the date" card. It lets guests know to put it on their calendars months in advance, and it also makes things official. "After people got the card, my friends all called and were really excited that someone in their circle was finally going to do a wedding," said one lesbian. "It made people happy. It made us know we were doing the right thing. It also helped enormously with the planning, since those who knew they couldn't attend told us."

Send these cards out to your guests about three to four months before the wedding, assuming you've finalized the date at that point. Give them even more notice if your event will be taking place close to a major holiday, on a three-day weekend, at a location that might get booked up early (say, Miami Beach in midwinter or San Francisco during Pride Week), or if you're planning a destination wedding.

Usually, save-the-date cards are informal. A postcard or standard single-sided invitation is fine, but you're welcome to be playful and creative if that feels right. For instance, some couples go all out with video trailers to grab their guests' attention and put the personalities of the betrothed center stage. Paperless Post and other electronic mail services are also perfectly appropriate for save-the-date cards. (See page 176 for more on electronic wedding invitations.)

The essential information this card needs to convey is: (1) your full names; (2) the date of the wedding; and (3) the city and state. For out-of-towners, you may also want to include information about airlines, hotels, car rental companies, and other travel arrangements. If you're planning to reserve a block of hotel rooms or want to recommend accommodations in different price ranges, go ahead and let your guests know this now (but also include it again with the invitation). Make sure the card itself says that an invitation will follow.

Sample of an informal save-the-date card.

Sample of a formal save-the-date card. Note that full names (including middle ones) are used; the date is written out—no numerals.

Note: Not everyone on your guest list has to be sent a save-the-date card. You don't need to send them to friends who live close by or those who don't need to worry about planning ahead. However, everyone who does receive one must also get an invitation.

Ordering Your Invitations

Timing is crucial when it comes to issuing invitations. Your wedding invitations should go out about six to eight weeks before the ceremony (perhaps a little bit less if you sent out save-the-date cards). If you're planning on printed invitations, figure out with your stationer how much time it will take to produce them. This includes the time necessary for reviewing the proofs (fixing mistakes if necessary) and assembling and addressing the envelopes—which for a formal ceremony or one with a large guest list can take as long as two weeks.

Be sure to ask your printer for a sample of your complete invitation package—fully assembled with any envelopes or cards—before accepting your order as final. This can take some time, but it's worth the effort. It's also smart to take this package to your post office to be weighed and reviewed in order to find out if there are any extra charges (for instance, a square invitation requires additional postage). While you're there, buy enough decorative stamps (plus extra) for all the envelopes, to avoid going back later.

When you confirm your order, you'll need to give the stationer a final number. Don't just request the same amount as your total guest list. While you don't need an invitation for every single person—couples living together

share, as do families with children under eighteen—do add some extras to your order for last-minute guests (and so you have a few left over as mementos). Extra envelopes are a must, because even the steadiest of hands make mistakes, especially when writing out dozens of names and addresses at once.

Invitation Styles

Between online stores and brick-and-mortar stationers, you'll find a wide range of printing styles to consider, including engraved, thermography, letterpress, or laser-printed. There are also the many weights and colors of paper to choose from, typefaces and fonts, the size of your invitation (and all of its component parts), and, finally, invitation wording for gay and lesbian couples. Since your invitation will be the first take on your wedding to prospective guests, it's important that it set the right tone—formal, semiformal, or casual—and that it evoke who you are as a couple. Perhaps you want to write them by hand, which is a very personal touch, or make them yourselves (if you're crafty in that Martha Stewart kind of way).

(For more on printing styles, see "The Essentials: Letter Writing 101," page 256.)

Invitation Basics

Certain things are fairly set on a wedding invitation, mostly for clarity. The names of the official hosts come first—although in LGBT unions, this is commonly the couple themselves—followed by the names of those getting married (if not the hosts), the date, the time, and the location.

The description of what's happening—a marriage, an affirmation ceremony, a relationship covenant, a commitment ceremony, for instance—is up to you and what's legal where you're getting married. Likewise, you'll need to make some decisions about the language on the invitation; it may range from a straightforward "so-and-so invites you to" to the more formal "the honour of your presence is requested by . . ."

If all of the guests invited to your ceremony are also invited to the reception, be sure to include the line "reception to follow," with details about time and where that will be. Otherwise, the invitation for the reception must be on a separate card accompanying the wedding invitation. In either case, anyone invited to the reception also receives a small envelope for the RSVP.

Here are some examples:

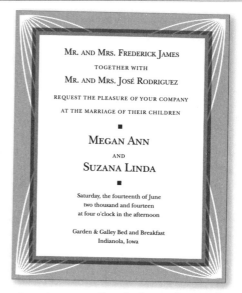

MR. AND MRS. FREDERICK JAMES
TOGETHER WITH
MR. AND MRS. JOSÉ RODRIGUEZ
REQUEST THE PLEASURE OF YOUR COMPANY
AT THE MARRIAGE OF THEIR CHILDREN

■

MEGAN ANN
AND
SUZANA LINDA

■

Saturday, the fourteenth of June
two thousand and fourteen
at four o'clock in the afternoon

Garden & Galley Bed and Breakfast
Indianola, Iowa

Formal invitation (from both sets of parents)

The order of the parents and the order of those getting married are completely up to you. Some resort to simple alphabetization. Others just flip a coin.

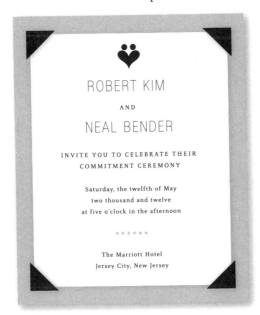

ROBERT KIM
AND
NEAL BENDER

INVITE YOU TO CELEBRATE THEIR
COMMITMENT CEREMONY

Saturday, the twelfth of May
two thousand and twelve
at five o'clock in the afternoon

• • • • • •

The Marriott Hotel
Jersey City, New Jersey

Formal invitation (from the brides or grooms)

You are invited to celebrate twenty years
of continual love at a commitment ceremony for

Suzana Rodriguez
and
Megan James

Four o'clock in the afternoon
Saturday, the sixth of September
Two thousand and fourteen

Brooklyn Botanic Garden
Brooklyn, New York

Semiformal invitation (from the brides or grooms)

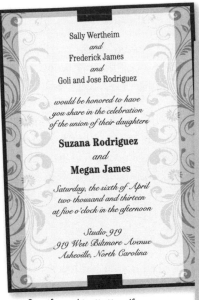

Sally Wertheim
and
Frederick James
and
Goli and Jose Rodriguez

would be honored to have
you share in the celebration
of the union of their daughters

Suzana Rodriguez
and
Megan James

Saturday, the sixth of April
two thousand and thirteen
at five o'clock in the afternoon

Studio 919
919 West Biltmore Avenue
Asheville, North Carolina

Semiformal invitation (from
both sets of parents)

Suzana Rodriguez
+
Megan James

INVITE YOU TO JOIN THEM AS THEY PLEDGE VOWS OF
love + faith
IN A CEREMONY OF COMMITMENT

SATURDAY, NOVEMBER 20, 2015, AT 1:00 PM
THE ROSE GARDEN, BERKELEY, CALIFORNIA

Informal invitation (from the
brides or grooms)

Dear Aunt Cynthia and Uncle Bruce,

Megan and I are planning to be
married on May 12 at 4:30 p.m.
at the Brooklyn Botanic Garden.
We really hope that you'll be able
to join us for the ceremony and
the reception to follow. (Please let
me know by May 2.)

Love,
Suzana

Handwritten invitation

QUEERY

"Beach attire for wedding guests"

Q This summer we're getting hitched on the Jersey shore, literally on the beach in the late afternoon. We want everyone to be comfortable and to be able to enjoy the day. How do we word the invitation to let our guests know that casual dress is fine—except that we don't want to see anyone in bikinis at the ceremony?

A The style of your invitation will go a long way toward helping your guests understand what kind of attire you have in mind. Certainly, you don't want a formal, engraved invitation. But suggesting that your guests be "comfortable" might be interpreted as shorts and sandals, which is not what you have in mind.

Generally, it's not appropriate to suggest dress on the ceremony invitation, but it certainly can be added to the reception invitation. In your case, I would add either "Festive attire" or "Casual chic," either of which should conjure images of linen slacks and jackets for the men and colorful summer dresses or coordinated skirts and blouses for the women. But you can also set the tone in the way you describe the event on the invitation: "The ceremony will take place at sunset on the beach" conveys the message that it's not a "come as you are" affair. In addition, tell your close friends and family members what you plan to wear, and give them some appropriate suggestions for your guests—in case they're asked.

THE ESSENTIALS

Wedding Technology Dos and Don'ts

Using e-mail for most wedding-related communications is frowned upon. By and large, it's considered too casual a medium for weddings, even though younger, more tech-savvy gays and lesbians are embracing it increasingly, even for such celebrations. For now, consider these guidelines:

- **Save-the-date notices:** Digital announcements that a wedding is being planned are more and more common and completely acceptable.
- **RSVPs:** If you want to give your guests the option of replying to a printed invitation by e-mail, go ahead. Ditto if you plan to use a personal wedding website, which can also collect and organize RSVPs.
- **Casual or last-minute invitations:** This is okay if you're inviting computer-savvy people to an intimate shower, informal reception, or a very hastily put-together wedding. You may be tempted to do a group blast ("Hey Friends: Jodie and I have decided to get married before the Supreme Court rules on the validity of same-sex marriage . . ."), but it's better to think of them as electronic, handwritten notes—so use a personal salutation ("Dear Sarah, Jodie and I . . .") instead.
- **Detailed logistical information:** Maps or hotel listings are often too bulky to fit inside your wedding invitation envelope. They're much more useful e-mailed or posted online anyway.
- **When to send electronic invitations:** Be ready with them at the same time you'd mail any printed ones.

The Invitation Package

An entire slew of stationery items can become part of what is known as the invitation package or ensemble. Most LGBT couples don't go all out, but if you're throwing a formal wedding, it pays to know about all the extra layers and flourishes in that traditional packet, so that you can decide for yourselves what to include. The invitation itself is of course nonnegotiable. Here's a rundown on all the other possible items that go into it.

ENVELOPES

Consider having your return address printed on the back flap of the envelope to make addressing them faster. Whose address goes there? That of the hosts of the wedding—at LGBT nuptials, more likely to be the couple than either of their parents. (If you don't live together currently, pick one or the other residence as your official wedding address.) The person living there should be prepared to keep track of RSVPs as well as any gifts received.

You'll need at least one envelope per invitation package, but sometimes two or even three. The first, or outer, envelope's function is simple—it's the one you address and stamp. The inner, or second, envelope serves a different function: it allows you to be quite specific as to who is invited. Let's say that you've invited your best friend, and she has a new girlfriend whose name you don't know yet. You address the outer envelope to your friend ("Ms. Linda Rich"), while the inner envelope would read, "Ms. Rich and Guest." That's how Linda knows she's being invited with a guest—without those words, she should also

QUEERY

"Invitations for gay couples"

Q I don't live with my lover, although we've been together for years. I've noticed that when straight friends are getting married, they send their invitations solely to one or the other of us—not even "plus guest." What's up with that? We're a couple, too.

A Straight wedding etiquette traditionally has dictated that non-live-in boyfriends, girlfriends, partners, and lovers are by definition less serious and don't "qualify" as significant others. And that's often true for straight couples: When they want to make a commitment, they tend to move in or make it legal. As you know quite well, non-live-in LGBT boyfriends or girlfriends or even unmarried same-sex partners may actually be fully committed yet unable to have an analogous commitment ceremony.

So, when deciding whether to invite a gay friend's partner, the litmus test for a joint invitation is to ask: Are they a committed couple? Since the answer in this case is yes, you should be invited together, regardless of your domestic arrangements.

Pass this along to your straight friends—and make sure they know the full name of your lover, so that they spell it right on invitations from here on after.

understand that she's being invited solo. The third envelope is intended for the RSVPs, or what's called the response card, and comes printed with the host's address (and has return postage affixed).

RECEPTION CARD

Reception cards are usually included when the reception is taking place at a different location than the ceremony itself. They can match the wedding invitation in style and language, or they can simply provide the address with a small note.

RESPONSE CARD

If you're asking your guests to let you know whether they're attending, providing a card makes that easy, not just for them but for whoever is tallying the RSVPs. There's no need to provide anything but the barest details on the card.

It's smart to put a number on the back of each response card and enter the same number next to that guest on your master invitation list because many cards come back without the guest's name being filled in. Doing this at first makes reconciling your list much easier.

Here's an example of a response card using somewhat traditional language:

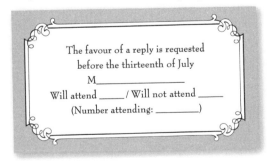

The favour of a reply is requested
before the thirteenth of July
M_____
Will attend _____ / Will not attend _____
(Number attending: _____)

TISSUE PAPER

Ink doesn't tend to rub off printed cards these days, so when tissue is added now, it's more for added elegance than to prevent smudges. It's generally used only when the invitation is engraved. If you choose to use a piece of tissue, it goes between the wedding invitation and reception card.

DIRECTIONS AND ACCOMMODATIONS CARDS

Instructions for how to get to the wedding might be necessary, especially for out-of-towners. Many couples like to suggest places to stay overnight in the area. Either streamline this information and have it printed on another small card, or include a line on your invitation or reception card about where to find such information online (see page 159).

Assembling the Invitations

Assembling the invitation package can be a bit daunting, and one of the first and most important questions to finalize is whether to use one envelope or two.

If using just one, which means there's no inner envelope, the invitation is placed with its front facing up. If it's a folded invitation, don't put any of the other pieces inside it: The

---

QUEERY

"Asking for cash instead of gifts"

Q We're wondering how to make clear on our wedding invitation that we don't want gifts— that we'd prefer cash.

A Ha! Straight couples have been wondering how to get away with this for decades. For better or worse, good manners still frown on the idea of "pay for play" weddings, even though it's perfectly acceptable to ask for and receive cash in lieu of a gift in some communities and ethnic groups. Furthermore, it's a big no-no to say *anything* about any sort of gift *on* the wedding invitation.

Nonetheless, there's room for invention here to get your wishes known. You can tell your closest friends and family members that you'd prefer cash gifts and that it's fine for them to tell that to others—although *only* if they are asked. If you yourself are asked directly, be honest. For instance, you could say "We already have enough stuff since we've just combined two households, but we're saving for a new bedroom set. If you can help us with that, great. But anything you decide will make us happy." Often it does help to have a specific item in mind so that guests don't think they're simply defraying your ceremony and reception costs.

Also consider a financial registry, which your bank may provide; these allow gifts to go toward stocks, bonds, and the like. (Or consider a honeymoon registry, which makes it possible for your guests to contribute to a honeymoon fund.)

QUEERY

"E-mail wedding invitations seem like a faux pas."

Q I recently received a beautiful electronic invitation for a friend's wedding, which I thought was bad manners. Have things changed?

A Traditional manners experts have issued a dictum: Using e-mail for wedding invitations is inappropriate. Period. They say it would be akin to picking up the phone to invite your guests to the most important event of your life: too informal. Many others these days are of a different mind—and I myself am on the fence.

There's definitely a generational divide here. Younger people generally eschew "high manners," while embracing technology to a greater degree than has been customary. So it's important for the wedding couple to think about whom they're inviting. If their guests are predominantly Gen Y or Gen Z, they likely use e-mail for a range of things, including invitations of other kinds; then I think it's okay to consider going electronic for this special occasion (but I recommend a premium service like Paperless Post). The same goes if the guest list is full of technorati; they will appreciate the effort for its digital and (sometimes) its green qualities. But if the guests are a bit more traditional, less addicted to e-mail, or multigenerational, I would say choose some form of printed invitation. So, yes, things are changing, but there's more to come.

---

reception card goes on top of the invitation, and on top of them goes the response card and envelope (the response card should be inserted, faceup, under the flap of the envelope), as well as any directions or other "accessories."

If you are using two envelopes, the invitation is inserted directly into the inner (or second) envelope, folded as above. Other enclosures are inserted in front of the invitation, starting with the larger items. All should face the back flap of the envelope—except for the response card as noted above.

All the individual pieces of the invitation ensemble should be readable from the same direction, so that when you take all the parts out of the envelope, nothing needs to be turned around to be read.

Addressing the Envelopes

One way to get ahead on your wedding tasks is to ask your printer if you can pick up the envelopes before the invitation and other elements of the package. That way, you can get a head start on addressing them—in a well-heeled script, of course. Some couples hire a calligrapher, which adds a sophisticated touch. You'll also find that invitation vendors offer envelope addressing services in a font and ink color that match your invitation, which is considered an acceptable alternative to writing the addresses out by hand. (Some online vendors offer this, too, by special request.)

A few general guidelines for addressing envelopes:

ASSEMBLING THE INVITATION PACKAGE

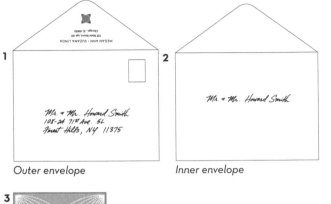

Outer envelope   Inner envelope

Invitation   RSVP card and envelope

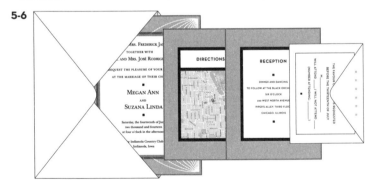

1. Address mailing envelope with the guest names and address. Take one assembled invitation to the post office and have it metered! Fully assembled invitations are heavier than a standard letter and odd shapes (square) may require extra postage.

2. If using an inner envelope, write the guests' names on the front using only the surname prefaced by Mr., Mrs., Dr. (formal), or with first names or family titles (informal).

3. Place invitation faceup. Lay tissue over the writing, if using tissue. When inserting a foldover invitation into an envelope, the fold goes into the envelope first. Accessories or enclosures are never inserted inside a foldover invitation.

4. Put a stamp on the response envelope. Tuck response card, faceup, under the flap of the response envelope with its flap overlapping the response card.

5. Layer enclosures in the following order from bottom to top: invitation, directions, reception card, and response set, from largest to smallest on top.

6. If you are not using an inner envelope, slip the resulting stack inside the outer envelope. The back of the invitation should rest on the inside of the flap as you insert the stack. When the outer envelope is opened, guests will see their names.

- Use each guest's full name, preceded by the proper courtesy title.
  - **Dr. Thomas Stephen Draper**
  - **Ms. Tamar Mutch**
  - **The Honorable Julie R. Lister**
- For couples who are dating, send each an invitation to his or her home address.

- For a gay couple that is committed, whether legally married or not, address them together on one line: "Mr. Eric Schweitzer and Mr. Andrew Owen." The use of the word "and" signifies their union. This is a departure from straight manners, which dictates that only legally married couples can benefit from this symbolic form of address. (By the way, it's up to you to decide whose name goes first.)

- Write out the names of streets, states, provinces, and other words in each address without abbreviations, despite what the post office recommends.

320 El Camino Road

Santa Fe, New Mexico 87501

- If you're including a second envelope (the inner envelope), there's no need to write out the address again on it, or even to include first names. Instead, it's just the guest's title and surname, that is, "Dr. Draper." Or you can be more familiar and just use first names, that is, "Thomas."

- Double-check the spelling of all names. Preferably, someone other than the person who addresses the envelopes should do this, as a fresh pair of eyes is more likely to spot mistakes.

- Don't even think of using labels. As a Chicago wedding planner stressed, "No, no, no. Wrong, wrong, wrong."

- If you have a wedding website, offer your guests the option of RSVP-ing there by adding a line like this on your response card: "You may also RSVP on our wedding site at . . ." You can collect meal choices and any other preferences through the site, too.

Placing a Newspaper Wedding Announcement

Many newspapers these days have renamed their traditional "Weddings" section as "Celebrations/Weddings" specifically to accommodate the growing number of LGBT committed relationships. In fact, since *The New York Times* first started accepting same-sex couple announcements in 2002, more than one thousand U.S. newspapers (nearly three-quarters of them all) now accept them, too.

Some newspapers run free wedding/celebration announcements on their style news pages and consider them to be editorial

---

QUEERY

"My boyfriend wasn't invited but I'd like to bring him along."

Q I just received an invitation to my best friend's commitment ceremony. I assumed that my new boyfriend was invited until I showed him the invitation, which actually did not have his name on it and didn't say "and guest." My best friend has met this boyfriend once.

A Nope, sorry. Boyfriend needs to sit this one out. It's clear that not including your boyfriend isn't an oversight, since even if your best friend didn't know his full name, he could have chosen to include him with "and guest." You should assume that while spouses and partners were invited, casual boyfriends and girlfriends have been left out, perhaps to keep the numbers down or to ensure that all guests have a strong connection to the couple partnering.

In your case, it sounds like this relationship is still in the more casual stage than the committed, and that your best friend has apparently classified it in that way. Let it go. But sign your gift card from the two of you.

in nature (such as *The Washington Post* and the *New York Times*), while others (like the *Los Angeles Times* and the *San Francisco Chronicle*) consider them paid advertising.

If having an announcement published appeals to you, follow the paper's guidelines (usually located on its website), which involves filling out a form with information about each of you. You'll be asked where you went to school and what degrees you earned, your current employer and job title, about your parents and their work, other background information, and when and where you plan to have your ceremony. You may also be asked to provide information about who will be officiating, your honeymoon destination, and where you plan to reside after the ceremony. Finally, provide a photo exactly as the newspaper specifies.

THE RECEPTION

Some gay couples find that the details of their receptions say as much about their commitment and their lives together as the ceremony itself, or even more. Food, music, bawdy toasts—these lively ingredients can make such a difference. Since your intention is to have a good time at your reception (and to provide the same for your guests), you'll need to make sure all the elements—including the menu, seating arrangements, music, wedding cake, and floral arrangements—have been arranged for and are in place. Then there's less chance of last-minute goof-ups and more of an opportunity for you to relax (perhaps) and enjoy yourselves (definitely) during the reception.

Planning the Menu

Many elements determine the menu for your reception. First and foremost, the kind of reception you envision will dictate some decisions. If it's a sit-down meal, you'll likely have at least three courses: salad/soup/appetizer, entrée, and dessert (your wedding cake). More formal receptions will have more courses and more choices within each course. On the less formal end, a complete meal generally isn't offered. Instead, passed-tray hors d'oeuvres are the norm; this form of service is perfect for a cocktail reception and usually the least expensive catered option. Buffets are appropriate for almost any kind of affair; they can be dressed up for a more formal event and dressed down for a lunch. Costs will vary by both the quality and quantity of foods served.

HIRING A CATERER

Whether or not you need a caterer depends on the number of guests you plan to entertain, the type of reception, and the venue. It's a good rule of thumb that you consider a caterer if you're planning to have more than twenty-five or thirty guests. But if it's a home wedding, there's no reason you and your loved ones can't make your favorite foods for everyone to enjoy. Some LGBT couples have potluck celebrations, which can have a nice, symbolic community feel.

You can rely on caterers simply to prepare and/or serve the food or to take care of the entire reception, from soup to nuts. That latter option entails arranging for the bar, bartenders and servers, the wedding cake, tables, chairs, linens, silverware, flowers—sometimes even a tent and parking for your guests. As with a wedding planner, you'll want to check out a caterer's references, have a signed contract, and insist that everyone working on your event is comfortable with an LGBT wedding reception.

If you decide to employ a caterer, interview the person in charge and do tastings of the dishes you're considering. Don't be shy about asking for this: It's standard operating procedure just about everywhere and gives you the opportunity to make your decisions based on what really matters—how the food is presented and how it actually tastes. Along with your partner, consider inviting a few friends or family members to participate in the tasting. This can serve a dual purpose. Perhaps the slightly homophobic mother of your fiancée happens to be a foodie, and involving her in the choice of caterer might help to warm her up. Alternatively, it can just be fun for you and your closest friends to pick and choose among a caterer's offerings.

Caterers know how people behave at weddings; if you want your guests to meet and greet each other with a drink in one hand and a small plate in the other, they'll steer you clear of their highly regarded but impractical-while-standing rack of lamb. Meanwhile, you know what your friends and family like; that's why it's important to choose a menu that will appeal to most of your guests' preferences and take account of their dietary needs or restrictions. While you can't please everyone, you can try your best (often by providing choices).

Last but certainly not least, your budget will help narrow the choices you have to make. (For more about hiring a caterer, see "When You Need a Caterer," page 273.)

Cash Bars

Cash bars, also known as no-host bars (where guests pay for their drinks), have become more common recently, especially as the economy

---

QUEERY

"BYOD = Buy Your Own Dinner"

Q **We received an invitation to a wedding reception recently with a card reading, "This is a no-host celebration." When I talked to one of the brides about it she said, "We couldn't afford to cover dinner, so this seemed the next best thing." We're shocked and thinking about not going. Isn't this rude?**

A Inviting a guest to any event, much less a wedding reception, means that you're hosting. Period. If a couple can't afford that, there are many ways to cut costs, so yes, it's rude to ask guests to pay for their dinners. That being said, if you are close friends with the couple, I would still go, celebrate their love, and enjoy the evening, but perhaps compensate for having to buy your own dinner by being more frugal on the gift. It also may help to think about it like this: There are rules of etiquette (like not charging your guests) and then there are *rules of etiquette*, like not punishing your friends because they messed up. A wedding is a once-in-a-lifetime event. Don't miss it over this.

has suffered. If you can, however, try to avoid going to this extreme by cutting costs other ways. Why? It's a general rule of good etiquette that when you invite guests, you host or treat them. Here are some ways to reduce your bar bill without resorting to a cash-bar policy:

- Limit the beverages you offer.
- Create a special cocktail to be served in your honor. Serve it but no other hard liquor (also offering wine, beer, soft drinks, and champagne). This will cut down on bartending costs as well as your hard liquor bill.
- Provide an open bar for a set period of time. Then switch to wine, beer, and soft drinks only.
- Find a place to hold your reception where you can BYOB. Not that you would ask your guests to do that, but so that you can provide wine and other drinks yourselves without the markup of a caterer or reception hall (but perhaps with a corkage fee). Generally, you'll want to find a venue like a church, museum, or public building that doesn't rely on reception revenue, so that they won't miss this part of the pie.

Choosing the Music

What genres of music do you both like? What tempo will set the right mood for your reception? Where should the band, string quartet, or DJ be located? If you want a dance floor, where should it be placed? For many, the music at a reception is just as important as the cake and the meal, so these questions are priorities as you plan the festivities. If this sounds like you, go ahead and take control.

Still, there's something to be said for not getting overly involved in the selection of *every*

single song. Indeed, this part of the reception is often best delegated to someone else. Ask a DJ friend or music lover to scope talent and to consult with you about styles and songs as the play list develops. Just make sure the technical details are set well in advance, or that the DJ has them fully under control. Some of the points to pin down, all of which should be in a written contract, are:

- The number of breaks to be taken
- The number of hours they will perform
- The attire of the DJ or band members
- Any charges for staying overtime
- Ability to take special requests
- Cancellation provisions—just in case you have to

Even if you've left the music details in someone else's hands, you and your fiancé(e) should decide on the song for your first dance. Take some time to think about what that special song will be when you inaugurate the dancing (usually after dinner) with a first (slow) spin around the dance floor alone. Maybe it's the romantic song you heard on your first date? Or when you went to see Rufus Wainwright or Alicia Keys in concert? Your style of dancing will depend on the music chosen; among the most popular are the fox trot, two-step, and rumba.

Here are some other important tips when it comes to your music:

- **Don't wait until the last moment:** Start thinking early in your planning about the kind of music you'd like (6 to 9 months ahead).
- **Ask for references:** It's important that your DJ has a good reputation and follows through on his promises.
- **Book your wedding at an off-peak day (or season):** This is a good way to reduce costs.

Ordering the Cake

Wedding cakes are among the most enduring of wedding traditions, perhaps because cakes represent fertility (symbolized by the grains or seeds in the ingredients) or because of the custom of feeding the first piece by hand to each other. Although you can have your reception without one, it's a sweet way to mark the occasion, whether you provide vegan cupcakes; multiple cakes in different flavors; a tiered white masterpiece with a same-sex wedding topper; or a dessert table with a variety of petits-fours, homemade favorites, or ethnic specialties.

The number of guests you invite determines the size of the cake. One to two tiers will serve up to sixty guests; three tiers will do for sixty to one hundred; you'll need at least four tiers for more than one hundred. Bakers who specialize in wedding cakes can help you with any necessary math; reputable ones will also allow you to taste the various layering and decorating options—not to mention actual forkfuls of as many different flavors of cake and frosting that interest you. When choosing a cake, two things matter: How the cake looks and how it tastes.

If your baker hasn't done an LGBT reception before and doesn't know where to get same-sex toppers, suggest sites like GayRites .net or Wedding Cake Toppers. Another popular item for decorating LGBT wedding cakes is monograms—the initials of the couple, sometimes encrusted with crystals, anything sparkly, or fresh flowers.

If you order your cake directly from a baker, your caterer may impose a cutting fee;

be sure to inquire about that. As with all your other vendors, sign a written agreement with the baker that delineates the size and type of the cake as well as the date and time of delivery.

Note: Some people buy a special knife to use when cutting the cake. It could be an extra touch for the photo opportunity when you cut the first piece together.

THE ESSENTIALS

Five Ways to Cut the Cost of Your Wedding Cake

If you haven't paid for a wedding cake before, get ready for some serious sticker shock. The average cost tops $500, with pricing usually determined on a per-slice basis. For example, a simple, small-tiered cake or a sheet cake will run you about $1.50 to $2 a slice; a high-end, multi-tiered confectionery may price at more than $10 per slice. (These prices are just rough estimates and will vary by region.)

To reduce the cost of your cake, think about these options:

- The less complex and the less decorated a cake, the lower the cost. Assembly and decoration account for much of a baker's time.
- While fresh flowers are a beautiful touch, they're also an expensive one. Be judicious in your selection if you go this route.
- Have your cake and eat it, too: If you want a grand-looking work of art, ask your baker to make several tiers from Styrofoam and decorate them as she does the rest of the cake.
- Don't take the traditional approach. Buy a number of different cakes, pies, and cookies and serve them buffet style. If you're having an informal wedding, ask your guests to bring a

special dessert to share with others.

- Ask your caterer whether she can also provide the cake; you may find yourself saving on cake-cutting and other service fees.

Seating Plans for the Reception

If you're planning anything bigger than a small reception, especially a sit-down meal, start working on a seating plan once you know about how many guests you'll have. You'll want to sketch out a map of your reception hall, tent, or barn and play with the arrangements, contemplating, for example, who would like to sit with whom and whom it might be best to separate (two exes perhaps). Usually, it helps to visualize the seating plan by drawing it the old-fashioned way, on paper, or by using a computer program that allows you to drop and drag your guests. All of this planning will make the reception run more smoothly—and help avoid a stampede for the best seats.

Traditionally, the wedding couple sits up front, facing the room, and the members of the wedding party either share the newlyweds' table or are scattered around the room. But don't feel bound to such a plan, especially if it feels too formal (certainly, make adjustments when you have close friends or family members who are separated and you think it would be better to keep them apart). As for guests, you can assign them specific seats at specific tables or—as is done more and more these days—just to a table, leaving it to the guests to seat themselves. This latter approach is less work for you and may result in more spontaneity in the seating arrangements. In any case,

here are some other useful suggestions about devising a seating plan:

- Put attendants at the same tables with their partners, but not necessarily next to each other.
- Same for other couples (married or not).
- Strategically place singles—so they won't feel left out.
- Make sure guests know at least one other person at their table. Suggest one of your attendants make other introductions before folks sit down.
- If you have infirm or elderly guests, be sure to place them where they will be comfortable and have easy access to any necessary services.

Consider including details about seating, whether it's a map or some other system, in your wedding program. Otherwise, place cards with guests' full names written by hand are a good idea; if it's a larger reception, number the tables and provide a list or individual place cards at the entry with each guest's table number.

Toasts

There are two types of toasts at a wedding reception: those to the newlyweds and those from the newlyweds. Here's a look at each kind in turn.

The best man, the maid/matron of honor, or those acting in those roles usually makes the first toast to the newly married couple. After that, you can go one of two routes. Either it's open season, with close friends; parents, siblings, and assorted family members, as well as others in the wedding party, college roommates, and work colleagues all joining in. Alternatively, you may decide to limit the toasts to a select—and tasteful—few. If that's the case, speak ahead of time to those you've chosen (or have your best man or woman do so), especially about when the first toast should take place and whether the subsequent ones are grouped or spaced out.

What makes a good toast for the brides or grooms? Start off by identifying your connection to the couple and then tell a little story, ideally a special memory of one or both that in some way speaks to their relationship or their marriage. Be funny if you like and certainly sentimental. But don't be overly dramatic—and keep it brief! (Three minutes is about the maximum.) Finally, don't tell secrets that aren't meant to be shared or that may embarrass the wedding couple in any way (like any kind of recitation of their previous relationships). One lesbian bride recalled, "My best friend got so drunk before the toasts that she was practically incoherent, which turned out to be a very good thing!"

As for the couples' toasts, unless you're the spontaneous type, give a little forethought about what you each want to say when it's your turn. This is a twofold process: One of you acknowledges all the toasts, and each of you toasts the other.

A good rule of thumb about the toast to your new spouse: Make it brief, loving, and not too risqué. One groom, known for being loquacious, relied on humor—when it came time for him to toast his new husband, he said, "I will keep it short," and then proceeded to let a fifty-page "speech" slip from his fingers to the floor, to the amusement of all (the pages were all blank).

WEDDING ATTIRE

When LGBT couples wed, these ceremonies range from down-home to a near state affair. You will find plenty of lace and taffeta at LGBT weddings (as well as less frilly fabrics) and generally lots of tuxedos—the latter are a favorite not only when gay men tie the knot but also among lesbians and transmen. On the other hand, LGBT couples also tend to bend traditional fashion rules for weddings, sometimes simply by mixing gender traditions or combining fashions in other unique ways.

What Two Brides and Two Grooms Wear

Before you go off and buy (or rent—see below) your wedding attire, it's important to remember all those decisions you should have made by now: How formal a wedding will it be? What season will it take place? What's your budget? Are there any religious or family traditions to consider (such as having your head covered or wearing your mother's wedding dress)?

Once you've answered those questions, you're well on your way. If you decide to buy your dress or other attire, be sure to give yourself sufficient time—months!—both to shop and to have any necessary fittings. Many couples start this process as soon as they've set the ceremony date. Even an off-the-rack dress or a new suit may need to be altered—sometimes more than once if you lose or gain weight.

LEVELS OF FORMALITY

Traditionally weddings usually fall into one of these three categories, which set parameters for what the couple (and their guests) wear:

- **Formal:** Black tie or white tie for men (tuxedos); a classic wedding gown (i.e., a long white dress with a veil). (For more about the details of formal wear, see opposite.)
- **Semiformal:** Dark suits (black, charcoal, or navy), white shirt, and tie for men; for women: a traditional gown, but with no train.
- **Informal:** Either a suit or a sports coat and slacks for the men, usually with a tie (unless it's a beach wedding or at an exotic destination); a cocktail dress, suit, or pants suit for women.

Variations exist for each level of formality. For instance, a semiformal or informal wedding in the evening is usually dressier than a daytime one. In warmer climates, linen and white suits are appropriate for men at any wedding other than a formal one; brides may choose gowns or dresses in lighter fabrics, too: linen, silk, and taffeta are good choices for both comfort and style.

YOUR OWN STYLE

Many LGBT couples create their own styles to suit their personalities and the nature of their ceremony—and some eschew any part of tradition. For instance, a couple having a domestic partnership at city hall may wear business attire (men: suit and tie; women: daytime dress or coordinated top and slacks) or a more festive outfit of their own choice. At a more formal wedding, you may find two brides, one in a traditional white gown, the other in a silk pantsuit. While there's no need to be matched, you'll want to find a way to complement each other. A Caucasian man who married his Asian partner in a commitment ceremony explained, "I wore a white linen suit, and Gerard wore a long white linen Nehru-style tunic with matching trousers."

RENTING YOUR WEDDING OUTFITS

LGBT couples frequently turn to renting their wedding attire as a cost-cutting measure (a new tuxedo or an upscale gown can cost more than you might imagine). Renting an outfit is easy, generally economical, and amazingly convenient (because it's fine if you return it with cake all over it). If you know you'll be wearing a tux, reserve yours several months in advance of the celebration, especially if the wedding happens to fall in prom or high-wedding season (late spring or summer). Look for one that

"I now pronounce you wife and wife."

fits you well, is not worn or faded, and reflects your style, whether classic or contemporary.

Women's tuxedos (which can also be rented at many mall tux shops) are becoming increasingly popular for lesbians. Usually, they're tailored and can be butched up or femmed down through your choice of blouse, shoes, and other accessories. A complete outfit includes tuxedo pants and shirt, as well as a silk bow tie with either black Mary Janes or patent leather flats. Some women opt for western-style tuxes, fitted white dinner jackets, as well as tuxedo skirts. Brides-to-be can also rent gowns—either in brick-and-mortar stores or online.

How Attendants Dress

How the wedding couple dresses informs what their attendants will wear. If the brides and grooms are wearing formal attire, so, too, should the attendants. Casual clothes—ditto. A rather unpopular wedding tradition is the "edict" that bridesmaids or attendants dresses should be completely identical. Such rigor certainly makes for uniformity in wedding photos, but the often pricey outfits are too often not what a guest would have chosen to wear— or would ever wear again. (If you're being asked to be in the wedding party, it's important to ask about your attire—and especially how much it could cost you.)

Generally, however, the dress code is more lax at LGBT affairs, except for the most formal ones. Many gay couples forgo the "matching" in favor of having attendants simply dress "alike." For instance, brides or grooms might suggest a color palette for the female attendants. In fact,

"I waited my whole life for you and for this day!"

many attendants are generally thankful for a little bit of direction when it comes to the actual shopping. Said one lesbian: "When my best friend decided to marry her girlfriend, I was thrilled to be asked to be an attendant, but even happier when she said the only rule was 'wear a black dress.' We all were able to choose styles that flattered our bodies. And I can still wear that dress!" Another benefit: The wedding party looked similar—and distinct from the guests.

Some LGBT brides and grooms will designate a particular rental store for members of the wedding party and perhaps even a specific tuxedo style. Play along, even if it's not your first choice in fashion. Of course, if you already have your own, simply accessorize it to match the others in the wedding party.

"What do the mothers of two brides wear to a lesbian wedding?"

Traditional etiquette calls for the mother of the bride (MOB) to buy her dress first and then let the mother of the groom know what she plans to wear. This is done to avoid matching dresses and clashing colors or styles. That advice is none too helpful in your situation, so here's what I recommend: If you've already been introduced to the other MOB, reach out to her. If not, you can ask your daughters to play intermediary, passing along the necessary details. (And it really doesn't matter which of you initiates the conversation.)

Keep in mind that the ceremony is about the brides; whatever you wear should not detract or distract from your daughter and daughter-in-law-to-be. Finally, it's not a competition between the MOBs (the same applies to the mothers of two grooms).

How Guests Dress

Guests offer their respect and support for the couple by neither competing for the limelight nor distracting the other guests by dressing off note or too "original." That holds true whether it's a theme wedding—for instance, with everyone in western gear and cowboy hats— or a high-church affair with organ music and formal attire.

When in doubt about what to wear to a particular wedding, pay close attention to the style of the wedding invitation. A formal wedding will usually be preceded by a formal invitation; similarly the invitation for a casual affair or one suggesting "festive attire" will be reflected in the invitation style, and perhaps in the actual language within the invitation packet. If you remain confused, talk to someone in the wedding party for guidance. (For more specifics on the types of outfits these categories entail, see "What to Wear to a Gala," page 338.)

Attire for Trans Brides and Grooms

Transmen and -women looking for something special to wear to a wedding—whether their own or somebody else's—may go the androgynous route, or amp up the masculine or feminine wedding traditions. Think frothy white gowns with endless trains and shiny black tuxedos with starchy collars. Tuxedos are classic wedding garb for trans men, not just because they make you look handsome but also because they shout out "gentleman" and "playboy" at the same time.

Whatever fashion route you favor, the shopping trips and multiple fittings that characterize so many weddings can be anxiety-inducing. Unfortunately, unless you have access to a rare trans-friendly clothing establishment or can afford to hire a designer of your own, you can expect some shade from store clerks. Wherever you shop, you may find the experience more pleasant if you're up-front ahead of time about being transgender.

Not surprisingly, shopping online can be a great solution for trans people. Large-size pumps are to be had for transwomen on the Internet, alongside dresses to suit broader and sometimes fuller bodies. And for transmen seeking a classic look, tuxes come in all sizes and shapes (see Resources, page 381).

If you do shop online, your best bet is to hire an LGBT-friendly tailor to put it all together nicely once your purchases arrive. Good fit is the key not just to "presenting" the way you want, but also to being a beautiful bride, a handsome groom, or a smart-looking guest.

WEDDING GIFTS & REGISTRIES

Giving gifts on the occasion of a wedding is not only incredibly helpful to a couple trying to set up a household without going broke, it's also a way to tangibly support their bond. LGBT couples hoping to set up a wedding gift registry at a few favorite shops are finding themselves ever more welcome (even if often they're asked to fill out forms that allow only for one bride and one groom). On the other hand, the many long established LGBT couples whose households are already bursting with "stuff" are wise to consider alternatives to actual gifts, such as donations to a favorite charity or even to a honeymoon fund. Just be careful about how you let your guests know.

Why Use a Gift Registry

It's hard to argue against using a gift registry if you're getting married—especially for gay couples who have been together for a long time before tying the knot. Do you really need another vase, blender, or coffee maker? Unless you tell your guests explicitly that you'd rather they donate to a certain cause, people will want to get you a gift, so help them help you.

Registries are also useful for friends who don't know your taste or what you may need,

---

"This bride won't match."

Q My girlfriend and I have been looking for wedding clothes for weeks! I really want to wear a nice, tailored suit (maybe even white) and she wants to go full Cinderella, with a gown and tiara. She says we'll look mismatched. I say I will look odd in a dress. Must we be matchy-matchy?

A Think back a few years to the famous wedding of Ellen DeGeneres and Portia de Rossi. Ellen wore an all-white outfit, including pants, dress shirt, and a vest, while her bride dazzled in a backless light pink dress. What both women shared: the same designer (Zac Posen), wedding rings (designed by Neil Lane), and their vows. Feel free to dress differently (like Ellen and Portia) or coordinate your outfits (same dress, different accents or accessories). Some women even go butch to the ceremony and femme to the reception, or vice versa. What you will want most is to be comfortable and to be happy to look at yourselves years later in photos or videos.

and they're a very efficient way of keeping track of who gave you what, which makes thank-you notes easier. Of course, no couple is obligated to use a gift registry, just as no guest must purchase a gift through it.

LGBT grooms and brides tend to register under both their names, so their account is easily accessible (for instance, if you are shopping for a colleague's wedding but can't remember her fiancée's name). Meanwhile the registries themselves have expanded to include a much wider range of potential wedding gifts, such as sporting goods, bed and bath products, wines, and just about everything for the garden.

The best approach is to sign up with one to three stores. It's better if these are establishments you actually shop at (either online or in person); at the least, they should carry the aspirational items you intend to build your new home around. These days, some online sites will group different stores into a single registry for you, which can be very helpful.

How to Sign Up

Despite the ever-increasing numbers of same-sex marriages and commitment ceremonies, signing up for a wedding gift registry in person can still be an uncomfortable experience. LGBT couples often find they need to come out again and again in an effort to make sure everything is set up properly. "I finally had to shout at the poor sales clerk," reported one recently married lesbian. "We're both dykes!" The most common roadblock for gay couples is a semantic one: in fact, registries are still generally called "*bridal* registries."

If you're not up for such in-person encounters—as much as they do serve to raise LGBT awareness—consider registering online with the Rainbow Wedding Network or one of many new such services. Many of the larger department stores have also begun to cater to same-sex marriages (especially in Canada, and in states where it's actually legal).

THE ESSENTIALS

What You Need to Know for Your Registry

Perhaps you've used registries for gift giving in the past, but have never had to set one up yourself. Here are some things to keep in mind when you do:

- Make sure that you choose gift items that will appeal to all budgets, but choose more items in the low-to-moderate price range.
- Consult with your partner on your choices.
- Choose national stores or chains when possible, as well as those with commerce-enabled websites. This will make shopping easier for your guests.
- Don't pressure anyone into using a registry, even if that's more convenient for you.

Letting Your Guests Know

Don't put your registry information on your wedding invitation. That's universally considered inappropriate. As old-school as it may sound, the matter of which stores you've registered with will usually have to be spread by word of mouth. As soon as you've opened your registries and built a wish list, let your family, close friends, and wedding party know the details and invite them to pass the word along—although, again, *only* when asked.

Be sure to set up your registries before you send out the invitations. If you set up a wedding website, include your registry choices there, although not necessarily front and center.

Alternatives to a Gift Registry

Maybe you don't need a registry. If you're having a small, intimate wedding, it's more likely that guests will know your tastes and needs. Or perhaps you'd rather your guests make a donation in your name than help restock your kitchen cabinets with new plates and glassware. More and more sites catering to LGBT weddings offer easy ways to invite your guests to make a charitable gift. Freedom to Marry, for instance, invites donations to the cause of marriage equality itself. (For a selective list of worthwhile LGBT nonprofits, see www.gaymanners.com.)

Honeymoon Registries

While some simmering controversy lingers about whether or not using a honeymoon registry is appropriate, the tide is definitely moving in that direction.

If you take this route and set one up, make the extra effort to delineate the activities the registry will pay for, whether it's skiing in the Tetons, swimming with the dolphins, or a grand tour of Europe's museums. On the registry itself, your guests can choose which activities they'd like to give you as a gift. When

---

QUEERY

"Is same-sex marriage selling out?"

Q **I've always thought that being gay is about taking a different road and having different kinds of relationships. So I was kind of WTF when two friends decided to marry. But *then* they registered for gifts and I went berserk (privately!). This makes me ask: Don't you think that gay marriage is really just a way to mimic heterosexual norms and institutions?**

A No, I don't. It seems to me that gay folks get married for all kinds of reasons—just like our straight friends and family members do. Some marry for financial reasons or health benefits; others as an act of political theater or to be recognized and counted as LGBT; while the great majority marry for love or companionship. And just having the right to participate in (or, if you prefer, "mimic") heterosexual norms and institutions is a crucial building block of equality.

If being gay for you means "taking a different road," then please do so. Your options are many, as long as you and your significant other come to a mutual understanding. But don't be judgmental about gay men and women who do want to marry— especially when there are so many others in this country who are trying to deny our right to do so.

As for the gift registry— aren't they entitled to the same generosity from their loved ones as straight couples? I think so.

things are costly, ask for multiple contributions, much as you would when listing a silver service (or anything special and expensive) in a regular gift registry. A lesbian bride says, "None of our friends had ever heard of a honeymoon registry, but when they read about it on our wedding site, most of them loved the idea of helping us see Canada from Vancouver to Nova Scotia."

Caveat emptor: Make sure your honeymoon registry is legitimate by checking it out with the Better Business Bureau. And note that nearly all of them will charge a hefty fee (7 to 10 percent) to either you or your gift-giving family, friends, and coworkers. You need to decide whether that service is worth it to you. (For more about planning a honeymoon, see page 155.)

A Guest's Guide to Gift Giving

Sometimes it's confusing to know when a gift is expected. But, remember, gift giving is always voluntary, as is the amount you choose to spend. Assuming you have received an invitation to one of the events below, here are some additional guidelines to help you:

- **Engagements:** Gifts are not usually expected at an engagement party, especially if a shower and wedding are to follow fairly soon after. Still, it's nice to bring a bottle of wine or a box of chocolates for the hosts. Toasts are always welcome, too.
- **Showers:** Bring a gift to a couple's shower, even though it's not considered mandatory. Pay attention to any shower themes. If you're invited to more than one shower for the same

QUEERY

"We want our wedding guests to help our favorite charity."

Q My boyfriend and I feel like we have what we need for our home. Instead of registering at Williams-Sonoma or Macy's, we thought about asking our friends to make a donation in our name to our favorite LGBT charity. Is this cool or is it like asking for cash?

A No, it's not like asking for a cash gift. In fact, I think it's wonderful when LGBT couples use their ceremonies as a way to help others in need, and especially nonprofits that serve our community. However, what you need to beware of is coming across as though you are *expecting* a gift. The best way to do this is to let your closest friends and family members know of the organization you support and, when they're asked what you might like for a gift, they could say "As a matter of

fact, if you'd like, they would appreciate a donation to The Trevor Project." Alternatively, you could put that kind of information on your website. Finally, while not considered "proper" by the high-manners folks, you could add in a separate printed card to your invitation package with the language above.

A note to gift givers: If you choose to go this route, be sure to let the agency know the name of the couple you're honoring so that they will be notified and you will be acknowledged.

couple—each party usually involves a different group of guests—you needn't give more than one gift. (By the way, if hosting a shower, consider choosing themes that include a wide range of price points, such as kitchen or bathroom parties.)

- **Weddings:** Wedding gifts are expected but not required. Use the couple's registry only if you want to. But if you send an "independent" gift, be sure to include information about where you bought it along with a gift receipt. It's best to send your gift in the mail or through a private delivery service to the couple's home—use the "signature required" or "delivery confirmation" options.

Although the traditional rule of thumb is that you have a year to bestow a wedding gift, why wait that long? As to how much to spend, the only rule is to spend no more than you can afford, and there's absolutely nothing wrong with going in on a gift with a friend or friends.

GIVING THANKS

As the couple getting married, you'll be the recipient of many gifts, some tangible, others not so. While it's important that you express thanks along the way—to friends who may have thrown you an engagement party or shower, to the various professionals who've helped make certain that your special day is just as you've imagined, and to those dear to you in the wedding party—you'll want to pay special attention to your thank-yous when it comes to wedding gifts.

What Couples Need to Know About Gifts

Gift etiquette has its complexities and it's better to understand them than get caught flat-footed. Here are some pointers:

- **Keep a record:** Be sure to note the item and whom it's from, and to keep the card with the gift until you have written your thank-you notes. A special notebook or an online spreadsheet is great for this, or delegate the project to a highly organized friend.

- **Remember your wedding attendants:** It's a timeworn tradition to give your wedding attendants some sort of gift for their service and support. Suitable attendant gifts appropriate for women and men include personalized cosmetic bags or flasks, a friendship bracelet, a picture frame, and engraved wineglasses or other glassware. In lieu of a gift, you can also waive the usual practice of asking attendants to pay for their own wedding attire or cover their hotel stay or airfare. Nevertheless, any such gesture to your attendants is really meant to be symbolic, so don't get carried away.

- **Expect only one wedding gift per guest:** If you received a significant shower gift or someone hosted a party for you or otherwise helped make your wedding happen, consider that your wedding gift. Don't expect anything else.

- **No gifts for "encore" weddings:** Don't expect gifts from friends who have attended your previous weddings or other commitment ceremonies (whether straight or gay); giving you a present upon your latest nuptials is entirely optional on their part. New friends may choose to give gifts at so-called encore weddings; while not required, this is often done.

Wedding Thank-You Notes

Anyone who gave you a shower or wedding gift needs to get a handwritten thank-you note. It's simply not appropriate to thank someone via e-mail or to send a mass e-mail to a group. Also, add to your list anyone who performed an above-average service or courtesy on the occasion of your wedding, such as your wedding attendants, the neighbor who let your guests park on her lawn, the caterers, the band, and even those who sent a note of congratulations but didn't attend.

Here are some basic tips:

- **When to send them:** As soon as possible after the wedding, but if you can, try and send notes before your ceremony for gifts that were sent ahead of time. Two to three months after the ceremony itself is the outside limit; otherwise, guests who sent gifts may wonder whether they were received.

- **Always add a personal message:** Even if you use preprinted or generic thank-you cards, a good thank-you note will acknowledge the specific gift and how you will use it. For instance, "Thank you so much for the blender. You know how much we enjoy making margaritas, and we hope that you'll join us soon. . . ." Avoid thanking someone for her "lovely gift"—she'll think you have no idea what was given. Do your best not to send thank-yous by e-mail.

- **Either of you can pen the notes:** Your best bet is to divide up the list and write the guests you each know best. Or figure it out another way, but make sure no gift-giver is left out. Best etiquette suggests that you each sign your own name and then pass the card to your partner for signing. However, if you write a note that starts like "Glynis and I have fallen in love with the _____," close by signing your name alone. While thank-yous can seem like a daunting task with, say, a hundred guests, if you each do about five per evening, you'll be done in less than two weeks.

For more on thank-yous, see page 261.

THE ESSENTIALS

Thank-You Note Don'ts:

- Don't decide how much you will write depending on how expensive you think (or know) the gift to be. All gifts are thanked as though equal.

- Don't gush, just say thank you.

- Don't mention it if you're planning to return a gift, nor if it's just not your taste. If you've already returned it, keep that information to yourselves.

- If you decide to regift an item, be very sure that you regift it to someone outside your immediate circle. If you're not putting the gift into circulation but keeping it in your closet for the right occasion, it's a good idea to tag it in case you forget who gave it to you.

- Don't delay writing them because you're waiting for photos or some other embellishment; just do it.

PART IV

CHILDREN

CHAPTER 7

Starting a Family

So Many Ways to Make a Baby

There's never been a better time for LGBT people to become parents. State bans prohibiting same-sex couples from adopting are falling by the wayside; there are more and more LGBT-friendly sperm banks and fertility clinics; and even the Family Medical Leave Act now explicitly embraces LGBT parents. All in all, this is what's considered the new normal when it comes to LGBT families.

But the path to parenthood (or the nursery) is still not an easy one. From the moment you decide to start a family to the day you bring a child home, you'll likely find yourself developing new and sometimes complex relationships with a host of individuals: a surrogate, an egg or sperm donor, perhaps an adoption birth mother, to say nothing of all those social workers, lawyers, and judges. And then there's your partner (if you have one).

While deciding to have children is a game changer for anyone, it presents an extra set of challenges—and rewards—for most LGBT people. Certainly, gay parenting has become far more common than it used to be, with millions of kids in North America having at least one gay parent. Still, the mere idea of LGBT people having kids can sometimes provoke resistance from family, friends, neighbors, and society at large. Gay male and trans parents in particular often face scorn, whether seeking parenthood alone or as part of a couple. And even the lesbian baby boom of recent years has yet to reach most rural areas.

No surprise, LGBT pregnancy, surrogacy, and adoption call for a particular kind of etiquette. How do you introduce your surrogate to friends? How do you deal with nosy questions like "Who's the father?" And how do you write an effective "Dear Birth Mother" letter? With a little forethought, you'll find your way—and leave a path for those who will follow in time. The truth is that the deliberateness usually required for LGBT parenthood has its advantages: You really have to *want* a child—there are very few accidental pregnancies or babies in the LGBT world.

GETTING PREGNANT VIA SPERM DONATION

Lesbians are getting pregnant in greater numbers than ever, thanks to a lot of individual chutzpah, a growing network of friendly sperm banks (not to mention other, more firsthand sources of sperm), and an increasingly supportive health care industry. Among the big issues lesbian mothers-to-be face are choosing between a sperm bank and a known donor, and, if they take the former course, whom to finally select among the blur of mystery men in the bank's database. Then, if you're coupled, there's deciding which one of you will actually carry the child.

By the way, getting pregnant is not limited to lesbians; it's also increasingly a means for gay men to start their families through a co-parenting agreement with a woman or by hiring a surrogate, as well as for some transmen to conceive.

Note: How to talk with your child about how they were conceived and the manners of grown children meeting their donors are covered in the next chapter—in particular, see pages 232 and 234.

First Questions

The process of getting pregnant can be joyful, stressful, or somewhere in between—for anyone, gay or straight, single or coupled. But lesbians—whether single or partnered—who decide to get pregnant find themselves facing a number of questions right at the start that involve matters that most straight couples don't ordinarily have to consider:

- If coupled, who will get pregnant (or pregnant first)?
- How will she get pregnant (insemination or sexual intercourse)?
- Will the donor be anonymous (usually through a sperm bank) or known (usually a friend or partner's relative)?

Often deciding who will conceive needs little discussion. One of you is interested, one of you isn't. If one of you is older, the tick-tock of your clock may be the deciding factor. As a lesbian banker explained, "My partner was older and really keen to be pregnant, so it definitely made sense for her to start our family. I was terrified. But three years after our son was born, I had our second, a daughter."

If the ticking of the biological clock doesn't settle matters, an entirely acceptable alternative is for both of you to be inseminated at the same time and simply see who conceives first. That strategy carries a risk: You might both get pregnant simultaneously—in the extreme, producing two sets of multiples.

Sperm Bank Etiquette

Many lesbians choose to work with a sperm bank because they want no one else involved in their family decisions, so the anonymity, and subsequent noninvolvement, of the donor is a big plus. Others use this approach when no one they know has the genetic qualities they're seeking in a donor, or who is comfortable with the level of participation the couple (or single woman) envisions.

In addition to anonymity, sperm banks offer convenience and an ever more detailed offering of donor details and online search options—and they come with a lawsuit-proof release of claim from the donor. They don't, however, offer the comfort that comes from knowing your child's biological father—intangible elements like personality, quirks, even values and morals.

The anonymity of a sperm bank donor also keeps the etiquette pretty simple. If you're using an online database, your only social interactions are with your doctor and your partner (or friend or family member) who is ideally helping you choose a donor. Not that it's always easy negotiating with a prospective coparent about which qualities matter most in an anonymous donor; you may pore over endless online details about this donor or that, and you may well disagree. One lesbian explained, "I wasn't interested in the number of graduate degrees the guy had, but Mary certainly was." Often couples will seek out the qualities of the nonconceiving parent in the donor. If you don't see exactly eye-to-eye, remember that there will be plenty of opportunities down the road to influence your child's personality.

The stricter your requirements, the narrower your list of options will be. A white lesbian birth mother whose partner is black recalls that they chose to work with the only sperm bank they could then find with more than one black donor. "As far as qualities in the donor, our choices were limited," she explained, "so we looked for a guy from the Caribbean, someone with an unremarkable family and personal medical history." Appearance and racial origins are a lot easier to determine ahead of time than personality, by the way. Sometimes, however, you can pay an additional fee to hear a donor's voice on audio or read through a longer file, which may provide more clues.

Note: Consider restricting yourself to LGBT-friendly sperm banks (of which there are now many) since most sperm banks are still set up with straight, infertile couples in mind. Even if you select your sperm online and it arrives overnight on your doorstep via FedEx, same-sex parents have experienced hassles in the past with non-gay-friendly institutions. (See Resources, page 382, for more information about LGBT-friendly sperm banks.)

THE ESSENTIALS

What You Can Learn About a Donor

While the characteristics you're seeking are certain to be personal, there's a wide range of information available to you as you make your donor decisions:

- Religious background
- Educational background
- Race/ethnic/cultural background
- Physical characteristics (height, weight, hair color, eye color, and more)
- Career/professional role
- Personal history
- Medical history, including genes for or exposure to sickle cell anemia, hepatitis B and C, all STDs (including HIV), Tay-Sachs disease, and many others

QUEERY

"Asking my married brother to be a sperm donor"

Q My girlfriend and I are thinking about asking my brother to donate sperm for a child that she would bear. He and his wife have two daughters already, and I'm really not sure how they'll respond. What do you think would be the best way to ask him?

A Your proposal certainly makes a lot of sense. Inseminating with a close family member is a great way for lesbians to make a baby that's truly part you and part her. Since he's married and has kids already, however, it's really important that you talk not just to him but to his wife. Invite them over or otherwise plan a get-together where the four of you can be alone. Then ask them with no nuance.

At first, leave lots of room to talk out what this would mean for both of your families. Present your preferences about his—and their—level of involvement as questions.

While you should remain firm if there are aspects of this proposal that you don't want to budge on, it's important for everyone involved to feel like they were in on the project from day one. In the end, if you can't persuade both halves of the couple to sign up, it's time to move on to plan B.

Selecting a Known Donor

If the thought of shopping for sperm is just too surreal for you, or if you want your child to know his or her biological father, consider asking someone you know to be a donor. Using a known donor has a lot of benefits, including a more thorough understanding of his medical and family history and better odds of success (assuming he's willing to provide the goods fresh, not frozen). It's also cheaper: Frozen donor specimens run hundreds of dollars apiece, and you may need six, eight, ten, or more.

There's also a tantalizing genetic angle: If a brother or cousin of one woman donates sperm that impregnates the other, the resulting child carries genes from both sides of the family. It's a great way to connect both women to their child by blood, and it approximates the experience of "making" a baby, at least genetically. Plus, you know the characteristics of the donor (smart, funny, weird), and have access to him if it becomes medically necessary.

However, relying on a known donor raises a whole new set of difficult questions, such as:

- Are you looking just for a sperm donor, or do you really want a coparent?
- Is he willing to participate to the degree you'd like (from forgoing his parental rights altogether to being a hands-on dad)?
- If the donor is married, how does his spouse feel about this?
- How common will the knowledge be who your sperm donor is?
- How does he feel about other people knowing he fathered your child?
- How and when will you tell the child about his participation?

STRAIGHT TALK

"My son is in his first year of medical school, and some lesbian friends of his want him to help them get pregnant. He's thinking about it, but I'm a wreck. This is my grandchild they're talking about, and I'd never even get to see the kid!"

It's perfectly understandable for you to want a relationship with your son's future child. But you may not know what role he plans to take with the little one. Many sperm donors who are friends with the moms-to-be decide to take an active, if not a legally protected, role with the child. If that were the case, you could be a grandmother not only in name, but in actuality (like helping with diaper changes, babysitting, and gift giving). So, start by asking your son some questions about the arrangements that are being discussed, rather than telling him how worried you are. Do your best not to pressure him or judge him, no matter what he or the prospective mothers choose to do.

Asking Your Potential Donor

It's an etiquette question Emily Post never had to answer: How do you ask a fellow to make a baby with you when it's not about sex? Before you even start the conversation with a potential sperm donor, be sure to give consideration to the preceding questions.

Once you've made some of the preliminary decisions, arrange to meet with your prospective donor in a quiet, comfortable place and lay out your situation plainly. Make it clear right away that you're requesting a favor—a huge one, in fact—but one that you wouldn't ask of just anyone. And be direct, along the lines of "Would you be interested in helping me/us get pregnant?" Be quite clear that you're not proposing having sex with him (unless you are). Lay out the basics of your vision for the future, focusing most of all on your preferences for his relationship with the child.

Even a yes deserves a good long talk eventually—but first: Celebrate! "I remember being so relieved that he said yes that I didn't want to ruin it with serious issues yet," recalls one lesbian. She and her future baby daddy savored the enjoyment of their decision, shelving the heavy talk for later.

By the way, should you be fortunate enough to have more than one contender, be sure you ask them in order of preference and wait to get a definite no before moving down your list to your next choice.

If You're Asked to Be a Donor

If someone asks you to donate sperm, first express your appreciation for being asked, then give some careful thought as to whether being a donor—involved or not in the child's upbringing—fits into your future. Think ahead as well as you can, not just to the proposed pregnancy and the bouncing baby, but also to the toddler, the school-age youngster, the teen, and finally the adult. Would you be able to handle what is being proposed about your contact with the child, involvement or noninvolvement in parenting decisions, and the rest?

If you're thinking of saying yes, be prepared to answer intensely personal questions about your health and to get tested for HIV and other STDs. Keep in mind that the process of handing off your sperm on a monthly basis until there's conception—ideally just seconds after you've produced it—can be a little awkward. If your life involves lots of travel or professional commitments that are hard to reschedule, be up-front about whether you can be relied upon to show up as ovulation cycles require. And if you are seriously considering participating, it's a smart move to consult an LGBT family lawyer—in fact, it's wise for both parties involved to do so at this juncture.

If your answer is no, speak up about it—your friend needs to move on to the next donor prospect on her list. Be aware that turning her down may be upsetting; if you're declining because you can't meet her requirements, however, say so. By being realistic, you're treating the request as respectfully as you possibly can.

Intrusive Questions

Once you've conceived from a donor—whether a known or unknown one—don't be surprised if you're asked, in a well-meaning but nosy way, a number of questions you'd rather not answer. (This will continue for years to come, by the way.) You may find the whole thing very irritating, but good manners often require that you rise above the occasion—and the intrusion—and treat the questioner with respect. Here are three such questions, with appropriate responses that could deflect the sting:

- **"Who was the donor?"** "We'd prefer to keep that private for now—that information really belongs to the child, so we'll wait until he's older and tell him what he needs to know."

- **"Do you know if the donor has other kids out there?"** "The process was really quite thorough, and we have all the information we need, thanks."
- **"What does the donor look like?"** "It was either Dennis Quaid or Randy Quaid, I can never remember which. . . ." A little gentle humor goes a long way.

Finding a Supportive Ob-Gyn

If you don't already have an LGBT-friendly gynecologist, now's the time to find one—ideally one who is an obstetrician too or can refer you to one. This is important not just for getting good care, but because your ob-gyn will be a central player if you're planning on inseminating at a fertility center (or even just want to talk through the options). A physician who is not fully supportive of your efforts is the last thing you need in any case, which is why it's certainly worth the effort to go out of your way to find a practitioner who is respectful not just of LGBT life but of your decision to parent.

Here's how to start:
- **Get a referral:** From friends, your regular doctor, or an LGBT resource center, whether online or at a community center or nonprofit.
- **Interview your candidates:** Talk about the doctor's experience with lesbian patients overall as well as donor-inseminated LGBT patients in particular. Don't discount going with someone who lacks LGBT experience but has a good reputation and is supportive and likable. Transgender people will have a more difficult time finding a doctor with relevant experience and may need to travel greater distances. But trans-friendly ob-gyns are out there.

- **If you don't feel comfortable with the doctor for any reason, trust your instinct:** Does the intake form ask if you are "single, married, divorced" or is there LGBT-friendly language, like "partnered"? If not, ask about this and explain why you're asking.

Infertility: Dos and Don'ts

If you have a gay friend or a couple who has let you know that they're not able to have children of their own and are considering infertility treatments, you'll likely wonder what's the right thing to say or do. First, acknowledge that you appreciate the trust your friend has shown by sharing this private information with you and be sure to respect his or her privacy in safeguarding what you know. And if they're not aware of relevant sites, a wonderful resource for LGBT individuals and couples seeking fertility options can be found at 10thousandcouples.com, which also provides up-to-date lists of gay-friendly fertility clinics, and BostonIVF.com, which has a special focus on helping LGBT families facing infertility.

Here are some other suggestions of what you can do:
- Ask whether they'd like you to follow up and, if so, check in from time to time. This can be as simple as calling, e-mailing—or just listening.
- Be aware that infertility treatments can be draining, time-consuming, and expensive. If there are specific ways you can help, do so. Some ways to assist include: driving your friend to the clinic for appointments, helping out with some the chores at home, or just

acknowledging that you may want to spend time differently at this juncture (whether to save money or energy).

- Be considerate in inviting your friend to a baby shower or child's birthday party. This may prove to be a difficult emotional situation for your friend—so give her the option not to attend (while letting her know that she's welcome).

- Understand that every failed cycle brings with it another loss of what's not to be—at least right now. There's both an emotional component to each loss as well as physiological and financial ones, too.

- And, finally, don't downplay a friend's infertility or make facile suggestions. For infertile couples and individuals, this is a challenging time—but one that they will get through. While there are other options available, recognize that some keenly want a biological connection to their child or want to experience pregnancy firsthand. Hold back on comments like "Oh, you can just adopt" or "We'll find you a surrogate."

Insemination-Day Manners

Inseminating with freshly produced sperm at the right time of your cycle is the most effective alternative to actually having intercourse with a man. Your donor ejaculates in a cup, and you—or your partner or a medical professional—can use an oral medicine syringe to send the swimmers on their way.

To make sure the day goes smoothly (along with next month's visit, and the ones after that), consider this checklist of key decision points and good manners:

- **Decide whether to inseminate at home or at a clinic:** Home is cozier and cheaper. But if you don't mind the clinical setting and the cost, consider inseminating at a fertility clinic; your chances of conceiving are higher and you and your donor get a little more distance from each other (perhaps you don't actually want him ejaculating in your bathroom).

- **If your donor is anxious, be sensitive:** Performing on command isn't always easy for men. If you're inseminating at home, make sure your donor has plenty of time, privacy (he probably doesn't want you to see *or* hear him), clean towels, and maybe a cold drink. **Note to donors:** You're responsible for bringing along any visual stimulation you might need or enjoy.

- **Be considerate of your donor's schedule:** You may need his services half a dozen times or more over the course of many months, and on a very specific schedule that matches your ovulation cycle. You're entitled to try to pin him down to certain dates, but don't give him grief about other obligations. Good faith is required by all.

- **Cover any of his costs on your behalf:** It's generally understood that you'll reimburse your donor for any and all costs associated with the insemination, unless otherwise agreed to. For instance, if your donor needs to cancel a flight to accommodate your ovulation schedule or even just to take a cab to the fertility clinic, that's on you.

The Old-Fashioned Way

It's not that common, but some LGBT pregnancies do occur as the result of intercourse.

According to a recent poll on my site, www .gaymanners.com, only 8 percent said they expected to conceive by having sexual intercourse. For instance, best-friend bisexuals may be willing to have sex once or twice in order to create and raise a child together—or help one or the other make a baby to raise with a partner. A woman in a lesbian relationship may have a one-night stand with someone who may or may not know he's being used as a sperm donor. Or maybe you're a transgender lesbian with sperm and a non-trans girlfriend who's ready to be a mom. Indeed, LGBT baby-making doesn't necessarily require a surrogate or a sperm bank—or even that anyone spill his seed in a cup.

So how do you approach this one? First and foremost, you need to be very clear about what you're doing, why you're doing it, and what kind of relationship, if any, you expect will come later. Ask each other tough questions:

- "What if you start a new relationship while I'm pregnant?" Will that change your involvement—or noninvolvement—in raising the child?
- "What if you fall in love with this baby, when you've planned to relinquish your paternal rights?"
- "What if we fall in love with each other, even though that's not part of the plan?"

Try to be as up-front and honest with a sexual partner as you would be with any known donor, asking all the same questions about his future relationships with you, your child, and your partner(s) that you would ask of a sperm donor. Don't make a rash decision and fall immediately into bed; take time for medical checkups, including HIV testing.

SURROGACY ETIQUETTE

Infertile straight couples have been hiring women to have their babies for a long time, and these days surrogacy is increasingly becoming the method of choice among gay men in the United States (but not as much in Canada, where a 2004 ban on paying surrogates has put a damper on the practice). Some transgender folks and lesbians struggling with fertility issues seek out surrogates as well—indeed, if you're unable to get pregnant yourself, surrogacy is the only way to create a child who's genetically related to you.

The legerdemain required here lies in dealing effectively and courteously with the fact that you're not "buying" a baby—you're making a contract with a living, feeling woman who will conceive and carry a child whom you will raise. You may also be hiring someone to donate an egg; infertile men will choose a sperm donor, too. Any or all of these people may become part of your extended family, with challenges ranging from how to choose among surrogacy candidates to figuring out how to respect your surrogate mother's personal lifestyle choices when they're not your own—and may not even be optimum for the baby.

Talking to Surrogacy Candidates

However you go about identifying a candidate for surrogacy, whether through an agency or on your own, take a good look at her file to see whether she seems to suit you before making an appointment to meet in person. The idea is to not waste her time—she's probably already gone through a lot of interviews and shared endless personal details about her own life.

When you do meet for the first time, thank her for all the effort she's gone to and for meeting with you. Try to make her comfortable with some small talk and then engage her in a conversation as you talk through your list of questions. This is a time to be gentle and friendly. Whatever you do, don't treat your meeting like an interrogation—this is, after all, a partnership that you're proposing. If all goes well, you'll be putting your signatures on a contract that may very well stand on shaky legal grounds, so having a common understanding is important for everyone concerned.

Finally, don't get her hopes up. A prospective surrogate recently described her frequent disappointments in a particularly emotional blog post: "It kills me whenever I get 'the Call' and they say, 'We decided not to pursue this journey with you' for some reason or another. It makes me feel totally rejected. After every call I am depressed and all emotional for a good month. It's just no good."

THE ESSENTIALS

Surrogacy Logistics

Careful research and planning is important for anyone considering a surrogacy contract, not just because a child is forever but because of the legal limbo of LGBT relationships (in most states) and surrogacy itself (in many states and in Canada). There are three basic decisions to make:

1. **Choose the sperm:** If you're a gay male couple, you need to decide whose sperm will fertilize your surrogate's egg. Genetic or medical reasons may decide this for you, or maybe one of you is very eager to be the donor. Or you can combine your "stuff" into a single "sperm cocktail" and leave it to chance.

2. **Choose the egg:** Some surrogates use their own eggs (where it's not against state law); others are implanted with an already fertilized embryo. Either way, keep in mind that your egg donor will be considered your child's biological mother.

3. **Choose the womb:** This is your surrogate—she'll be carrying your baby for nine months, after which time you become the parent(s).

QUESTIONS FOR YOUR SURROGACY CANDIDATE

Meeting with a prospective surrogate is your best opportunity to talk about the kind of social relationship your child will or will not have with her. Medical and legal questions matter too, but they can also be discussed by your agency or by your lawyer.

Remember that this is a two-way street, so you will have some questions to answer as well. Here are the key questions for *you* to ask:

• Do you want to keep your identity a secret from the child, or do you see yourself as part of the child's family? Are you open to changing that decision later, based on the child's needs?

• If you don't want contact, are you willing to write a letter to the child now, to be read years later, about yourself and your life?

• Will you commit to keeping us up-to-date on how to contact you, in case we need you in the future?

- How much will you be telling your own family about this surrogacy?
- How do you feel about having such a close connection with an LGBT family? Do you have LGBT friends or family members?
- How can we be involved in our baby's health during the pregnancy?

Finally, make sure you understand her fee (if she has one); whose name goes on the birth certificate; and the amount of contact you'll have with her during the pregnancy and after the birth—although these items should be in your contract as well (and finalized by your lawyers).

THE ESSENTIALS

Finding a Surrogate

There are plenty of surrogacy agencies out there to assist in this matchmaking process—especially if you live in California or Florida. Not all surrogacy agencies are gay-friendly, so ask about their experience with LGBT clients, if they don't tout that openly on their website. It's also smart to request the names of a number of their LGBT clients to talk with directly (the agency would need to get permission to release any contact information—or simply provide yours).

Know that using an agency can be an expensive option, but they do provide much needed assistance from agencies screening prospective surrogates and clients for emotional readiness, to overseeing legal and medical matters, to handling any glitches along the way.

If you want a more personal touch or want to save on agency fees, launch a surrogate search on your own. You may meet the right woman in the course of your day-to-day life. If not, try placing a classified ad on sites catering specifically to surrogate searches. Here's an example of one such ad:

> ## WANTED
> ## SURROGATE MOTHER
>
> Hello. My partner and I have been in a long-term relationship and we are registered domestic partners, 25 and 28, and are seeking a woman or lesbian couple who would love to help us out in expanding our family. We are both healthy and educated, and have stable full-time jobs. We have tons of love to give and want a bundle of joy to call our own. There will definitely be compensation, which we will work out.

Whichever route you take to identify a surrogate, be sure to work with an attorney who's well-versed in the patchwork of laws regarding LGBT parenting. Because surrogacy contracts are illegal in many states, many LGBT couples find themselves unable to predict what their legal rights are regarding a child they've conceived this way.

During the Pregnancy

If you've agreed to have personal contact with your surrogate during the pregnancy, be sure to treat her like an equal and with respect. She may have different lifestyle habits than you're accustomed to; that comes with the territory. Definitely don't interrogate her by asking if she's eating healthy food, exercising, smoking, or drinking (although most contracts will cover the latter two points). If she lives nearby, try to be helpful by doing some grocery shopping or providing some meals—as long as she's okay with that. The idea is to show consideration and interest in her overall well-being and health—not just the baby's—and to respect her independence.

No matter what your contract says, you won't have total control over what happens during the pregnancy. Also keep in mind that your surrogate is having a major physical, hormonal, and psychological experience. She may change her mind about having you present at doctor visits, for example, or start calling you all the time for additional help and support that you hadn't planned to give. Do your best to remain flexible.

When there are hiccups, there's nothing wrong with gently reminding her of the terms of your arrangement. For instance, if she hasn't been in touch as previously agreed, you could say, "We'd love to hear how you're feeling and how things are going, every week. We hope you're still okay with that part of our agreement."

You may also find that you want more contact than you anticipated back during your contract negotiation. It's okay to ask your surrogate if she's open to that, but better to focus on her than solely the baby: "We're so excited about this pregnancy—we'd love to see you even more than we thought! Can we take you to dinner, or shopping for maternity clothes?" Also consider inviting her to your home, or ask if you can meet her somewhere in public, like a park or the mall. But be prepared for her to say no to these new requests.

"Guys, everything is okay, really."

QUEERY

"Don't mean to be pushy, but can't I ask the surrogate if she's pregnant?"

Q **It's been three weeks since our surrogate was inseminated—by now that home pregnancy test could be changing colors—and we haven't heard from her. We're going crazy! May I call her?**

A Your anxiety is understandable, but calling might seem intrusive. If you used an agency, call your contact there instead of the surrogate and ask whether there's any news.

If your relationship is directly with the woman, sit tight for a few more days. When you do call, be sure to phrase your inquiry as one about her. Don't just ask, "Did it take?" She'll know why you're calling, and she'll probably tell you what she knows, or when she expects to do a pregnancy test. But don't hang up without specifically arranging your next contact—will she call when she knows, or can you call again on Saturday? That way there's no pacing back and forth, at least not until you're headed for the delivery room.

Introducing Your Surrogate

If your relationship is purely contractual, and neither you nor the surrogate is interested in an ongoing postbirth relationship, then consider keeping your surrogate separate from the other people in your life. This will make the relationship clearer to each of you and help avoid the possibility of the surrogate developing an unexpected attachment to you (and/or your partner).

However, it can certainly be difficult not to become friendly—after all, you'll be seeing a fair amount of each other. Perhaps you'll decide to try mingling a little. How do you refer to this woman who's such an integral—yet unusual—part of the family?

When making an introduction, be sure not to reduce her as "the surrogate," as though she has no other identity. Instead, try language such as "I'd like you to meet Sarah Nielsen, who works at the local library and has two children. We're thrilled that she's helping us by carrying ours." Be sure to identify her fully, including her surname, as you would other friends.

If you do plan to continue socializing after the baby is born, then go ahead and introduce her to close friends and family. You may both enjoy allowing "grandma" a peek, for instance, or want to include your surrogate in meals or other activities at your home. Recalls a gay father of two children born to the same woman: "Our surrogate stayed with us in the final few days of her pregnancies. She got to meet our friends and they, her. We played together, watched movies, prepared and ate meals, and really got to know each other better. Those were very exciting and nerve-wracking times."

STRAIGHT TALK

"I'm single and have agreed to be a surrogate for two nice men, but I'm really not comfortable telling my neighbors that they're gay. What should I say?"

I hope you know this already, but you don't need to explain to your neighbors that you're acting as a surrogate, much less anything about the couple you've agreed to carry a baby for. If neighbors ask you about your pregnancy, simply thank them for wishing you well—even though we both know they were really asking "Who's the father?" since you're single.

On the other hand, if you like the idea of sharing your experience with other surrogates, check out the message boards on sites such as Surrogate Mothers Online (www.surromomsonline.com), where there's even an area targeted to women carrying babies for gay couples.

Postpartum Manners

After the birth, when all is said and done, send your surrogate a well-thought-out thank-you note, with some photos of your new baby. Tell her how much you appreciate what she did for you—helping to create a new family. If this marks the end of your contractual relationship, and all parties are ready to move on, then close the door and start parenting your little one. If you've specified ahead of time that you'll have sporadic contact, follow through as necessary.

SAME-SEX ADOPTION

A doption is quickly becoming the most frequented path for gay men trying to create families, and is increasing among other LGBT people as well. While adoption is, in the end, all about you and your child, you'll find yourself developing a variety of new relationships until the proceedings are finalized. Among them will be social workers, birth mothers, attorneys, and maybe even international adoption specialists. A paramount question for LGBT people undertaking an adoption is understanding with whom it's advised to be out—and when you're better off not mentioning that you're LGBT.

The Importance of Who Adopts First (in a Couple)

When married straight couples adopt, both are automatically considered the child's legal parents, with the result that each has all the rights and responsibilities that come along with parenting. Should they break up, their parenting rights are not terminated—unless a court expressly takes that action. In states that don't allow same-sex marriage, the situation is very different for gay and lesbian parents: Only the biological or *first* adoptive parent is considered the legal parent. The other partner has no inherent legal rights or standing vis-à-vis the child. In the event of a breakup, that parent would have no custody or visitation rights.

In that light, the question of who adopts first is an essential decision about the legal guardianship of the child. Yes, in some states, there are many legal options for the other partner to become a legal guardian, but these take time and the approval of the first adoptive parent.

Usually this process works quite smoothly. Here's how a gay dad with an adopted newborn described his experience: "We really had no logical way to choose who would be the parent, so we just decided that my partner would adopt our baby and then I will do a second-parent adoption. Case closed."

But at other times, much heartbreak can ensue. In 2010, the North Carolina Supreme Court invalidated a second-parent adoption, claiming that such adoptions are not allowed under state law. This decision came despite the fact that much of the court testimony indicated that it was in the best interest of the child to be placed with the second parent and not his biological mother.

THE ESSENTIALS

Agency or Private, Domestic or International?

E ach route to adoption has its own rules, but the final arbiter of who can and can't adopt is a judge in your state or provincial court. Here's a primer on your options:

- **Agency adoptions** match birth mothers with prospective adoptive parents by collecting background information on both sides, and then sharing it. The agency handles all the details and a judge reviews the file, making the final determination.

- **Private adoptions** are just that—private. In many cases, a pregnant woman or teenager approaches a doctor or lawyer to find a suitable family to adopt her baby. You'll still need a social worker to proclaim you fit to parent and a judge to sign off on the adoption.
- **Foster-to-adopt arrangements** usually involve an older child who is placed in a home on a trial basis, with hopes for a permanent adoption. Many LGBT people find this route the easiest, since children in the foster care system can be hard to place; any homophobia in the legal system usually takes a backseat to the needs of the child.
- **International adoption** involves first getting an adoption approved in another country and then grappling with immigration rules to bring the child home to your own country. Gay couples cannot legally adopt in many foreign countries,

but "unmarried" individuals often do so without revealing their orientation. Then, if you're partnered and live in the right state or province, the other prospective parent can pursue a second-parent adoption.

The Home Study

No matter what kind of adoption you're undertaking, the home study will be a crucial part of the process. The intensive, months-long look at your life and household determines whether or not (in the eyes of the authorities) you are suitable for parenting. If you've signed on with an adoption agency, a social worker will call to set up a time for a home visit. These agencies have long been known to be aggressive in their adoption investigations

QUEERY

"Evangelical sister is against our adoption."

Q My sister is a born-again Christian and the mother of five. My girlfriend and I are in the process of adopting, and my sister constantly tells me that we're going to have really messed-up kids because we're lesbians. Last week my sister asked us, "How could a child grow up to be normal in a gay household?" What in the world do I say to her?

A Well, it depends on how available your sister is to having her mind changed. You could explain to her that all the research shows that children of lesbians and gay men turn out just as well as other kids and that there's no evidence to suggest that we're unfit to be parents. It's also true that one's sexuality does not make for a good or bad parent; what matters most is your ability to create a loving and caring environment. Or you could suggest some reading, if you think she'd be open to that,

or offer to take her to a PFLAG meeting.

But the truth is that you may not actually resolve this issue until you have a chance to show her by example. I'm going to guess that the day your sister sees that your kid is pretty much like any other is the day she'll understand. Knowing gay people—and, in your case, knowing the children of gay people—seems to be the number one factor when folks who started out homophobic decide to finally accept us.

when it comes to LGBT cases. As same-sex adoptions are becoming more common in the United States and Canada, however, many of these agencies and case workers have become advocates for gay families—they've watched the babies and children they've placed grow up and they like what they've seen. Still, it's important to do your homework and find an LGBT-friendly adoption agency (see Resources, page 381). If you're doing a private adoption, a court-appointed social worker will perform the home study.

Home studies ask for a huge amount of information to be turned over, starting with your birth certificate, proof of any marriages or divorce, and documentation about your income, investments, and mortgage or lease payments. And that is only the beginning. This is not a time to hedge in any way about what's going on in your family: Be honest about your sexual orientation or gender identity so that the social worker will best be able to describe your family situation in the reports that follow. Soon enough, if all goes well, you will be asked to provide references.

Before the home visit itself, be sure to scrub the bathroom, run the vacuum, and take care of any known safety hazards. During these visits (often there may be several), offer refreshments and comfortable seating. Be yourself and as relaxed as you can be under the circumstances.

THE ESSENTIALS

The Struggle for LGBT Adoptions

In the United States, individual states generally have the right to limit adoption because of one's sexual orientation or marital status. Historically, Utah, Arkansas, and Florida have had the most injurious restrictions when it came to LGBT adoption. For example, Utah doesn't allow adoptions by individuals not in a "legally valid and binding marriage," although single gay people may adopt as long as they're not in a gay relationship. Similarly, in 2008 Arkansas voters approved Act 1, which banned anyone "co-habitating outside of a valid marriage" from being foster parents or adopting children; this statute was overturned in 2010, however, paving the way for LGBT couples to both adopt and foster.

For more than three decades, adoption by lesbians and gay men in Florida was prohibited by state law; in 2008 the state's supreme court struck down that statute with an opinion stating that the law violated equal protection rights for the children and their prospective gay parents. The ruling added that no rational basis existed to prohibit gay parents from adopting, especially since the state allowed them to act as foster parents. Late in 2010, the ruling was upheld, and then-Governor Charlie Crist announced that the state would no longer enforce the ban on LGBT adoptions.

In Canada, adoption by same-sex couples is legal in every province and in the Northwest Territories.

Asking for References

At some point in the adoption process, you'll need to provide letters of recommendation from friends and neighbors (not relatives) to help establish your suitability as a parent. From time to time, this effort can unearth some negative comments that you didn't expect, like those from the "nice" couple next door who may be happy to chat with you about *their* kids but don't approve of LGBT parenting. It's a good idea to make sure you know prospective references' views on gay adoption before you ask for a letter of recommendation; this can be done either be asking directly or in a more general way by discussing the legal and procedural challenges gay people have in adopting—and gauging their reaction.

When you do ask, be sure to give the person some time to think about it; if there's any reason this person doesn't feel comfortable writing you a reference you don't want him or her to do so anyway. Here's one way to go about it: "I (or we) would like to ask you a personal favor—I'm considering adoption, and the home study requires references from people who know me on a day-to-day basis. Would you mind thinking about writing such a letter? You can let me know next week if you can to do it."

Letters should be in the author's own words, but a social worker can provide a list of questions and topics to cover, such as:

- How long has the person known you, and in what capacity?
- Do they consider you a friendly and stable person?
- Have they seen you with other people's children?
- Do they think you have good judgment, especially in handling challenging situations?
- Do they think you will make a good parent?

A prompt thank-you note to anyone who writes a letter of reference is a nice touch.

THE ESSENTIALS

A Sample Reference Letter

It's actually quite helpful to provide a template, such as this one, to those whom you're asking to write on your behalf. Let them know it is simply meant to help them organize their thoughts and that they can and should personalize it to your situation.

To Whom It May Concern,

I am writing to express my unequivocal support of _____ and _____ as prospective adoptive parents.

I came to know this couple because their five-year-old son, _____, was in my own son's preschool class and the two became fast friends. Subsequently, the _____ became close with my husband and me, and we all spend a good deal of time together socially.

I have witnessed firsthand the loving attention they show toward their son. They have provided him with many opportunities for self-discovery by way of music classes, gymnastics, and other organized activities. But even more important, _____ and _____ are truly hands-on parents. It is such a joy to see _____ crawling around the yard on his hands and knees growling like a dinosaur, just because he loves seeing _____ laugh. And not only is _____ great with his son; he is one of the most compassionate people I have ever met. When I or someone else in our playgroup is in a pinch, he is the first to step in and offer to drive, visit a sick friend, and so on.

Together, this couple is just amazing. Of course, they have occasional disagreements like any normal couple, but they are truly best friends. They treat each other with mutual respect and have created a stable, secure home for _____.

_____ would be so excited to welcome a new baby brother or sister into this loving household. It is my strong desire that _____ and _____ be able to expand their family through adoption.

Sincerely,

Auditioning for the Birth Mother

In most agency adoptions, you'll be asked to prepare a dossier about your background life to present to the agency or, in an open adoption, to a birth mother, which includes a letter.

Most birth mothers review a stack of applications, then narrow their list to a few to interview personally.

Many LGBT parents confess to being terrified of writing the "Dear Birth Mother" letter, worried that they'll be rejected immediately on the basis of sexual orientation alone. The truth is that a whole range of facts and even personality quirks come into play in a birth mother's decision to go with a particular couple or individual. Also, don't discount the possibility that the birth mother may actually be *looking* for a gay couple.

If you're selected for a personal interview, that probably means you're one of three or four candidates in the running. When you do meet, greet the woman respectfully and acknowledge your gratitude for having been chosen for a face-to-face discussion. You'll cover many topics at this first meeting, and while you're not the one doing the interviewing—she is—consider working these questions into the conversation:

- How does she feel about contracting with LGBT people as the prospective parents?
- Does she have LGBT friends or family members?
- Is her family supportive of her plans, and are they gay-friendly?
- What kind of relationship does she envision having with the child and with you over the years?

When it comes to the birth mother's questions, answer them directly and honestly. The goal is to find the right fit—so being open and making a connection are paramount.

THE ESSENTIALS

What Goes into a "Dear Birth Mother" Letter

The general idea of these letters is to let your charm, integrity, and reliability shine through, while making it as clear as possible what kind of life you're offering this child. Be open about being LGBT, but also show evidence of your love for children as well as your commitment to raising a happy, safe, supported youngster.

Two prospective gay dads who posted their "Dear Birth Parents" letter started this way: "We are intellectuals (but not nerds!) and so we tend to prefer quiet, bonding activities rather than sports and athletics." But they also promised, "We are a loving couple who can offer a child a welcoming home with all of the opportunities a child needs."

A few more tips for your letter:

- Even though everybody in the industry calls it the "Dear Birth Mother" letter, don't do so when addressing your prospective birth mother. That's considered presumptuous because you haven't yet been selected. Use "Dear Friend" instead.
- Describe yourself—and your partner or children if you have either—and do your best to explain what's important to you and how you like to spend your time, perhaps by describing a typical Saturday.
- Talk about where you live—what kind of community, neighbors, and friends you have in the "village" that will be raising your child; describe your family and your relationships with them.
- Sketch out your thoughts about what kind of contact, if any, you see your future adopted child having with the birth mom. And be clear whether this is firm or open to discussion.

- Speak simply and from the heart—be clear, and don't write more than a couple of pages.

You've Been Chosen!

Congratulations! A birth mother has selected you as the parents for her baby—or by some other means, an agency has matched you with an older child. When you get the call, this news is tremendously exciting—although it's natural to be a little nervous-making as well.

The next step is to continue working out the details of your relationship—contractual and otherwise. Keep in mind that this isn't just about you, your partner, and the birth parent(s); this is about the child you're going to raise. Your child will have questions about his or her origins, so be sure to keep that in mind as you figure out your relationship.

If you're adopting a newborn, you'll likely have months to negotiate the rules of the road before the actual birth takes place. Initiate a discussion about how much involvement and support the birth mother expects you to provide (and be sure your attorney covers the legal points of your arrangement); you should also be direct about your expectations and hopes as well—but remember, she's calling the shots.

One final note: Talk with the birth mother in advance about what will happen on the day the baby is born: Who will be present at the birth, how much time (if any) will she spend with the baby, and how will the hand-off play out? Be prepared for some bumps along the way, and remember that this is still her baby until she relinquishes the child to you.

STRAIGHT TALK

"My lesbian cousin is adopting a little girl from Russia without telling the agency that she's gay. Is that unethical?"

As you may or may not know, the fact that your cousin is a lesbian prohibits her from adopting from many countries overseas. In my book, that's unethical. The good news is that most countries (including Russia) don't question a prospective parent's sexual orientation when it comes to adopting, which means as long as your cousin provided all the required information and did not file any false documents, there is no ethical issue.

READY OR NOT

No matter how you're creating your family, the time will come to reach out beyond your immediate circle and tell others that you're expecting a child. Whatever the joys for you of these exciting months, be careful about reaching out to potentially unsupportive family members, friends, and colleagues—people to whom your baby-making may seem like a violation of God's will, a science experiment, or a reason to fire you from your job. By contrast, make a big fuss and celebrate extra with those who are completely behind you.

Then, as the time comes for your child's arrival, make sure you're completely ready (or as ready as possible), whether that means determining who will be in the delivery room—often with a larger cast of players to

"Who's your baby's daddy?"

Q Being a pregnant lesbian wasn't really an issue for anyone but my family and friends until the past couple of weeks, when I started showing! But imagine my surprise—and outrage—when a coworker patted my belly and then asked me a number of questions about the father (she knew I was single), notably, "Who is he?" What should I have said?

A Pregnant women have long borne various invasions of their privacy. Alas, neither you nor I am about to change any of that, even though it *is* inappropriate behavior. But what happened to you is also the result of a naive assumption that all pregnant women are straight, which I'm guessing is what upset you most. As for what to do, even though you can't change people's preconceived notions overnight, you can be better prepared for this question the next time. In fact, there's nothing wrong with saying "I'm sorry, that's my business," or joking "Are you saying I'm fat?" If you want, try a more genuine explanation, such as "I used a sperm bank and, by the way, I'm a lesbian." I would bet that your colleague would think twice before asking another pregnant woman the same question. And you would have done your duty for the day in coming out to her.

---

choose from than in a straight birth—or planning for that first eye-to-eye meeting with an older child you're adopting.

Letting Others Know

Some prospective parents start blogging about their quest from day one, never omitting a single detail of the journey, while others hold their cards closer to their chests. These more circumspect types may fear that the adoption process could fall apart at any time (and it could), leaving them babyless after such fanfare, or they worry about having to explain to others that a birth mother or surrogate mom changed her mind at the last minute, reliving the anguish publicly.

For those who come out early with their news, e-mail is a great way to keep friends and family up-to-date. "As we started the process with our adoption agency, we sent e-mails to our families letting them know what we were doing and sent them updates along the way," reports one gay dad. Other LGBT couples create their own websites, posting regular updates and photos, too. Being in touch like this can bring home the excitement to friends and family members.

Not surprisingly, the situation is quite different if one of you is actually carrying a child. Most pregnant women—or men hiring a surrogate—wait until the beginning of the second trimester before making their news official because of the higher incidence of miscarriages early on. Still, you might want to tell a few close friends that you're expecting—if so, ask them to keep it to themselves until you let them know otherwise.

Miscarriage and Stillbirths

If you've told friends or family members that you're expecting (however you're expecting) and a miscarriage takes place, you'll want to let them know what's happened. It can be as simple as a phone call or a brief e-mail. If you're in the mood for visitors, let them know that—and if you're not, explain that you'd like some time to mourn and heal. As noted above, more miscarriages occur in the first trimester, which is why some keep the news of a pregnancy quiet until the beginning of the second trimester.

When you lose a child at birth, there really are no words of comfort that can ease the pain.

Talk with those friends and family members on a need-to-know basis and give them permission (or not) to keep others informed.

When a friend tells you that she's miscarried or lost a baby during childbirth (or that a surrogate has), acknowledge the loss by sending a card expressing your sadness. Don't let your discomfort with the loss tie your hands, literally or metaphorically. One blogger posted: "It is good to send the card. It is thoughtful. Let them know you are sorry for their loss. If you are comfortable with it, let them know you are available if they want to talk about it. Some people do and some don't. You can try calling and see what kind of reaction you get." A woman who miscarried late in her pregnancy was appalled and hurt that her friends ignored what had happened: "The silence was deafening, and it did not make it easier for me to mourn my loss."

QUEERY

"Breaking the good news at work"

Q **If I were pregnant, it would be one thing, but when and how do I tell people at work that we're expecting, since it's my girlfriend who's pregnant and I obviously don't appear at all with child?**

A If you need a role model for this exercise, put yourself in the shoes of one of your straight male colleagues. What would he do if his wife were pregnant? He'd be elated and go around the office hugging and backslapping his (male) colleagues until everyone knew. Okay, so maybe that's a bit 1960s, but he'd certainly be spreading the joy. Before you do the same, however, remember that in some jurisdictions LGBT people don't have the same workplace protections and can be fired for simply being gay. Assuming you think your job is secure, start by sharing your happiness with colleagues you're closest to. Keep it simple: "By the way, Shelley is pregnant and we're expecting in June" pretty much lays out all the information folks need to know. (As you may have noticed, this phrase also serves as your coming-out announcement to colleagues who don't know.) Maybe you'll want to skip all the *Mad Men* male bravado, but there's still no harm in stocking up on cigars.

If you do reach out, you'll want to stay away from some common clichés that only seem to rub more salt in the wound; these include comments like "It just wasn't meant to be," "At least he didn't suffer," "I know exactly how you feel," or "You're young; you can always have another baby."

STRAIGHT TALK

"I was never very accepting of my daughter's sexuality, but now that she's almost due I'd like to end our estrangement. How can I do that?"

Since it sounds like your differences had to do with her being gay, the first step is to let your daughter know that you're ready to move beyond your prejudices, to stop judging her, and to be 100% supportive of her decision to be a lesbian mom.

Sometimes actions are as good a place to start as any. Offer to take your daughter shopping for maternity or baby clothes. Ask her whether she'd like help setting up a nursery or throwing a baby shower. See if she'd like you to cook dinner once or twice a week. Follow up your actions with words, apologizing for your past judgments and sharing your hopes for a future relationship. Understand, though, that it may take your daughter some time to come around— although often the smile of a newborn is often enough to cement things all on its own.

Telling Family

Keep your expectations in check when telling family members your news. While they may have long accepted—or embraced—your sexual orientation and even welcomed a partner into the family, that doesn't always guarantee a warm response to the prospect of your parenting. Adding a new member to the clan affects everyone in it—and it outs them, too, in a way. Your mother may not have told all her friends, neighbors, and extended family members anything about you and your life, for instance, and if she suddenly has to announce a new grandchild to her circle of friends, she can no longer maintain the fiction that you're living with your BFF.

In fact, some people officially come out to their family only when they're about to become parents themselves. "We'd been living together for eight years," says a lesbian named Anne, "took all our vacations together, even visited each other's families at holidays together." But Anne's partner wasn't out to her family. "They surely must have known, yet nobody ever mentioned it, and she was content to leave it that way. But when we decided to adopt a child, she ended up having to come out as gay *and* announce our plans at the same time."

THE ESSENTIALS

Parenting Leave for Gays and Lesbians

Under the Family Medical Leave Act (FMLA), eligible employees are permitted to take up to 12 weeks of unpaid leave during any 12-month period for 1) the birth or placement of a son or daughter, 2) to bond with a newborn or newly placed child, or 3) to care for a child with a serious health condition. The 1993 FMLA has always been clear about covering children who are biological, adopted, foster, or in step-families. Until 2010, however, there was confusion as to whether the law applied to same-sex parents, specifically those who might not have a legal or biological relationship to the child. In a recent ruling, the Department of Labor clarified that the FMLA *does* include employees who seek time off to care for a child they are involved in parenting *regardless* of their legal or biological relationship to the child. Many LGBT advocates considered this administrative ruling to be a significant win for same-sex parents who, as the Department of Labor asserted, "often in the past have been denied leave to care for their loved ones."

Canada, like most other industrialized nations, offers employees of all sexual orientations *paid* maternity or parental leave. In Canada, it's 17 weeks, with payments coming out of a national fund that employees pay into, much like unemployment insurance in the United States.

Labor Day Etiquette

LGBT parenting often involves extra adults and unique combinations of rights, responsibilities, and emotional attachments. Deciding who gets to be there for a birth, for instance, can kick up all sorts of questions—as well as insecurities and resentments. One expectant mom reports, "My partner and I are excited about the upcoming birth of our child, but we can't figure out who gets to do what that day! My mother *and* her mother want to be in the labor and delivery rooms with us, and so does our sperm donor. How do we keep things manageable without hurting any feelings?"

The key is working all this out ahead of time—and deferring to the wishes of the birth mom. While a child's official parents have all the rights postdelivery, birth mothers who are giving up a child for adoption and surrogates are entitled to privacy and whatever sort of birthing experience they choose. A crowd hovering in the delivery room may even seem like harassment to some.

Whatever you decide beforehand, keep in mind that the experience of labor itself can change a woman's mind on just about anything. If you're the one who is pregnant (or her partner), don't hesitate for a moment to adjust your bedside rules midstream.

Meeting Your Child

For a parent who is adopting, there may be no greater joy than greeting your son or daughter for the first time. No matter what kind of adoption you undertook, it will have been a long and expensive journey, colored by angst and ecstasy, frustration, and anticipation.

Manners are not likely to be anywhere on your list of priorities when that day finally comes, whether you're meeting your baby in the hospital nursery, or catching your first sight of your older child sitting in a chair with a social worker at an adoption agency. But there is, in fact, a right thing to do in a situation such as this: Simply be very grateful to the birth mother, the social workers, your references, your partner, and anyone else who helped you reach this day.

If you're meeting an older child, leave the adoption talk to the adults for now. There's also no need to discuss your sexual orientation or gender identity—unless that has already come up as an issue and the agency or social worker thinks you need to discuss it directly with the child. Nor is this a time to make promises to the child; an adoption is never final until a judge has signed off on it. Talk to the child about the present, not the past or the future. For example, if you know she likes to read, ask about her favorite books. If it's sports, what does she play? Study ahead of time so that you will know more about the interests of the child and bring along games, age-appropriate clothes, and some food and drink that may be appealing. Your job that day is to connect, as best you can, and to do your best to make the child feel comfortable and secure.

CHAPTER 8

LGBT Parenting

How We Raise Our Kids

For more than thirty years, Florida banned adoptions by lesbians and gay men because it considered us "unfit;" only in 2010 did we become eligible to adopt in the Sunshine State. In Alabama, not so many years ago, the State Supreme Court unanimously ruled against a lesbian mother of three in a custody case on the grounds that "homosexuality [is] an inherent evil" rendering her, as the court said, "unfit." Fortunately, the situation isn't quite so dire in all states: Most permit LGBT *singles* to adopt, although the rules for gay couples and second-party adoption vary widely. By contrast, same-sex couples in Canada are free to adopt in all provinces and the Northwest Territories.

Despite obstacles, millions of LGBT people have become parents in recent decades. Most of these mothers and fathers know what a long litany of legitimate studies, reports, and articles emphatically conclude: Their children differ in no way from children raised by others, period. Every major professional medical association is also in agreement—from the American Psychological Association to the Child Welfare League of America. In fact, the U.S. National Longitudinal Lesbian Study reports that same-sex parents are in fact better parents.

Still, the fact that you are LGBT will affect every aspect of your child's life, whether you're a single parent or raising a child with your partner. From the time your little one begins making friends in the neighborhood to the day that you suggest ways for your daughter to fight off anti-gay teasing and bullying from her peers, you're not just solving problems, you're teaching tolerance and, most important, respect—and self-respect.

Indeed, this is the highest calling for good parenting etiquette: communicating the manners and mores you live by to the next generation.

First Celebrations

The first ceremonies honoring a child's life are joyous affairs in LGBT families, not only because they're intended to celebrate the arrival of your son or daughter but also because they affirm the importance of your family and community. Remember (as though you could forget), it's usually been an extra challenge to get to that point.

As in straight families, friends and relatives of LGBT parents often gather for a baby shower or naming ceremony to show their commitment and support; but there's often an added poignancy to these ceremonies, with two moms celebrating the bris of their son or two dads being honored at a shower as they wait for an adoption to become finalized. Much of this etiquette is quite new for LGBT parents and their gay friends, many of whom have not participated in the straight version of these rites. While these first ceremonies often stand on heterosexual tradition, lesbians and gay men have found ways to tweak and reinvent them to suit two moms or two dads or whatever configuration your child will eventually call "family."

Baby Showers

New baby on the way? Time to party! (And get gifts!) It's true that receiving presents is one of the main reasons for having baby showers. New parents need lots of stuff, and the gesture of helping supply the requisite soft blankets and snuggly onesies amounts to a welcome to the child and congratulations to his or her parent or parents. Traditionally, baby showers were a celebration of the expectant mother herself, but times have changed and now many celebrate both prospective moms and dads, which is also a fine model for a lesbian or gay baby shower.

Back in the day, tradition also called for a friend, in-law, coworker, or cousin to host the shower; no one in the mother-to-be's immediate family could do so because it was considered tacky. The rules are a lot less stodgy now, and pretty much anyone (except the expectant parents) can host these days—that is, send out the invitations, plan the food, and cover the costs. Here are some shower basics:

- **Timing:** Parties usually take place four to six weeks before the baby's due date. Because it's not always possible to know with certainty when an adoption will be finalized, in those cases, consider having the shower after the child is safely home (see also "Adoption Showers," below).
- **Invitations:** These generally go in the mail three to six weeks ahead of the shower date. If you're sending electronic invitations, which are perfectly acceptable, e-mail them at the same time. For surprise showers and last-minute ones, a phone invitation is fine, too. If you're throwing a shower for an LGBT couple, make sure that the invitation mentions both mothers or fathers (when there are two).

Example of a more casual shower invitation (and for a single parent)

Example of a more formal shower invitation

- **Guests:** Hosts should check with the expectant moms or dads about whom to invite, but LGBT tradition is to invite both male and female friends, gay and straight. Showers are meant to be intimate, with friends and family mingling and talking together, so don't let the guest list get too long. If you're hosting for a friend and feeling guilty about limiting the number of guests, remember that the mom-to-be's coworkers or the dad-to-be's fellow volunteers at the soup kitchen may be planning their own showers (or suggest just that).
- **Gift registries:** If the prospective parents have signed up for a gift registry, it's a smart idea to mention it in the invitation. (To be even more helpful to your guests in their gift selection, note the gender of the expected child—when known—with a line like "It's a girl!")

Adoption Showers

Timing an adoption shower can be tricky: You want to be sure the adoption is close, but you don't want to wait so long that the moms or dads have already bought all the gear they need. And then sometimes, especially in overseas adoptions, the adoption process can drag on and on and—*suddenly*—the parents receive an e-mail, finding themselves on a plane the very next afternoon. Be sure to check in with the parents-to-be for their guidance on dates.

For some parents, having the little tyke home by the time of the shower is a distinct advantage because you'll know the child's size (helpful for gifts) and he or she can be part of the festivities. There are other reasons: "I didn't want to have a shower before we had a baby because it just felt like tempting fate," said one

"Must I invite my surrogate to the baby shower?"

Q Even though we've previously decided that we won't have an ongoing relationship with our surrogate mother, I'm feeling uncomfortable not having invited her to our child's baby shower. She's done so much for us, and I don't want to hurt her feelings. Should we just go ahead and add her name to the list?

A No, I wouldn't suggest you do that. Including her in this family situation will send a mixed message—is she part of the family after all?—and likely be confusing to her and your guests. Remember, there were reasons you decided to keep your worlds apart, as much for her benefit as yours.

Not surprisingly, for this reason among others, a surrogate may be thrown a shower by her own friends and families, which is a nice way to honor both her and the pregnancy. If that's the case, be sure to send a nice gift (but not a baby gift) and your well wishes.

adoptive gay dad. And your friends and family can meet the new arrival, too, which is why they're often referred to as "Baby as Special Guest" showers.

If the child will be at home by the date of the shower, word the invitation accordingly.

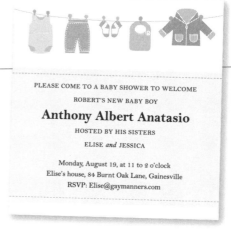

PLEASE COME TO A BABY SHOWER TO WELCOME
ROBERT'S NEW BABY BOY
Anthony Albert Anatasio
HOSTED BY HIS SISTERS
ELISE *and* JESSICA

Monday, August 19, at 11 to 2 o'clock
Elise's house, 84 Burnt Oak Lane, Gainesville
RSVP: Elise@gaymanners.com

Example of a less formal shower invitation

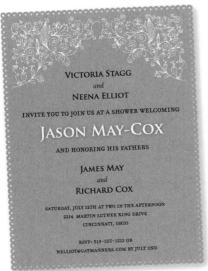

Example of a formal shower invitation

VICTORIA STAGG
and
NEENA ELLIOT
INVITE YOU TO JOIN US AT A SHOWER WELCOMING
JASON MAY-COX
AND HONORING HIS FATHERS
JAMES MAY
and
RICHARD COX
SATURDAY, JULY 12TH AT TWO IN THE AFTERNOON
2214 MARTIN LUTHER KING DRIVE
CINCINNATI, OHIO
RSVP: 513-555-1212 OR
NELLIOT@GAYMANNERS.COM BY JULY 2ND

Shower Gifts and Games

As mentioned previously, registries are especially suited to baby gifts because the parents-to-be are likely to have a list of items they need for their little one.

If you do set up a registry, be sure to choose plenty of low- to medium-cost items, alongside the higher-ticket ones like a car seat or a cashmere baby blanket. Guests should also feel free to go off the list—or just opt for plain old cute—if they are so inspired. (I recently gave some friends an adorable onesie for their baby girl, which said on the front: SAVE THE DATE FOR MY BAT MITZVAH. JUNE 2023.) Or gift givers can get creative by putting together the beginnings of a photo album or scrapbook. (Note to relatives and close friends: If you think of it, wrap up a little gift for any small brothers or sisters who may be prone to early-onset sibling rivalry.)

Shower games are a traditional—and famously embarrassing—way to entertain party guests between all the unwrapping of gifts, socializing, and eating. It's a good idea for the party's host to check in with the expectant parents about what sounds fun and appropriate for their crowd. Definitely plan any games out a little ahead of time, as you'll need to pick up a few things to make it a success. Here are four classic favorites—easily tweaked to suit an LGBT group:

• Put out white onesies and some paint for your guests to decorate them or have them write gay parenting slogans such as "I was hatched by two chicks."
• Provide colorful cards and invite guests to write messages to the baby to be included in the Baby Notebook that may already be in the works with details from the pregnancy, surrogacy, or adoption.
• Have a faux diapering contest between the two prospective moms or dads. The parent who finishes second has to do the diapering for the first year. Okay, not really. But it can be fun to watch two novices race the clock.
• Play *Baby Jeopardy!* between the expectant parents, with questions like: "For $200: Pertussis is the clinical name for this common childhood condition." [Answer: What is whooping cough?] Or "For $1,000: The baby bible *What to Expect When You're Expecting* has been translated into this number of languages." [Answer: What is thirty?]

Favorite Baby Shower Gifts

You've been invited to a baby shower and need to buy a gift. Go ahead and recombine a set of Mommy Loves Me/Daddy Loves Me bibs into same-sex versions if you like. But don't forget gay parents need a lot of the same goodies that all new moms and dads do. In case you haven't been to many baby showers or you simply can't bear the predictability of shopping from the registry, here are some can't-miss baby gifts:

• Picture frames and photo albums
• Adorable outfits in a range of infant sizes
• Soft, cuddly blankets
• Keepsake editions of beloved children's books
• A small rocking horse or rocking chair
• A growth chart
• Piggy bank, complete with lucky coin
• Terry cloth stuffed animal
• Almost anything personalized with the child's name—wall hangings, treasure boxes, and even step stools are sweeter when they come engraved with a name.

Except for personalized items, it's always a good idea to include a gift receipt with your package. The blankie you've selected may be precious, but it could also be the tenth one the new parents receive. So don't take it personally if they swap it for something they need more—like diapers.

QUEERY

"My mother-in-law the monster-in-law"

Q My spouse's mother stopped talking to us as soon as she found out we are adopting a young child. She doesn't think we'd be "good enough parents." With the adoption approaching, some friends are planning a baby shower. Here's the question: Should they invite my monster-in-law?

A In theory, any granny should be invited to her daughter's baby shower even if she's the Creature from the Black Lagoon. But pulling the silent treatment and openly questioning your parenting abilities is a little over the top. My suggestion is that you use the occasion of the baby shower (and of course the child's imminent arrival) to reach out to her by adding her to the invitation list you give your friends. She's obviously not going to get suddenly unhomophobic (though don't rule that out for later), but she may be more open to having contact now than you think. Kids are capable of melting even a monster's heart. And who knows: Your mother-in-law also may be a teensy bit embarrassed by her behavior and too ashamed to speak up without prompting, so this could be the perfect opportunity to mend fences.

A NOTE TO PROSPECTIVE PARENTS

In case you're wondering, yes, you need to send out thank-yous for any gifts received at a baby shower. Make sure someone at the event itself keeps a list of all presents received (matched with the gift giver) so that you can either write or e-mail a thank-you specifically mentioning the gift received. It's wise to send these notes as soon as you can—before parenting duties overwhelm you.

And don't forget to thank your shower hosts—either with a note or a small gift.

Naming Ceremonies, Baptisms & Brith Milah

"When I went to my baby nephew's naming ceremony at the LGBT synagogue in New York, my jaw dropped when I saw the love and support from this community," a straight aunt explains. In fact, LGBT parents use naming ceremonies (and other rites of passage) as a way to invite a community of friends and neighbors to affirm their family by welcoming their child. Sometimes these ceremonies have another symbolic meaning inherent in them: That is when a nonlegal parent takes on responsibility for her partner's child in front of their community. While there's nothing inherently legal about these ceremonies, there are plenty of rules to lean on if it's a religious ceremony.

If you're a godparent at a christening, your responsibilities include saying a few words at the ceremony itself and gifting your godchild (both then and on future occasions). You'll also be asked to take a lifelong, special interest in the spiritual development of the child; while an honor, this is not a role to take on lightly.

Meanwhile, some Jews have godparents; others don't. This depends on the family and on the bris. It's not unheard of for the godparents (also referred to as guardians) to carry the baby (literally) to the circumcision table or, if at a naming ceremony, to play a starring role. No matter, always be sure to talk with the parents and clergy beforehand to understand any specific expectations or additional duties.

Naming ceremonies are more and more common now at LGBT religious institutions such as the Metropolitan Community Church, DignityUSA (Catholic), the Gay Buddhist Fellowship, Integrity USA (Episcopal), and the World Congress of Gay, Lesbian, Bisexual Jewish Organizations. But they also take place in a traditional religious institution, where rituals and gender roles may not be very flexible.

Nonreligious ceremonies are usually simpler and less weighted by tradition. There may be a reading selected by the parents, and instead of godparents, a sponsor or mentor. Secular Jewish ceremonies often skip the circumcision involved in a traditional bris or have it take place in a hospital and do the naming separately. If contemplating an old guard temple or church, be sure to discuss your sexual orientation ahead of time so that there are no surprises—except those your little one brings to the day!

FOR THE PARENTS

In making your plans as the parents, be sure to ask how you can adapt the traditional ceremony to fit your family, and how godparents or sponsors will be respectfully incorporated into the ceremony if they, too, are LGBT. Even in the most traditional houses of worship, there's usually a concerted effort to help guests from different traditions feel comfortable.

You may be pleased at how little resistance you encounter when trying to plan one of these ceremonies through a place of worship. One lesbian couple experienced some anxiety about approaching their local Catholic church before their daughter's baptism, but were surprised, even amused, by the results. "It was hysterical to find out that they were willing to list both of us as parents on the baptismal certificate," recalls one of the mothers, "but they refused to include the name of the godmother, who is straight but a Mennonite. They could deal with lesbians, but not a Mennonite."

FOR GUESTS

As a guest, if you're not sure what's going on, take a cue from those around you (for instance, cover your head at many Jewish or Muslim services). It's not unusual to be somewhat anxious in attending a ceremony of a different faith than your own—or, if you're straight, being a guest at your first LGBT naming ceremony. No matter which, you'll likely discover that there are only small differences between types of services.

KIDS, TWEENS & TEENS

Raising children when you're LGBT is in many ways identical to doing it in other families. They need to be diapered, fed, taken to school, scolded, praised—and loved. But there's also some invention required in defining your family and everyone's role in it—especially if you're including a surrogate or sperm donor.

When it comes to children and families, other manners books dwell on topics like "getting children off on the right (and mannerly) foot" or "teaching table manners." Here the more pressing issues are: defining our roles (and what we're called), dealing with outsiders' curiosity, and even the occasional insult about your sexual orientation or gender identity, especially in front of—or to—your kids. The right manners will also help make sure your children can deal with such issues themselves, equipping them with the social tools and skills for handling a sometimes hostile world.

The "Other" Mother

Being the mother in a lesbian couple who hasn't actually given birth to your child may make you the lightning rod for questions about the legitimacy of your role in your family—sometimes even in the eyes of other LGBT folks. Dealing with such attitudes in your community, school, or workplace can be a major source of discomfort if not handled directly and consistently by both parents. One especially challenging situation is in-laws who don't think of you as their grandchild's other parent but rather as the girlfriend their daughter happens to live with. "Other" fathers deal with many of the same issues.

While the law may not always consider the "other" mom or dad as a legal guardian, good etiquette doesn't make such distinctions: Blood ties don't make

one of you more of a parent than the other; good and consistent parenting does. If someone asks you who's the "real mother," feel free to reply "We're both her moms," even if that results in a puzzled look. Repeat as necessary, but gently. Some straight people still don't get the idea that Heather can have two mommies, so it falls on us to educate them along the way.

As a parent in a same-sex couple, it's important for both of you to make the effort to be extra-clear by using phrases like *"our* family" or *"our* kids" with friends and strangers alike. Then get going on finalizing a second-parent adoption, if such a legal option exists in your state (see page 232).

What to Call LGBT Family Members

There's a lot of latitude and invention in how you—as gay parents—may ask your children to refer to you, as well as to sperm donors or birth mothers who remain part of an extended family. These forms of address may be confusing to outsiders—straight or gay—who also

"We are family . . ."

may have questions about how to refer to each, or all, of you. The straight aunt of two nephews explained, "It took me a couple of years to learn the distinction those young boys seemed to know instinctively—that one mother was 'Mama' and the other 'Mommy.' I always got confused and was never sure who they were referring to."

YOUR KIDS' NAMES FOR YOU

Your child may come up with something organically, but there's nothing wrong with making suggestions. A few favorite styles:
• Mom and Mommy
• Daddy and Papa
• Mamma and Mom
• Daddy Mark and Papa Patrice
• Mommy Sue and Mommy Maria

HOW OTHER ADULTS REFER TO YOU AS THE PARENT

For other adults, you are the two mothers/moms or the two fathers/dads, period. You're not *adoptive* mothers or fathers, nor *donor* dads. If anyone calls you the "adoptive mother," take the person aside and explain that that phrase makes you sound like a less-important or less-qualified parent. (By the way, the same holds true for straight couples who may have adopted; you're both the "parents.") The only time it may be helpful to qualify your parenting status is if there's a question about the "birth mother."

YOUR CHILD'S SURROGATE, EGG OR SPERM DONOR, OR BIRTH MOTHER

In most circumstances, a very basic "This is our friend Amelia Sanchez" will do. If someone asks how you know each other, reveal only as much as you, the person, and your child want shared. "David helped us start our family" or "Amelia carried Max for us for nine months" are both quite clear. (For more about your kids meeting a surrogate, donor, or birth mother, please see page 234.)

THE ESSENTIALS

Protecting Your Child's Future

Until same-sex marriage and gay adoption are available nationwide, most LGBT parents in the United States would be wise to protect their rights and clarify their wishes through other more sanctified legal agreements. The following four documents are the key ones to inquire about (they're available on websites such as Rainbow Law) and discuss with an LGBT lawyer or with groups such as the National Center for Lesbian Rights (NCLR). Also look into executing property or domestic partnership agreements if such protective mechanisms are available where you live.

It's worth noting that because same-sex marriage and gay adoptions are legal in Canada, there is no such list of recommended documents for LGBT parents to sign.

Regardless of which side of the border you live on, executing a will and power of attorney are considered key documents for all parents.

1. **Parenting (or Donor or Surrogacy) Agreement:** This states your arrangement with a sperm or egg donor or a surrogate. It may not hold up in either a U.S. or Canadian court if contested, but you should document and sign your joint understanding. The idea is to prompt a full discussion of rights and responsibilities between all parties.

2. **Second-Parent Adoption:** In the United States, this type of adoption gives full parental rights to the partner who didn't give birth or the partner whose name wasn't on the initial adoption papers—without taking any rights away from the original parent. In Canada, same-sex couples can adopt together and non-birth parents using a sperm donor or surrogate can put their names on a baby's birth certificate, so this issue comes up less often.

3. **Power of Attorney:** Especially in states where gay people can't marry or adopt, it's wise for the blood-related parent to officially designate the other parent as qualified to make medical and educational decisions for minor children in case the first parent is incapacitated. (One should also execute and sign a health care proxy, which specifies who makes decisions about your own care in such a situation, as well as a living will, which lists specific directives about medical interventions.)

4. **Last Will and Testament:** This document is important to *any* LGBT person who owns property—or even has a bank account—and wants to make sure her partner is the legal beneficiary and not her parents or siblings. In the context of gay parenting, it's an absolutely critical tool for lesbian and gay parents who aren't able to secure a second-party adoption; what happens is that the legal parent designates her partner as the official or legal guardian of the child. **Note:** The blood relatives of the legal parent could, upon your death, still contest such a custody arrangement because of their genetic link to the child. That's why it's wise to contact an attorney well-versed in gay family law.

STRAIGHT TALK

"I'm confused: How do I refer to the two dads down the street when I meet them and when I talk about them?"

Well, when you speak to them, why don't you just call them by their names? If you haven't been introduced yet, go ahead and do so. As for how you refer to them in absentia, I imagine you're a bit tongue-tied because of the novelty of the situation to you. The etiquette here is actually quite simple. Try this: "I was at the PTA meeting last night, and I was talking to Sam's parents [or Sam's two dads], Mike and Jason." You certainly don't need to get into which of them might be the legal parent, even if you are privy to that knowledge. It's not relevant. Your straight friends might still raise an eyebrow of surprise at the notion of two dads, but they'll catch on quickly. Last point: Please don't talk too much about them behind their backs.

Family Histories

All LGBT parents will want to talk with their child at some point about how their family came to be. Explaining that your child was adopted or born through a surrogate or sperm donor can be a lot for a child to understand, depending on his or her age. While this is not unique to LGBT families—straight parents have been dealing with these conversations for a long time, too—being LGBT adds another layer to the conversation.

One lesbian mom explains: "When our elder son turned twelve, we told him that we had used a sperm donor to get pregnant, and now we're waiting for our nine-year-old to get a little older. But we worry that she'll hear it from her brother or someone else first." That's why most parenting experts recommend starting this conversation early on, in age-appropriate terms, and letting the story evolve as the child grows up. If you handle it this way, it's more likely that the child is hearing his own story directly from you instead of learning partial, inaccurate, or biased details from another relative—or from a kid down the block.

As an example: If you're two white dads with Hispanic sons or a mixed-race couple with a child resembling only one of you, talk about those differences when you start getting questions or think your kid(s) will understand. As with the other LGBT aspects of your life, don't present racial or ethnic issues as a problem; emphasize instead that it's something that makes the child special with a wider cultural background to draw from. These conversations not only help your children to understand their own backgrounds, they also teach them about diversity, tolerance, and acceptance.

A gay man of Indian descent, who recently adopted a black child with his white partner, says they're embracing every aspect of their new multicultural family with much enthusiasm. "It's important for us to feel like our racial differences are something exciting and not something that needs to be explained away," he says.

Being a Family Role Model

Teaching manners to children is an ongoing task, and in LGBT families it's a process that goes way beyond "please" and "thank you," "no eating spaghetti with your hands," and "keep muddy sneakers off the nice, new sofa." Your kids also need to know how to react to nosy questions, rude assumptions, and remarks that are downright hurtful.

This is yet another form of behavior that you can model for them. Take, for instance, showing your children that you have pride in them and your family. For some gay families, this is as simple as both mothers coming to parent-teacher conferences or participating in Take Your Child to Work Day; for others, it may mean marching with PFLAG in your city's Gay Pride parade. As your kids get older, continue to be a role model for them, but also take the time to strike up conversations about homophobia and transphobia in language they will understand.

Coming-of-Age Ceremonies and Tween Birthday Parties

Many of the same rules apply for parents hosting coming-of-age ceremonies as they do for their services for babies or young children. Some parents choose to work within the boundaries of a beloved institution while others find an "alternative" place of worship that's more supportive of an LGBT family than the one they grew up in. There are also ways of making a fuss about an adolescent child's momentous day well outside churches and synagogues. Yet the purpose is always the same: to mark the passage from childhood to adulthood and to affirm a child's community.

There are countless traditions for coming-of-age ceremonies, both religious and secular, but among the most common in North America are the Jewish celebration of bar or bat mitzvah, Catholic and Protestant first communion, and the Latin culture's *quinceañera* or *quince años* celebration. Guests generally bring a gift to any of these—bestowed not at the service but afterward, at a reception.

What you give can be pretty much anything you think the young woman or man will like (more about that below) or else cash, a gift certificate, or a donation to a favorite charity. But sometimes a religious gift is also called for. For instance, for a girl marking her fifteenth birthday with a *quince años* ceremony, it's customary to present a rosary, cross, or Bible. A friend of mine always gives *The Torah: A Modern Commentary,* a sixteen-hundred-page book by W. Gunther Plaut, to anyone celebrating a bar or bat mitzvah.

Deciding what to give at a nonreligious celebration such as a birthday party or sweet sixteen is actually often more challenging. It can be tough to keep up with what's cool for kids at that age. Here are some suggestions on how to select a good gift for a child, whatever the occasion:

- **Ask the child's parents:** Chances are the kid maintains a list of what he or she wants, and the parent would be happy to have you do some of the fulfillment.
- **Ask a clerk:** Big-box stores won't offer much help, but sales reps in small specialty stores have lots of ideas about what's appropriate for different ages. The more you know about a child (she plays sports, for example, or he's a big animal lover), the better suggestions you'll receive.
- **Give cash or a gift card:** Tweens and teens in particular will appreciate being able to choose their own gifts.

Remember, get a gift receipt for whatever you buy. Duplicates happen, and fads can change quickly; what is a must-have today may be quite passé by next month's party.

Children Who Want to Meet Their Sperm Donor

Many LGBT couples specifically choose sperm donors who agree ahead of time to meet their biological offspring when they come of age. These are known as "identity release" sperm donors, and they have made a commitment to be identified when your child reaches eighteen. While it's impossible to know whether your child will want to exercise this option, it's a good one to secure for her just in case.

If your child chooses to exercise this right, she would initiate contact with the donor through the sperm bank. It's smart for you to help your child think through what kind of relationship she envisions—to be realistic and even consider the possibility of being let down. Disappointment can come in many flavors, such as that experienced by the two teenagers in the landmark film *The Kids Are All Right,* who discover that their sperm donor is a real person with real flaws alongside his good qualities. Or, as one lesbian mother explained, "We chose a known sperm donor so that our son could have this option and we always referred to him as 'bio-dad'—like a very distant relative. When our son was ready, we learned from the sperm bank that bio-dad had fathered many other offspring, which really changed our understanding of what that relationship could be."

It's important to note that any contact with a sperm donor is completely at the child's

QUEERY

"White mom, black child"

Q Both my partner and our adopted son are black—and I'm white. How do we let people know the "white lady" is part of the family too? I often feel left out.

A This mistaken-identity situation is pretty much built into your family structure, and not unfamiliar to *all* families under similar circumstances. You may need to accept that people are going to jump to conclusions, so just jump in, explain who you are, and make sure your partner does the same.

For instance, introduce your child by saying, "I'd like you to meet my [or our] son. . . ." When all three of you are out, be the one who pushes the stroller. Or, if your work schedule permits, consider being the parent who picks him up at school. When he greets you as "mama," others will quickly take note of your costarring role in the family.

As your son grows up, you'll need to keep explaining to him that there are lots of variations on how families look. He'll see that within his own extended family, but it's your job as parents to help him understand how wonderful all that is.

---

option; donors are never given the identity of the mother, couple, or child.

WHEN SPERM-DONOR SIBLINGS CONNECT

Having a sperm donor dad with other progeny can be a real boon, especially if your children are open to meeting their half-siblings. In many cases, the children enjoy the process, even making friends. Finding these other kids—through sites such as Donor Sibling Registry—can be exciting for everyone involved, not just because of the likely genetic similarities but because it may mean a broadening of your family. (It may also be helpful in the event your child needs a medical procedure requiring a "match.") It's increasingly doable, with more and more donors signing agreements permitting their offspring to contact them once they reach eighteen.

Still a word of caution: Just like connecting with a sperm donor himself, the experience can

be positive or negative. Here are some suggestions to facilitate the process:

- Making contact is best approached with reasonable expectations including the possibility that the half-siblings don't get along or, worse, that it kicks up family tensions in one household or the other.

- After you (or your kids) have found the necessary contact information, take it slowly. Suggest to your children that they write a letter to a half-sibling to see whether there's interest in meeting. This is often a better option than simply making a phone call or sending a quick e-mail, which gives the recipient little time to think through the vast array of emotions that can arise upon contact from a half-sibling.

- Assuming all parties agree to get together, then it's time to make plans to meet. But note that connecting the children of a sperm donor (or egg donor or surrogate) often brings together very different kinds of families, because of the scattershot way that they find themselves at a particular donor clinic. Sometimes, for instance, this is a straight family's first connection to a gay one—or you may find stark class or racial differences. With any luck, however, your kids may become best friends for life.

STRAIGHT TALK

"I think my kid is gay; can I ask him?"

There are many conversations a parent has to initiate, but this isn't one of them. If your child is gay, you'll have that talk when he or she is ready. However, if you're wondering—and even if you aren't—take whatever opportunities present themselves to make clear that you're open and accepting of all sexual orientations and gender identities.

Believe me when I say this is a great message for all young people to hear. As an example, my mom often invited a gay colleague of hers to dinner when I was a teen—and before I was out. And when I was ready to talk, Dr. Scrivener became a mentor. You could even discuss some of the LGBT characters or actors on TV and make it clear that you support diversity of all kinds.

Asking open-ended questions may be a way to build up to a conversation, but you don't want to pressure your child in any way. Rely on vague questions like "Is there anything that you'd like to discuss with me that we haven't talked about?" or "I see you have some new friends. What are they like?"

Finally, consider attending some PFLAG meetings yourself so that you become more aware of LGBT issues in general, and in particular of how to help your son or daughter should she or he decide to come out to you. I wouldn't tell your child you're doing this, however.

Talking with Your Child About Gender Identity

If your child is way outside so-called gender norms (think haircuts, clothing style, or behavior), try to avoid getting overly agitated about it—especially if your child is not. And slow down. The instinct for many parents is to rush ahead with some strategy, even perhaps advocating a "choice" of which gender the child should now embrace, when simply learning to live with ambiguity can be the best plan. The most helpful role for a parent is usually to help your child see things in a less binary, less male-female way than what he or she has likely picked up from the media and other influences.

Don't ask big, heavy questions that are beyond your child's immediate experience or that suggest there might be some kind of problem, such as "Do you think you're really a boy?" Instead, explore the immediate situation in a supportive way that makes it clear you don't think anything's wrong with your child. If your daughter says, "I want to dress like a boy," for instance, ask "What does dressing like a boy mean to you?" If the answer is "baseball hats," point out that lots of girls wear baseball hats, too, and that girls dress in all different ways.

Your tween or teen may need immediate help dealing with the outside world, and you can be instrumental with that. Try to find the balance between protecting your child from potential harassment and frightening them. Simply acknowledging "People can be weird about these things" or "I know it can be confusing" or "People sometimes say mean things" can be more helpful. And do your best to empower your child to speak up in such situations without being confrontational. Your child might, for instance, respond to another young person's hostile comment by saying, "Well, you may think that, but I don't." If your child is the victim of any sort of name-calling or bullying at school, however, talk to administrators immediately and report incidents to the police if advised. (For more about bullying, see the following section.)

Finally, consider doing some research about the range of gender-inclusiveness programs being instituted in schools around the country now; there are good alternatives to the way that children are so often divided up by gender or addressed as "boys and girls," such as simply saying "kids" or even "girls, boys, both, or neither" in progressive communities. And however you choose to proceed, don't underestimate the power of telling your child "I love you so much" or "You have my unconditional support."

PRIDE & PREJUDICE

Well-intentioned curiosity about your LGBT family is one thing, but bullying and discrimination are quite another. Depending on where you live, having kids in an LGBT family can put all of you more at risk for subtle or overt homo or transphobia, whether from neighbors, at school, or in the course of your own day. These may be difficult moments for both generations and even more so if your family is also dealing with racism or some other form of prejudice. All of these challenges are much more easily handled if you've laid a foundation of pride and done the groundwork for open communication in your family.

Is It Homophobia?

If you're an out family and don't live in a neighborhood where LGBT families are common, you'll likely be the talk of the town, at least at first. And the first time your young child gets turned down for a playdate, you may well wonder if it's because you're gay. Don't jump to the conclusion that any slight is based on homophobia. Sometimes parents just don't click with one another—and in the earliest years it's compatible parents, not compatible kids, who are the social glue.

As you meet new parents, try to get to know them, whether that's doing the daycare drop-off or watching the holiday pageant together. You'll learn more about each other as you interact, and you can also use these conversations to sound out attitudes that may affect the acceptance of your child. At the same time, be open about your relationship and your family and try to gauge the reaction. If you get a bad vibe, back off for now. If all looks promising and you're interested in developing an adult friendship that will spill over to your children, go ahead and invite them over for a family get-together. One of the beauties of having very little ones is that you get to pick their friends. You won't always have that power, so use it now to steer them to gay-friendly pals.

If your child is older and you happen to know a friend's parents are not fully accepting or even openly hostile to LGBT people, don't try to end the friendship between the kids. Instead, use it as an opportunity to talk with your child about these issues. Ask him to tell you about things he may have heard that he doesn't understand or that bother him, especially as they relate to your being LGBT. Don't close the door on the possibility that these neighbors may one day turn their attitudes around—perhaps because they got to know your family.

"My husband and I are Orthodox Jews and to us homosexuality is unnatural. Now, our twelve-year-old son has been invited by his friend to a sleepover, but we don't think that he should go because the parents are lesbians. What do we tell our son? And what do we do about the invitation?"

It must be difficult to tell your son no to an invitation as innocuous as this one. I'd recommend that you think it through a little more. Allowing him to become friends with this other fellow doesn't mean you need to compromise your beliefs or even condone the mothers' relationship. If anything, I'd hope your son will be exposed to all kinds of people and ideas as he grows up—not just those he encountered at home.

If you still decide this isn't right for you, I think you owe your son an explanation. Talk to your son about your religious beliefs, although I hope that you will allow that not

all Jews or members of other faiths feel as you do about homosexuality. As for the invitation, contact the moms promptly, thank them for the invitation, and let them know your son won't be able to make it. No further explanation is necessary. In fact, I'd avoid one.

What's Not So Funny About "That's So Gay"

Using "gay" as a synonym for "lame" or "stupid" has become common among kids all the way from middle school to college and has even inspired a public service campaign, ThinkBe4YouSpeak.com, to draw attention to the problem. "In becoming an ally, you promise not to use homophobic words and phrases—such as 'that's so gay'—and to educate others when you hear them being used," explains comedian Wanda Sykes.

Comments like "that sweater is so gay" actually have nothing to do with sexuality per se, and young people often use such language without even being aware of the implied slur, which is a large part of the problem. Gay kids, kids perceived to be gay, and straight kids with LGBT parents are most susceptible to these kinds of homophobic messages that can create an environment for LGBT bullying and sometimes violence. A recent study by GLSEN (the Gay, Lesbian and Straight Education Network; see page 383) reported that nine out of ten teens who are LGBT said they were verbally harassed in the past year, and almost half said it was because of their sexual orientation.

One lesbian describes how she has stopped teenage nieces and nephews in their tracks several times when they've "slipped" in front of her. "You mean a stupid party?" she'll ask (or sweater, or car, or whatever is "so gay"). "You're using gay to mean *stupid*? Can you just remember please, when you do that, that you're calling *me* stupid?"

WHAT TO DO AS A PARENT OR TEACHER

As a parent or teacher, if you hear anti-LGBT comments from one of your own or from another child, find the time to have a short conversation about how words hurt people. If a parent, take your child aside, making sure not to embarrass him in front of his friends, and discuss the issue. A teacher can use such an episode as a "teachable moment" for the entire class without naming names. Explain that using hateful language, even if it seems humorous to you, encourages anti-gay bullying and harassment. Point out that the chain of violence against

VOX POPULI

If you're a family with same-sex parents, what do you do about a Mother's or Father's Day card project at school?

"There's usually a male or female familial figure nearby who can fill the 'aunt' or 'uncle' role."

"This is more a learning experience for the teacher and classmates as to the realities of life around them. It is an opportunity to graciously acknowledge the potential that everyone's life does not fit the mold often asserted by society."

"Go to the teacher and give her some info from PFLAG and a copy of *Heather Has Two Mommies*."

"Ideally, the school would present Mother's Day as 'This is a day we do special things for important women in our lives, like our moms or grandmothers or babysitters, or any woman who is a special friend.'"

QUEERY

"What does Mother's Day have to do with my family?"

Q **Our son, who has two dads and no mom, came home from school this week and said that his fourth-grade class will spend an hour making Mother's Day cards. He didn't know what to say to the teacher. How can we help him here?**

A This is actually a pretty common scenario, since these days a majority of North American families don't conform to the classic nuclear mold. Some school districts have reacted by modernizing that little ritual (along with the Father's Day version, of course), either by changing its name ("Parent's Day") or simply by telling kids to make a card for any relative.

In your case, I'm not sure it's your son's job to speak to the teacher. If he insists on doing it himself, perhaps suggest he say something like "I don't have a mother but I want to make a card for my dads." Alternatively, contact the teacher yourselves. Explain that your son is uncomfortable with the assignment and suggest some options for doing things differently (if the teacher doesn't take the lead on that). In your particular case, that could be a Father's Day card to you in May and a second card to your partner on Father's Day itself. Or the teacher could make sure that the assignment suits any family situation.

QUEERY

"Kids who tell anti-LGBT jokes"

Q **Our son is now in his teens and has been telling his friends anti-gay jokes (one of their mothers told us). What do we do? Even if we weren't gay ourselves, I would have trouble with that.**

A Do you know any teenage boy who's not a little embarrassed by his parents? He might very well be telling short jokes or "your mama's so fat" jokes, if he didn't have the gay thing as fodder.

But I'm going to guess that your son is a little self-conscious about having gay parents. Consider raising the topic, not in anger or hurt, but as something that has you concerned. You could tell him, "Anti-gay jokes may seem funny at first, but they give people the idea that making fun of or even hating gay people is okay." The idea is not to lecture him, but to get him to talk about his feelings. And you might need to have this conversation more than once.

LGBT teens begins with young people learning from their peers, teachers, and families that it's not acceptable to disrespect and taunt others. If there is a Gay-Straight Alliance, or a similar club in the school, suggest that the offender attend some meetings. These student-led groups specifically work to address anti-LGBT name-calling, bullying, and harassment in their schools. (To find out if your school already has a GSA or to get information on how to start one, register at www.studentorganizing.org.)

STRAIGHT TALK

"I teach fifth grade, and every fall we study genealogy and create what are called 'family trees.' I have a new student this year who has two moms, and I think he's adopted. How do I talk about this topic appropriately in class?"

First of all, kudos to you for being sensitive to this subject. The family tree project can be a tough one for adopted children—actually for anyone whose roots don't match the classic format, whether that means kids with two LGBT parents; single parents of any kind; or grandparents and any other adults serving as their guardians.

There are lots of options for tweaking this lesson, many quite creative. Some nontraditional families draw their family trees as bushes, with a tangle of parents, birth families, and sperm or egg donors. Others approach this as a more traditional exploration of genealogy, showing the lineage of the two moms or two dads, begetting the student. Still others add a second tree trunk for the birth family.

The wisest approach is to discuss the lesson with the child's parents in advance so you can develop a plan as partners. In fact, don't be surprised if the mothers approach you directly about the larger topic of how their sexuality may affect their child at school. No doubt they're worried about potential name-calling or bullying. As for the family tree lesson, this topic has likely come up for them already, so they may have some good ideas on how to handle it smoothly.

Let the parents know that you respect their family structure and want to honor it in a way that instills pride in their child—which is, after all, the whole point of the lesson.

Finally, when it comes time to start the project, do your best to explain to the whole class that families come in all different shapes and sizes, even presenting some varied examples that include gay families and others. And then see where your new student takes the exercise himself, with your guidance if necessary.

Teasing, Bullying, and Harassment

Rising LGBT visibility—of kids and adults both—makes open conflict all too common these days in public settings. It even happens in so-called gayborhoods like Brooklyn's Park Slope, where you'd think kids would be sensitized to this issue. "Our kids still get harassed at school," one lesbian there says. "They hear things like 'Wow, your family's nasty.'"

Meanwhile, social media sites like Facebook and MySpace have created new opportunities for teens to ridicule and torment one another. Well-publicized cases of young people being harassed online, sometimes with tragic consequences, have raised awareness of online bullying. Although it's not a specifically LGBT issue, the Internet has become one more venue for such harassment.

If you're the parent of a child who is being subjected to teasing, bullying, or harassment,

---

QUEERY

"We want to help other kids fight bullying."

Q **It's been so upsetting to us queer kids at my middle school to hear about all the teen suicides lately and the awful bullying going on. One guy I know got punched in the face recently and his Facebook page was smeared with homophobic comments like "faggot." What can we do to help our friends?**

A It's really admirable that you want to reach out to other kids; whenever there's a series of highly visible gay teen suicides (and unfortunately, this happens far too often), lots of people ask that same question. My advice is quite clear: It's everyone's responsibility to help fight public and private expressions of homophobia and transphobia, especially when violence is involved or could be anticipated.

The truth is that you and your friends may already be doing the two most important things: being yourselves and supporting one another. But in the case of your friend, you could help him by suggesting that he talk to his parents or school officials about that assault—and yes, he was *assaulted*. I know that can be hard to do, but you can't stop a bully unless he (or she) is called on it.

That Facebook mess is an example of how "direct" confrontation has its place: Without saying anything threatening or targeting individuals by name, go ahead and post some supportive messages on the guy's page. Please also report the individuals making the hateful comments to Facebook, who will cancel their accounts.

remember that revenge is neither good manners nor acceptable adult behavior. Instead, start by talking about the problem at home. The Park Slope mom went back to her kids and asked, "Do you feel your family's nasty?" You may also want to explain that kids get teased a lot about being gay or trans, or having gay or trans parents—even when neither they nor their parents are. "This isn't really about you," you can tell them. "Other kids get it all the time."

Nevertheless, if a schoolyard incident seems like more than a one-off scuffle, talk to your child's teacher or the principal, as well as other parents about whether the school needs to institute an anti-bullying program (good ones have been put together by GLSEN—see page 383). See whether your state protects school kids under an LGBT anti-bullying statute—federal civil rights statutes may also apply. Also do what you can to make sure your kid has access to kids from other LGBT families—it will help him or her realize there are other children in the same boat. Such friends may give your child valuable advice on how to deal with these kinds of issues—or you may find that your son or daughter is more likely to take the advice from a classmate than from you.

THE ESSENTIALS

Violence Against Our Kids

Eighth-grader Lawrence "Larry" King had it rough. His classmates at E. O. Green Junior High, north of Los Angeles in Ventura County, routinely picked on him. "Hey, you gay kid, you want to wear lipstick?" was a typical taunt, according to one of Larry's friends. Another classmate told the *Los Angeles Times*, "You'd hear, 'Faggot! Hey, faggot!' That was happening in every class." The middle-schooler's friends say that the anti-gay slurs and vitriol only grew worse as the young man began to come out more visibly, wearing makeup and girls' boots with his school uniform. A month after Larry turned fifteen, he came to school at 8:30 A.M. as usual, and as the other students unpacked their lunches and books, a classmate put a gun to the young man's head and fired two fatal shots.

The Human Rights Campaign, the largest LGBT civil rights organization in the United States, explains that "sexual orientation remains the third-highest recorded bias crime in our country, which underscores that anti-gay hate crimes are a very real problem nationwide." Shannon Gilreath, a law professor and author of *Sexual Politics: The Gay Person in America Today*, adds, "Physical violence begins with bullying, name-calling, and homophobic remarks. When nothing happens to someone [for making slurs], it escalates to violence."

If you fear that your child is at risk of being hurt, don't hesitate to contact school authorities immediately. Even when schools don't visibly embrace or support LGBT students, they do not allow violence and should work with you to protect your child. It's often a smart strategy to meet with school administrators as a precautionary measure to establish a relationship—and explain to them what you know about the link between anti-LGBT slurs and violence. Another option is to recommend that the school conduct an anti-prejudice workshop for its entire student body. These workshops, covering issues of racial and ethnic minorities as well as LGBT people, can engender important conversations and even help raise awareness of LGBT and other discriminatory issues that will serve your child and countless others.

"I want to know about any good organizations that work with young people who are struggling with coming out, especially gay teens who are the victims of bullying and other forms of anti-gay harassment. The news continually mentions gay kids committing suicide and it seems as though things just get worse daily, not better. I just can't sit back and watch it anymore. As a parent, what can I—no, what can we—do?"

There are a number of things parents can do to help these kids. To begin with, let your child know that it's okay to be gay, lesbian, bisexual, or transgender (even if he or she isn't). Young people who find acceptance at home enter the world with a much stronger sense of self. Such messages also teach tolerance toward classmates. A mother of two teens wrote, "I sincerely hope that my children and their peers will be tolerant and decent humans as they mature, and will know to stop others from tormenting and abusing anyone for beliefs and actions that may be different from theirs." We all have skin in this game and it's up to each of us to teach our children well—and by example.

When it comes to schools, there are a number of protections we can all advocate for (with thanks to GLSEN—see page 383— whose pointers I've adapted here):

1. Schools should adopt comprehensive anti-bullying policies that include sexual orientation and gender expression as protected categories. Then harassing fellow students for being gay or being "too" masculine or feminine is officially forbidden.

2. Teachers, administrators, and support staff at the school should undergo training, so that they can understand, identify, and address anti-LGBT bullying and harassment.

3. Schools should support student efforts to address these same issues by encouraging the formation of student organizations that provide a safe and supportive environment for all, or by participating in the National Day of Silence, the annual day of action to protest the bullying and harassment of LGBT students and their supporters.

VOX POPULI

If you have a school-age child, what advice are you giving him or her about how to deal with bullies (who threaten them or others)?

"Kick their ass!"

"I would get my kid involved in activities out of school to build his confidence in something that he loves and excels at. I would also speak privately to the principal and teacher and ask them to monitor it better without causing a scene."

"Stand up for yourself. Never give your lunch money away (or whatever)—once you do, it's over."

"Our school has an anti-bullying program and they take it seriously. But I still practice with my second-grader, so that she's got her responses ready. And if it ever does start, that little bully won't know what hit him when this mama bear comes at him!"

4. Schools should provide age-appropriate curricula to help students understand diversity and respect difference in the schools and society as a whole.

As for organizations that can help young people, the aforementioned GLSEN does wonderful work in this field. If you know of any LGBT person at risk of taking his or her own life, immediately contact the Trevor Project, the leading national organization focused on preventing suicide among LGBT youth; their hotline is 866-4-U-TREVOR. The federal government also has resources—notably, an initiative called Stop Bullying Now! that offers movies, games, and information about bullying and how to prevent it.

FAMILY BREAKUPS, LGBT-STYLE

When parents separate, the matter of whether they are gay or straight may be the last thing on anyone's mind. But sometimes a specifically LGBT situation—even the process of coming out—can fuel the split. Putting children into the mix complicates everything. Divorce is generally so hard for kids to go through that, no matter what the cause, it's a time for more communication rather than less in your family. And more handholding. And more loving. If your children now face the drama of a custody battle or getting used to a new stepfamily or some other new configuration of the LGBT parenting puzzle, how you deal with each other—and how you talk with your children—becomes even more crucial.

Talking About Separation/Divorce

If you and your partner have decided to split up, make sure your kids hear it from you first. Ideally they should learn it from both of you at the same time, with the focus being on them, amid repeated clarifications that the separation has nothing to do with them. Your children also need to understand the basics of what's going on between parents, including that your breakup has no connection to your being LGBT (if that's the case).

Time is often the great healer here. Says the lesbian mom of a child who was six when she split with her girlfriend, "It was a constantly evolving conversation for the first couple of months during which time she continued to hope that we might get back together. But after a year or two, when everyone settled into the new routine, those conversations seemed to fade away."

What you say—and continue to say on an ongoing basis—can set the stage for an easier healing process:

- Explain what changes your kids can expect. Will one of you be moving out? Will you have joint custody?
- Reassure them repeatedly of your love for them. Do this individually and collectively.
- Stay open to their questions. While they'll likely have questions right away, don't be at all surprised if they continue to as time goes on. Do your best to answer them—honestly and without blame or rancor.

• Do not overshare or try to make your child an ally against your former partner or spouse.

LGBT Child Custody

With LGBT relationships already on shaky legal ground in the United States, child custody and visitation issues present additional challenges for parents seeking remedies through the courts. Whenever possible, LGBT family-law experts recommend that couples who are parting ways find a solution without involving lawyers or judicial institutions. In the United States, laws vary tremendously from state to state, and these laws are ultimately interpreted by individual judges—any one of whom may be hostile to LGBT families. (With gay marriage legal throughout Canada since 2005, custody disputes between same-sex parents don't stand on such unfirm ground there. But transgender parents often still face discrimination in the courts of both countries, and it's not uncommon for them to lose custody of their children.)

"From the very first day of our breakup, we both agreed to make the children's well-being our top priority," says a lesbian mother who separated from her kids' birth mom a decade ago. "We both vowed never to fight in front of them or ever bad-mouth each other to them. We also agreed to maintain a united front as parents no matter what, which has involved everything from attending parent-teacher meetings together to discussing appropriate punishments when one of the kids was developing behaviors that needed to be addressed."

To her list of commitments, add two more:

• **Make a solid parenting plan that works for each of you—and your kids:** Who will pick them up from school on which days? Who has them on which weeknights? Where will they spend the holidays?
• **Don't use the child as a pawn:** For instance, if only one of you has legal custody, don't deny the other parent visitation rights. This kind of action only serves to hurt your child. If you have any residual anger with your ex, it's best dealt with privately—or with a professional therapist.

New Relationships

After any divorce, straight or LGBT, it's a good idea to be circumspect about introducing a new love interest to your children. If you were previously in a heterosexual marriage or relationship, take the time to come out to your children first. Let them absorb this one piece of news before you formally present a same-sex partner. Then, generally, it's best to wait until you and your new beau agree that your relationship is serious. Once you decide it's time for your new girlfriend to meet your kids, be honest: Don't pretend that she's just a friend or a colleague. Kids have an uncanny way of figuring this out anyway.

Of course, the ages of your children will affect the timing and wording of your introduction. "Mommy's new friend" will do just fine for the preschool set, while you'll need more nuanced language for older kids. One lesbian mom used lingo for her very young children from—of all places—princess stories. "We started using the expression 'my one true love' to mean a spouse of either sex," she says. "They got that the relationship was different than other friendships, that it was extra special, without having to know about the sexual element of it."

Stepfamilies and Blended Ones, Too

Perhaps you've stumbled into an LGBT family—surprise! Lots of gay or trans men and women didn't plan on raising kids until they happened to fall in love with someone who already had them. Welcome to your new stepfamily. Says one such lesbian stepmom, "While I never sought out motherhood, becoming a part of my new family has brought me joys I never would have imagined. And some headaches, too!" Or you may be blending kids and pets to create a whole new family—your very own gay Brady Bunch.

In either case, it can be awkward to become friends and/or a parental figure to a new lover's children. Kids are not always predisposed to accept or love someone they may perceive as being an "outsider" or who may be interfering with their reunion fantasies if their parents split up. LGBT partners are discovering the challenges of creating new families, which straight parents and stepparents have been facing for a long time now. "I am not trying to diminish anyone's role or relationship with the kids," says one lesbian stepmom, who is now one of three moms for two young children. "We all have a place. It takes a village. And I'm part of the village."

Here are some basic considerations for starting off on the right foot with your partner's children:

- **Be clear that you're not replacing their other parent:** As such, you might not even want them to call you "Mom," "Dad," or any near equivalent. Instead, let them call you by your first name—this makes sure there's no implicit confusion.
- **Talk about who makes decisions in your family and who doesn't:** For instance, if your partner expects you to oversee their behavior, does this mean you can also punish the kids when you think it's appropriate? Make sure the children understand the arrangement.
- **Explore their interests:** Find out what they like and engage them—as authentically as possible. Children can sniff out a dishonest (or uninterested) adult right away.
- **Get involved in their lives:** Go to school plays or soccer practices. Help them with their homework. Make time for them. Also, don't forget to include them in your own activities. Invite them to go hiking or biking, to watch a movie, or to help you prepare dinner.
- **Be open with them:** If you feel that they want to talk about your sexuality or gender identity, answer their questions honestly and directly, but keep their age in mind (if you're unsure, ask your partner for guidance on how much to share with any younger kids). Continue to lead your life as an openly LGBT person and they will learn who you are—even countering stereotypes about gay people they may have brought to the table.

PART V

EVERYDAY LIFE

CHAPTER 9

The Art of Connecting

Introductions, Correspondence
& Communications

Imagine these awkward scenarios: that first moment between our partners and parents; completely blanking out on the name of someone you've had sex with; being on a date with a new girlfriend and running into an ex; figuring out who should receive a condolence note when an LGBT friend dies; or determining whether a young person's coming out is worthy of a special card.

Don't panic—send that card, and then read on. Fortunately, Emily Post was correct when she wrote, "Manners are like primary colors; there are certain rules and once you have those you merely mix, i.e., adapt, them to meet changing situations." That's why there *are* guidelines for how best to connect and reconnect with other LGBT people, family members, colleagues—and friends and acquaintances of all kinds. That's why there is practical advice when it comes to utilizing e-mail, texting, chat, or Facebook. And why there are still times when it's respectful and more meaningful to pen a handwritten note or letter. For instance, when expressing thanks, a written note shows appreciation for the original gesture, whether it was a weekend away or the caregiving a good friend may have provided.

In the end, however, it's not the medium that matters most, but the message and your sentiments. Just as it is not always vital to rise from your chair when someone enters a room—as long as you are smiling, and inviting, and make direct eye contact—an e-mail brimming with gratitude is far better than no communication at all.

Making Introductions

One of the main reasons for the popularity of the "missed connections" section of Craigslist is that many of us don't know the basics of making introductions—which means we miss certain opportunities. These skills are crucial for all areas of life, whether professional, collegial, or romantic. Yet, there's no need to pretend that the basics of introductions are rocket science; you'll see here that they're actually pretty straightforward and easy to deploy. And remember to speak clearly when making an introduction and to listen carefully when meeting someone new.

The Order of Introductions

Most manners books carry on with page after page about the hierarchy of introductions and correct forms of address. But most of us don't know whether you introduce our first lady to the Queen of England, or vice versa (nor how to formally address the Chief Justice of the United States). While some may find this impardonable, in daily life it rarely matters if you get the minutia of introductions wrong. Let's forget all those complicated rules, which really boil down to this: *Introduce "inferiors" to "superiors."*

It's as simple as that, whether you're family members, friends, work colleagues, or royalty. In practice, this means you say the name of the older or otherwise more senior person first— for instance, you address your mother and then your new girlfriend: "Mom, I'd like you to meet my girlfriend, Lola Lillien. Lola, this is my mother, Ann Strauss." Similarly, at work: "Mr. Chief, this is Andy Holden, our newest sales associate. Andy, this is Mr. Chief; as you know, he's the CEO." In the case of introducing an ex to your new squeeze, say your new squeeze's name first and present your ex to her. No need to shout out her position in your life; it should be clear enough by your body language even if you are not actually holding her hand or showing some other form of light affection.

WHEN TO STAND UP

When it comes to standing for introductions, we believe in the premise of gender equality. Women stand up for men and vice versa. Nevertheless, it's still appropriate to rise for anyone more "senior" than you—that means a person who is older or whose title or rank is higher than yours.

Common sense comes into play here, too. For instance, if you have a physical disability, a desk in front of you, a plate of food on your lap, a baby in your arms, or some other impediment, it's not necessary to stand—simply do your best to be outgoing and welcoming. Standing is a sign of respect, but so is making eye contact, shaking hands with a certain enthusiasm, and simply offering a warm greeting.

Take Action

If you're at a social function—like a cocktail party, a class reunion, or a benefit—and no one else takes the initiative to introduce you to others or themselves to you, there's no need to be a gay wallflower. Even though this is a challenging situation for most of us (the shyness gene really kicks in), find the chutzpah and make a move yourself. Simply walk over to someone who looks interesting, attractive, or engaging, make quick eye contact, put out your hand, and say "I'm _____. Nice to meet you."

If someone introduces him or herself to you in this way, take the gambit: Give your name in return and ask a question to jumpstart a conversation. What you ask can be as simple as "How do you know the host?"; "What kind of day did you have?"; or, if you're at the same school, "What class are you in?"

One caution: If a group seems very involved in a conversation, don't just barge in. Observe (without staring) and bide your time nearby until you see an opening, a quieter or transitional moment when you can make your move. Or seek out someone else to introduce yourself to.

What Puts You on a First-Name Basis

When deciding whether to use just a first name or your full name, take cues from the social setting you're in. For instance, it might be too formal at a college dance or a summer barbecue to use more than your first name.

Professional situations always call for first and last names, often with some added information like the name of the company you work at and what you do. For instance, I might say, "I'm Steven Petrow—a journalist and book author." Any additional information makes it easier for new acquaintances to fire up a conversation.

Then there's also local custom to follow—in some parts of the country, like the South, it's completely de rigueur to use your full name and even to include maiden names or other middle names. For example, my friend Allan Holderness Davis, from Richmond, Virginia, prefers the perfect troika of all three names. By contrast, out West, where social and professional spheres both tend to be more informal, in a social situation you'll often be fine introducing yourself with just your first name.

Forgetting Someone's Name

When you're introducing yourself, be sure to speak up and take the time to clearly pronounce your name—especially if it's not a very common one. This is an important point because one of the most common problems with introductions is that people so easily forget the names of new acquaintances. To avoid this, it helps to have heard it well pronounced in the first place.

It's all too common today for people when introduced to reply using a diminutive or a nickname as though they hadn't heard how their new acquaintance presents herself. If you're among the many who often have trouble remembering, try this approach: Focus on the name and repeat it back. For instance, immediately after meeting Georgina Sweet, say, "Georgina [or Ms. Sweet], great to meet you." However, the more you worry about forgetting someone's name, the more likely it is that you will forget. If that happens to you, here are some other approaches to get you out of the "no recall" zone:

- **Introduce yourself with your own name right away:** Even when you know you've met previously, declare your name and the other person's more likely to say his in response. "It's great to see you again. It's been a while. I'm Lars." "Lars, ditto. I'm Eddie."
- **Attach a mental picture to a name:** Perhaps the best idea is to look at your new acquaintance while repeating the name in your head. You'll be attaching the name to a visual image. Similarly, create a picture in your mind using the person's name; in the case of Georgina Sweet (above), imagine something sweet, like a Georgia peach, in association with her name.
- **Ask for the name to be spelled out:** This is especially useful if someone has an unusual or complicated name. Simply say, "Would you mind spelling that for me?" Use the additional

time to pay close attention; you might even "type" it out in your head to create another mental picture to attach the name to.

- **Ask a friend to help you:** "What's the name of the guy in the gray suit over there?" This is what friends are for. Reciprocate whenever you can.
- **Stall or just skip it:** Start in with some chitchat and hope that your acquaintance's name will spontaneously reappear in your brain's database. Stalling can also buy you time; if you're lucky, someone else will join the conversation and say to the no-name person: "Hey, Josie, I'm so glad you're here!" Bingo.
- **Fudge what you say:** If you're not 100 percent sure whether you've met someone before, say, "Good to see you" rather than "Nice to meet you." "Good to see you" covers both new introductions and those whom you've met previously. In fact, it's not a bad idea to use "Good to see you" all the time.
- **Admit defeat:** There's no harm in simply coming clean and acknowledging "I'm sorry, I know we've met before, but I don't recall your name." Similarly, if you run into someone whom you've met before and he seems to have forgotten your name, *don't* say, "You don't remember me, do you?" Just introduce yourself again.

Don't Shorten People's Names or Create Nicknames

It's fairly common today for people to use diminutives and nicknames without thinking twice. If someone introduces herself as "Jessica," don't take it upon yourself to then refer to her as "Jessie"—or even "Jess." If you're

Jessica and someone calls you Jess, either live with it, gently say, "I prefer to go by Jessica," or try some light humor: "I've even managed to get my parents to call me Jessica now that I'm a big girl."

"We're straight, in our fifties, and about to have a gay couple stay with us over the holidays. We really don't want to put our foot in it, so to speak, so what's the right way to introduce our gay friends to others?"

Introduce them as you would any other couple. In making introductions, it's not necessary (or appropriate) to make a comment or statement about someone's sexual orientation, as in "and, you know, they're *lesbians!*"—not that you would ever do that!

I can understand, however, that you may want to clarify to others that they're a couple. So if you're not sure how Maria and Robin like to refer to each other, ask them ahead of time, before introducing them to your other friends. Then you'll able to say "These are my friends—Maria Miccozzi and her wife, Robin Stevens."

Introducing Your Partner

What to call your significant other when introductions are being made may be the single most vexing etiquette question there is. Miss Manners punted on this conundrum, referring to it as the "Great Unsolvable Etiquette Problem"—and she was worrying only about heterosexuals. Congressman Barney Frank once argued, "Gay men and lesbians need a term that would do for us what 'Ms.' did for women."

It's not merely a matter of choosing one of the available terms, since different people often use the same word to mean different things. For instance, some say "lover" to mean "sexual playmate," while others use the word to mean "life partner."

Before you're out in the world together, discuss with your "partner" how you'd like to refer to each other: boyfriend/girlfriend? partner? companion? lover? spouse? There's no right or wrong here; it's really about your joint comfort level. Then, assuming you want new friends to understand the nature of your relationship, be clear in your introductions. For instance, "This is my boyfriend, John," or "This is my spouse, Margarita."

Using the word "partner" can be confusing to some and lead to other questions, mainly: "What kind of partner? Do you work together?" Many choose to clarify this by using the phrase "life partner" (as opposed to "business partner"). But in some circles, the term is quickly gaining wide recognition on its own.

By the way, it's not unusual for couples to refer to each other differently depending on whether they're in the LGBT or mainstream world. For instance, some couples choose to use "boyfriend" or "lover" in a gay environment, and "partner" or "friend" in a more mainstream crowd. If you've had a civil union, domestic partnership ceremony, or wedding, consider using the language the law allows, like "husband and husband."

QUEERY

"Meeting Mummy and Daddy dearest"

Q In a few weeks, I'm going to my new lover's parents' place for the first time and I'm not really sure what to call them. What do you suggest?

A This question has puzzled many a heterosexual couple and it's no less challenging for LGBT couples. The best advice is for your partner to ask his folks what they'd like you to call them. Is it Mr. and Mrs.? Sylvia and Samuel? Mom and Dad? Without that information, it's always safest to start out most formally, saying "Dr. Garcia" or "Mrs. Eppel." Depending on the parents' level of formality, they may say "Oh, please call us Sylvia and Samuel," but if they don't say something like that, don't make that leap. Also, remember that relationships mature over time and that your lover's parents may drop the formal affect once they've gotten to know you a little better.

COUPLES WITH DIFFERENT LAST NAMES

If you and your partner have different surnames, be sure to say both when making introductions. For instance, "I'm Louise Hobbes and this is my wife, Michelle Drake." If you share a last name and are a couple, the way you introduce yourselves can help clarify any confusion about your relationship. For instance: "We're the Drakes—Louise and Michelle."

STRAIGHT TALK

"The other day I was at a party and this person reached out to shake hands with me and introduced him or herself as Morgan. By the name and appearance, I wasn't sure whether I was talking with a man or woman. What was I supposed to do?"

Shake hands. Say hello. And refer to him or her as Morgan. A person's gender identity hardly matters in an introduction.

Social Kissing

"All these variations of kissing are driving me crazy," a gay realtor with a number of LGBT clients said recently. "Some guys greet me with a peck on the cheek. Others try to be European with a two-cheek or even three-cheek kiss, and then there's the terribly sophisticated air kiss. I especially hate when I find myself forced to lock lips with a near stranger."

"Mwah!"

254

It's true that all greetings—and LGBT ones in particular—do seem to be incorporating more and more physical contact. In North America, this trend has been influenced by what's common practice (and good manners) in most Mediterranean countries, Latin America, and the Middle East, as well as the many immigrant communities in the United States and Canada.

It's a delicate matter dodging social kisses, whether you are opposed to physical greetings in principle or it happens to be the height of flu season. The best thing to do in such a case is reach out to shake hands the moment you meet (whether for the first time or if you know your friend to be overly familiar), as a preemptive move. If you're the kissing type or it's just an engrained habit as part of your culture, don't assume everyone likes to be so bussed.

Here are some other suggestions to help you avoid too much social kissing and yet remain civil:

- **Keep to simple handshaking or try the two-handed clasp:** Either of these approaches is fine, with the latter being a bit more effusive. Or, as you get to know one another better, you can give each other a quick embrace.
- **Use the air kiss:** The basics of air kissing are simple: it's the pretense of a kiss. You faux kiss your friend (or colleague) by placing your cheek near your friend's and making the "mwah" noise with your lips. Meantime, you grasp each other's arms or shoulders, creating a dead zone between you.
- **Be a forceful one-cheek kisser:** This is a particularly useful maneuver if you're greeting a known lip kisser. As you approach, sharply turn your face to one side to avoid a direct hit.

A final note to gay men greeting straight men: Some straight guys are still squeamish about body contact with other men, let alone actual cheek kissing. Instead, try the "I'm not gay" three-pats-on-the-back approach.

THE ART OF LETTER WRITING

Certainly, we all write fewer letters than we used to or than our parents did, which isn't to say that we communicate less or that such a trend is necessarily a bad thing or that it's yet another marker of the end of civilization. Nevertheless, there are still some occasions when putting pen to paper is more appropriate—and meaningful—than either e-mailing or typing a letter to send via snail mail.

When to Write

People are often confused about when it's necessary or important enough to write a letter. There are two basic situations that call for you to put it in writing:

1. If you think the recipient might want to hold on to what you send as a keepsake. For example, many of us like to save notes of condolence and congratulatory letters marking commitment ceremonies, graduations, coming out, and the like.

2. When it's appropriate to help convey the seriousness of the matter at hand. The

handcrafted care of a note or letter is a symbol of your sincerity and your effort. When you write an apology, for instance, the receiver can see that this is not a string of bons mots you just dashed off on your keyboard—it's a note you put considerable thought into. The respect inherent in the act of handwriting a letter adds to the strength of the words themselves.

The most important element of a well-written note or letter is the sentiment behind it. Before you put pen to paper, think through what it is you want to say; after all, there's no delete key or cut-and-paste function. Some letter writers start by crafting a short outline of points they want to make or even write a rough draft first. If you forge right ahead and find yourself crossing out a lot, it's better to start over.

THE ESSENTIALS

Letter Writing 101

One of the benefits of taking pen to paper is that you're able to express your individuality in the stationery (and ink) you choose to use. If you're an environmentalist, you may choose from all-cotton papers (no trees felled here!); if you're a traditionalist, you'll probably be drawn to more classic fonts and paper colors. Whatever your personal style, here's what you'll need:

- **Pen and ink:** Of course, you can use any pen that you happen to have on hand; however, if you're going to go to the trouble of writing a letter or note, try to choose a good-quality pen that is comfortable to use and looks good on the paper you'll use (for instance, it doesn't "bleed" or run into the paper). Generally, black

and blue inks are the most readable and the most formal. Certainly, stick to one of those colors when writing a condolence note. By contrast, at holiday time, you can be more playful, even choosing red or green ink. Or choose an ink color that feels right for your personality or what people refer to these days as your "personal brand."

- **Paper:** Choose paper that's better than the run-of-the-mill paper in your printer. Texture, weight, and the percentage of cotton combine to create finer papers. Traditionally, letter-writing paper comes in muted colors such as white, light blue, light gray, or cream, but it's fine to choose any color you like as long as the ink you then use on it is legible. In addition to the cotton papers mentioned above, recycled papers are a great "green" option (see "The Essentials: Green Papers," page 259).

- **Printing:** For those who plan to be writing notes or letters regularly, think about investing in printed stationery rather than using blank note cards or plain sheets of paper. The entry "Personal Stationery" (right) explains what forms of stationery are available and what you might have printed on them, but here's the skinny on how stationery can be printed:

  - Engraving is the gold standard—the most expensive and most formal means for printing your name and address. A metal die or plate is created that literally indents or "bruises" the paper.

  - Thermography is next "best," less costly but just as nice to most eyes. Thermography uses heat to attach the ink to the paper and may have a slightly glossier sheen than engraving.

  - Letterpress, with its attention to beauty and craftsmanship, is an excellent option that has enjoyed a resurgence in recent years.

• Laser printing: Many people today choose this method, also known as offset printing, whether done on their home computers or at a local copy shop. This is the least expensive means of all and can look just fine, especially if you use a higher-quality paper and a distinctive font.

Personal Stationery

If you're going to make an investment in stationery, your best bet is to start with what are called "correspondence cards"—one-sheet cards of heavy stock—which are usually 4¼ by 6½ inches, with your name or initials centered at the top. (By the way, no titles—like Mr., Dr., or Ms.—go on these cards.) These are especially useful for quick notes, thank-yous, and even short condolences. One great advantage of having correspondence cards is that, because of their compact size, you don't have to worry about writing very much—but you still get credit for coming up with a personalized message.

For men, the standard writing paper is what's known as a monarch sheet. This measures 7¼ by 10½ inches and traditionally comes in the monochromes gray, white, and ecru. Women use monarch sheets as frequently as men today; the slightly smaller traditional women's writing paper has virtually fallen out of use. The classic colors for women have stayed closer to the muted tones: light blues and grays, white, off-white, or ecru. As mentioned before, choose a color that you like, even bright fun ones, as long as it nicely highlights your ink choice.

If the stationery is for personal correspondence, center your name at the top and don't

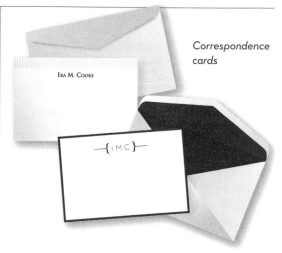

Correspondence cards

IRA M. COOKE

{ I M C }

use any honorifics. Again, that means no Mr., Dr., or Judge. (Just because your mailbox may be inundated with return labels from various charities that use these honorifics incorrectly doesn't mean that's the right way to do it.) Personal stationery is just that—*personal.* It's optional whether to include your mailing address, phone numbers, and/or e-mail address (these are not included on correspondence cards).

On professional or business stationery, it's appropriate to include any advanced degrees or other titles, like M.D. or Ph.D., but the honorifics "Mr." and "Ms." are still not appropriate.

An example of professional stationery

JOAN B. ROTHSTEIN, M.D.
75 MADISON AVENUE, SUITE 201
NEW YORK, N.Y. 10016

THE ESSENTIALS

Rules for Monograms

Correspondence cards (and some personal stationery) often get printed with your initials in type at the top. There are actually rules on how such monograms should be handled, and here they are (if only this were as easy as ABC!).

In general, use either two or three initials (first, middle, last, or first, original family name, new last name). That is, unless you have a name that makes an unfortunate acronym, like my friend Susan Ostwald Barnes (SOB); she uses her middle name, Jessica, for the center initial (SJB).

As for presentation, there are two common approaches:

1. Each of the initials in the same size in consecutive order (SJB).

2. The last name is in the center, larger than the other two letters, see examples below.

If your last name is hyphenated, as in Richard L. Oz-Garcia, your choices would be RLO-G or rO-GL; see sample below.

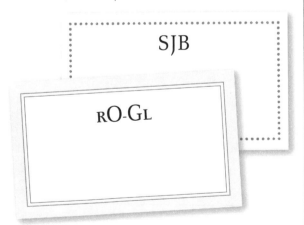

Monogram variations

Stationery for Couples

LGBT couples have a wide variety of stationery choices reflecting the many ways we choose to showcase our names. The most common choice of personalized stationery is a folded note card, which must be at least 3½ by 5 inches when folded (or the postal service will reject it).

Here are some examples:

Couples or house stationery

THE ESSENTIALS

Green Papers

If you're concerned about your carbon footprint, choose stationery using recycled papers with as high a post-consumer waste (PCW) content percentage as you can find and afford. A PCW number of 100 means it is 100 percent recycled. Another good option is to choose papers made from cotton, as opposed to wood pulp; cotton is also superior in terms of both strength and durability. Cotton paper is typically graded as 25, 50, or 100 percent cotton. Usually, the cotton percentage of a piece of paper can be checked by holding it up to the light and looking just below the printer's watermark.

NOTES & CARDS

When writing a letter feels over-the-top, notes and cards will often do just fine. It's easier and often more fun, whether picking out a birthday card that sings "It's Raining Men" or keeping a box of "one size fits all" (no message inside) notes at home. You'll find lots of choices in online stores as well as your local stationers. Choose cards that reflect not only your personality but the event at hand. And don't forget that the mere act of putting a sealed envelope in the mail is still recognized as a sign of genuine thoughtfulness.

Holiday and Other Greeting Cards

Millions and millions of greeting cards are sold every year in North America. We send cards for Mother's Day, Father's Day, Gay Pride, Halloween, anniversaries, birthdays, Hanukkah, Christmas, New Year's, and many more occasions. Although many of these cards have pre-printed sentiments in them, it's more personal to add some original words of your own. Even if what you pen is as simple as "Happy Birthday, Lover!" or "I'm so sorry to hear that you're not feeling well. Get better!"

When it comes to the end-of-year holidays, it's easiest to choose cards that have winter imagery—or a family photograph—and are appropriate for anyone of any faith (or no faith). If you're Christian or Jewish, you might want to buy two different kinds of cards: a "Season's Greetings" or "Happy New Year" set and others with religious imagery or verbiage that say "Merry Christmas" or "Happy Hanukkah." The former can be sent to anyone on your list, including those of all faiths, while the latter can be reserved for those who celebrate the specific holiday featured on the card. After all, why take a chance on offending anyone when the idea is to make a warm gesture?

The Importance of Signing Greeting Cards

Traditionally, manners books had much to say about the signing of greeting cards. Admonitions included the wife's name must precede her husband's; don't use honorifics or titles; and when there are kids in the family, the father's name must come first. These days, the most important rule—and the one most often overlooked—is to take the time to *actually sign your names,* even if they are also preprinted. One gay man explains, "When I get a holiday card that has no personal greeting or signature, it feels as impersonal as junk mail. Why even bother?"

Take the effort to personalize the card by signing your name and adding a salutation, like "Dear Aunt Meg and Serena." For extra credit, jot a short personal message (even if it's on the back of a flat card).

For same-sex couples, it makes no difference whose name comes first in signing—assuming it makes no difference to the two of you. If the card is sent to your friends or family members, just use your first names. If sent to business acquaintances, use first and last names. If you have children, you have two choices: "The Smith-Varvatos Family" or "The Smith-Varvatoses—Paul, John, Paulette, and Johnny," with the children listed in birth order from eldest to youngest.

Holiday Newsletters

While there are those who love reading of friends' and relatives' doings in holiday newsletters, these annual updates are also easy to mock. One lesbian reports that her aunt exploits every member of her family in her yearly summaries: "Her Christmas updates have included one son's painful divorce and another's inability to get his wife pregnant. She violates everyone's privacy."

If these letters are part of your family tradition, keep these dos and don'ts in mind:

- **Don't start off with "Dear All":** Write a personalized salutation at the top of each one.
- **Keep them short:** Whether on paper or via e-mail, a half to a full page is sufficient. Really, it is.
- **Send them judiciously:** Don't mail out to everyone you know, just those whom you think will actually care about your news.
- **Don't brag:** Granted, this is a major reason people write them, but try your best to keep it in check.
- **Don't be a downer:** Too much bad news (illness, war, the economy) can ruin the best of holidays.

"Gay couple (plus cat) contemplate a holiday photo card."

Q Many of my straight friends send holiday cards with their kids front and center. Since my partner and I don't have any offspring, can we send a card with just us as the cover models? We could add in our cat if you think that would help.

A Most holiday photo cards feature kids ("aren't they adorable!") or vacation destinations ("look at how fabulous we are!") as key elements. But there are limits: It's actually pretty rare that couples alone—straight or gay—pose for their close-ups without a supporting player. Since equality is all about parity, I'd say do go ahead with your close-up—just don't forget your cat ("isn't she beautiful?").

One last note: If you're not already out, this is a quietly effective way to do so. Imagine the photo: two husbands and their cat in front of the fireplace. ("The warmest of holidays from Justin, Benji, and Garfield!")

- **Respect your family's privacy:** Always ask for permission before revealing others' personal affairs.
- **Include photos:** Especially nice are snaps of important events like vacations, weddings, anniversaries, and other milestones.

Many of these holiday updates are now sent by e-mail, often with attached photos. If that's convenient for your recipients, then go ahead and save yourself the cost of printing and postage.

Thank-You Notes

Even if you expressed your appreciation for a gift or an act of kindness at the time you received it, it's still a must to follow up with a short note of thanks, mentioning the gift specifically ("We really love the stainless toaster oven") and how you will use it ("Every morning we'll think of you").

If the gift has been mailed to you, a thank-you note is even more necessary. Keep in mind, however, that for a present of a certain magnitude—say, a "big" wedding gift from your parents—it's best to first make a phone call and express your appreciation orally ("We're overwhelmed by your generosity"); then follow up with a proper pen-and-ink note.

There are other times when expressions of thanks are welcome, even if no gifts are involved—for example, if a good friend has been very supportive during the illness of your partner, or your sister has stood by during your coming out or a nasty breakup. Here again, the point is to take the time so that your "thank you"—whatever form it takes—reflects your gratitude. It may be a note or an e-mail.

Sometimes these days, we're all so busy that we forget to write a thank-you right away. (By the way, try to send thank-yous as soon as possible and within a week to ten days.) If, for whatever reason, you haven't been terribly prompt in expressing your thanks, don't let your embarrassment get in the way. Apologize for the delay and then express your gratitude.

Addressing Invitations to Lesbian and Gay Couples

Whenever you're sending out invitations—whether it's to a housewarming, a surprise birthday party for your best friend, or your wedding ceremony—it's very important before you start addressing the envelopes to get the exact spelling of the names of your guests and their correct addresses. Once you've nailed down those details, you can move on to each addressee's title and other details.

With so many LGBT couples formalizing their relationships, whether through marriage or other ceremonies or simply by living together, there is ever greater confusion about how same-sex couples should be addressed. Certainly the traditional heterosexual model of listing the man first—which plenty of straight couples eschew by now as well—doesn't apply.

Allow the following tips to be your guide, but remember that it's up to you to assess the degree of formality in your particular situation.

- When LGBT couples are *committed,* legally or not, but have different last names, their names should be placed on the same line and joined by the word "and" to signify their partnership:

Informal:

Jayson Klein and Roberto Shiver

Formal:

Mr. Jayson Klein and Mr. Roberto Shiver

• If a couple shares the same last name, it's even simpler. Again, honorifics are used on more formal invitations:

Informal:

Ophelia and Meredith Seehusen

Formal:

Though there are actually a number of options in this instance—the best choice being the form the couple prefers—the most common variation is this:

Ms. Ophelia and Ms. Meredith Seehusen

Devotées of very high manners might opt for Mrs. and Mrs. Ophelia Seehusen, or as Miss Manners has suggested, Mesdames Ophelia and Meredith Seehusen. This last approach, however, seems way too formal for anything other than a state affair.

STRAIGHT TALK

"Which name goes first in the salutation of a letter or e-mail to a gay couple?"

It doesn't matter which name goes first, unless it matters to one of the recipients. It is amusing how some couples come to be known as "Rich and Jim" or "Molly and Vicki" rather than the other away around. Despite some common misconceptions, there is no rule that says names should be listed alphabetically (although my friends with names closer to "A" continue to insist otherwise). If you know a couple with their names in a particular order, it makes sense to address them that way.

Sympathy Notes

Writer's block or an outpouring of emotion often gets in the way when it comes time to sit down and write a letter of condolence. It's difficult trying to put feelings of sadness or sympathy into actual words. Yet cards or letters expressing your condolences can be very soothing to their recipients, who will have them, hold them, keep them, and read them aloud to others. If you do send a preprinted card, personalize it to some degree with your own sentiments, no matter how short or to the point. If you're writing a family member or loved one about a loss, consider adding in your note that "no acknowledgement is necessary" so as to relieve them of that additional burden.

In today's electronic world, it's okay to quickly acknowledge someone's passing in an e-mail or even a text message; for instance, you could write, "I'm so sorry to hear about your loss. Let me know what I can do." Or if someone has posted a death notice on a newspaper website, or on Legacy.com, feel free to add in your thoughts in the comments section or send them privately through the service (if the funeral home's website has posted details of the services, you can usually post comments there, too). Nevertheless, this does not satisfy the need for a note of condolence; do your best to send one within the week.

FOR RECIPIENTS OF CONDOLENCE NOTES

If you're the grieving party and have received condolence or sympathy notes, try to thank your correspondents in a timely way, say two to four weeks after the services are completed. If someone made a contribution to a charity, sent flowers, or took care of your dog for a spell, be sure to thank them specifically for those gestures. (For more about sympathy notes, see page 373.)

Congratulatory Notes

It used to be de rigueur to handwrite notes for a wide range of milestones—everything from high school and college graduations to a first job or promotion, even the receipt of an award or some other professional success. Today, it makes more sense to consider how you *usually* communicate with colleagues, friends, or family, and then to deliver your congratulations that way. If, for instance, you regularly correspond on e-mail or via a social media site, it's acceptable to send your good wishes that way—but it's still nicer to send an actual note.

But do consider sprucing things up a bit—say, if you're in the habit of using all lowercase letters in your e-mails, be more formal in this note by using upper- and lowercase (and definitely use the spell-check). Or send one of the "Congratulations" e-cards offered by many electronic card websites.

Notes of Apology

When you've hurt someone's feelings inadvertently, such as by forgetting a birthday, or, worse, you've purposely said, done, or written something snarky or mean-spirited, an apology is called for. Usually, it's best to pick up the phone and actually make personal contact. The swiftness of e-mail and texting can be satisfying; nevertheless, in cases where an apology and explanation is necessary, these quick means can sometimes make the situation worse because it's so hard to convey emotional nuances digitally.

However you choose to apologize, make sure you actually say the words "I'm sorry" or "I apologize for . . ." and take responsibility for the action. In addition, try to make amends. If you spilled red wine all over your sister's tablecloth, offer to pay for the dry cleaning. If you broke something, offer to replace it.

ELECTRONIC COMMUNICATION

No twenty-first-century guide to the manners of correspondence would be complete without considering e-mail, texting, Facebook, and the other digital ways we keep in touch. It may not surprise you to know that electronic communication is easy to flub: There are so many ways to be rude if you lean too much on technology and forgo the human touch.

E-mail Dos and Don'ts

The two main rules for polite e-mail communication are straight from "real" (or what's known as offline) life: Be kind; and don't use language that may offend. The third rule bears repeating even though you've probably heard it thousands of times: Think twice before you hit the SEND button.

Beyond that, keep in mind that there's a lot more room for misinterpretation in the digital realm, so be careful.

As for e-mails themselves, don't forget that they can be widely misunderstood: Gentle ribbing can be seen as hostile sarcasm, a flirtatious comment may become evidence for sexual harassment, and so on. Even when carefully choosing your words doesn't make your message 100 percent clear, add an emoticon or an acronym (for instance, ROTF—"rolling on the floor"—indicates humor). As silly as these symbols may seem, they can help communicate your tone and mood.

Neither smiley faces nor a little self-editing may be enough for some e-mails—such as those telling your family that you're gay or transgender, writing to an ex you're still angry with, or criticizing someone else's work. In these kinds of cases, the best advice is to save the draft and then take a break—sometimes as long as a full day. Time has a way of not just calming your nerves but clarifying in your mind whether your words are the right ones.

Once you sit back down at the computer and decide it's all right to hit SEND, keep in mind that your e-mail may be forwarded and reforwarded without your okay—in fact, without your knowledge. Here's one that eventually made its way to me and so many others: "My partner is the biggest a—hole in the world! His birthday wasn't special enough for him so now he won't even eat the dinner I made for him. Maybe I should have hired Ricky Martin to play for him? I bet he would have complained about that too!"

A few more general e-mail tips:

- **BCC:** Use BCC (blind carbon copy) when e-mailing a group of people who likely don't want their e-mail addresses known to strangers. In the workplace, BCCs are great for making sure an assistant can follow along discreetly while sensitive business is being conducted. But BCCs can backfire when someone forgets who's seen what or replies to the wrong e-mail address and mistakenly reveals that they were secretly copied and that you were indiscreet.

- **Forwarding:** Likewise, be careful about using the FORWARD button, especially if you're forwarding an entire thread of a conversation. Who knows or can recall what evil lies at the start of an e-mail thread?

- **Workplace sensitivities:** What you type on a home computer in view of your girlfriend, sister, dog, parents, or roommates is yours to sort out. Certainly, be careful and considerate about what you share or reveal (but you know that already). In the workplace, however, there are additional concerns because others may be able to see your screen, not to mention that your company's IT staff can track your every keystroke. Be sure to review your company's e-mail and web viewing policies regularly. Running afoul of them or offending someone is not just in bad taste—you could lose your job over it.

- **Adult-only content:** If you're the type to send adult-themed e-mails or photos, at the very least put a warning in the subject line: "Do not open at work" or "NSFW" ("not safe for work") to alert your friends to the nature of the material you've just sent. Better still, send it to a home e-mail address instead of a work one.

- **Sexual orientation and gender identity/expression:** If you work in an office where your sexual orientation or gender identity is either not known or not approved of, you'll need to be extra careful about e-mails you write (and receive) as well as any websites that you visit, as these may out you. It's wiser to create and use a nonwork e-mail account (remember, if you access it at work, your privacy is still not safeguarded).

Also, don't forget that just about any site that you visit on your work computer will be stored in your cache or on your network's hard drive. Even if you're out and proud, be careful where you click on the Web, because some straight colleagues may wrongly interpret LGBT-related sites as sexual or provocative in some way—however far from the truth that may be.

All About E-cards

Many people send electronic cards these days to their wired friends—and with their animations and even audio tracks, some of them can be quite special. E-cards are becoming increasingly acceptable for a range of special occasions, including holidays, graduations, anniversaries, and birthdays. If anything, what matters most is whether the recipient will appreciate such a card. However, e-cards for weddings and condolence notes fall outside of this zone—those you must write (at least for now).

As you would with any other card, take the time to personalize the message on an e-card and definitely avoid sending a mass distribution to all your friends, with no personalization whatsoever. Doing so makes it look like you really couldn't be bothered, and if you can't be, well, then don't.

THE ESSENTIALS
Digital Etiquette 101

The rules for using technology to communicate with other people are unwieldy and elusive. It's hard to keep up as each new device shifts etiquette in some new, unforeseen direction. Nevertheless, here are some basic guidelines worth keeping in mind:

- **Texting:** Friends don't let friends text and drive (even if it's not illegal in all states). And when you're in a meeting or social group, resist the temptation to pick up your smart phone and start tapping away. It's not just that your attention is elsewhere; eye contact is completely impossible.

- **Sexting:** Don't! If you text a picture of your naked body, even just one part of it, to a friend, it's pretty much the same as posting it permanently on the Internet. People caught up in the sexting frenzy of late may well be chagrined in the future to find out how widely these photos are distributed—especially if they get in the way of a scholarship or a job. Also, in some states sexting is against the law.

- **IMing:** Always ask someone if it's a good time before plunging into an instant messaging session—for instance, "Hey, Michael, do you have a sec to go over the plans for the Bisexual Brits party on Friday?" This applies to both personal and professional uses of this highly efficient yet sometimes distracting method for communicating in real time from your computer desktop (or PDA). Other rules here: Watch the "availability settings" (for example, is your friend "busy"?); don't try out any obscure IM acronyms unless you suspect the other person is familiar with them; and keep your messaging brief.

• **Facebooking:** Facebook is great for keeping in touch with friends, networking for social and work reasons, and promoting events. Use status updates sparingly, however; Twitter's the place for blow-by-blow commentary on the progress of your day.

• **Tweeting:** Tweeting more than a few times in an hour or a dozen times a day is annoying. You risk losing your followers, no matter how funny or fingers-on-the-pulse you happen to be.

CHAPTER 10

Social Occasions

At Home & Out on the Town

O ne of the greatest transformations of the past generation has been the ever growing inclusion of LGBT people in corporate life, churches, federal and state offices, and professional athletics—as well as in the pages of magazines from *Sports Illustrated* to *Better Homes & Gardens*. We're also living in greater numbers than ever in the suburbs and rural enclaves— joining neighborhood picnics, carpooling our kids to school, and volunteering. The change in attitudes has been profound, explained Joe Solmonese, head of the Human Rights Campaign, to *The Washington Post*: "We're talking about our community's willingness and comfort level living anywhere. And not just our own community, but society's view has changed so much in the last few years." In short, we're visible in unprecedented ways, able to come together and heed the advice of E. M. Forster, the twentieth-century gay novelist who admonished, "Live in fragments no longer. Only connect."

And connect we do, whether that means heading out to the local bar with our best pals, grabbing a bite to eat on the fly, being a good houseguest or—with a bit more formality—hosting a dinner or attending a gala. But even when our goal is simply to have a good time, such get-togethers can be fraught with social pressure and needless anxiety, for entertaining veterans and social novices alike.

Before delving into what's different about entertaining in the LGBT world, it's important to know the very basics. If you want to throw a cocktail or dinner party, how do you pull together a compatible—and not combustible—group? When is it okay to use electronic invitations—and when not? What's the best way to deal with guests' special diets? What do you do about late guests, those who drink too much, and those who bring uninvited dates along? Then there are all the details involved in actually putting together such parties and dinners, not to mention the creativity required to stay within a budget or pull it off in a small apartment.

Not surprisingly, we set the table, order our restaurant meals, and make our guests' beds pretty much like straight folks. Nevertheless, specific LGBT hospitality issues do crop up all the time, and not just in summer shares at classic gay vacation spots, with their own long-established and unique customs. For instance, is it okay to have all-gay parties? What do you do when your gay friends hit on your straight ones? Will straights and LGBT friends mix comfortably at a sit-down dinner? And what

should you do if you encounter anti-LGBT discrimination at a local restaurant?

Speaking of eating out, restaurant etiquette can be another delicate, if not challenging, matter. You've likely been stymied about the rules for dividing a check, what to tip, and deciding how much to spend on a bottle of wine with people you don't know very well. Also needed: advice for overnight guests and hosts alike, who face myriad situations requiring sensitivity to one another's needs.

Household and restaurant manners are, of course, very much susceptible to cultural and generational variations, and also morph from town to town. One young lesbian's laid-back potluck—or a gay couple's multicourse dinner party—may be another's culinary and social nightmare. But once you grasp the essential courtesies involved in hosting and in being a guest, the rest is—almost—easy.

BEING A GOOD HOST

Whether you're throwing a simple pizza party or a dinner for eight, and whether it's takeout, catered, or home-cooked, there are always a lot of details to look after. For starters: Who, what, where, when? How will everybody get along? Themes are nice—say, Mexican for Cinco de Mayo, barbecue for the Fourth of July, or cocktails for Pink Saturday (the Saturday night of Pride weekend in many cities). All this is up to you as the host, and the way to start is by considering the pleasures and preferences of your guests. If everybody has a good time—and you manage to put everything together on time and within your budget—that makes for a successful get-together. It also ups your chances of actually being able to enjoy the party yourself.

Selecting Your Guests

It's said that designing a first-rate guest list requires the talents of a diplomat, psychologist, and chemist combined. Not true: All it takes is some basic consideration, common sense—and a good address book, meaning friends, family, or colleagues you like and believe will get along together well.

Naturally, it's a bonus when most everyone on that list is a good guest, too. You can often sniff out troublemakers ahead of time. A gay restaurateur who also hosts a lot at his home says, "I never invite people who I think have an unpleasant history, or just know will not get along."

Some kinds of parties practically dictate their own guest list. If it's your best friend or partner's birthday, count on inviting her closest friends and family members. If it's your neighborhood watch group or a reunion of your buds from last year's AIDS Ride, just take a quick look at your e-mail distribution lists: You've got your party. However, be careful not to cherry-pick a list—if you invite only some of the folks in a particular group, word is likely to get around and you may wind up with a manners' black eye.

For other types of parties, just invite people you enjoy spending time with or want to get to know better. Ideally, you should be sure they'll each bring *something* to the table, whether it's a keen wit, amusing stories, the ability to listen, a contagious joie de vivre—or just a nice bottle of wine.

Still, it's important to put some thought into the equation. For instance, extroverts need listeners, not rivals, so don't invite a tableful of boisterous talkers to a small dinner. Similarly, a roomful of taciturn guests invited for cocktails can inadvertently extinguish all attempts at spirited conversation. You may find that at times you want to host what a friend of mine calls an "everyone party," like his annual winter solstice get-together. For that kind of event, it's a good rule of thumb to mix and match your guests: peppy and calm, straight and LGBT, male and female, Republican and Democrat, older and younger.

"I hope that's Andrew's foot—not Alicia's—playing with mine."

QUEERY

"Guess who's coming to dinner? Your ex!"

Q It's said that the LGBT community is an army of lovers and ex-lovers. So, how do you handle invites and—God forbid it's a dinner party—seating arrangements when you know that so many of the guests are former lovers?

A First of all, as a host, you need to remember that your guests' comfort comes first. Just because you want to invite all your exes, and your friends' exes, doesn't mean you should. Masked or unmasked bitterness, rage, or jealousy can quickly tank the best of parties. But if you're committed to this potentially prickly guest list, be transparent. You don't need to tell each guest which of his or her exes will be present, but if you're asked, 'fess up. Then it's every man and woman for him- or herself. Some will simply decline to attend, but at least everyone will know what lies ahead.

Seating arrangements are an entirely different thing. You really can't just put a group of unhappy souls at a table and ask them to break bread together. If you insist on inviting those with complicated relationships, I'd suggest using place cards and putting those with a bad history far enough away from each other at the table—or, if the party is big enough, at separate tables.

Of course, you'll also find that there are times when you want to socialize with just your gay friends, your work colleagues, or (for an election night party) compatible political bedfellows. What's important here is not to publicize such a gathering to everyone you know, because some might not understand why they haven't been invited. For instance, one straight woman in a small community felt left out when a close lesbian friend had an all-gay dinner: "She kept saying it was only for the gays in the gayborhood, but I couldn't imagine saying that you'd have a 'straight only' dinner."

In addition, if you're on Facebook or another social media site, be considerate of your friends, who may be hurt if they see photos and other tidbits of the great time you had *without* them.

All About Invitations

When it comes to invitations, here are two rules to keep in mind: The more formal the event, the more traditional the form of invitation. And the more formal the event, the more advance notice you'll want to give guests. As examples, gala benefits and other fundraisers often require a long lead time. Dinner on the weekend or a next-day brunch invitation can be completely informal—and obviously impromptu.

For a big to-do, such as a milestone birthday or an anniversary dinner, begin by letting your friends know the date as soon as possible; three to six weeks is plenty of time (you could even send out a quick "save-the-date" e-mail or card). Then follow up with an actual invitation. If you're throwing a dinner—say, to celebrate your wife's promotion or to share a sit-down meal at your home on a Saturday night—try to do your inviting a week or two in advance, whether electronically, by telephone, or via a preprinted invitation, which can be store-bought or printed on your computer. If it's a casual brunch or barbecue, calling, using e-mail, or texting—anywhere from a couple of days before to almost the last minute—is just fine; you can also use your favorite social media networking site to round up friends on the spur of the moment. If it's a last-minute get-together, let your guests know that fact; otherwise, some may think they were on your B-list and have been invited only because you had A-listers cancel.

THE INVITATION ITSELF

Now that you're set on the timetable of when to do the inviting, it's time to put some thought into how you'll do so. Depending on your personal style and how formal the event will be, you have a wide range of invitation choices:

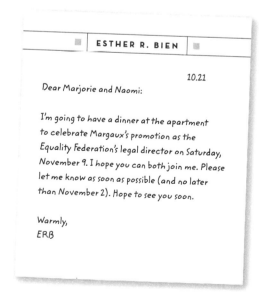

ESTHER R. BIEN

10.21

Dear Marjorie and Naomi:

I'm going to have a dinner at the apartment to celebrate Margaux's promotion as the Equality Federation's legal director on Saturday, November 9. I hope you can both join me. Please let me know as soon as possible (and no later than November 2). Hope to see you soon.

Warmly,
ERB

- Preprinted party invitations, where you fill in the details.
- Electronic invitations, like those from Paperless Post or Evite.
- Handwritten invitations, perhaps in the form of a short note, such as the example adjacent.
- Engraved, thermographed, or laser-printed invitations.

No matter what form of invitation you choose, make sure to convey the following:
- The date and time
- Your address
- The kind of party (e.g., cocktail, potluck, holiday dinner, surprise)
- The host or hosts
- What, if anything, to bring
- Directions, if necessary
- How (and when) to RSVP

STRAIGHT TALK

"How do I address my party invitations to a lesbian friend and her partner, when I don't know her partner's name?"

Unless your friend goes through partners so fast that today's lover might well be tomorrow's ex, shoot a quick e-mail to your friend saying something like "I don't seem to have your partner's full name in my electronic address book. Could you please send it to me?" Alternatively, send the invitation to your friend, using her name and the words "and partner" in the address line. In that case, if your friend is a good guest, she'll reply along the lines of "I'd love to come and bring Dani, too. Just so you have it, her full name is Dani Shapiro. Thanks for asking us both."

Electronic Invitations

Some people consider electronic invitations less meaningful than their hard-copy counterparts—unsuitable for events of any kind and barely worthy of an RSVP. And that reaction comes from unlikely quarters. Explained one twentysomething blogger: "There's nothing that equals a well-thought-out and personalized printed invitation. And if it's a particularly pretty invitation, I'll even keep it after the party."

But online invitations are efficient, less expensive, and better for the environment. Increasingly, LGBT people make use of them for a wide variety of occasions, even their weddings and commitment ceremonies. Perhaps because we've been early adopters of many new technologies, we've also been at the fore of the movement toward online invitations. To meet demand, companies such as Paperless Post have created an elegant line of electronic invitations for all occasions—and they are blessedly advertising-free.

If you decide to use electronic invitations, you'll often have the option of making the invitation list public. Think carefully about whether to do so. Sure, your guests might like to know who else is invited, in case they want to carpool or go in on a gift with someone. Or if you have feuding friends or exes, you won't have to go to the trouble of notifying them. But you may also want to afford your guests some privacy or just not have others decide whether or not to attend based on who's coming.

Inviting Your Single Friends

Believe it or not, traditional etiquette used to require having an even number of guests at formal dinners. For instance, at a sit-down event, a single guest could throw off the seating plans for even the most adept hostess. While that rule is thankfully long gone, when an LGBT host lives in a world of coupledom, inviting singles can present some challenges (and if you're the lone diner among duos, you can definitely feel like the odd man—or woman—out). One considerate work-around is this: Invite two singles and each will have a natural ally.

Sometimes there's kind of a de facto exclusion of single people by couples. A gay man who's encountered this explains, "After my lover and I broke up, it seemed like I lost my dinner parties, too. As a couple we fit in nicely with all the others. As a single man, I truly became the third wheel." Too often, someone who's recently been widowed or divorced gets dropped from social gatherings when he or she most needs to be included. Couples, be welcoming to your single friends!

The Importance of Your RSVP

RSVP is an initialism for the French *répondez s'il vous plaît,* which means "please respond." It's as simple as that, and if you receive an invitation that says RSVP, do just that. Not only is this is a matter of common courtesy, your host needs to know how many people to prepare for. It's hard to make sure everyone has a good time if you expect a dozen and find thirty people at your door—or the other way around.

Ideally, answer an invitation right away, or note the deadline on the card and then follow up in time. If the invitation says, "Regrets only," then the host will assume you're attending *unless* you call or e-mail otherwise (nonetheless, it's always a nice gesture in such cases to say you'll come, and it will help your host do a better job of planning).

When you receive an electronic invitation, please RSVP as requested. Just because you see that twenty or two hundred people are on the guest list, don't let that deter you from responding in a timely way. Also don't fall prey to the online phenomenon whereby "yes" means "maybe" and "maybe" means "no." Finally, many of us today seem loath to make any advance commitments—perhaps hoping that a better invitation will come along.

While you don't have to make a witty remark in the comment field, if you're not able to attend, it's thoughtful to give a brief explanation just as you might had you received a printed invitation. Keep it simple, like "We'll be sorry to miss this gathering, but we have a previous commitment." In addition, it's important to use the service itself for your response, as opposed to sending a separate e-mail or making a phone call. Part of the value of these services to the hosts is the ability to keep track of who's coming to an event and who's not, in a neat, well-ordered manner.

By the way, if you're the host and have not heard from your guests by the time your RSVP date has come and gone, don't hesitate to call or e-mail them directly and ask.

When You Need a Caterer

Certain kinds of parties pretty much require hiring outside help, whether it's a lone bartender or an entire professional catering staff. Perhaps you're expecting more people than you can easily handle without becoming a kitchen servant yourself—or you simply want to be able to enjoy your party and guests. A lesbian painter who likes to entertain explains how she decides about catering according to the size of an event: "Sometimes, my wife and I just put out eight to ten different hearty appetizers on the counter and let our friends help themselves. They know that wine's in the ice bucket and just about everything else is nearby. Call it 'self-serve' cocktails." At other times, like the holidays, this couple serves more complicated fare and mixed drinks "and we usually bring in some help."

If you're considering hiring a caterer, here's where to start:

- **What will it cost?** Get an understanding of a caterer's price range. Are prices itemized according to the foods you choose or is there a fixed charge per person? Does that price include incidentals, such as glassware and linens, as well as tax and gratuities?

- **How much staff?** If you're considering bartenders and/or waitstaff, ask how many the caterer would recommend for a party of your size. Find out what their hourly rate is and whether there's a minimum number of hours you need to hire them for. Don't forget to discuss what you'd like the service staff to wear. For a more formal affair, both male and female staff are best dressed in a white shirt, black bow tie, and black pants. For a more casual event, khakis and a pressed, button-down shirt are fine.

- **Can you do a tasting?** Once you've narrowed down your menu, ask if you can arrange a tasting to help with your final decision.
- **Will the menu be prepared in your home?** Or at the caterer's facility? Make sure you have a clear understanding of this beforehand so that there aren't any surprises.
- **What's not included?** If it's a large party and you need extra tables, chairs, plates, and silverware, will the caterer be able to provide them directly or help you arrange their rental? Be sure to discuss the costs involved.
- **Does the caterer have a business license?** This would ensure that all local health department rules and regulations had been met and the owner has the appropriate liability insurance.
- **Does the caterer provide alcohol?** If you are planning to provide the spirits yourself, ask the caterer whether there will be a corkage fee.

Finally, before making a commitment to a particular caterer, ask for the names of some previous clients and talk with them. Even if they report being completely satisfied, they may have some suggestions for helping you get the best possible experience.

Dinner Parties

LGBT people have a long tradition of hosting dinner parties. During more closeted times, when being out as a group in public was uncomfortable—and sometimes even dangerous—coming together at home over plates of food and bottles of wine was the ideal way to socialize. To this day, enjoying the personal touches of home while sharing the fruits of a well-stocked table makes for a very pleasant evening.

Traditional types will be happy to know that dinner parties are one area where some hosts still lean heavily on classic etiquette, such as which knife or fork a guest uses. Nonetheless, if you are such a traditionalist, be patient with your guests—inevitably, some will slip up. Keep in mind that, in the larger scheme of things, your guests' choice of cutlery is really not that important. What matters is how hospitable you are as a host and the mutual enjoyment you find with your friends and loved ones at your table.

Planning a Menu

These days, the first step in planning what to serve your guests is to determine whether anyone has any major food allergies or special diets—vegetarian, vegan, lactose-intolerance, gluten-free, etc. If you don't know already, a quick call or e-mail will do just fine. For instance, you could write, "I'm working on next week's dinner menu and just wanted to know if you had any food allergies . . . ?" Better to do that than have a PETA-friendly guest announce as you're serving veal Prince Orloff, "No dead baby cows." Be careful, however, because once you open your metaphoric kitchen door, you may also be deluged with concerns about simple carbs, beef that's not grass-fed, farmed fish, nonorganic produce, and so on.

Which brings up the most important manners issue for dinner guests here. If a host is considerate enough to ask you directly about what you cannot eat, stick to food *allergies;* refrain from going overboard with food *preferences.* After all, being invited to a dinner party is not like going out to a restaurant—you don't get to pick and choose (nor do you have to pay). Explained a gay maître d' who also entertains a lot at home: "I get so many special requests that are too difficult to accommodate, so I'll make sure there's at least one no-carb vegetable dish and call it a day—or dinner."

Once any food-allergy information is in hand, consider these questions as you prepare your menu:

- **What is your budget?** If things look tight, you might extend it by asking friends to bring wine, dessert, or appetizers. Alternatively, you could choose a less expensive dish to serve as an entrée.

- **How many courses will you serve?** In part, this decision depends on how formal an event it is, what your budget is, and the time you have to prepare. Most hosts start by deciding on a main course and then determining the side dishes that will work best with it. If you have any questions, there are loads of cooking/party planning websites—or revisit your favorite cookbook.

- **How much of the food can be prepared in advance?** You may be able to prepare a soup course a day or so before, make a dessert, marinate the entrée, or prep the veggies. You can also check off some other items from your to-do list whenever you have some free time—everything from setting the table, picking up some flowers for the table, or deciding which wines to serve.

- **What is in season and local this time of year?** Go to a local greenmarket a day or two before to see what the local farmers are selling—and ask them for ideas and recipes.

- **Are you cook, caterer, and host?** If so, keep it simple or think about getting some assistance from a friend with the preparation and cleanup.

- **What else will you need for the evening?** Cut flowers, a bowl of fruit, or even an arrangement of pine cones makes for an attractive centerpiece. Stock up on the drinks you'll need, both alcoholic and non. Make sure you have both coffee and tea available for the end of the evening, including decaffeinated and herbal options.

The Table

Don't know which fork to pick up first at a sit-down dinner? Perplexed about which course is supposed to bring that little spoon into play? If baffled, you're certainly not alone. And remember: It's no faux pas to make a mistake out of ignorance; it is, however, a serious violation of good manners to call someone out for such an infraction. A gay real estate agent complains, "Just the other night, I came to the dinner table and couldn't tell which was my place setting, much less my fork and knife. I panicked and then was admonished by my host for getting it wrong!" Bad host.

What follows is generally considered the "right" way to set your table; keep in mind that very few of us set a table like this on a daily basis—even a weekly one. And if you do deviate from the accepted formal practices and do it your own way, that's fine, but clue your guests in by letting them know which utensil to use with each course.

DISHES

At a very formal dinner party, place settings begin with a decorative plate known as a charger. The charger is often fine china, although it can also be made of wood or even leather. These plates are generally twelve inches in diameter and act as a base plate for all courses except dessert, although sometimes chargers are removed even before the first course is served. Because they're meant to be both decorative and somewhat protective of either the tablecloth or table, use them as you like. At less fussy affairs, for instance, their inclusion can help dress up a table. Ironically, although they are considered plates, no food actually ever rests on them, and for that reason they are rarely microwaveable or dishwasher-safe.

Unless it's a casual or family dinner, each new course is served on a different plate (or in a new bowl) with the bread plate placed to the left of the dinner plate so that it is close to the tines of the fork that is farthest to the left. Place the salad plate diagonally to the upper left of the dinner plate, or, if it's a first course, right on top of the charger.

Before serving a dessert or cheese course, clear all dishes from the table, including salt and pepper mills, condiment dishes, and wineglasses (unless a guest asks to keep hers).

CUTLERY

Silverware is one element where you might want to restrict your creativity, if only to avoid confusion. Cutlery is generally used "from the outside in," which is to say the fork farthest to the left is for the first course served. If you're going to serve salad first, place the salad fork to the left of the dinner fork. If the courses are reversed, reverse the positions of those forks.

FORMAL PLACE SETTING

1. Napkin
2. Salad fork
3. Dinner fork
4. Dinner plate
5. Dinner knife
6. Teaspoon
7. Soup spoon
8. Bread plate
9. Butter knife
10. Place card
11. Dessert spoon
12. Cake fork
13. Water goblet
14. Red wineglass
15. White wineglass
16. Coffee cup/saucer

DINNER NAPKIN FOLDING TECHNIQUES

The Bishop's Hat Napkin Fold

The Standing Fan Napkin Fold

The Fleur de Lys Goblet Fold

The Pyramid Napkin Fold

The Basic Silverware Pouch

The Basic Napkin Ring Stuffer

The same holds true for knives. Place one knife for each course to the right of the dinner plate, blades facing "in," with the one to be used first farthest from the plate. If you're serving soup as a first course, place the soup spoon to the extreme right of any and all knives. The butter knife is placed on the bread plate's upper rim.

Finally, the dessert fork and/or spoon are placed directly above the dinner plate, horizontally, with the fork pointing right and the spoon left. In general, don't place coffee spoons on the table until coffee cups and saucers are brought out at the end of the meal.

GLASSWARE

Set water glasses just above the dinner knife, with any wineglasses to the right of the water glass. Unless it's a casual dinner, guests generally leave all glassware they had been using for aperitifs in the living room or on a side table.

NAPKINS

Set napkins to the left of the forks, not underneath, if you have enough room on the table. If space is an issue, as it is in most of our apartments, placing the napkins under the forks or on the service plate is fine. Traditionally, napkins are folded into rectangles, with the fold facing the plate.

Apartment Dining

The traditional rules for setting a table have been devised with the notion of an expansive dining room table in mind, if not a whole staff of servants to help you. If you're an apartment dweller, live in a cozy house or condo, or simply have a smaller table and only the help of a friend or two to count on, don't hesitate to improvise.

Here are some other ways to arrange your place settings for tighter quarters:

- Bread plates can be omitted; salad plates can go on top of the dinner plate; and cutlery can even be elegantly arranged on top of your main plate, wrapped nicely in each napkin.
- If you have a limited selection of cutlery, don't sweat it. Salad forks are fine for fish or dessert as well. A teaspoon is just right for coffee and will do nicely for dessert, too. A tablespoon easily replaces a soup spoon. As for selecting the proper knife: If it cuts, use it.
- By the way, the reason to use different utensils is not to show off your silverware, but to provide a clean implement that does not carry the taste of one course over to the next. If you run short, just clean them between courses.
- As for wineglasses, in a perfect world you'd set a different glass for each new wine to be served and match the glass to the type of wine. In the real world, do your best with what you have.

Seating Arrangements

You'll be glad to know that modern manners no longer dictate that you seat your guests boy-girl-boy-girl. Instead, place each guest adjacent to those you think they'll enjoy talking with, especially if they have shared interests. As a general rule, seat couples and close friends separately, the idea being that they get many other chances to talk to each other and a dinner party is an opportunity to meet new people. If you're setting someone up, sit that person next to the intended, not across the table. Think strategically where you'll place left-handed guests so that both they and their dinner partners are comfortable. Here are some other suggestions for successful sit-downs:

- If it doesn't matter to you where your guests sit, just say so—although if you want to reserve a seat at the head of the table or close to the kitchen for yourself (or your partner) let them know that, too, or lean that chair against the table.
- If you have a specific seating plan in mind, either use place cards and ask your guests to find their names, or help direct each guest to his or her seat.
- If there's a special guest (also called a guest of honor), place that person to the right of one of the hosts or, if you're the only host, at the opposite end of the table.

Potluck Dinners

Potlucks—sometimes called covered dish suppers, when every guest brings a dish—are a relatively easy way to entertain family or friends and not spend hours in the kitchen preparing in the process. Here are some tips for potluck hosts:

- **Get organized:** There are several ways to do this. You can ask your friends to tell you what they plan to bring, and then do a little finessing to make sure you don't wind up with five green salads and no main courses. You can also make assignments by category, such as appetizers, salads, main courses, desserts, drinks, and other necessary items like napkins, utensils, cups, charcoal, or ice. A fair and easy way to make such assignments is to use an alphabetical system (that is, those whose names begin A through D bring appetizers; F through H, salads and so on), but in that case do a quick inventory of where your guests' names fall in the alphabet—you don't want to have too many hors d'oeuvres and too few main courses.

- **Be specific:** You may need three desserts, but you probably don't need three pumpkin pies. Let your guests know how many servings you expect them to provide. You could say, "Please bring enough for about eight."

- **Create a label:** Hosts can consider providing slips of paper (or place cards) so that dishes can be properly described, especially to those who might have food allergies. For instance: Brownies (Nuts), Vinaigrette (Mustard), or Trifle (Alcohol).

And here are some tips for mannerly potluck guests:

- **Be ready to serve:** Arrive with all your slicing, chopping, and baking already done—otherwise, the kitchen could become mayhem. Reheating a dish in the host's kitchen is okay, but let him know that ahead of time. With different dishes requiring different oven temperatures, he may have to coordinate the order in which guests do their final prep.

- **Presentation matters:** Don't serve your deviled eggs from a Tupperware dish or your frisée salad in a mixing bowl. If you can't transport your contribution in a decorative dish or platter, bring one along and do a quick transfer before putting it out on the table.

- **Don't come empty-handed:** If you're not a cook or your best-laid plans have gone awry, pick up a prepared dish at a market or deli that corresponds to what you intended to make. If you have time to put it in your own serving dish, all the better. (In this case, however, don't go one step more and claim that you're the chef!)

QUEERY

"I didn't invite their kids to my dinner party."

Q I was completely shocked when two of our gay friends showed up for a dinner party with their twins in tow. I hadn't mentioned kids in the invitation and the table was set for eight—four adult couples. I did the best I could, but I don't think I hid my irritation very well, especially when the twins complained about the caper sauce I served on the fish!

A Here's the underlying problem: You have too few kids in your life. Otherwise, you'd know better than to invite two parents to dinner without addressing the kid issue one way or another. It pays to be explicit in such an invitation, writing or saying something like "It will be the eight of us on Saturday. I think you know the other couples," or "It's just the big people this time. No little ones."

Of course, one of the parents should have asked ahead of time whether it was okay to bring the twins. But I can imagine they felt horrible when they saw a table set for eight adults—or I hope they did. And I trust that the parents apologized profusely in the moment and in their thank-you note, as well.

Finally, about that caper sauce: Don't blame the kids for not taking to that. I suggest keeping emergency provisions in your cupboard—like macaroni and cheese—for the next set of freeloading toddlers.

THE ESSENTIALS

Six Tips for Being a Good Host

1. **Get your home up to snuff:** The house should be clean, the table set, and you should be ready to greet your friends when the doorbell rings. Plan the evening so that you can enjoy your friends. Too many hosts "work" their parties without stopping to really participate.

2. **Make sure the kitchen is under control:** Some hosts prefer to have all the cooking done ahead of time, so they can pour drinks, make introductions, and mingle. Others feel that if you are serving really fresh food (like a well-prepared pasta dish or a fish course), you have to finish your cooking once guests are present—right before sitting down to eat.

3. **Introduce your friends to one another:** Having taken the time to invite compatible guests, make sure they get to meet one another. In parties under ten, try to introduce each new person to at least one other. If you can't do that as they arrive, take some time shortly after to circulate and make introductions as necessary.

4. **Ask questions of your guests and listen to what they say:** Sometimes it's easy to forget that making and deepening connections is the underlying purpose of entertaining, whatever kind of event you're hosting. Make sure you do that and help others do so as well.

5. **Know your guests' preferences:** Is someone vegan? On a wheat-free diet? Do your best to accommodate them without making it too hard on yourself.

6. **Don't push alcohol on nondrinkers:** And don't out your alcoholic friends to others. If you plan to serve foods prepared with either wine or liqueur, make that known to *all* your guests—not just to those whom you know to be nondrinkers, as you don't want to single them out publicly.

COCKTAIL PARTIES

A good mix of personalities and the right combination of drinks and hors d'oeuvres make for great entertaining. Maybe your gay and straight friends finally meet one another; your ex has such a good time that she doesn't care anymore that you're marrying someone else; and even your boss enjoys himself, finally realizing you're gay and being totally cool with it. And if the idea of throwing a cocktail party seems either too grown-up or just not your style, think of it more along the lines of having friends over for drinks and conversation. It's not necessarily expensive, it's easy to pull off, and fun for all—in a word, simple.

The Basics

Sure, it's always drink time somewhere in the world, but cocktail parties generally begin between 5:00 P.M. and 7:00 P.M. and last for two to three hours, ending in time for guests to have dinner elsewhere or return home having drunk and eaten some light hors d'oeuvres. But there's no rule saying you can't start midafternoon or simply invite friends over for a post-prandial drink.

Depending on your budget, your guests, and the occasion, you may decide to serve a full bar, just fizzy drinks (champagne or sparkling wine and water) or various wines, beers, and soft drinks. Always make sure to have some nonalcoholic options available for those choosing not to drink that evening as well as for friends who never do. If you plan to serve mixed drinks, it's a nice touch to do some research ahead of time about your guests' drink preferences, whether margaritas, Manhattans, daiquiris, or cosmopolitans, to make sure you'll have all the ingredients on hand.

Here are some other suggestions for throwing a successful cocktail party, whether intimate or for a big crowd:

- **Make sure you have enough ice:** Both to chill bottles and cans and to use for drinks.
- **Try to have a variety of glasses on hand:** If it is within your budget (and you have room), either buy or rent an assortment of glassware, which can make your evening more festive. Plan on having two glasses available per guest, since we all tend to lose ours. A typical assortment would include wineglasses for wines (there's no need at a cocktail party to get into red versus white wineglasses); champagne flutes for sparkling wines; martini glasses for martinis and Manhattans; straight-sided highballs for tall drinks like G&Ts or Tom Collins; and low highballs for water, juice, and other soft drinks. If this sounds too ambitious or out of your price range, don't worry: Any combination of glassware is perfectly fine, including plastic if that fits the occasion (like a poolside party).
- **Make sure your bar is well stocked:** What you're serving will determine what you

need. You may decide on a "house" or theme drink, and if it's a complicated one such as a mint julep or mojito, it's smart to make these ahead of time or to employ a bartender. If you're sticking with just wine and beer, plan on about half a bottle and about three cans, respectively, per person—unless you've invited heavy drinkers, in which case plan for more.

- **Rearrange the furniture:** Add or remove chairs. Turn a table to the wall. Make more space for mingling. Do what you can so that people can socialize in groups.
- **Don't forget about edibles:** Make sure you have some food to serve, whether an assortment of nuts, a cheese plate, crudités and a dip, shrimp cocktail, or hot hors d'oeuvres. Keep food bite-sized, provide plates for hot appetizers, and always have lots of napkins. It's not good form to serve alcohol by itself—for obvious reasons.
- **Keep the phone number of a local taxi company on hand:** It's your responsibility, as the host, to make sure an inebriated guest doesn't get on the road. In most states, it's also your *legal* responsibility, one not to be taken lightly.

THE ESSENTIALS
The Well-Stocked Bar

Start with the basics: a bottle each of gin, Scotch, rum, bourbon, and vodka. That will cover most of your friends' needs. Buy decent brands that you enjoy—or premium ones that a friend especially likes. Don't feel compelled to buy the most expensive brands, and avoid the least expensive. (Don't make the faux pas of pouring low-cost replacements into a high-priced bottle in order to save money. Your guests with discerning palates will know instantly.)

For wine, assume that a standard (750 ml) bottle of wine will, depending on how you pour, yield about five glasses. Usually, hosts provide red and white wines (or a dry rosé during the warmer months), but if you're excessively worried about spillage, pretend that your home is an art gallery and serve only whites. For a more complete bar, also buy one bottle each of tequila, sherry, dry vermouth, and sweet vermouth.

For mixers, opt for six-packs rather than liter bottles, since the soda will lose its fizz soon after being opened. The essential mixers are club soda or sparkling water, colas, ginger ale, orange juice, tomato juice, cranberry juice, pomegranate juice, and tonic water. Make sure you have a selection of sugar-free mixers, too.

Finally, stock your bar with these garnishes and condiments (often a good bartender will bring them along): cocktail olives and onions; maraschino cherries or liqueur-infused marinated cherries; lemon and lime juice; angostura bitters; pepper; coarse salt; superfine sugar; Tabasco; Worcestershire sauce; and horseradish.

Hiring a Bartender

If your cocktail party is going to be much larger than fifteen or twenty guests, it's time to consider bringing in additional help (even if there are two hosts and both of you mix a great cocktail). To find a good mixologist, start by asking friends and colleagues for recommendations. Caterers or other food service professionals are also a good source. Or ask a favorite bartender at a club or restaurant to do some moonlighting for you. If all else fails, look around online. If you're planning a larger party (forty people or more), consider having two barkeeps, with the bars set up strategically (that is, in different rooms) to avoid a massive line at one of them.

Here are some other considerations when staffing a bar:

- **Hire a professional:** A good bartender will have memorized her mixed-drink recipes and not need a guide. If you have a cocktail or two that you know and like, ask your prospective bartender to mix one up and see if it's to your liking.

- **Make sure your bartender comes equipped:** The better ones bring their own tools: wine and bottle openers; a cocktail shaker and strainer; a jigger; a long-handled spoon; a clean towel; and a knife for cutting garnishes. You're responsible for everything else.

- **Set parameters:** Explain ahead of time how full you'd like wineglasses to be poured; you don't want your bartender to overfill glasses, running down supplies and getting your guests drunk. But you want to be generous enough.

- **The details are important:** Be sure to ask if she'll be cleaning up her workspace at the end of the evening and if there's a minimum number of hours that you must book. Don't hesitate to ask for help determining how much and what kind of alcohol you'll need for your party, and be clear about what you want her to wear (a black bow tie and white shirt, or, for more casual events, a white button-down shirt and khakis, or even a black T-shirt and black pants—whatever you like).

THE ESSENTIALS

Dos and Don'ts for Hosting a Successful Cocktail Party

DOS:

- Make sure you have enough food and alcohol for your guests. You'll want about six to ten hors d'oeuvres per person.

- Serve all guests their first drink personally (unless it's a very large event) and, if it's a casual party, tell them they can serve themselves from then on. If it's more formal, direct them to the bar.

- Create a welcoming ambiance. Make sure your home is clean and uncluttered and that you have a place for coats and bags. Dim the lights, fire up the candles and music, and consider having some fresh-cut flowers.

- Introduce guests to one another. Be on the lookout for shy or orphaned guests and bring them into the fold.

- Remember that you're a host first and foremost, not a server or bartender. Spend time with your guests.

DON'TS:

- If you have pets, don't let them run free as though they own the house (even though they do). You never know who has an allergy or just doesn't like cats or dogs jumping on their laps or slobbering on their nice outfit.

- If someone spills wine or otherwise makes a mess, don't overreact. Take care of it the best you can in the moment and then deal with the rest later. Don't make a guest who's spilled feel worse than he probably already does.

- If guests bring wine or other edibles, there's no need to serve them. You've put together a menu—stick with it. Save the rest for yourself or for another party. It's actually considered rude for a guest to "request" you serve what she's brought along, since it is meant as a gift for you.

- Don't worry about when people will leave. As soon as the food runs down, most guests will get the idea. And if you stop serving the booze, they'll be out the door before you know it.

- Be sure not to overimbibe yourself.

Good Guest Behavior at a Cocktail Party

As with all social occasions, there's a short list of good manners for guests at a cocktail party.

- **RSVP on time:** Even though it's "just" cocktails, your host still needs an accurate headcount. (You do want to be sure to have enough to drink, don't you?)

- **Don't bring flowers:** A cocktail party is one case when the generous impulse of bringing flowers is better squelched. The reason? It's cumbersome for a host to deal with your flowers while greeting other guests, making introductions, and fetching drinks. Bring a bottle or box of chocolates instead.

- **Dress for the occasion:** If it's right after work, come in your business attire. Otherwise, take a clue from the invitation. Some parties are more formal than others and the invitation often holds the answer (it might even say "semiformal" or "business attire"). In choosing your shoes, bear in mind that you may be on your feet for several hours.

- **Bring your business cards:** Cocktail parties fall squarely between the personal and professional spheres. Normally, you wouldn't network (at least not openly) at a seated dinner, but a cocktail affair is fair game for this kind of socializing.

- **Master the art of mingling:** The best way to reconnect with friends and reach out to new people at a party depends a lot on the event and the crowd. But many of the same basics apply: Pay genuine attention to what people say; look them in the eye; and make an effort to engage in conversation, even if you're shy. (For more about this, see "Getting Friendly," page 28.)
- **Thank your host when leaving:** Follow up within the next day or two with an e-mail or short note.

These suggestions can easily be extrapolated to other kinds of parties, too. (For more on good guest etiquette, see below.)

GUEST ETIQUETTE

The worst thing about being a bad guest is supposed to be that you won't be invited back. Just as awful, however, is the possibility that you've ruined someone's party. Listen up, guests: *It's not that hard.*

Here are the basics: Get the date and time right; RSVP; pay attention to who has been invited (perhaps your boyfriend is not actually being asked to accompany you, for instance); and behave as you would in your own home—only better.

Problem Guests

Problem guests seem epidemic in an era where informality reigns and an anything-goes attitude about social events makes it hard for some people even to make commitments. With all that in mind, it is possible to handle the most troublesome of guests, no matter what kind of affair.

THE NO-SHOW

As a host, what do you do when a guest simply does not turn up? If it's a large cocktail party, carry on as planned, but keep your phone close by in case it turns out your guest needs directions or has had some kind of mishap. If it's a smaller party, like a sit-down dinner, you're likely to have a period of time set for before-dinner drinks. Keep to your schedule and if by the time dinner is ready to be served, do so. If they are complete no-shows, send an e-mail the next morning, asking, "Is everything okay? We were expecting you for dinner last night."

As a guest, there's really no excuse for failing to be in touch if you can't make it. Unless an emergency makes you absolutely unable to be in contact, there are simply too many ways to reach out these days not to say something, if only to text: "Ill. Can't make it. Call u tomorrow. So sorry." Even if your apologies are last-minute or after an event has started, let your host know. Otherwise, besides being aggravated, he or she may be worried. Then, follow up within a day or so with a call or note of apology.

THE LATE GUEST

People used to joke in the gay community about HST (homosexual standard time), based on the tired stereotype that we needed extra time to primp and preen, so we couldn't possibly be expected to arrive promptly. But excuses or not, the fact of the matter is that

"When gays hit on straights"

Q Not long ago I was hosting a "mixed" birthday party—gays and straights altogether. One of my gay friends started flirting pretty seriously with a straight guest—he practically glued himself to this fellow. Should I have told my gay friend he was barking up the wrong tree?

A No, you did just the right thing by staying out of it. What I imagine happened is that your gay friend found out the truth soon enough.

It's also possible that you were wrong about your "straight" friend's sexuality. Although I'm not Alfred Kinsey, what really interests me about your question is that it implies that we all live with just one label and one fixed sexual identity, which really isn't the case. What you think you may know about a friend's sexual identity may actually be limited or incorrect.

I say if two *single* people are flirting, good for them. Let them enjoy the frisson and see where it leads. We're all adults now.

---

there's only one way to deal with people who are late, and that's to go on without them—after a reasonable period of time. "Reasonable" pretty much depends on what the invitation said. If, for instance, you had announced an open house from 2:00 P.M. to 6:00 P.M., guests are not required to be punctual, although it's considerate for them to show up with enough time left to make more than an appearance. On the other hand, a dinner set for 7:30 P.M. means guests should arrive within fifteen minutes of the appointed time. Smart hosts will send out an e-mail reminder a day or two ahead of time so that guests will remember to come at the right hour (as will most electronic invitation websites, which dispatch timely reminders).

Hosts should, however, assume that people will run late; if your invitation says "dinner at 7:30," don't actually plan to serve people then. Allow for some wiggle room—forty-five

minutes is both long enough and not so long that people will become famished or inebriated. Should your tardy guest arrive in the middle of a dinner party, serve the course that is currently being enjoyed by the rest of your guests (if it's an informal gathering of close friends, you can make up a plate of everything he's missed).

If you're a guest who is late, reach out to your hosts via the means that is most likely to reach them *at that time*. If they're BlackBerry or iPhone addicts, send an e-mail or text. If their landline is in the kitchen, call that. When one means fails, try another until you make contact.

By the way, there are no bonus points to guests who show up early since your hosts may be in a last-minute frenzy of either making final preparations or getting dressed. If you arrive early, cool your heels by taking a walk or having a drink in a nearby bar.

THE UNEXPECTED GUEST

Sometimes it happens that you open the door, expecting to see *one* particular guest, and there she is with a date or a friend in tow. No doubt you're muttering to yourself, "Didn't she see that the invitation was only addressed to her?" No matter, they're both here now and your job is to make *them* comfortable. Offer drinks and—while they're saying hello to your other guests—figure out where you can squeeze in another place setting at the table and take stock of your food offerings. With any luck, you've planned for a bit of leftovers; if not, just serve everyone a little less.

TIPSY GUESTS

At one time or another, every host has had to deal with someone who's drunk too much. It's not an enviable position. Whatever you do,

remember that your party isn't a time for judgments. Once you recognize there's an issue, job one is to make sure that your guest is okay and gets home safely.

Here are a few other things you can do:

- Cut the person off and start serving soft drinks, water, or coffee. Do it quietly and without embarrassment. If you have sugary, carb-rich foods, which absorb alcohol, serve him some of those. None of this will make your guest less drunk or more able to drive, but it will start the process of sobering him up.
- Don't try to control what a drunken friend is saying or get into a debate or heated discussion. It's usually a no-win situation. Let the person go on and, if necessary, take her into another room, especially if she is starting to embarrass herself or causing others to feel uncomfortable. Be kind and gentle.

Queery

"Help for a drunken friend"

Q My boyfriend and I went to a posh cocktail party hosted by my best friend, George, who, truth be told, has a problem with alcohol. Late in the evening, pretty darn wasted, George felt my boyfriend up. BF made a big scene and insisted we leave. We're both furious, but what should we do?

A Well, what are you furious about most? That your best friend can't control his impulses? That he accosted your boyfriend publicly? Or that your boyfriend thinks you didn't stand up for him? A troika of manners dilemmas.

It's easiest to wag your finger at George: He violated your boyfriend's body and your trust—and may well be an alcoholic. Make a coffee date and tell him how you feel about what happened that night. I also suggest doing a little asking and listening, however. While I can understand that you're

furious, it sounds like George may need help more than you need retribution.

As for your boyfriend, he has good reason to be upset at both you and George. Why was it left to him to make the move to leave? I'm sorry to say it, but that was really your job, and you let him down. Take the initiative now and say two of the most difficult words in the English language: "I'm sorry." Then explain that you're sorry you didn't stand up for him when he needed your assistance. After all, that is—in part—what boyfriends are for.

THE SMOKER

According to various studies, one in three LGBT people smokes. This fact poses numerous problems for hosts. One blogger explained how he and his partner dealt with the issue: "We've decided our house will be no smoking, even though most of our friends smoke. Why should our house stink? I've told them all that they can smoke out in the garden, but that's it."

Most of your smoking friends will abide by the rules of your house, but it's best to state them early and often. If you've just moved or created a new rule, let people know that your home is now a smoke-free zone. Or do what a friend of mine did: Have an artist carve a NO SMOKING placard and hang it on your front door.

You'll also need a plan for friends who are smokers, especially if you're in an apartment. Do you have an outdoor porch or balcony? Do they need to go down ten stories and smoke on the street? Provide ashtrays when appropriate.

If you're a guest who's a smoker, be sure to always check with your host—and not your fellow guests—before lighting up. Explained one horrified guest: "We had just finished dinner when Heather pulled out her cigarettes and lit up. She asked no one and continued on with another cigarette before the host called her into the kitchen 'for a little help.' There was no more smoking after that."

Getting Your Guests to Leave

Often, parties run later than expected. This should in part be viewed as a tribute to your hosting skills, but it can be awkward when your guests linger, whether you've hosted a long dinner party or a fast trot of a cocktail party. What's the best way to get your partiers to grab their coats and head out the door?

One option is to simply be very direct. One half of a couple I know has no qualms getting the attention of the room and saying loudly, "Thank you for coming. We can't wait to see you the next time" as a curtain call for the evening.

Unfortunately, such a shout isn't the best of manners; most of us need to rely on other, more subtle methods. Try one or more of these:

- **Start with the invitation:** Specify an end time—for instance, say "Cocktails from 6:00 to 9:00 P.M." At the very least, you're giving your guests advance notice that there is a witching hour.
- **Serve coffee:** That's a well-established hint that you're now in the shank of the evening.
- **Make like a nightclub:** Turn up the lights and start to play louder, fast-paced music as an audio cue to your guests, who no doubt have witnessed other last-call moments. Alternatively, if you think your guests will notice, turn the music off and let the sounds of silence speak volumes.
- **Enlist a friend to help you out:** More often than not, the first person or couple to take leave starts a stampede out the door. If your evening is running long, pull a good friend aside and suggest she help you break things up.
- **Start cleaning up:** This is on the more aggressive side and is recommended only with close friends and family. However, if you clear the table, load the dishwasher, and pack up the leftovers, even the least savvy of guests will get the hint.

If all attempts fail, then leave it to your partner to wind things down (if you have one and she agrees) and say good night.

EATING OUT

There's lots of room for misunderstandings and gaffes—some even causing offense—when you are dining out, whether it's a business lunch, a group of LGBT friends celebrating together, or a romantic tête-à-tête with someone you met on Gay.com. Do you split the check? If so, how? Who chooses the wine (and what price range is okay for all)? What if you encounter homophobia—or transphobia—while dining out? And most important, how can you make sure you have a great restaurant experience—with a date, a group of friends, or in just about any situation?

When There's No Host

Many of us celebrate our birthdays, new jobs, anniversaries, and other important milestones en masse at a favorite restaurant. (One day I hope a young person's coming out will be honored along the same lines.) If a partner or friend is acting as the host, the situation is usually pretty straightforward; he or she makes the major decisions—where to go and how much to spend on wine—and takes care of the tab.

However, the event can get dicey when that person is just the organizer—the "no-host host," if you will—and is not picking up the bill. Any number of things can go amiss. For instance, a diner needs to leave early and throws down some bills to cover his share—except that when the check comes, it turns out that amount wasn't enough; a nondrinking contingent decide that they're not comfortable paying

for anyone's liquor bill; or someone orders a very expensive entrée and expects the group to defray the cost.

What to do? It's smart for the no-host host to plan ahead—when the invitation is being made—by establishing some guidelines about how to deal with the check. If the plan is separate checks, let it be known. If the intention is to treat the birthday gal or the anniversary couple (with everyone sharing in the cost), be clear about that at the outset, too. If you're invited in such a manner and don't want to participate, then politely decline, claiming another obligation.

Another smart solution is for the no-host host to talk with the restaurant manager ahead of time about creating a special dinner (with choices for each course) for a fixed price. That can significantly reduce the cost for all involved and also add some certainty about the required contribution. If this becomes the plan, let your friends know about it ahead of time, so that, aside from the bar bill, they will know the cost of the evening.

An e-mail invitation to a no-host celebration

THE ESSENTIALS

Dividing the Bill

Here are some ways to split the check, especially when there's no host. Mind you, no one way is necessarily the best; it really depends on your group of friends.

- **Ask your server for separate checks:** This is not allowed at some restaurants, so be sure to make the request right up front, before you start ordering.
- **Pass the check around and have each person do the math himself:** Make sure to allow for tax and tip. One of you then needs to count it all up at the end to make sure that not only is the bill covered, but the tip is sufficient.

- **Choose someone to play "banker":** That person will have the job of determining what you each owe. While this can be a thankless and difficult job, it works well when the designated numbers person has good math skills.
- **Divide the bill equally:** Even if you've ordered very differently from one another, this is a great way to avoid counting pennies. Make sure to include the tax and tip before you divide things up. Keep in mind that if you're dining with a friend or a group whom you see regularly, the cost will probably even out over time. Nevertheless, do speak up if things are consistently uneven, and be sensitive to changing circumstances—for instance, if one of your friends has just lost her job, don't make her pay a share of your truffle risotto.

QUEERY

"No gay smooching allowed in the restaurant."

Q Last month, my partner and I were at a very nice bistro. After a glass of wine, I took his hand and held it across the table. Soon after, I gave him a peck on the cheek and then excused myself. After I returned, the maître d' told us we had to leave because we had been "inappropriate." He admitted it was because we were a same-sex couple. I didn't want to make a scene so we left. What could we have done and stayed within good manners?

A I completely understand not wanting to make a scene, but if something like this ever happens again, I suggest kicking the ball upstairs right away by asking to speak to the general manager or owner. Explain what happened and why it's a double standard. Stay calm, but be forceful.

If you don't find any resolution this way, there are several options to consider. Go online and write a review; start with the "Rants and Raves" section of Zagat Online or go to Yelp.com. If the restaurant has a Facebook page, post your comments there and ask your friends to support your position.

All this will get the manager's attention soon enough. Since it *is* legal to discriminate based on sexual orientation in most parts of the United States (but not in Canada), sometimes we have to resort to the court of public opinion and community pressure. And if enough of the community joins you in an online protest, the restaurant may soon understand that we can vote with our dollars just as we can vote at the ballot box. As a last resort, you could call the ACLU or an LGBT-friendly legal firm to see whether it can provide assistance.

Ordering Wine for a Group

With the straightforward choice of red-versus-white a thing of the past, the task of ordering wine can sometimes be a nightmare, even for an oenophile. Now, everyone wants a favorite varietal: syrah, pinot gris, or tempranillo. If that's the case, better to let your companions order by the glass. If consensus seems doable, perhaps there is a wine aficionado in your group who is suited for this task. (By the way, it's always fine to ask your server or the sommelier for a recommendation.) When friends or couples don't know one another very well (which is to say, they also don't know each other's budgets), it's a good idea for the decider to ask someone else (and not her own partner) for "approval." For instance, she could tentatively choose two different wines, at different price points, describing and pointing them out on the wine list to one (or more) of her dining companions.

With friends you eat out with often, it's a lot simpler: Stay within the dollar range you usually spend. If you want to splurge, ask them before you order.

By the way, if you're at a table of wine drinkers and don't plan to imbibe, just place your hand or fingers over the glass as the server approaches and say "No thanks." There's no need to turn the glass upside down. When it comes to paying, the polite thing for the drinkers to do is suggest that they cover the bar tab themselves, especially if it's a significant amount.

Who Orders First

You may have noticed that in many "nicer" restaurants women still tend to have their orders taken before the men. Some say that's

QUEERY

"Dinner à trois"

Q Sometimes I go out to dinner with my boyfriend and his rich ex-lover, and the ex always insists on picking up the tab. It really bothers me, because I know he's just trying to impress my boyfriend. How do I take control of this situation without making a big deal out of it?

A First, I'd suggest you start by talking with your boyfriend about this unorthodox arrangement, explaining how it makes you feel. Then, it's really up to him to speak with his ex. Still, there are other ways to master the problem at hand: Take the initiative. Invite them both out, saying definitively, "And it's my treat" (naturally, choose a restaurant that you can afford). Another idea is to surreptitiously give your credit card to the host and ask him to put the tab on it, rather than bring a check to the table. While visiting the men's room, sign the check and when you get back to the table, you can announce that the bill is all taken care of.

In short, you need to find a new mathematical model. This is why threesomes—in bed and out—almost always leave someone out.

a vestige of sexism (and they're right), but such an approach is simply supposed to be a courtesy. When it comes to same-sex couples, we're more likely asked to order in a sequence of the server's choosing. Your server may start with the person seated at the "head" of the table, with the eldest or youngest, or even with the one he judges to be the best potential tipper. What matters most is that he collects the orders in a way that can be remembered.

If you're on a date, with a colleague, or with your parents, it's a nice touch to indicate to the server that you'd like him to start with your dinner companions—again, as a courtesy.

Who's Got the Check?

There's rarely any question about who pays when the terms "host" or "guest" have been used—or one person has clearly invited the other(s). So, if you intend to take someone out, it's best to signal this directly. For instance: "We'd like you to be our guests"; "Please let us be the host for your anniversary celebration"; or "Will you be my date at dinner on Saturday?" Then, when the time comes, it's easier to avoid that moment where the check sits on the table almost radioactively.

Even if you've been invited out to dinner, it's still nice to make the small gesture of reaching for the check when it comes. Chances are you'll be rebuffed, but in case there's been a miscommunication, at least you won't look like a freeloader. If you like, offer to pay the server's tip, take care of after-dinner drinks, or pay for the cab, coat check, or parking. Most important, don't forget to say thank you. And you could say, "The next time, dinner is on me."

THE ESSENTIALS

A Guide to Restaurant Tipping

There's nothing special about LGBT tipping, but most of us could stand a refresher from time to time. As a big-time restaurant owner explains, "If you want to be fondly remembered by the waitstaff, someone whom they're really happy to see walk through the door, being friendly and leaving an above-average tip is all you really need to do."

Here's what's considered standard for good service, although you can certainly go beyond these suggestions for exemplary care:

THE MEAL	15%–20% of the bill (before tax)
YOUR BARTENDER	$1–$2 per drink or 15%–20% of the tab (whichever is higher)
COAT CHECK	$1 per coat, more if it's an upscale place
PARKING ATTENDANT	$1–$3

By the way, you can tell a lot about people by how they treat a server—in addition to the way they tip. Whether on a business dinner, out with friends, or on a date, be mindful of treating your server (and the entire restaurant staff) with courtesy and respect—and not as personal servants.

Some of us also regard servers as fair game for flirting or hooking up with. If that describes you, think again. First of all, paying attention to someone other than your dining companion is not so nice. Second, most of us on the job don't like being hit upon while working. Third, how good is your gaydar?

HOUSEGUESTS

Whether you're a guest at a friend's home, your colleague's summer cabin, or a family member's cozy apartment, being an overnight visitor requires extra alertness and sensitivity to other's needs. As a guest, your job is to make your stay as low-maintenance as possible for your host—no demands for 600-thread Egyptian cotton sheets or pillows with your preferred mix of down and goose feathers. (If you *must* have a certain pillow, bring it along with you.) Also, no special meals. Above all, remember that a private home is not a hotel.

If you're the host, your job is to make your guests feel welcome—whether you have a sprawling, three-story house on the beach or a city flat where your visitors sleep on a pullout couch.

In addition to these basics, guests will benefit from advice on specifically gay situations, such as visiting your family as a same-sex couple and understanding the "house rule" on tricking.

Extending an Invitation

If you're planning to invite a gay friend or group of LGBT friends to stay with you—for a long weekend, the holidays, or a birthday celebration—give careful consideration to the mix, just as you would at a dinner party. For instance, don't invite two ex-lovers at the same time (unless you're 100 percent certain things are okay between them), or friends who you know have a strong dislike for one

another. One host explained, "As much as I wanted both Lance and Vince to stay with us for the July Fourth weekend, they simply can't be civil with each other, so I chose one over the other." Even if it's a more casual invitation, like "Why don't you spend Saturday night with us after the theater?" pay attention to the following considerations, which will help make sure both you and your company enjoy the visit:

- **If you have a partner, make decisions together:** One of you may like to have overnight guests more than the other. Sometimes you just may want the house to yourselves. Either way, it's wise to talk together, set parameters, and put guest visits in your joint datebook or online calendar.

  Note: Roommates and housemates (if you have them) deserve to be looped into these discussions as well.

- **Be specific in your invitation:** The more precise you can be in setting the timing of a visit, the less likely there will be any confusion by your guests or resentment on your part. If you're inviting friends for the weekend, let them know whether you expect them to arrive in time for Friday dinner or not until Saturday morning. Similarly, set the end point at the start. "We're really looking forward to seeing you and Samantha this weekend. Just so you know, we'll have lunch at the house on Sunday and then plan to go back to the city." Samantha and her girlfriend should understand that to be their exit cue and make their plans accordingly.

- **Make any necessary disclosures before your guests arrive:** It's important to ensure that your guests have the right expectations. Do you have any pets that might set off a friend's allergies? Is it a nonsmoking or nondrinking house? Is the housekeeper coming at 8:00 A.M.? Will your guests be sharing a bathroom—or even a bedroom—with someone else? If so, let them know ahead of time in a direct fashion, for instance, "We've also invited our friend Gail to join us this weekend. I hope you won't mind sharing the guest bath with her. I promise you she's not a bathroom hog."

- **Be ready for your guests:** Make sure the house is clean, the beds are made, and towels are laid out, and leave some time for those last-minute touches.

  Among the niceties that distinguish a great host from a good one are, in the bedroom, a vase of fresh flowers, an extra blanket, reading material and a reading light, and an alarm clock or clock radio; and, in the bathroom, shampoo, a new toothbrush or disposable razor, a new bar of soap, and other basic body products.

- **Lay out your house rules:** Once your friends arrive and are settled, give them a quick tour and let them know of any special house customs or rules.

  For instance, "We all have breakfast at 8:00 A.M. on the porch." Or "Feel free to help yourself to anything in the refrigerator or bar, but I'm saving those strawberries for tomorrow's margaritas." Or "Please strip your bed on the day you leave." Slightly more obsessive hosts who have frequent weekend guests write up their house rules, leaving them on the dresser. However, houseguest etiquette to that degree is perhaps better suited for a B&B than your own home.

STRAIGHT TALK

"First off, I'm heterosexual, and I want to know how to avoid inviting a gay friend's live-in boyfriend as a houseguest. I'm not homophobic; I just don't like the guy."

It's always refreshing when people dislike others because of who they are instead of what they are. But seriously, the truth is you have two basic options. One is to embrace the old saying that "feeling follows form." That means invite the boyfriend, engage him, entertain him, and hope that through your actions as a good host—and his as a good guest—you'll come to like him better. Your other choice is to find a time when you happen to know the boyfriend will be away, and invite your good friend then. But, as you know, that's not foolproof—and it also might be quite transparent.

The Dutiful Houseguest

Whether you're an overnight guest or a week-long visitor, there are some basic considerations to being a good guest when staying over. First and foremost, be considerate of your host. Arrive on time. Leave as planned. Don't pretend that you're at a resort and expect to be taken care of (starting with the basics—make your own bed in the morning). If it's just an overnight visit, bring a hostess gift; if you're staying for two or more days, offer to take your hosts out for dinner or make them a special dinner at (their) home if you think they will enjoy that. Then, once back home, write a thank-you note and think about how you might reciprocate for your host's generosity in the future.

Here's how to make sure that you're a guest who's invited back:

- **RSVP promptly:** When you receive an invitation, respond within two or three days. If you're unclear about your plans, let your host know that so he can hold the invitation or reschedule you for some other time. Keep in mind that it's very bad form to ask, "Who else is invited?" Saying that makes it seem like your response is contingent upon the answer, rather than the invitation itself.

- **Ask what you may bring:** Also ask when you are expected to arrive and depart, and whether you can help with something in particular, such as preparing or shopping for a meal or transporting other guests.

- **Don't be a fair-weather friend:** If the weather is poor, do not cancel at the last minute, because that looks like you value the beach or the ski slope more than you do the company.

- **Come as you are:** If you're single, don't ask to bring along another guest. If you have a dog or cat, leave the critter at home unless it's explicitly invited.

- **Make your mark:** Bring an upbeat attitude. Contribute to your visit in the best ways you can: Are you good at mixing drinks? Are you a bewitching storyteller? An energetic brunch chef? Can you wash dishes? (Yes, you can!)

- **Be adaptable:** If things aren't to your liking, don't complain. If an "issue" can be easily remedied, such as an extra blanket procured or the air-conditioning adjusted, ask politely.

- **Respect your host's schedule:** While staying with friends or family, don't make other plans without consulting them. If you know others in the area, talk with your host(s) about how best for you to see them. Don't worry: Most people will be happy to have a little down time, but do ask.

- **No tricking without prior permission:** Don't bring a stranger back with you unless you know it's okay.

- **Send a thank-you note:** After the visit, no matter how well you know your hosts (even if they're your kids or your parents) and no matter how much you thanked them upon leaving, send a thank-you note (or e-mail). In

QUEERY

"My boyfriend wants to have sex while we're houseguests, but I think it's rude."

Q My boyfriend and I are going to be visiting some close friends at their apartment next weekend. He really likes the idea of getting hot and heavy while we're there; I think it's rude to have sex at someone's place when you're a guest. What do you think?

A Although some think it's disrespectful to one's hosts to have a private pleasure-fest in your room, I think it's fine as long as you're able to keep it quiet. That means: no moaning, no screaming, and no running to and from the bathroom naked. Lock the door, and use a towel to avoid stains or other tell-tale signs. If you bring toys, remember to pack them up on departure, especially if you've hidden them in a dresser. And definitely don't mention "it" at breakfast, even in the most general or cute way—although your hosts may pick something up from the looks on your faces.

I do suggest, however, that you save your more complicated rites and rituals for the privacy of your own home, or for a hotel.

your message, be sure to mention any specific nice touches or extra efforts that your host went to on your behalf.

THE ESSENTIALS

The Right Hostess Gift

While there are some social occasions where a hostess gift (the traditional term, but these days one could just as well be presenting a host gift) isn't mandatory (such as a cocktail party or a casual brunch), overnight stays—of whatever length—call for one. Even if you think your host has everything, here are some ways to approach the challenge. If she has a favorite leisure-time activity (say, cooking, golf, gardening, or viniculture), find a small gift on that theme, one that indicates you gave it some personal consideration. Still stumped? If you are staying more than one night, then during your visit take note of what your host might actually want or enjoy and purchase it (or order it online for later delivery). Here are some tried-and-true ideas almost anyone would appreciate:

- A houseplant or orchid
- Long-stemmed candles
- A picture frame (later on you can send a photo from your visit)
- A box of gourmet chocolates
- A couple of bottles of wine
- A nice set of dish towels for the kitchen
- A collection of herbs and spices
- Homemade jams, cakes, muffins, or breads (wrapped up nicely)
- Barbecue tools (especially if you're visiting in the summer)
- Specialty coffees or teas

What do you think makes a good guest?

"Get out of the house and/or stay away from the host for a certain amount each day."

"Be careful with your lube. One time some male houseguests left a huge lube handprint on my expensive guest sheets!"

"If you want full service, stay at a hotel!"

Asking Whether You Can Bring a Date

It's bad form to ask to bring an additional person if you're going to be someone's houseguest, just as it is at dinner parties and weddings. More likely than not, your host already has figured out the room assignments; for all you know, you may have been designated a twin bed or be sharing a room with someone else. If you've recently started dating someone new—and your host doesn't know—he certainly will learn so by the end of your visit. With any luck, you'll both be invited the next time. (A good way to ensure this: Invite your host over as your dinner guest so that he can meet your new beau.)

Still, if a host is asked whether another guest can be accommodated, it's perfectly acceptable to say, "So sorry, we really don't have room. Perhaps another time." End of discussion.

Guests Who Stay Too Long

As Ben Franklin famously said, "Fish and visitors stink after three days." One hopes that guests know not to overstay their welcome, but if the day of departure is looming and you see

"Looking for a skier to seduce at my friend's cabin."

Q I've been invited to my friend Dave's ski cabin for a gay ski weekend, but I don't ski! I'm single right now and wouldn't mind sitting in the main ski lodge and chatting up the skiers as they come off the slopes. But how do I ask Dave if it's okay to "entertain" at the cabin—if I find someone—and skip the ski lessons?

A Presumably Dave knows that you don't ski and asked you to come along because he takes pleasure in your company. But it sounds as if you're more interested in using the cabin as a love nest for some après-ski activity than as a place to spend quality time with your friend. When you're a houseguest, some rules are pretty standard, like take short showers, recycle, strip your bed before you leave, and no tricks, please.

If you insist on asking, start with this question first: "Will I have my own room?" Then you can move into the specifics of what you have in mind, but be careful—Dave may not like where the conversation is going.

---

no signs that your guest is inclined to leave, here are some other things you can do:

- **Don't be shy:** Ask about your guests' departure. If the morning arrives when you understood your friends were leaving, yet they make no move to do so, ask what time they expect to get going. If you're so inclined, as an incentive, offer to put together a lunch or snack for them to take along. If they had planned on staying longer, your question will act as a gentle reminder that the clock is running down.
- **Explain that you'll need to get back to work:** And that while you've enjoyed the visit, you're sure they'll understand.
- **The guest room is needed for others:** Perhaps you're expecting some new friends shortly and you'll need to get the room ready for them. If untrue, this is a permissible white lie.

- **Extenuating circumstances:** On the other hand, if your guests have been grounded by bad weather or some other act of God, or a guest has become ill, be patient. Do what you can to help them make new plans, and continue to be a good host.

Guests with Special Needs

Houseguests with medical or other personal issues that may affect a visit should let the host know beforehand. For instance, a friend who has HIV notes that, whenever possible, he asks for a bedroom with its own bathroom so that he can keep his meds private. It you are allergic to cats or dogs, you may be able to visit if the host can keep the pets out of your bedroom for a couple of days before your arrival and during your stay. (Still, bring along your own antihistamines.) Likewise, if you have certain food preferences, it's your responsibility to buy any necessary staples rather than asking your host to provide, say, low-carb, gluten-free, or sugar-free foods.

The bottom line if you're a guest with special needs: Don't be shy about your needs when it comes to your health, but remember that this is someone else's home. The more you can do to take of yourself, the better—and the more likely you are to be invited back.

Family Visits

When expecting a visit from family members, think about the kinds of activities they would enjoy but that might also introduce them to your gay life and friends. When I was first out to my folks, I threw a small party in their honor when they came to visit, inviting my closest LGBT (and straight) friends. My gay pals did remarkably well at putting my parents at ease about my sexual orientation and being ambassadors-at-large for LGBT life.

Here are some other ideas for hosting family:

- Some cities have walking tours of their gay districts, like San Francisco's "Cruising the Castro." This can be an enjoyable way to spend several hours together while your family learns about local LGBT history and culture.
- If you belong to an LGBT church or temple, consider going to services together. If you're on a gay sports team, invite your siblings or parents to a game or meet.
- Check out a gay or lesbian film that you feel will be both educational and good entertainment. Be sure that any film you all go

to is "appropriate" for everyone's taste and sensibility.

- If it's Pride season, take them to the parade. Even better, see if they'd like to march with a group like PFLAG. Keep in mind, however, that for every lesbian-mom-with-stroller, you risk a buttless-chap situation. Explain that it's all in good fun and about diversity and pride.
- Visit a museum exhibit about gay life. Three notable ones are the Stonewall Library and Archives in Ft. Lauderdale, the James C. Hormel Gay & Lesbian Center, located in San Francisco's main public library, and the Canadian Lesbian and Gay Archives in Toronto.
- If your community has an LGBT center, check out what's on the calendar; you'll likely find an event of interest to all.

Visiting Your Family

If you and your significant other are planning to visit your parents (or other family members), make sure you've had the bedroom discussion—that is, one bedroom or two—before your arrival and that everyone is satisfied with the outcome. Many parents will have no qualms about a same-sex couple sharing a bed; others may insist that you sleep in separate rooms (just as some parents don't allow unmarried straight lovers to share a room until the wedding). While you may not agree with your parents' decision, you'll need to accept that they are entitled to enforce whatever rules they like in their own house. If their decision is not to your liking, you still have some choices: You can decide to acquiesce and stay in separate rooms; you can stay at a nearby hotel or with friends; or you can choose not to visit at all.

Just don't leave this conversation until your arrival.

"My daughter and her lover are coming from South Carolina to spend the holidays with my husband and me. Do I put unmarried lesbians in separate rooms when they come to visit?"

My first instinct is to recommend that you treat your daughter and her partner (that is to say, unmarried gay partners) the same way you would treat unmarried heterosexual overnight visitors. If you don't want unmarried couples to sleep together under your roof, that's your prerogative and those are your morals. But don't set household policy based on sexual orientation. That's discrimination.

However, there's another dimension in this case. Your daughter and her partner are not allowed to legally wed in South Carolina (and most other states). So, if they are a committed couple in every other way, don't hold this technicality against them. I'd say it's a shared room and bed for them.

SUMMER SHARES

Whether it's Provincetown, Fire Island Pines, the Russian River, or Rehoboth Beach, there's a long tradition of summer group housing rentals in the LGBT community. Historically, these gay vacation spots permitted a measure of freedom not usually found in day-to-day life back in the city, and they still do—though in return you're generally required to give up a little privacy and show extra patience in the face of crowding, sharing, late-night music, and all the rest. Despite their casual ambience, however, these summer enclaves have an etiquette of their own. By the way, most of the following suggestions also apply to other group vacation adventures, whether a house in France or a cycling tour through Canada's national parks.

Making Summer Plans

Seasonal households may contain anywhere from a handful to twenty housemates, some previously friends, others complete strangers at the outset. Even though those long out of college may find the communal-living aspects of a summer share a challenge, as will be adapting to the dictates of majority rule, the pleasures of relaxing in an LGBT-friendly resort can definitely be worth it. The success of a seasonal house depends most of all on participants' ability to create a community—stepping up to their responsibilities, and beyond them.

Many summer households start up the year by convening a meeting in the spring to make sure all new members are properly introduced to one another, to choose weekends and roommates (if not to start some early cruising), and to agree on a set of house rules. Whether at the beach, in the mountains, or in a small country town, the writing of these rules can make international diplomacy look easy. Here are some of the questions to consider in your house regs:

- **When does the season start and when does it close?** Who is responsible for opening and closing the house? When are payments due? And what's the understanding for renewing the following year?

- **What exactly does a quarter, half, or full share entitle you to?** Can you make trades later on if your plans change? How are the holiday weekends (like July Fourth, Pines Party weekend, and Labor Day) divvied up? (Seniority in the house usually prevails on these valuable three-day stretches.)

- **How will bills be paid?** Will there be a house fund that covers all basics (nonalcoholic beverages, food staples, utilities, for instance)? How will inequities be dealt with (if they will be dealt with at all)? Is alcohol included in the general house fund? (See "Dividing Expenses," below, for more about this.)

- **Does the house have policies regarding alcohol and drug use?** What about smoking?

- **Are there rules or extra charges for overnight guests?** Either old friends or new sex partners? Is it okay to have friends out during the week (when presumably fewer will be in attendance)?

Nevertheless, rules can go only so far. Take note of the personality types you encounter as a summer house's occupant list is being set up. If you're the head of the household (see page 300) or already onboard and interviewing potential housemates, turn potentially difficult or incompatible candidates away. If you're looking for a share, don't cast your lot with a group where you don't feel good about the mix of personalities.

Dividing Expenses

There are several ways to approach the money question. Some households agree to share and divide all costs equally, while others buy staples and specific meals together, leaving the rest of the shopping to each individual. Household accounts can be settled weekly, biweekly, monthly—or however the group decides. Still other households share only the roof over their heads, with each member responsible for all of her own needs.

If there's going to be any sharing, set up a system. Maybe there's a pool to which everyone contributes and takes from as necessary to buy food, alcohol, and miscellaneous household items. Alternatively, each member spends what's necessary, putting receipts with her name on it in a jar or in a basket. At the designated time, all receipts are added and divided. For this reason, it's a good idea to designate a household accountant. It needn't be someone with an MBA, but your ideal choice has people skills almost as good as his math skills. Once the rules are set, it's the accountant's job to make sure the bills are paid and that weekend spending is properly handled.

If you owe money at the end of a weekend, don't leave without paying. If you're

QUEERY

"I don't see why nondrinkers should help pay for the house booze."

Q I'm new to my Cherry Grove share this year and I realized at the planning brunch in the spring that everyone is expected to pay for the house alcohol. No exceptions. That wouldn't be a problem except that I don't drink much, and some of these guys knock it back! Is that fair?

A Is that fair? No, it's not. But the more important question is: Is it equitable?

Sure, you drink less. But do you eat more? Or are you a carnivore? Maybe the pool heating bill comes from the joint account and you're in it daily and some of the others view it as a Hockney painting to be admired from afar. This is equitable (balanced), which is different than fair (equal). The most important thing, however, is that you go into the season being comfortable about the house rules. If you're unsuccessful in bending them in a way that pleases you, the best decision might be not to join this particular house.

going to leave before the weekend's expenses are tallied, pay more than what you think you owe. It's easier to get refunds from the collective pot than it is to do an additional collection once you've departed. Plus, it's just not fair to stick others with more than their share.

Annoying Housemates

Every seasonal household has its annoying housemates. The question is *how* annoying, and what's the infraction? If it is a violation of one of the basic rules—say, smoking indoors when that's prohibited, hogging the bathroom while others are waiting, or bringing home an overnight guest to a shared bedroom—someone needs to play cop.

Usually there is a head of household—either the owner of the house or the primary lease signer. If there is an issue, it's best if he

talks to the alleged offender privately, explaining the problem and reiterating more appropriate behavior. (Stop smoking inside. Stop using the bathroom as your private hair salon. Don't subject your roommate to your sexual hijinks.) This is usually an easier, more dignified solution than involving the entire group in an all-hands meeting (nonetheless, some groups prefer the latter approach).

More often than not, though, the annoying housemate is just that—and not a rule breaker. She's got a negative attitude, her sense of humor really isn't funny, or she's just not considerate. If you can't bear it, then have a one-on-one chat about the problem and try to resolve it that way, without any accusations or embarrassment. It's possible she's completely unaware of having habits that rub people the wrong way. Here are some of the most common annoying archetypes along with what to do in each case:

The slob: *He treats the entire house as though it's his own, leaving wet and dirty clothes everywhere. Although he makes a faint effort at doing his chores, his level of cleanliness is so low that it makes little difference. Generally, the slob is unaware of his state.*

WHAT TO DO: Make a chart listing each housemate on one axis and the cleaning chores to be done on the other. Determine who is responsible for which and when they are to be done.

The control freak: *You know the type—organizing, cleaning, fretting, complaining, and, in general, insisting his way is best no matter what.*

WHAT TO DO: Remind him that it's summer and that country or island life is meant to be enjoyed at a different pace. Remind him that people have different ways of enjoying their domesticity. Be firm—if not perhaps a little controlling yourself with this type.

The sexual athlete: *This type has no problem picking up a guy at the beach and bringing him back to the house for sex—in the pool, the living room, or the bedroom he shares. He's generally unaware of the hour and of volume control.*

WHAT TO DO: Make sure your house rules are comprehensive. Some households don't allow sex between housemates. Some don't allow tricks to be brought home. Still others put condoms and lube on the communal shopping list.

The semiresident guest: *In any household, an occasional overnight visitor may be fine (check your house rules). But such behavior becomes inconsiderate if a housemate starts bringing her new girlfriend around—and around—eating dinner, watching TV, and otherwise becoming a regular presence in the house. That's called taking advantage of your friends and their goodwill.*

WHAT TO DO: Work out some form of payment or barter arrangement with your housemates. Perhaps your friend can buy the weekend's food or make a special dinner. Or pay the utilities. Or limit her visits.

CHAPTER 11

On the Job

LGBT Workplace Etiquette

It's one thing to be out of the closet among friends, family, and your neighbors, but often quite another to "be yourself" at work. Currently, it's perfectly legal to fire someone based on sexual orientation in three-quarters of the states; furthermore, only a handful of states provide transgender people protection from workplace discrimination. In Canada you can't be fired for being gay, but only in the Northwest Territories is that protection explicitly extended to transmen and -women.

Nevertheless, being out in the workplace has become the de facto norm for a great many of us in recent decades, reflecting the positive strides of the LGBT civil rights movement. Making reference to a same-sex partner in a job interview is often a viable option now. A majority of Fortune 500 companies provide domestic partner benefits; some of them even provide paid leave for the new LGBT parent who is not giving birth (which was unheard of until recently). Figuring out when and where it's okay to be out without affecting your career can still be a head-scratcher, and often requires stepping gingerly through an antiquated and discriminatory office culture. You'll want to scope out the scene where you work or want to work. Upon landing a new job, you'll need to determine whether to deploy little tricks like "pronoun shifting" when your private life comes up, or, on the contrary, if it's okay to bring your boyfriend or girlfriend to a company function.

By following these basics of LGBT workplace etiquette, you're likely to earn the respect of your colleagues day by day (performing your job duties well is also a prerequisite). With changing mores, let's hope that workplace discrimination against LGBT people will soon be a thing of the past; until then, greater protections of LGBT people on the job are needed, such as the proposed federal Employment Non-Discrimination Act, which would prohibit job discrimination on the basis of sexual orientation or gender identity.

JOB HUNTING

In addition to all the usual elements to worry about when seeking a job, LGBT people generally face an additional set of hurdles throughout the process. First, you have to determine whether a company is likely to be gay-friendly. And then, you have to ask yourself such questions as: Just how out do you want to be? Can you wait until you get the job to reveal your sexuality or gender identity? Would you be okay about working in an environment where you can't be yourself—in exchange for an upward career move? These are very personal decisions to make, but as you fine-tune your résumé and cover letter, and embark on interviews, they can have a big effect on how soon you land a new job that's right for you.

Finding an LGBT-friendly Company

There's already a lot to think about when seeking a new position—questions about roles and responsibilities, title, salary, the kind of work the company does, its location, benefits, and who your boss and coworkers will be. Looming prominently alongside these factors for many of us is whether the company is LGBT-friendly. LGBT workplace advocates say that your job satisfaction and productivity will get a definite boost when you can be yourself, that is to say, out. By contrast, tolerating day after day of anti-gay or anti-trans treatment—or even just a vague sense of discrimination or exclusion—will wear down most of us, whether the job is a vehicle for creativity or just a way to pay the rent.

LGBT-friendly companies usually provide equal benefits, which is a big plus, so that you can put your partner on the company health insurance plan and become eligible to take parental or bereavement leave. Nevertheless, in the United States, the most LGBT-friendly companies generally do not compensate gay employees for the additional taxes incurred on health benefits for a partner. Unlike with straight married couples, the federal tax code treats these benefits as additional income; in fact, this gay tax penalty can be quite hefty. (Google, Kimpton Hotels, and Cisco Systems are among the first firms to "gross up" an employee's wages to cover the penalty.) Then there are the less tangible elements of the work day, like being able to talk openly about your life with your colleagues, taking a date or partner to company events, or even just showcasing a photo of you and your boyfriend or girlfriend on your desk.

It's noteworthy that many companies go out of their way these days to recruit LGBT employees, with managers and interviewers stressing in early encounters the same-sex benefits they provide. These employers generally find that to remain competitive, providing these benefits is not only the right thing to do, but good for business, too.

THE ESSENTIALS

Seven Ways to Learn More About Gay-Friendly Companies

The number of LGBT-friendly companies has jumped significantly in the past decade, but because of the dearth of federal and state protections for gay employees, it's even more important to try to find out whether a specific company is LGBT-friendly:

1. Consult the Human Rights Campaign's (HRC) Best Places to Work list as well as its Corporate Equality Index. This gay advocacy group rates hundreds of companies based on benefits and nondiscrimination policies, and also looks at such issues as diversity training, LGBT philanthropy, and whether there are LGBT employee or affinity groups.

2. Check out one of the websites that match LGBT-friendly companies with LGBT candidates, such as ProGayJobs.com.

3. Visit one of the many job fairs now geared at making those matches, including national membership groups such as the National LGBT Bar Association and events such as Atlanta's Southern Comfort Conference, an annual event for trans people.

4. Google the name of a company you're interested in to see what kinds of donations it may have made or political affiliations it may have. In 2010, for instance, Target, with a 100 percent rating from the HRC Equality Index, appalled many LGBT people by lending financial support to an anti-gay politician in Minnesota.

5. Network to find someone who works at the company or organization you're eyeing. "I happened to know this guy at ——— who is totally out at work and even has his boyfriend on the health plan," says one job seeker of his dream employer, "so I knew they were cool." Don't forget to ask if the company has an LGBT employee group.

6. If you're out, raise the matter directly in interviews, especially if asking about benefits or diversity, with a question such as "Is the office environment comfortable for lesbians and gay men?"

7. Another option is to come out to your interviewer less directly, whether casually mentioning a partner, or some LGBT volunteer work, and see what kind of reaction you get. With any luck it will be "It will be great to have your partner join us for the holiday party this year."

Are You In or Out?

Times are improving and there's a lot to be said for LGBT visibility in the job-seeking process. Employment discrimination based on sexual orientation and gender identity is harder and harder to defend—both ethically and economically—as the job market fills up with proud and qualified LGBT applicants. Even the U.S. military has finally dropped its long-standing discriminatory policy regarding gay and lesbian service members; not surprisingly, this is a nonissue in Canada. But the strongest argument of all for including LGBT items in your résumé may be that you can identify supportive work environments more quickly—where you're likely to be hired anyway. In other words, by being visible, you're screening them as much as they're screening you.

As much as times have changed, it's not uncommon for job applicants to edit the LGBT out of a résumé—for instance, not mentioning a summer volunteering with the National Gay and Lesbian Task Force or your role as a fund-raiser with the Bisexual Resource Center. Although few LGBT career counselors support this strategy in theory, they do say it can be effective when applying for jobs at more conservative companies. There's no doubt that there's a lot of regional variance on this issue, as well as a generational one—younger hiring managers are usually more likely to be LGBT-agnostic, if not LGBT-friendly.

There are other reasons some decide to keep the gay off their résumés, too: You may still be in the closet with your family or trying to maintain a separation between your personal (out) and work (closeted) lives. Also, not coming out on your résumé gives you the option, once on the job, to decide if you feel comfortable being out in this specific workplace.

Dos and Don'ts for Cover Letters

Your decision about how out to be on your résumé will probably apply to your cover letters as well. However, keep in mind that personal matters are less appropriate in these letters than on résumés, so be mindful of how much you reveal about yourself unless it's *directly* related to the job you're applying for.

In general, don't mention such upcoming events as any surgical procedure (including a gender transition) or your same-sex marriage, even if it affects when you'd be available for an in-person interview or able to start a new job. This is not because you should hide the information, but because it's not relevant, any more than it would be for a straight applicant to mention an impending surgery or soon-to-be nuptials.

Whether you are applying for your first job out of school or already in midcareer, these suggestions will help you write a great cover letter:

- **Put your best foot forward:** The cover letter shouldn't restate your résumé but rather pitch your skills and experience as they relate directly to the job at hand. Find out as much as possible about the position and the company before you sit down to compose it. Talk yourself up by citing your accomplishments and make clear how you could benefit the company. Do not brag or exaggerate. Grab your reader's attention with simple, direct language.

- **Do your homework ahead of time:** Try to find out the name of the hiring manager and address the letter or e-mail directly to him or her. This information may be available from a company roster, the job description, or the HR department.
- **Be concise:** In general, keep the letter to one page, or three to four paragraphs. It's bad form to go on at length, and you run the risk of drowning your best points in a sea of verbiage.
- **Proofread it for typos:** Even better, have a friend or professional copy editor review it. Don't simply rely on your PC's spell-check function.

LGBT Networking

Among the pluses of being an out job seeker is the ability to draw on connections with other LGBT people, relying on them for everything from learning about open positions to providing references. Despite its being known humorously as the "gay mafia" or the "lavender network," this web of out LGBT professionals functions like any other workplace network, helping members find jobs or simply make professional connections.

Also consider joining a relevant professional association, such as the National Lesbian & Gay Journalists Association, the Gay and Lesbian Medical Association, or the National Organization of Gay and Lesbian Scientists and Technical Professionals. Most of these groups offer formal job fairs, professional development programs, and informal networking. There are LGBT professional associations for nearly all of the major career disciplines. (For a complete list, see www.gaymanners.com.) There are also professionally based LGBT networks in most U.S. and Canadian cities, which you can easily find by doing a quick online search. Social media sites like LinkedIn and Facebook also maintain such networking groups.

THE ESSENTIALS

Using LinkedIn to Keep Your Private Life Private

In a few short years, LinkedIn has become the gold standard among social media sites in the professional sphere. Legitimate business networking sites like this one are especially helpful for LGBT people who want to draw a line between their personal and professional lives and avoid sharing colorful details—such as Facebook relationship updates or risqué vacation pictures—with your coworkers. Even if you're out, you may not want everyone in your office to know you went to the gay rodeo or played a mean game of drag bingo this past weekend. (Facebook's "groups" option, however, does allow for greater privacy protections.)

If you receive a friend request from a colleague on Facebook or MySpace, you can reply along the lines of "I prefer to keep work life separate from my personal one. Why don't you contact me on LinkedIn?"

Workplace Attire & Grooming

Whether coming in for an interview, your first day on the new job, or deciding what to wear on a daily basis, how you present yourself in the workplace is crucial. As much as we like to say that books (and people) are not judged by their covers (and their clothes), that's usually the case. And that's why it's important to choose clothing to suit your job and to be well groomed and generally put together. Also, show respect—and self-respect—by exhibiting good posture, offering a firm handshake, and looking people in the eye when you speak. If you have visible tattoos or piercings you'll need to determine whether you'll reveal them or not.

If you're not out professionally, there's one additional question to consider: Do you want your attire to out you?

What to Wear for the Interview

Before you even step into an office for your first interview, make an effort to find out how your potential new colleagues dress at the company in general and at your specific level of seniority. Try to glean clues from visiting the workplace beforehand, looking at its website for candid shots of employees at work or a posted dress code, or asking a friend or colleague in that business for advice. Then, take whatever you've learned to heart and

emulate it as you dress for your interview (even taking it up a notch). For instance, one large corporation's dress code states women may wear only small stud earrings or smaller hoop earrings, while men cannot wear any earrings. Long fingernails are prohibited, as are dirty ones or nails painted in a color that is not "natural."

Not surprisingly, transgender workers are often the most affected by strict workplace dress codes, especially in fields involving customer contact: Traditionally, either you're a man or a woman, with no gray areas allowed. As a result, some trans men and women, as well as butch lesbians and effeminate gay men, often make an extra effort at conformity during the interview process. When in place, anti-discrimination laws that include protections for what's called gender expression help ameliorate this situation by prohibiting employers from assessing job applicants or employees with such non-work-related criteria. But those protections are still rare.

If you have doubts about which way to dress, it's best to err on the conservative, overdressed side. Those of us who wouldn't even consider wearing a suit to work often put one on when we're looking to be hired. But consider the company itself closely: What you might wear when interviewing for a position at Google or a barista gig will certainly differ from how you suit up for a bank, law firm, or CPA consultancy. The idea is not to impress but rather to *not* annoy or distract anyone.

If you're one of those who bristle at the idea of shaping his or her sartorial sensibilities "just" for an interview, keep focused on the goal of landing a good job. You'll have plenty of opportunity to imprint your personal style on your work clothes once you've been at your new position for a while and figure out the right balance between being professional and being yourself.

THE ESSENTIALS

When You Care to Look Your Best

With the exception of so-called lipstick lesbians, gay women are still stereotyped as bad dressers, or at least unimaginative ones. At the same time, gay men are supposed to be born fashion designers, aspiring runway models, and hair stylists. The real story is that there are those LGBT people who have the style gene and others who don't (just like our straight friends). So, if you're in need of some basic instruction, follow these guidelines. At the very least, your fashion and grooming capabilities won't be what hold you back—in fact, they may help you advance to the next level. Feel free to adapt these suggestions as necessary to the job, to the company, and to your own taste.

WOMEN
- Keep the fragrance and the makeup light.
- Choose a well-fitted outfit—a suit if appropriate—that's fairly conservative in terms of style and color.
- Coordinate your blouse with your outfit or suit.
- No superhigh heels or flashy, noisy jewelry. Wear a watch so you can keep track of the time, but don't look at it too often.
- Make sure your nails are well groomed (and clean) and that your hairstyle looks smart and professional.

- If you're in a dress or skirt, wear black, tan, or other neutral hosiery.
- Carry a briefcase or portfolio.

MEN
- Wear a conservative suit, either in a solid color or pinstripes. Sometimes a good sports coat, tie, and dark trousers work as well.
- A light blue or white button-down shirt will go with almost any outfit. Make sure it's nicely pressed.
- Find a nice, clean tie; patterns are okay as long as not too distracting. If you're seeking a creative position, choosing a tie with flair can be a plus.
- Wear polished, professional-looking lace-up shoes or loafers. The former are appropriate for just about any white-collar position; loafers are a more casual shoe.
- Socks shouldn't stand out. Nor should your ankles. Dark colors are safest.
- Don't forget a belt and watch, and keep other jewelry to a minimum.
- Watch the aftershave or cologne.
- Pay attention to your nails, and make sure you've gotten a haircut recently.
- Carry a briefcase or portfolio.

Facial Hair

While it's generally acceptable for men (including transmen) to sport a soul patch or a two-day growth of beard in many workplace environments, be sure to find out if there are any official policies about facial hair (sometimes available on a company's website). As an example, one major U.S. corporation has only recently allowed moustaches, which it states must be neatly trimmed, no longer than the corners of the mouth, and grown during your vacation. Sideburns cannot pass the earlobes. Got that? Many police departments also allow, if not encourage, moustaches, but you'd find that untrimmed beards are prohibited because they're said to look unprofessional.

Tattoos and Piercings

As has happened with facial hair, workplace policies regarding tattoos and piercings are morphing rapidly. Although they're still banned in some workplaces, in others they are considered on a par with haircuts as simply another way to distinguish oneself. As one manager put it, "It doesn't matter to me if my employees show off their body art, because it doesn't mean they work less, make them stupider, or leave them any less of a person."

So much of this depends on whether you work in a staid corporation or at a Web development shop. In the former case, the overall principle is that employees not call unnecessary attention to themselves (this is the same rationale for the corporate frown on visible cleavage on women, or an expanse of chest hair on men); in the latter, the underlying rationale is "Please be sure you're presentable when you have a client meeting."

You'll also want to consider these questions: If you cover a tattoo or remove a piercing, will you be comfortable in that office environment? If you don't, will you fit in? Will you be seen as too much of an individual and not as a team player? Or, will this help you to be viewed as a creative iconoclast (that's usually a good thing)?

QUEERY

"Setting aside the real me for an interview"

Q **Usually when I'm applying for a job, I set aside the real me—the butch dyke, if you will—and dress up a little feminine (hair, suit, everything). As I get older, doing this makes me feel less and less comfortable, as though I'm not being true to myself. How do you suggest I dress for interviews?**

A That's a tough question. Ideally, it's best not to disguise yourself or to appear other than who you are. Still, there's something to be said for having your "interview suit"—and doing some extra grooming—especially because we all know how others' prejudices can work against us.

Think of it this way: The idea is to take appearances completely out of the equation, so that you can explain your qualifications and sell yourself without distraction. Once you land the job, you can be freer in how you dress. You're not selling out to adopt a more mainstream look for the interviews; this is just another step to get you in the door.

In my experience, most people try to pick up a company's dress code once they start working there. But if you don't think you can do that—or if you want to dress butch all the time—then go ahead and dress that way for the interview. If the company can't take it, you're wasting your time considering this particular employer.

THE INTERVIEW

By definition, job interviews are stressful. You're meeting new people, putting your best foot forward, and trying to show that you can both fit in and be a standout. For LGBT people, there's also the question of whether or not to come out, if your résumé hasn't already done that for you. Do you refer offhandedly to a same-sex partner, for instance, or ask about domestic partner benefits? There is no one answer to this, as it all depends on you and on the particular workplace.

Getting Ready

You may find yourself being asked about your résumé, skills, work history, management style, leadership abilities, and much more. Questions may play to your strengths or to your weaknesses, and they can even do a number on your self-esteem. All work-related questions, even when challenging, are fair game.

To do your best, no matter what the job, here are some suggestions to be well prepared:

- **Decide ahead of time whether you will be in or out:** You'll feel much less stressed if you've charted a course of action that you can follow and spend no time second-guessing yourself.
- **Practice makes perfect:** Think about the types of questions you're likely to be asked during the interview and either write out or practice your answers aloud. Consider asking a friend to conduct a mock interview with you so that you can get an honest critique. In your responses, be sure to use specific examples

of your accomplishments that showcase your skills and experience.

- **Do your homework about the company and the position:** This will help you answer such standard questions as "Why do you want to work here?" and "Why are you right for this job?" Make sure you know how to correctly pronounce the interviewer's name and then use it during your meeting.

Then, on the day of the interview:

- **Be punctual:** For a job interview, this means being ten minutes early so that you won't be rushed or disheveled. Make sure you build in extra time for rush hour traffic, parking, getting lost, and the like. You may even want to take a practice drive before the day of the actual interview or figure out which subway/bus lines are fastest. Being on time will signal that you're responsible and value other people's time. If you realize you're running late, call or e-mail ahead and let your prospective employer know. Then apologize in person at the start of the interview.
- **Listen as well as speak:** Answer the questions put to you, recounting your experience and skills. Use concrete examples whenever possible. Don't forget to pay attention to your interviewer's visual cues, body language, and any instructions. (If she seems bored or distracted, wrap it up.)
- **Acknowledge what you don't know:** If an answer escapes you, say directly without embarrassment: "That's a good question. Let me think about that." If you come up with

a response later, return to the topic. If that doesn't happen until after the interview, reference the question in your follow-up e-mail and supply your answer then.

- **Be sure to send a thank-you e-mail:** Unless applying to a stationery store or some other tradition-bound organization, e-mail is the medium of choice these days for this kind of thank-you. If you saw more than one person at the company, send a personalized e-mail to each one—not a mass e-mail.

Legal Protections

Numerous laws in the United States and Canada delineate topics that are off-limits during an interview, including questions about age,

marital status, and overall health, as well as (in some jurisdictions) sexual orientation and gender identity. Hiring managers and most bosses know to steer clear of these topics. However, if you are asked an inappropriate or illegal question, here's what to do. First, make sure you've understood the question by asking the interviewer to repeat it. If she insists, explain that it's your understanding that such a question is inappropriate. If that response doesn't help matters, your best bet is talk to a supervisor or the HR department after the interview.

When it comes to specific questions about your sexual orientation or gender identity, it's good to know when such questions are illegal:
- If you live in Canada.
- If you're interviewing for a U.S. federal

QUEERY

"Out at home; in at work"

Q I was on a job interview at a high-tech firm and the hiring manager, who seemed really friendly, asked if I knew some mutual colleagues, all of whom happened to be gay. I did, but I felt like she was trying to find out about my sexual orientation. Although I am out in my private life, I prefer not to talk about it in the office.

A If an interviewer asks you directly if you're LGBT, she's ethically and legally out of bounds. But the situation you described sounds neither illegal nor particularly rude. It's actually standard practice to inquire about any working relationships you may have had with other colleagues. In fact, she may have even

planned to ask them whether you'd be a good fit for the job in question. Perhaps past incidents of homophobia—not to mention the general climate against LGBT people—have colored your reaction, but don't assume the worst in your interactions with straight people. Sometimes a question is just a question.

government job (governed for gay men and lesbians by an executive order since 1998 and for transgender people since 2009).

- If you live in one of the U.S. states or municipalities that says so.
- If the company happens to be governed by nondiscrimination rules of its own.

Speaking Up About Being Transgender

Before interviewing for a new job, most transgender people evaluate whether to reveal that they've transitioned or intend to. If you choose not to reveal these details, keep in mind that even though it's definitely a private matter, an astute interviewer may find out as a result of physical cues, security checks, résumé curiosities (a big gap in your job history, for instance), or from talking with previous employers who refer to your prior identity.

Whether or not you plan to speak up, do your due diligence about the company's policies regarding gender identity issues:

- Does the company prohibit discrimination based on gender identity and expression?
- Does it have a commitment to gender-identity diversity training?
- Are there supportive gender-transition guidelines in place?
- Are there other trans men and women who work there currently?
- Does the company provide partner and other benefits to all LGBT people—specifically, transgender-inclusive insurance coverage?

With each "yes" answer, you move onto firmer and firmer ground if you decide to reveal your trans status.

COMING OUT AT WORK

In the event you got your job without coming out or have so far simply avoided any conversation about your personal life at your job, the time may come when you want your colleagues to know that you're LGBT. It's good to understand the circumstances that may push you toward taking this step and, if you do decide to do so, how to go about it. (For more information about coming out, please see Chapter 1.)

To Tell or Not to Tell

These are some of the many and varied circumstances that might lead you to decide to come out at work:

- Your company has nondiscrimination policies in place protecting LGBT people.
- You're discussing your respective families or personal lives with a straight coworker and decide that *not* revealing that you're L, G, B, or T would amount to appearing less than candid or even dishonest—or, along the same lines, you just don't want to hide your sexuality or gender identity anymore.
- Your work is related to an LGBT issue in some way and you think you could do a better job—or help win new business.
- Your company has an LGBT affinity group.
- An event is about to happen in your personal life, such as a birth, marriage, or gender reassignment surgery, which may affect your job or simply seems important enough to share with the people you spend so much time with.

- Others have come out recently at your workplace and your colleagues seem unfazed—even better, they welcomed the news.
- Your supervisor thinks that, being on the face of it single, you can work weekends or travel regularly because no one is waiting for you at home.
- The stress of being in the closet threatens to affect your work, and perhaps even your mental health.

How to Come Out

Once you make the decision to come out, don't make a big show of doing so. That kind of approach detracts from the notion that you're a professional first, who understands that the job at hand takes precedence over important personal issues. At the same time, remember that your character and honesty are two of your most important assets; let's hope your employer will see your coming out as a virtue, too.

There are a number of ways to let your colleagues know more about your sexual identity without having to have "the talk" (that is, make an announcement to all and sundry) or be accused of flaunting "your lifestyle":

- **A picture's worth a thousand words:** If you're partnered, put a photograph of the two of you on your desk—nothing oversexy, but one that definitely says "couple." If you're asked about it, explain matter-of-factly, "Oh, that's my partner, Janie." Most straight people understand what "partner" means, but you could also say "life partner," "girlfriend," or "wife."

QUEERY

"A gay boss ponders coming out to job seekers."

Q **I run a small insurance company with my life partner, and I just had a recent hire who quit on the spot once he realized that I'm gay and that we're a gay-owned business. Do you think it's appropriate for me to reveal my sexual orientation earlier, when I'm interviewing candidates? I hate to go to all the effort to bring a new employee in—and then lose him.**

A Usually, I'd say that personal proclamations of any kind are neither professional nor necessary, but yours is an interesting twist. I can certainly understand that if you're going to go to the time and expense of making a hire, you want your investment to pay out and not have the new employee jump ship over this kind of issue.

Still, there are other ways to determine if an applicant is likely to be comfortable in your business besides making an explicit statement about your sexual orientation. During the interview, ask about the candidate's experience working with diverse groups and be up-front about your company's commitment to diversity. Talk about your organization's values and workplace culture as another way to make it understood that having a diverse workforce—in terms of race, ethnicity, sexual orientation, and gender identity (citing them as examples)—is not only accepted but valued. Last but not least, there's nothing wrong with mentioning nonprofits or advocacy groups that the company supports, such as your local LGBT center or the AIDS Walk in your community.

- **"Oh, by the way":** Work it casually into a conversation. For instance, if colleagues are talking about their weekend plans or summer vacations, pipe in with a comment like "My boyfriend, Tim, and I are thinking about going out to California this summer." This clear acknowledgment of your same-sex boyfriend says it all.
- **Bring up real-time events:** If you don't have a partner, mention a gay-themed play you saw or a current LGBT-related news story. Bring up these topics within the context of other water cooler conversations. If there are no homophobic red flags in the banter that follows, it's a short jump to "Actually, I'm gay." Rather than thinking of this as a political statement, think of it more along the lines of a colleague mentioning, "Actually, I'm pregnant."

"It'll be our fourth anniversary next week. ♡"

Keep in mind that, unless you ask the people you've talked with to keep your news a secret (and even then there's no guarantee), word will travel. If you're not ready for that, then wait.

STRAIGHT TALK

"Why does my coworker in the adjacent cubicle have to display so many things that say 'gay'? He's got a gay rainbow flag, several photos of himself and his partner, and even a poster from the movie Milk. It's a gay-friendly office, so I'm not sure why he has to be so loud about it. By the way, I'm not alone here; some of the other straight guys here feel the same way."

Here's what I'm wondering: Why do you need to display so many things that say "straight"? Okay, that was rude—sorry—but do you see what I mean? Don't you or your straight colleagues put up art or knick-knacks that in one way or another show people "being" heterosexual? Pictures of girlfriends or boyfriends perhaps? What about a movie poster with, say, Jennifer Lopez or Jennifer Aniston? Or that plaque on your office wall commending you for years of service to the Boy Scouts of America, which prohibits gays from participating either as members or leaders?

My point is that many of the objects we're used to seeing around—and read as neutral—actually do convey lots about us and our identities. You may not be aware of what your decor says to others, and he may not be aware about what his says to you. Instead of stewing about it, why not walk around that cube wall, ask him to coffee, and start up a conversation about some of these issues? But, first, take a quick look around your own space as well as those of your straight coworkers, because those who live in glass cubicles shouldn't throw . . . well, you know.

Joining an LGBT Affinity Group

Workplaces of all kinds have LGBT-related affinity groups these days, not just big companies with high-profile efforts to foster diversity and "inclusiveness" (like CBS News with its group, Angle). The benefits of LGBT affinity groups in terms of visibility and the improvement to relevant company policies and benefits are hard to dispute. The very formation of these groups has often helped usher employees out of the closet.

Joining up can help advance your career through networking; it can even improve your social life. Some LGBT affinity groups go beyond the social sphere to influence employee policies in the company as a whole and even advance public positions on political issues. General Motors' GM PLUS, which stands for People Like US, started out as an after-work club in the early 1990s, but eventually helped put the company on record in support of the federal Employment Non-Discrimination Act. If you're out of the closet in your workplace, consider attending one of the group's events to test the waters.

Role Models on the Job

If you're one of a few out LGBT people in your workplace, you may become everyone's go-to person for all things gay. This can be both a

---

QUEERY

"Transitioning at work, and starting to worry"

Q **I'm not out with my colleagues about my impending transition from male to female. I have a therapist and a good support system of friends, but am starting to worry about what I'll do if there's a bad reaction at work. What's the best way to start this process while avoiding the most discomfort possible, for everyone involved?**

A I'm really glad to hear that you have supportive friends and a therapist to help you through this. I suggest using that network to find other people who have transitioned at their jobs, in order to make sure that you've thought everything through. Especially if no one in your circle has firsthand knowledge about this, you might chat with others online about their experience. In addition, if you haven't already (and just in case things go awry), it's probably a good idea to talk to a lawyer who is well versed in these matters. If you plan to stay at your current employer, definitely talk with someone in human resources (and certainly your boss) about finding a way to tell colleagues about what's to come. Their support is crucial.

What you're doing is not for the faint of heart. Many people switch jobs when they switch gender identities in order to start completely fresh.

privilege and an albatross. To a certain degree, these are the responsibilities that come along with newfound rights. For those LGBT people in more senior positions, take note that both our straight colleagues and other gay employees may look to you as a role model—albeit in different ways. Explained one gay HR professional, "A mentor who can relate to your background can be useful in helping you get ahead." In fact, whether or not you've ever been mentored yourself, now is a good time to consider actively helping other LGBT people as they come out and work their way up the ladder of success.

Introducing Your Significant Other

Perhaps you've already hinted at a "we" when discussing your weekends with workmates or you've been displaying a photo of the two of you on your desk, which is to say you've been hinting at being gay. At some point, you may want to give some thought as to whether your partner should be more than just a Monday morning talking point or the other guy on your health insurance policy—and actually show up as your date to a company event.

One way to test the waters and make an introduction is to have your partner stop by for lunch or come up to the office after work and meet colleagues informally that way. Or if you're certain you work in an LGBT-supportive firm, invite your spouse to the annual summer picnic or the "families-invited" river cruise celebrating your company's new merger (and bring the kids, too).

In addition to being fully out with your colleagues, the introduction of a partner can also be a great way to further bond with friendly colleagues. Explained one bi woman: "I was really excited when the people at work finally got to meet Patricia because I felt like they were finally seeing the real me, the personal me. Several colleagues made a point to say how glad they were to have met my significant other."

When You're Expecting

With more and more LGBT parents starting their own families, it's not uncommon for gay moms and dads to be feted with workplace baby showers or to bring the cute infant in to work to be ooh and aahed over. Although even a homophobic coworker can be won over by the sight of your smiling baby or the simple news that you're pregnant, keep in mind as you go forward with your plans for a family that it might not all be a breeze. There are still many people who don't believe gay people should be parents, and not all companies will embrace your new family as you might hope (although, according to the latest surveys, more and more Americans are accepting—even welcoming— of same-sex couples with kids). Here are some important points to consider along the way:

- **Beware of sneaky employers:** Discrimination is rife against prospective parents, not just LGBT ones, with the number of lawsuits on the rise. And a really unethical employer may choose one prejudice to cover up another. For instance, perhaps your boss doesn't care that you're gay as much as that you're about to take on a new "project" (starting a family) that could interfere with your time and productivity at work. It's even possible he could fire you for being LGBT—rather than for being pregnant—without violating the law.

- **Understand your company's benefit package:** Review the policies on parental leave for newborns, adding children to your health insurance, and providing life insurance for your family, especially since these rules are often not written with the needs of LGBT people in mind. For instance, if your partner is bearing your child, are *you* eligible for family leave? If the two of you are adopting, but *you're* not the primary adoptive parent,

can you add your child to your health insurance policy? And if your company benefits are deficient, are those at your partner's job any better? Often, gay-friendly companies, especially smaller ones or start-ups, will make certain accommodations for expectant gay parents. You may even find yourself the impetus for a policy change or two, if current company policies have been written from a straight perspective and the human resources department is interested in making them more equitable.

QUEERY

"Is it anyone's business at work how I had kids?"

Q When my colleagues ask where my kids "came from," do I need to be specific about my partner's insemination from an anonymous sperm donor? I'd really rather not, but I can't figure out exactly what to say.

A Although there's often much curiosity about this subject, how you "got" your kids should be irrelevant to the people you work with. But that doesn't stop coworkers from asking! And the truth is that different rules apply to these odd "relationships" we form at work. Your coworkers may not be friends or family, but you sure see them a lot. Because of that and because you may rely on them for everything from supply room access to career advancement, comfortably answering too-personal questions is a skill worth perfecting.

Start out by considering whether you want to provide a complete answer or simply an adequate one. This probably depends on how closely you work with (and how well you know) each other, as well as on

whether you're ready to be out to him or her about your sexual orientation. Full disclosure might be something like: "My partner and I adopted Jane, and I had Freddy myself." By contrast, "Jose's from my first marriage" answers the question politely without sharing a lot. Sometimes, using the word "partner" without saying much else is a good way to avoid details, yet answer the question sufficiently, such as "My partner and I adopted" or even just "I'm raising them with my partner."

Whatever you say, remember that you have no control over how other people will react and who else they will tell. Play it easy, and don't forget that LGBT parents are becoming more and more visible—your officemates may not actually be as surprised as you think.

• **Go "off-the-record":** If you decide to go ahead and talk about the child that's coming your way and are worried about the company's reaction, make an appointment with human resources to learn as much as you can about any obstacles you might face (and ways to overcome them) before bringing the topic up with your supervisor. One HR executive added, "Be clear that you want such a conversation to be unofficial and off-the-record so that it does not go into your file."

THE ESSENTIALS

Parental Leave

Most U.S. and Canadian workplaces allow employees to take time off to deal with parenting issues such as a birth or adoption. This is an important, but still limited, form of support for working families, although it's worth noting that the United States is the only Western nation that doesn't mandate *paid* leave. Under the U.S. Family and Medical Leave Act companies are required only to give *unpaid* leave; nevertheless, three states (New Jersey, Washington, and California) and the District of Columbia offer paid parental leave through state insurance funds, and a few others offer short-term disability insurance to birth mothers.

Beyond that, it's up to individual employers to decide whether to offer parental leave; one factor is whether it's financially feasible to provide this benefit. In companies that don't, another option is to use different forms of leave, such as sick days or vacation time, for parenting time off.

On top of all that, when this benefit does exist, the company might not immediately see that you're eligible: The National Center for Lesbian Rights points out that many LGBT parents often face resistance in being able to access parental or family leave, even when it's unpaid.

DISCRIMINATION & OTHER WORKPLACE ISSUES

Discrimination. Office romances. Sexual harassment. These are just some of the issues LGBT people deal with on the job. If anything, it's important to understand workplace law—federal, state, and local. When it comes to office policies, be sure to do your research, because some companies specifically exclude LGBT people from various protections. In any case, it's not just whether you have the tools to fight back but also how you choose to react that can make the difference.

Office Romances

While office dating poses its share of challenges for straight people, lesbians and gay men can face additional obstacles if one or both of you is hiding not just the romance but the fact that you're gay. "I'll always remember the first stolen kiss we had in the supply closet," says a gay talent agent about his now longtime partner. "Of course, part of the

QUEERY

"She's cute, but we work together!"

Q I think the new copy editor at my newspaper is a lesbian and she sure knows I am (everybody does). She hasn't actually said anything, though, and doesn't show up for our company's LGBT events. Is it okay if I just ask? She's really cute, by the way!

A I hate to burst your bubble, but did it occur to you that she might not be rushing to come out just because she can tell you think she's "cute"? Some people have a really bad reaction to flirting at work, and most companies have policies in place prohibiting unwanted sexual advances. Of course, there are many other possible explanations for her not being up-front about her sexual orientation: Maybe she's the private type; maybe she's had bad experiences in the past with coworkers knowing her business; or maybe she's not even a lesbian.

In any case, no, don't ask. It's not your business. Aside from that reason, she's someone you may need to work with or otherwise benefit from as an ally—no matter whether she's straight, gay, or bi—so act professionally. Furthermore, especially in a workplace situation, it's better to let relationships unfold organically. If she wants you to know more about her personal life, I'm sure she has the capability to do so. Better that than you press forward and she files a complaint with human resources against you.

---

thrill was that we were still both in the closet," he joked.

When starting a flirtation or romance with a colleague, rational thinking often goes right out the window. However, if at all possible, take a step back and consider the pros and cons of what you're doing. In some instances, your job could depend on it. Here are some pointers:

- **Keep it professional:** Don't meet for tête-à-têtes during office hours, flirt with each other in meetings or company events, or spend work time e-mailing or IM-ing. (Remember, every stroke you type can be retrieved by the IT department, and whatever you write is all technically company property.)
- **Keep it private:** Even if you can find an out-of-the-way corner or office, you're wise to take it outside and off hours.

- **Know your company's policy:** The rules on office dating vary widely from company to company, so make sure you know them. Some firms prohibit intra-office romances across the board, which means you could be fired for having one. Others say it's fine, as long as one of you doesn't report to the other. Still others have no rules whatsoever, or they apply only to heterosexual couples. Don't take your "right to love" for granted.
- **Be wary of dating those who work for you:** Even if there's no ban on dating a direct report, be especially circumspect about such relationships because they could open you up to all kinds of issues—from charges of favoritism to a big legal drama if the relationship goes south. For the same reason, avoid dating your manager or boss.

- **No surprises:** If your relationship starts to get serious (progressing beyond flirtation and into multiple dates), it's courteous to let your supervisor know the minimal details about your intra-office romance (assuming you're not in violation of company policy). It's much better for her to hear it from you than from someone else.
- **Consider the future:** Perhaps the greatest risk of an office romance is what happens if it ends. If you break up, how will it feel to be in meetings together? At the company holiday party? When one or both of you start dating again? Talk about these possibilities early in your relationship and do your best to agree to some ground rules, such as not bad-mouthing each other or discussing your relationship at work or with colleagues.

"Do you think anyone knows we're dating?"

Sexual Harassment

It was only recently that same-sex sexual harassment became widely accepted as *real.* The law now extends its protections to all of us, regardless of gender or sexual orientation. If you believe that you're a victim of sexual harassment on the job, start by talking informally and off-the-record to a human resources manager or company ombudsman (someone who you think is generally supportive), to decide whether to file an official complaint.

At the same time, make sure you have clearly rebuffed any aggressive actions by saying no to the person harassing you, or have otherwise communicated the fact that the behavior in question offends you or makes you uncomfortable. This communication can be in person, by letter, or through e-mail. In addition, throughout the process, keep a diary of what's going on, including dates, times, places, and what exactly has been said and done.

Nearly every person who has been sexually harassed finds it a very isolating experience, regardless of the circumstances. It often feels like *you've* done something wrong, when in fact you're the victim of someone else's inappropriate behavior. Reach out for support from friends or from a hotline such as the Sexual Assault & Domestic Violence Hotline (1-800-494-8100) or 9to5: National Association of Working Women (1-800-522-0925).

If the steps above don't start to resolve the situation, then consider the following actions:
- Report the sexual harassment officially to your employer. Keep a copy of any paperwork

you submit. Follow your company's sexual harassment complaint process or file a charge with a state or federal agency.

- Contact an LGBT legal rights group such as the National Center for Lesbian Rights or Lambda Legal to find out your options for reporting the incident.
- Meet with an attorney who specializes in employment law, to discuss filing a civil suit against your company and/or the person harassing you.

THE ESSENTIALS

What Is Sexual Harassment?

Sexual harassment is disruptive, illegal, and upsetting to its victims, no matter how you slice it: straight-on-straight, LGBT-on-LGBT, straight-on-LGBT, LGBT-on-straight, or any other combination. The official U.S. definition is "unwelcome verbal, visual, or physical conduct of a sexual nature that is severe or pervasive and affects working conditions or creates a hostile work environment." In the workplace it can take many forms, but it usually means unwelcome sexual advances, requests for sexual favors, or other verbal or physical infringements of a sexual nature, such as sexual bribery—whereby your job or promotion is made contingent on sexual favors.

Sexual harassment can also be experienced as sexual joking, the appearance of sexually explicit graffiti or objects (like posters) in the workplace, the display of Internet pornography, the sending of sexually graphic e-mails, or bullying or intimidation of a sexual nature.

Note: If you tell a company officer, like a vice president or the CEO, that you've been sexually

harassed, U.S. federal law requires that a formal investigation must be launched (there is no such requirement in Canada). Make sure you're ready to take it to that level before speaking to someone who's above your HR department or your supervisor.

LGBT Discrimination

A Latina transwoman worked for sixteen years as a deputy sheriff before being fired for cross-dressing in private (she presented as a "he" at the time). "The direct impact of the discrimination I experienced has been devastating on so many levels," she wrote on a blog. "I don't have a college degree or any other skills except law enforcement. I contacted attorneys, but they said I had no legal protections."

As of this writing, neither U.S. nor Canadian law explicitly protects transgender people from job discrimination. Gay and bisexual people fare somewhat better, with protection throughout Canada and in a handful of states, but this form of discrimination is still pervasive. A 2010 survey reported that 23 percent of gay employees said they had been harassed at work, 12 percent have been denied promotions, and 9 percent were fired because of their sexual orientation or gender identity.

What this means is that, in many circumstances, it's not just that you can lose your job for being gay or transgender but that complaining about anti-gay or anti-transgender discrimination can also get you fired. Still, if you don't speak up about your mistreatment, you can be fairly certain that it will continue unabated, affecting not just you but probably others.

QUEERY

"My gay boss tells creepy sex jokes."

Q My boss and I are both gay, and sometimes he creeps me out with little jokes that are definitely sexual. I love my job. In fact, I like working for him in every other way. How can I make him stop without getting fired?

A Unfortunately, it sounds like the joking won't stop unless you say something. What you need to decide is whether you want to talk to your boss about it directly or go to someone in the human resources department. If you can start with him, that's probably for the best, especially since it sounds like you have a good working relationship overall. Plan what you're going to say, then schedule a meeting with him. At that meeting, explain that sometimes his jokes make you feel uncomfortable because they're about sex and that doesn't feel appropriate in the office.

Don't make an official complaint, but do take notes afterward about what's gone on and how the meeting went. Keep this memo to yourself, just in case.

If this conversation doesn't change his behavior, then it's time to include other company officials. But take the time first to understand the legal definition of "sexually harassed" so that you're clear what you're complaining about. Sexual harassment is a very serious charge; if you intend to formally accuse him, you need to consider the possible effects on his career and reputation—as well as yours.

CHAPTER 12

Out & About

Our LGBT Lives

More than forty years after the Stonewall Riots, day-to-day life has been completely transformed for gay, lesbian, bisexual, and transgender people. We're out and about in ways that some of us only dreamed of, and that others never imagined could or would exist.

Our integration, if not acceptance, into the mainstream goes beyond what can be measured; in fact, it seems commonplace. On television, Ellen DeGeneres is one of the most popular personalities with both gay *and* straight audiences, and Rachel Maddow is respected as an anchor whose sexual orientation matters little. Openly gay teachers can be found in more and more of our schools; LGBT politicians from both sides of the aisle are out in record numbers; and lesbians and gay men are now on the cusp of being able to serve openly in the U.S. military (that's already been the case in Canada for years). And the announcement by Chaz Bono (previously Cher's daughter, now her son) that he was transitioning made the cover of *People*, where his story was treated as just another piece of celebrity news. He continued with his LGBT activism without missing a beat.

It's gratifying that we're finally able to see ourselves openly reflected in and reflected by the culture, from the "silent generation" of seniors, to baby boomers, to Gen X, Y, or Z. With such changes continually upending the gay rules of the road, we need an up-to-date map to better navigate our way: to know how to travel safely and comfortably at home and abroad, not to mention the etiquette of gay cruises, LGBT resort communities, and your local health club.

When it comes to fund-raising for our causes, there are specific steps to take in being successful—yet not overbearing—in convincing your friends to donate. And don't forget that there are plenty of ways to give back without giving dollars and cents. Although political manners aren't new per se, their inclusion here is a rarity in a book of this nature. What are the dos and don'ts of political protest—including outing, civil disobedience, kiss-ins, and the marches that carry their own historical legacy of gay pride? And what's the smartest way to respond to anti-LGBT hecklers—without compromising your safety.

Lastly, because the holidays raise so many questions about traditions and gift-giving—and can raise tensions between family and partners alike—you'll likely need some hand-holding there as well. This is particularly true as we create new holiday rituals that reflect our family circumstances—whether dear friends, our partners and kids, or our biological relatives.

TRAVEL

Traveling as an out LGBT person is no longer the anxiety-producing guessing game that it used to be (in most countries, at least). There are now tours, hotels, and even entire towns devoted to LGBT vacationing. The best way to approach an imminent trip is to tap into the wealth of available information, whether that means talking to an LGBT-wise travel agent, consulting online resources, or reaching out to friends who have been there and done that before. Find out what's fun to do, but also consider your safety and what restrictions on your independence you're willing to tolerate. Wherever you're going—and whether it's for vacation or work—it's always smart to have a general awareness about the climate for LGBT people.

North American Travel

When traveling around the United States and Canada, don't take for granted that LGBT life is as you know it in urban meccas like New York, Toronto, or San Francisco. Not only do different states have different legal protections for LGBT people (although this is less of an issue in Canada), you'll also find that cultural and social norms vary widely, too, depending where you are in the United States.

While visiting big cities, don't think that all neighborhoods afford the same sense of safety and acceptance. While it may be fine for you and your girlfriend to hold hands on Melrose Avenue in West Hollywood or in Montreal's Le Village, that may not be the case in other parts of L.A. or Montreal.

Wherever you go, whatever you do, the most important rule you can abide by is to make sure you're safe. When you're figuring out your itinerary, find out what you can learn about a particular area by asking these questions:

- Is it okay to be out and visible?
- Are public displays of affection acceptable? Is this true for two men? Two women?
- Where are the gay bars and clubs, and are those areas safe? How vigorous is police enforcement in cruisy areas?
- Will checking into a local hotel or B&B with a partner raise eyebrows, disapproval—or worse?
- Have there been any recent hate crimes or other violence against LGBT people?
- When abroad, are there any specific legal protections for gays and lesbians? What about for trans people?

Making Reservations

Sometimes you and your boyfriend may find yourselves checking into a motel only to stand before an intimidating heterosexual asking "How many beds?" In most cases, however, you can avoid this scenario by planning ahead. The easiest and smartest way is to book online, where you can select the kind of room, and the size of the bed you prefer.

Many same-sex couples also purposely list both their names on the reservation, so that it will be clear to expect "Adam and Steve" or "Hannah and Eve." This strategy is especially wise if you're staying at a smaller inn or a bed-and-breakfast, one where the proprietor makes the rules, or in a locale not known to be especially gay-friendly. If, when you give your partner's name, everything seems fine, then

---

QUEERY

"We're not sisters, we're lesbians!"

Q **When I travel with my girlfriend, people always assume we're sisters. Classic, huh? The problem is that it sounds so confrontational if you answer, "No, we're lesbians." Is there another way?**

A Coming out is a process that continues even when you think you're already out. This is especially true when you're traveling and meeting new people, and even more so when small talk inevitably leads back to the fact that you're gay. For instance, when my seatmate on a plane asks me what I do for a living, I'll reply that I am an author. Invariably, the person then asks, "What do you write about?" If I'm going to be honest, I'm going to say "Gay and lesbian issues"

and out myself. Sometimes that's followed by silence, which can make for a long trip sitting next to someone who's been discomfited by my simple statement of fact.

However, there's nothing confrontational about saying who you are or what you do, especially when asked. If you were to use more charged language, like "We're dykes," that could sound in-your-face to some. Also consider options like "We're girlfriends" and "She's my partner." Or, "We're married."

"Yes, I said one bed for the wife and me!"

your stay is likely to go fine, too. However, if you're suddenly told there's no availability, you'll know you weren't going to be welcome anyway.

For some additional certainty that your stay will be with a gay or gay-friendly business, look to see if the establishment belongs to the International Gay and Lesbian Travel Association (IGLTA) or if it's a TAG-approved hotel (tagapproved.com), the dual gold standard in the travel business. Or visit sites like OutTraveler.com and GayTravel.com. Nevertheless, keep in mind that just because a hotel is listed as "gay-friendly" (a marketing term) doesn't always mean it will be in practice. To be sure, call before you confirm any reservations to make sure there's truth in advertising, and look even more closely at online reviews from LGBT travelers.

THE ESSENTIALS

Twenty Gay-Friendly North American Travel Destinations

While there are dozens, maybe hundreds, of cities and communities coast-to-coast that are LGBT-friendly, here are twenty that would likely make anyone's list:

Atlanta

Austin

Chicago

Fire Island Pines/Cherry Grove

Ft. Lauderdale

Key West

Miami Beach/South Beach

Montreal

New York City

Palm Springs

Philadelphia

Portland (Maine)

Provincetown

Rehoboth Beach

San Diego

San Francisco

San Juan

Vancouver

Washington, D.C.

West Hollywood

Travel Abroad

The importance of safety can't be overstated when traveling overseas, especially since you may find a dearth of LGBT legal protections.

Equally necessary: Respect the local customs and traditions. This means understanding how those you'll meet, from innkeepers to cab drivers, feel about gays and lesbians and what the prevailing religious or political attitudes are vis-à-vis gay and transgender people. Expect a wide range of reactions to public displays of affection, for instance, and find out if there are specific customs or laws that would affect you, such as not wearing shorts in a mosque or covering your head in certain countries.

If you're working with an LGBT travel agent or have joined an online gay travel forum, ask directly how gay-friendly your prospective destination is and specifically whether there have been any recent instances of hostility or violence against LGBT people. Also ask about hotels, restaurants, rental car companies, and out-of-the-way towns and cities. Keep in mind that what may be acceptable behavior in a nation's capital may be viewed unfavorably in outlying areas.

If you're having difficulty finding out this kind of information, e-mail your hotels under consideration, asking the general manager or concierge to assist you. As with domestic travel, if you find resistance to your questions—or a distinctly unwelcoming attitude—that's likely a sign of what to expect in person. Outing yourself like this can be uncomfortable, but it's much better to understand the lay of the land from the safety of your own home.

THE ESSENTIALS
Countries to Avoid If You're LGBT

It's wise to consult the U.S. State Department or a website specializing in gay travel before going to any country where you are not completely sure of local statutes affecting LGBT people. The laws—and political factors affecting how much the laws are enforced—change all the time. For instance, being LGBT is currently punishable by the death penalty in these countries:

Iran
Mauritania
Nigeria (northern)
Saudi Arabia
Sudan
United Arab Emirates
Yemen

Dozens of other countries, ranging from Jamaica and Grenada in the Caribbean to Morocco in North Africa, imprison gay men and lesbians. Torture is not unheard of in some locales. Then there are nations such as Zambia and Zimbabwe that jail gay men but have no objection to lesbians. Check back again before you leave for updates—for instance, Uganda has been considering instituting the death penalty for homosexual activity.

Transgender Air Travel

Heightened security and additional screenings at airports have a disproportionate impact on transgender travelers, who, according to the U.S. National Center for Transgender Equality (NCTE), face "increased scrutiny, harassment, and discrimination." The NCTE suggests three ways trans people can attempt to mitigate some of these issues:

1. **Make sure the name you use for your airline reservation and ticket exactly matches the name on your identification:** If it doesn't, get an updated ID before you travel.

2. **If your face doesn't resemble the photo on your ID, get a new ID with an updated photo:** If you are still concerned about identification issues, carry a letter from your physician explaining why you don't look like your picture.

3. **Is your stated gender different than your appearance?** It's often quite difficult to change whether you're listed as male or female (known as a gender marker) on an official ID, but that doesn't generally cause problems at the airport, if only because U.S. Transportation Security Administration or Canadian Border Services agents may overlook the discrepancy. But that's hardly a foolproof situation. The State Department currently requires a physician's letter certifying that the applicant has "undergone appropriate clinical treatment for gender transition" to declare a new gender on a passport.

Trans people who carry syringes for injectable hormones are generally advised not to check them in their baggage, so you'll have them with you when you arrive at your final destination. However, if you go through security with them, be sure to have either a prescription or a note from your physician.

Finally, certain types of clothing, shoes, binding materials, prostheses, or jewelry may cause you to receive additional, unwelcome, and often unfair scrutiny. Airport metal detectors are extremely sensitive and may be set off by piercing jewelry, metal-boned corsets, underwire bras, and metal binding materials.

QUEERY

"Turned away from the inn"

Q My partner and I were in the U.K. last summer. When we got to our B&B the proprietor took one look at us and said, "Gays aren't allowed" and refused to honor our reservation. We were too stunned by his rudeness to react in the moment. What would have been the proper thing to do?

A No matter how much planning you do, same-sex couples should be prepared for all sorts of negative reactions when not on their home turf, ranging from surprise to snickers or even epithets from locals who aren't used to seeing LGBT people or families. In general, I'd suggest you not engage (if only to keep safe), move on, and enjoy your time elsewhere. But in Great Britain, you also could have filed a complaint with the appropriate authorities, since it's illegal there to discriminate on the grounds of sexual orientation. And if you're not a shrinking violet, you can always call the local press and make your case directly to the public. That's perfectly proper under the circumstances. You won't get to sleep in the bed you reserved, but one day some other couple might be so fortunate.

And full-body scanners can bring unwanted scrutiny. Try to dress so that you can avoid additional screening procedures and delay. If you wear a binder or corset, consider finding one without metal clasps for travel purposes.

Medical Issues

If you have a chronic disease or disability, talk with your physician before leaving home about the various scenarios to prepare for: What if you lose your meds or just need more? What if you need medical attention for a condition—especially one that may be stigmatized, like HIV/AIDS or another STD? To anticipate some of these situations, many LGBT travelers keep their meds in carry-on baggage and take duplicate prescriptions along just in case. Others keep two stashes, one in their carry-on bag and another in their checked luggage. It can also make sense to bring a doctor referral with you when you travel; one well-reputed source is the Gay and Lesbian Medical Association, the world's largest and oldest association of LGBT health care professionals.

While the United States has abolished its policy of barring people with HIV from entering the country, many other countries still have HIV travel restrictions in place. Examples include Armenia, Brunei, China, Iraq, Libya, Moldova, Oman, Qatar, Russia, Saudi Arabia, South Korea, and Sudan.

In fact, when overseas don't be surprised if you're told you'll need a physician's letter testifying to your overall "good health" just to use a public pool. Plan ahead if you're counting on doing laps—or just splashing around.

Special Considerations for Women

When it comes to travel, most cities in North America and Western Europe are considered safe for women to visit; public transportation is also generally not dangerous; and women's rights in Europe are at least equivalent to those at home, which is helpful in case you wind up in trouble there.

Even so, there are some travel issues that more directly concern lesbians, transwomen, and bi women travelers—whether at home or traveling abroad:

• If a hotel listing says that it's "gay-friendly," that doesn't necessarily mean you'll be comfortable there, because such language usually means "gay men." Instead, look for hotels and inns that market themselves as being for "women only" or, more openly, for "lesbians and gay-friendly women."

• When in doubt, try to talk with other women who have traveled to your destination to get their insights about cultural nuances and local customs, especially those between the sexes.

• If a situation feels unsafe, leave. Be guided by your intuition. If you're not sure whether a man is trying to be your friend or has sexual or violent intentions, remove yourself as quickly as you can from the scene. It's better to offend someone than to risk being hurt.

• Give a copy of your itinerary to a family member or friend before you leave. Some women and trans travelers decide to check in every three or four days—usually by e-mail—to let friends at home know everything is okay. Decide ahead of time what the protocol should be if you don't get in touch.

Gay and Lesbian Cruises

The gay cruise experience has diversified significantly in recent years, with lots of different ways to set sail. For instance, you can go as a gay single or a couple on a predominantly straight cruise, join an LGBT group aboard a mainstream cruise, or take an all-gay or -lesbian sea adventure, which to many can be very reaffirming. Regardless of the type of cruise, LGBT people are often surprised by how friendly life on board can be, with shipmates saying hello as if in a small town. Also, cruises are catering to a more and more international clientele, so they've also become a great way to meet potential friends from all over the world.

If you're considering this kind of vacation, here are some basics to be aware of:

- **Types of cruises:** Be sure to choose the type of cruise you think you'll be comfortable on. The number of passengers varies with the size of the boat, for example—would you rather be onboard with 125 to 150 men (or women) or several thousand? On some cruises, you'll have the opportunity to spend ample time in various ports of call; on others, the idea is to stay largely aboard. If you've chosen an all-gay cruise, you're likely to find a lot of the action centered around the pool (by day) and the dance floor (by night). Some of these cruises have a second-night party where those who are aboard seeking fun (read: sex) and those who just want to relax (read: read) can sort themselves out.
- **Dining options:** Usually you're assigned to a particular dinner table for the duration of the cruise, although sometimes there's what's called "anytime dining," which gives you a chance to sit with different people or in different restaurants. If you're unhappy or uncomfortable with your assigned dining companions, speak to the maître d' about moving to another table—and let him make the excuses to your former tablemates. Some cruises are more dressy than others; usually, you'll be sent information about the dress code. (For more on formal wear, see page 338.)
- **Special groups:** Some gay cruises cater especially to singles, couples, leathermen, gay naturists, bears, or many other affinity groups. For example, Olivia runs lesbian cruises all over the world now, but there are all-women and mixed-gender LGBT trips as well as through other companies. One of them, Sweet, is a new cruise and tour company for lesbians and their friends that specializes in "voluntourism" experiences. Not to leave out the kids, R Family Vacations (the company Rosie O'Donnell founded) offers LGBT families and their friends group travel on the high seas.
- **Solo travelers:** If you're traveling by yourself, you may be able to defray some of the cost by finding a roommate through the cruise company itself. If you do this, you'll need to agree to respect each other's privacy, which means coming to a mutual understanding of how or when visitors will be received.

Traveling with an LGBT Tour Company

One way to guarantee that you'll be traveling to places that are gay-friendly or at least gay-tour-tested is to sign up with an LGBT tour company. There are dozens of them, if you count the LGBT-focused travel departments of many airline companies. Toto Tours, DavidTravel, and Out Adventures are just a few of the better known.

Not only are you traveling as a mini-community when you're on such a tour—with safety and travel expertise provided by the operator—you also can choose between a wide range of experiences, from the adventurous to the posh. Another big advantage is that because these tour operators are connected to local gay vacation groups, they have more inside information about your destination than you could glean on your own. On the other hand, you'll be paying a premium for this kind of service.

Nudist Clubs and Vacations

Gay nudist resorts are often subject to a variety of misconceptions, with the top two being that public sex is rampant and that they are dirty or unhygienic. In truth, most of these resorts have rules that prohibit sex—or even heavy public displays of affection—in common areas and require clothing in dining halls and other areas where food is present.

In choosing a nudist vacation, ask questions beforehand about these issues and others, including the gender breakdown. Same-sex "segregation" is usually practiced in LGBT resorts as a way to keep guests comfortable and allow each facility to cater to its own particular clients.

Nude Beaches

In the United States, public nudity is generally illegal, so it can take some digging to determine which beaches are nudist or clothing-optional and how they are governed (or not) by local or state laws. Keep in mind that most clothing-optional beaches are nude by common practice only, meaning you may still be subjected to harassment or arrest by local authorities. The situation in Canada is different because the laws are more permissive about nudity overall, and sunbathing and swimming in particular.

More often than not, there tends to be an LGBT presence at nude beaches. Many gay nudists say that finding that particular section of the shoreline is usually quite easy—and comfortable for everyone. As one California lesbian put it: "Nudists don't ogle as much, even when they're straight guys." A good online resource to find nude beaches around the world is Nude Beach Guide (www.beachnude .org), and About.com has a state-by-state guide. Even better, ask some local friends.

LGBT Resort Communities

Scattered around the United States and Canada are a batch of vacation communities, many right on the beach, that cater to lesbians and gay men. Among the four most well-known are Provincetown, on Cape Cod; the Pines and Cherry Grove, on New York's Fire Island; Key West, Florida; and the Russian River area just north of San Francisco.

What's most notable about these communities is that gay people are clearly in abundance if not the majority, which is an unusual, albeit comforting experience. There is definitely a feeling of safety for LGBT vacationers in these enclaves that's hard to find at mainstream resorts. A gay man who has been vacationing in Fire Island Pines for more than a decade says, "Because it lies at the edge of the world, it may be the only place on the planet where it is absolutely safe for queers to hold hands in public." Nevertheless, it's still important to make sure you understand what's acceptable and where, especially when it comes to public sex. (For more about LGBT vacation spots, see "Summer Shares," page 298.)

STRAIGHT TALK

"I'm wondering what you think about the idea of lesbians and gay men going to their own communities for summer vacation. It actually feels a little 'separatist' to me."

It sounds as though you think this phenomenon smacks of potential bias against straight people, but that's not really the case. It's more about simply preferring to spend time, even just for a few days, with others like yourself. Think about it this way: Families with kids often like their own vacation spots. Straight singles often do, too. Even seniors. Sometimes, it just makes sense to be in a more homogeneous group. Families vacationing together can share the babysitting; single straight men and women no doubt find it easier to hook up when that's the focus; and seniors, likewise, have different interests and needs of their own. It works the same way for gay people. There's also the matter of wanting to feel safe and not having to deal with any sort of homophobia or, for many lesbians, sexual come-ons by straight guys—especially when trying to relax on vacation.

AT THE GYM

Health clubs and gyms have long been important in the LGBT community, playing an increasingly central role in recent decades, sometimes supplanting bars and often competing with the Internet as friendly social centers, cruisy pickup joints, or even backrooms for not so covert sexual escapades. In cities like New York, Los Angeles, and San Francisco, gym memberships are held "by a huge percentage of the gay population," writes social critic Erick Alvarez in his recent book on gay gym culture. Not surprisingly, much like the bars before them, what gym you belong to has become another measure of social, if not economic, status. At the same time, lesbians and trans men and women have found themselves unwelcome at some of these clubs, highlighting the sometimes fragmented nature of the LGBT community.

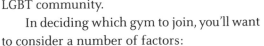

In deciding which gym to join, you'll want to consider a number of factors:

- Do you feel welcome?
- Do the membership dues fall within your budget?
- Does the gym meet your fitness needs as well as your social ones?
- Is it close to your home or work?

More often than not, you can get free passes to try out local clubs, which is a great way to get a better feel for the members, staff, overall atmosphere, services provided, and rules.

Basic Health Club Etiquette

Good gym etiquette is more or less the same whether you go to a predominantly LGBT health club or a straight one. However, you may find a more lax environment at certain gay clubs—for instance, shirtless (male) bodybuilders and a higher sexual temperature in general. Explained one yogi who's a member of a gay male gym: "It just kills me that even though my club has a zero-tolerance policy on sex, nobody wants to do anything about it. Guys, please do it at home!"

You don't need to go very far to find a club's rules, which are usually posted in the facility as well as online. Here are the ones you're likely to find in most gyms and clubs:

- Wear deodorant.
- Keep cologne and other scents to a minimum.
- Only use cell phones as necessary; obey rules prohibiting locker room photographs and video.
- Rack your weights when you're done with them; it's fine to hold on to them in between sets.
- Limit your time on cardio equipment if others are waiting.
- Don't hog the equipment, and allow others to work in with you.
- Wipe down your equipment with a towel after use.
- Keep your grunting to a nonintimidating level.
- Share swimming lanes as needed.
- Don't make judgments about others.
- Don't engage in sexual activity.
- Dress for safety: No sandals or other open-toed shoes in the weight room; wear supportive or protective gear as necessary.
- No shaving in the steam room or sauna.

QUEERY

"Mirror, mirror on the wall, who's the biggest of them all?"

Q **Some of the muscle gods at my gym spend an inordinate amount of time flexing in front of the mirrors. Isn't this just another form of bragging, "Hey look at me!"—or worse, pure narcissism?**

A My guess is that you're an ectomorph like me, so that whatever tendencies you have toward narcissism, they are not manifested by prancing and flexing in front of a crowd. Sure, there may be some testosterone-driven competition between bodybuilders that accounts for their posing, just as golfers boast about their birdies and Scrabble players, the number of triple-score words in a game. Everything in moderation.

Still, there's also a legitimate reason for your muscle gods to check themselves out: The best way to see a muscle group is to flex it. And how do you see your pecs? That's right, you take your shirt off. A competitive bodybuilder explained to me: "Anyone who is training for a bodybuilding competition should be practicing his posing at least an hour per day." Nevertheless, this man admits that some guys do indeed pose "just to show off." But, hey, nobody's forcing you to look at these guys!

Flirting and Cruising

Sure, health clubs are social centers in the LGBT community, so why shouldn't you make friends or find dates along the way? Of course we should, and that's why flirting is a welcome aspect of gym culture. However, don't cross over into the kind of hard-core cruising that can make your intended—and even others—uncomfortable.

What's the difference? It's flirting when you make eye contact with someone as a way to start a conversation, keeping (mostly) to nonsexual topics like workout routines or how great he or she looks. (If he's interested, he'll flirt back, but if he says he needs to get back to his next set or that his husband is waiting for him, back off.) But simple flirting becomes aggressive cruising when you're touching someone inappropriately, you're encroaching upon him (say, in the sauna), or you're in the steam room and your towel tents up. If you find mutual interest, take it outside the club as a next step.

Body Odor and Scent-Free Policies

"Whenever she came within about fifteen feet of me, I started to get a throbbing headache from her perfume," recalls one regular gymgoer of a fellow member she shared a workout room with recently. In fact, health club managers say that one of their biggest challenges is limiting colognes and other scents. Because the topic is hard to raise with a member, they usually wait for a complaint. One manager explains, "If I can smell it and I'm within three of four feet, it's too strong." To avoid becoming an issue yourself:

- Know your club's policy and be aware of your own body odor as well as any perfumes/colognes you use. Some clubs even prohibit specific products.
- Don't use cologne to mask body odor; once you've worked up a sweat, that's double trouble.

If someone's scent is overpowering, talk to the club manager about the problem. The manager can discuss gym policy with the member, suggest a shower, or in a worst-case scenario, ask the offending person to take a hike—instead of the planned workout.

QUEERY

"Swooning for my trainer"

Q I always fall in love with the trainers at the gym. They are so dykey and buff! I'm thinking of asking out my current trainer, but my friends say that's not a good idea. Any advice?

A Listen to your friends! You're probably writing to me only because you hope I'll say, "It's fine to have a sexual relationship with a professional you pay for *other* services." Sorry, I'm not granting you permission. Dual relationships are confusing by definition; add in the color of money and you're in real trouble.

Locker Room Sex

If you're a gay or bi man, it will come as little surprise that casual sex in locker rooms, saunas, and whirlpools happens a lot at many predominantly gay gyms (and just about every YMCA I've ever set foot in). Some claim it is part of their gym experience; others find it unsanitary or otherwise offensive. There certainly are times during the day when sexual activity seems to peak—for instance, mornings after the prework crush, right after lunch, or in the late afternoon on weekends.

These days, many clubs have zero-tolerance policies when it comes to sexual activity on the premises, and violating them can result in punishments, as one gym's rules put it, "up to and including membership termination." If that isn't enough to deter you, Google the term "locker room sex" and you'll find plenty of links to real-life gay sexual hijinks filmed unbeknownst to the participants. Not only is it good manners to steer away from this kind of public play, but it's smart, too, if you care a whit about your reputation or worry about a starring role on a YouTube video.

COMMUNITY GIVING

An ever widening range of nonprofits serve our community, providing crucial resources, fighting for our rights and legal protections, and offering services for everyone from youth, seniors, and immigrants to members of the armed forces. These organizations also depend on the time and energy of LGBT and straight supporters alike, through events like bar fund-raisers, AIDS rides, and star-studded galas. In particular, HIV's scourge—now entering its fourth decade—has added a whole new dimension to the notion of "community giving," having brought together lesbians and gay men in unprecedented fashion. Of course, gay people give to important causes that are not exclusively ours—climate change, the arts, health-related causes, and religious institutions, to name a few.

There are few more generous things to do with your time than give to these causes and coax others to do so as well. As Victor Hugo wrote, "As the purse is emptied, the heart is filled." And you'll be glad to know there's essential etiquette when it comes to asking friends and family members to donate to organizations you care about, hosting fund-raisers, holding silent auctions, and even saying no to a worthy request.

Asking Friends to Donate

It makes perfect sense that if you find yourself supporting a cause, you'd want to ask friends and family members to contribute as well. Certainly these agencies rely heavily on individual donations. However, many of us are uncomfortable asking.

First, convince yourself that asking is not greedy, pushy, or aggressive; it's just *asking.* Keep in mind that the key building block of any ask is that you believe in the organization's mission and are able to explain it. Sometimes you do the asking in person; other times you craft a letter or e-mail. But the important thing is to explain the good work that this particular organization does and why it needs help. Don't be shy or reticent. Remember, you're acting as an ambassador for those in need.

For instance, if you're soliciting on behalf of the National Women and AIDS Collective, a coalition of HIV-infected and -affected women activists, make sure you can discuss the disproportionate number of cases of HIV/AIDS among women and the dearth of funding sources. Rely on a combination of facts, statistics, and your own reasons to care.

Here are four basic steps to follow when fund-raising:

1. **Make the case:** Take the time to research and explain to your friends, family members, and colleagues why this particular organization matters—and matters to you. Even if someone can't make a donation, you'll raise awareness of the cause or perhaps encourage your friends to give another way, such as by volunteering time or in-kind goods.

2. **Close the deal:** If you've written a letter or sent an e-mail, follow up by phone about a week later. Ask potential donors if they've received your correspondence and if they have any questions. Help them understand concretely how their donation will matter and how they'll be recognized—perhaps with a newsletter mention or with a plaque (for bigger contributions). Then summon your inner moxie and ask them if they'll be able to help: Sit back and wait for the answer.

3. **Offer your thanks:** Even if you're not successful, thank your friends for their time and the opportunity to talk about your cause. If they do decide to make a gift, send a thank-you note or e-mail within the next two or three days, and make sure the nonprofit agency does, too. (Its letter should specify that the

QUEERY

"Uneasy about asking for donations"

Q My partner and I would like to be table captains at the annual dinner of a gay rights group in our city. We haven't done this before and feel a little queasy asking our friends to join us and pay some big bucks, even though it's for such a worthwhile cause. Any suggestions on how to write them about this tactfully?

A It's great that you're willing to step up. And your question is not an unusual one by any stretch. A philanthropist friend reports that he's constantly struggling with this issue, even after captaining umpteen tables. So, instead of focusing on your queasiness, try focusing on what a worthwhile cause this is. As you know, being a table captain is a crucial role at such events, because without you it's pretty much impossible for the organization to reach its fund-raising goal.

Here's how I would start such a letter to friends (with thanks to the Human Rights Campaign):

I'm hoping that you can participate in something really important to me, and important to our community. I have signed up to be a table captain for the [fill in your organization]. If you've been to one of our events in the past, you know what a fun, inspiring, and empowering time it is, and I'm sure this year will also be great. As a table captain, I have committed to filling the ten seats at the table, and would love to have you join us. . . .

Remember to reach out early, several months before the event. If you can't fill your table, usually the organization will try to fill empty seats.

donation is tax-deductible, and your friends should retain it for their tax records.)

4. **Use social media sites:** It's been said that if you "friend-raise," the funds will follow. In that vein, develop your social networks and use them—strategically—to raise dollars for the organizations you care about. Be sure to thank any donors individually, not en masse.

Good Charity/Bad Charity

You can never be too sure about where you are placing your money. While most nonprofits in the LGBT community are legitimate (as are most, in general) and do excellent work, it pays to keep in mind the following questions:

• **Is your money going where you think it is?** Make sure you are giving to the organization in question. Sometimes, disreputable groups try to siphon off funds by concocting similar-sounding names. Double-check the information you're given by examining a group's official website.

• **How does the group spend its dollars?** Do some online research and take note of the watchdog websites that now exist, such as Charity Navigator and the American Institute of Philanthropy. Take some time to understand how a certain agency spends its funds. Another great source for this kind of information is give.org, which is operated by the Better Business Bureau and has information about thousands of charities and nonprofits.

• **Is your donation tax-deductible?** Make sure that it is (if that matters to you) by asking if the agency has 501-(c)-(3) status. This is the official IRS recognition that a group is a charity, and

contributions to such organizations are tax-deductible to the extent allowed by tax laws.

• **Are you being pressured?** Don't fall for high-pressure tactics, especially over the phone. Ask for information to be sent to you or for the URL of the group's official website. Pay by check—made out to the nonprofit and not to an individual—not cash. Even better, call in your credit card number to the main office, or do so online at the official website. Alternatively, if an organization has set up a PayPal account, use that.

When You Have to Say No

It's easy enough to say no when the phone rings at the dinner hour and a faraway voice asks you to contribute to an organization you've never heard of. But it's quite another thing to turn down a friend's request to support a group she cares deeply about. Naturally, you can give only what you can afford—or to causes you believe in. Here's how you can turn down such appeals with appropriate finesse:

• "I've given all that I can for this year. You're welcome to ask me again next year."

• "I'm only supporting LGBT [or fill in the blank] organizations right now, especially with the fight for marriage equality being so expensive."

• Or if you want to hedge: "I'd like to know more about your organization. Please go ahead and mail me information about its mission and accomplishments, as well as what percentage of my donation would go to direct services."

• Even if you can't make a cash donation, you can volunteer your time or skills. In fact, sometimes having a hardworking volunteer show up is just as valuable for organizations as receiving a check or monthly pledge. Volunteering has benefits for you as well— for instance, it can put you in touch with others who have a like-minded passion. It can also be personally satisfying. (For more about the benefits of volunteering, see page 349.)

(For more about the benefits of volunteering, see page 349.)

THE ESSENTIALS
Five Other Ways to Give

Not everyone will be able to make a cash donation, but there are lots of other creative ways for you to help out and that you can suggest to others:

- Film a short video to persuade your friends and family members to donate to your cause, and post it on YouTube, your Facebook page, or e-mail it.
- If you run a business, agree to donate a percentage of the proceeds from your sales. Be sure to publicize it.
- Hold a garage sale of your own or organize your block to do one together and then donate the proceeds.
- Instead of a birthday or holiday gift, ask your friends and loved ones to make a donation to your favorite organization. Alternatively, have a party at your home and mention the charity of your choice in the invitations—or make a pitch during the event and pass the hat.
- Join an AIDS ride or breast cancer walk and ask your friends to support you.

Silent Auctions

Many LGBT organizations feature silent auctions, either as stand-alone events or as part of a gala or other fund-raising event. The objective is simple: to raise more money for the benefiting agency.

If you're attending a silent auction, here are some important rules to play by:

- Don't underbid an item. Minimum means minimum.
- Make sure you overbid properly (for instance, sometimes a bid must be at least $5, $10, or $50 higher than the previous one).
- Be prepared to pay with a check or credit card at the conclusion of the auction. There's nothing messier for a nonprofit than trying to track down payments due after an auction.
- Don't get upset if you lose out on a particular item. Silent auctions are meant to do good and be fun. Stay with the spirit.

What to Wear to a Gala

It's not always easy to figure out what's appropriate to wear to what sort of charity function and how much sartorial leeway is permissible. Even the language on invitations, which can run from "black tie" to "business casual," with "festive attire" thrown in from time to time, isn't always prescriptive.

Here's a rundown of some of the basic invitation terms for charity events and galas. As with all sartorial advice, take what you need and leave the rest.

FORMAL ATTIRE

The language on the invitation to a formal event could say exactly that, or it might say "black tie" or "white tie." This is definitely one area where the rules are a little more complicated for men.

For Men

Traditionally, "formal attire" calls for a black tuxedo jacket with matching trousers (pleated or flat front), black bow tie and cummerbund, a white wing-collared tuxedo shirt, black patent leather pumps (with grosgrain bows on them for the full effect), and black dress socks (preferably silk). Got that?

Typically, jackets are single-breasted and ventless with ribbed silk facings. You have three lapel options: the shawl collar, the peak lapel, or the notched lapel. However, if you're chafing under these conventions, there's room for a little creativity: Exchange the black bow tie and cummerbund for something with a pattern or a coordinating color. You can also ditch the patent leather shoes in favor of plain black leather dress shoes.

These days, traditional black tie can often feel a little "yesterday," especially in fashion-forward cities like Los Angeles, New York, and Miami. If you're more stylish, today's well-dressed man can also show up in a black suit, spread collar white shirt (no pleated fronts, please), and a skinny black or metallic tie—no more cummerbund and no more matching sets of bow ties and cummerbunds. John Bartlett, the noted menswear designer, suggests, "Keep it simple and masculine and spend your money on a good suit rather than a tux." (In warmer climates or during the summer, you can opt for a white dinner jacket, flat-front or pleated black trousers, and a black cummerbund.)

If the invitation states "black tie," stick with the traditional tuxedo. Meanwhile, white tie" indicates the most formal of occasions. According to protocol, white tie should be worn only for events after dark or 6:00 P.M.

(whichever comes first). This outfit consists of a black tailcoat, horizontally cut away at the front, with matching black trousers that have a single stripe of satin and are worn with suspenders. Add to this a plain white, stiff-fronted shirt, wing collar, white bow tie, a white, low-cut waist (preferably made with cotton Marcella, although silk is fine, too), knee-high black silk socks, and black pumps. Ready to party now?

For Women

If you're going old-school, this is the time for a formal evening dress (a gown) or an uptown cocktail dress. Traditionally, women were advised to make such an outfit more "creative" by adding colorful boas, brooches, or a fine shawl. Today's smart lesbian should "avoid looking too prom or down-market," John Bartlett cautions, by ditching those dated accessories; instead, focus more on a striking piece of jewelry, and wear high heels. Alternatively, don a sleek suit with a white shirt and tie or a black velvet Nehru jacket. Mixing and matching from both feminine and masculine styles makes for a sophisticated look.

BUSINESS ATTIRE INVITATIONS

Sorry, but the rules are definitely vague in this category. Generally, business attire means looking "professional," which will mean one thing for an attorney and quite something else for a filmmaker or a fashion designer. It's a relaxed look, but still dressed up a bit more than if you weren't going out at all.

For Men

Tradition would see you in a dark business suit with a white or light blue shirt, a fairly conservative tie, and coordinated leather shoes; or in a sports coat or blazer, with an open-collar shirt and no tie. If you want a more contemporary look, choose a well-tailored suit or a combination of a tweed or navy blazer with black or gray flannel trousers. Consider a brighter-than-usual shirt-and-tie combo (rep stripes and paisley are good bets), well-made wingtips, and a discreet belt. Another good choice is dark denim jeans, a well-cut shirt, and a blazer.

For Women

Wear a cocktail dress, a nice skirt and top, or a well-tailored pants suit. If you want to dress more like a celebrity, think about two-piece suits with brightly colored turtlenecks or a simple T-shirt for layering. Sometimes a men's-inspired pant with high heels or a fitted men's black blazer over a knit dress can be just the right look. John Bartlett adds, "Don't accessorize too much. It will make you look older."

FESTIVE ATTIRE (AKA DRESSY CASUAL)

Often used in holiday party invitations, "festive attire" is another invitation term without a clear definition. It suggests that both men and women sport a bit more sparkle or pizzazz than they might ordinarily. If you receive such an invitation during the winter holidays and you're more the traditional Brooks Brothers or Talbots type, haul out your reds, greens, and tartans (but don't go overboard). For more fashion-forward guys, anything from a sports coat and slacks to a dressy sweater or "conservative" turtleneck and nice trousers or dark blue, black, or even white jeans, depending on the season. For women, you'll be safe in just about any outfit ranging from a short cocktail dress to a smart skirt and top, a tailored suit, or a dressy blouse and jeans. However, if this all sounds too upper-crust or is just not your style, tweak your normal attire with a fun scarf, a pair of catchy earrings, or some glitter makeup. In the end, festive is more about attitude than fashion.

POLITICAL MANNERS

Activism is frequently about stretching the boundaries of manners—both to provoke and to bring attention to an issue. At the same time, there is something very civic about being a "good citizen" and participating in public affairs as well as public demonstrations. LGBT people have a long history of being advocates and activists, ever since the battles against homophobia and, more recently, transphobia became full-fledged civil rights movements. We stood up at Stonewall; we protested against the FDA's slow approval of HIV drug treatments; and, in the first decades of the twenty-first century, we've been marching, lobbying, Facebooking, and conducting protests in the fight for marriage equality—and other issues.

If you do choose to participate in some direct action, whether blogging about an issue you care about or going out and getting

QUEERY

"Not ready for pink triangles on my car"

Q **What do you think of people who put a pink triangle or a rainbow bumper sticker on their cars? My partner and I have been debating this for a couple of weeks. I'm uncomfortable telling the whole world that we're gay, but he says that the more visibility we have, the better off we'll be in the long run. I understand his point of view, but I keep reminding him that we don't live in San Francisco and that LGBT people are the victims of hate crimes in our state.**

A Let's start with your first question: When I see a car with an LGBT bumper sticker it signals to me that these folks are gay and out. That visibility makes me happy, be it on a Subaru, MINI Cooper, or F-10 pickup. It sounds like the issue in your case is that you and your partner are not equally out or simply have different ideas about how loudly you want to show that off to the world. I'd suggest you first talk together about what makes you uncomfortable and why.

But you're right that the homophobic landscape varies greatly in this country and that first and foremost you want to be safe. It's one thing to be tooling down Market Street in San Francisco with a pink triangle affixed to your car's rear and another to try that in—well, I won't name names. But the truth is that your partner is also right. Visibility is vital in the LGBT community; and in large measure that's how we've gotten as far as we have.

So, how about a compromise? The two of you could affix a less LGBT-flag-waving decal to your bumper, such as the Human Rights Campaign's iconic equal (=) sign—a choice like that provides the visibility your partner seeks, but more subtly.

arrested, remember that activists and other politically active people need to follow certain codes of behavior in order to get the job done as part of an effective group. As critic Malcolm Gladwell wrote in *The New Yorker*, "The moment when one protester deviates from the script and responds to provocation, the moral legitimacy of the entire protest is compromised."

Outing

Outing, the practice of dragging or pushing someone out of the closet against his or her will, is generally considered a major violation of an individual's privacy and LGBT community norms. Simply stated: Outing of family, friends, or colleagues is not good manners because of the disrespect it evidences. In general, a person's sexual orientation or gender identity is a personal matter, as is the decision to come out or stay in the closet. Outing has also encouraged the notion that being LGBT is something to be accused of or incriminated by.

In the political realm, outing is a controversial tactic—deployed by both gays and straights—aimed at publicizing a gay person's camouflaged sexual orientation in order to damage his or her reputation or highlight acts of hypocrisy. U.S. Congressman Barney Frank, among many others, has vociferously and rightfully argued that outing is both appropriate and called for when a gay political figure is actively working against LGBT issues such as the right to marry or adopt, funding HIV/AIDS research, or providing legal protections in the workplace. He said, "The right to privacy should not be a right to hypocrisy. And people who want to demonize other people shouldn't then be able to go home and close the door and do it themselves."

Civil Disobedience

The idea of civil disobedience is to highlight an issue by purposely and peacefully breaking the law—in a way that doesn't hurt anyone but simply inconveniences them, such as blocking an entrance to a building or resisting arrest. The Indian political and spiritual leader Mahatma Gandhi popularized this strategy, and the Reverend Dr. Martin Luther King Jr. brought it to the United States during the civil rights movement. The LGBT community has also deployed it with great success over the years, notably with ACT-UP's efforts in the 1980s and '90s to fight for increased funding for HIV/AIDS research and the speedier development of new treatment methods.

At first, it may seem like civil disobedience is on the wrong side of manners, but breaking the law for a higher calling is neither unethical nor bad manners—unless the idea is to foment violence or curb free speech.

It does pay, however, to follow these rules when it comes to acts of civil disobedience:

- **Teach others:** Be sure that a major thrust of your effort is to educate others about the need for reform. Whether on an individual level—by speaking to those around you—or as part of a communication strategy, take the time to explain your position, your values, and your reasons for breaking the law.
- **Respect others:** All those you come in contact with, including police officers, legal observers, the media, and those whose businesses you are disrupting, deserve to be treated with respect—even if they are not being respectful to you or your fellow protesters.
- **Be on time:** Civil disobedience is a form of political theater (often, the schedule of a protest is worked out among the organizers, the police, and the media), and timing is everything when it comes to political theater.
- **Criticize constructively:** Tactics and goals are usually all up for discussion, but alienating your fellow activists is not smart or effective.
- **Don't act out:** Your decision to commit civil disobedience doesn't give you license to violate other community norms or standards of behavior. For instance, getting drunk or high or name-calling is not only inappropriate but counterproductive.

Kiss-ins

While definitely a disruptive political tactic, a kiss is not meant to break any laws. The idea, simply, is to explicitly violate the usual rules for public displays of affection by having a crowd of protesters pair up and smooch, whether in a church to oppose its policies on condoms or homosexuality, at the state legislature to protest opposition to same-sex marriage, or outside a restaurant that has anti-gay policies.

Follow the same rules you would for any act of civil disobedience, but remember a few other things, too:

- **Be clean and kissable:** If that means breath mints, so be it.
- **Share the joy:** Don't hog the best kissers. If everyone else is moving on to a new partner, it's time to let go.
- **No tongues, please:** You're making a political statement, not engaging in foreplay.

Gay Pride

The famously flashy annual celebration known as Gay Pride or LGBT Pride or simply Pride has changed a lot in recent decades. It started out as a political commemoration of the 1969 Stonewall Riots, when the police raided a New York City bar (as per their regular routine) but this time the gay and transgender patrons fought back. The weeklong liberation party that it has pretty much turned into—with a smattering of political issues—has spread to scores of cities around the world.

There are no hard-and-fast rules about how to participate in Pride, except that diversity and its close cousin outrageousness rule the day. It's not a time for judgments, especially within our own community. You can get involved through a community organization promoting a particular cause or help decorate some elaborate float representing a neighborhood bar—or you can just join the parade. For straight people, Pride can be a special occasion, too, even if it just means supporting your

LGBT friends from the sidelines or marching with a group like PFLAG.

As for the anti-LGBT protesters that sometimes show up along the route, the best thing to do is ignore them. However, also let them serve as a reminder that Pride is not celebrating the end of homophobia or transphobia, at least not yet.

STRAIGHT TALK

"I'm so outraged that most gay people still can't get married in this country that I've decided to abstain from straight weddings until the laws change. What's a good way to let my friends know this without hurting their feelings?"

That's very bold of you. Making personal sacrifices can be a powerful way to make a political statement, especially if you're able to publicize your decision in some way. But I'd suggest you not let your activism or political beliefs get in the way of long-standing friendships; there are plenty of other ways to express your violent disagreement with the status quo. In that same vein, I'd hope those straights who oppose gay marriage wouldn't let their views prevent them from attending a same-sex wedding of a family member or close friend.

In any case, it sounds as though your marrying friends will take the brunt of your decision, and they're really not the ones who should be penalized. But here's an idea: Make your gift to them in the form of a donation to one of the LGBT rights groups advocating for same-sex marriage.

THE ESSENTIALS

Political Demonstrations and Gay Pride Parades

Parades and pride marches, from the annual LGBT festivities to local trans and dyke events, are part and parcel of our political culture. If you decide to join in, here's what you need to know:

- Keep in step. Adjust your pace to suit the people around you.
- Don't engage in name-calling if heckled.
- If you're blowing a whistle, don't do it in someone's ear.
- Don't hold up the line to cruise someone on the sidelines—unless you're able to march and flirt at the same time.
- Respect all public safety officers and follow the law.
- Be gracious if someone wants to cross the street between marchers.
- Share your water and sunscreen.

QUEERY

"In search of a Gay Pride dress code"

Q **I'm looking forward to my city's pride celebration later this month but wondering if you have some suggestions on a dress code for those in attendance. Here's why I ask: On a day when our community gets so much attention from the news media, I think it's a shame that so many of us don't present a more wholesome face to the country. Why do so many gay men and lesbians need to show up in full drag or leather?**

A I hope you're not suggesting I ask Dykes on Bikes to refrain from kicking off pride parades in cities across the country. While they're certainly front and center for logistical reasons (after all, you wouldn't want to march in *front* of them), there's also another more important explanation: They are symbolic of the defiance, freedom, and, yes, gay pride, that was birthed during the Stonewall Riots in 1969. Ever since, they, along with groups dressing in the particular styles you mention, have been criticized for presenting a "face" of LGBT people to the world that's too provocative.

I'd suggest that there is a time and place for everything. Pride festivities provide a brief moment every year to recall Stonewall, which we do happen to owe to a group of drag queens and trans people, among others. Even the current marriage-equality movement is about inclusion and diversity. If the more mainstream parts of our community push the leather and drag communities to the side, literally and metaphorically, we'll have erased the essence of gay pride.

At the same time, I think the reason we have other advocacy groups that do present a more "wholesome" front—complete with suit and tie—is that they're more effective in Congressional hearings and in state legislatures across the country.

CELEBRATING THE HOLIDAYS

D espite all the commercials depicting happy families and bucolic cityscapes, the holiday season can be frightful for many LGBT people (and straights) because it often involves travel, financial stress, anxieties about gift giving, and a host of family tensions—not to mention the temptations of too much food and liquor. Then, add to that wintry mix the inflexibility that so many have around certain "traditions" ("But we've always had Christmas dinner at 1:00 P.M.!"), and you begin to understand what so many of us face. To boot, many of our core LGBT questions come to the fore: Are you out to your parents or siblings? Will the real you be welcome at home? If you have a partner, is she accepted? And, how does *her* family feel about you? Or are you single and fear facing yet another holiday season without a beau?

Fortunately, there are three actions you can take that go a long way at this time of year: Plan well and early; develop a healthy dollop of patience; and finally, practice the art of flexibility—and you may find that it's New Year's Day before you know it.

Partner Versus Family

For LGBT people, the usual dilemma of deciding where to spend the holidays is deepened when families are unaccepting of our partners, adding to the stress of that stretch between Thanksgiving and New Year's. Or perhaps

VOX POPULI

Do you sometimes get poor treatment from your family over the holidays?

"My family expects me to leave my girlfriend alone on the holidays to be with them."

"I feel very fortunate that my chosen family has done their personal work and sacrificed their comfort to know more about the world. My biological family lags far behind."

"My family wants me to act like I'm straight in public so I don't embarrass them, especially during the holidays."

"I just discovered my family is having a lunch at one of the sister's. My [gay] husband and I were not invited. I am upset, but it just makes me realize how much more I love my husband."

you're wanted at one or both families but are seeking to establish new holiday rituals of your own. If there are any rules governing these kinds of decisions, it's these two: (1) Invent what works for you (and your partner); (2) Communicate your plans to friends and family early and often.

Here are some other unlikely-to-offend solutions for this time of year:

- **No one says couples *have* to be together every holiday:** Many gay and lesbian partners spend their holidays apart. Some LGBT people are not out, so bringing along a partner just won't work. Others don't get to see their parents and siblings much during the year and relish the chance to spend that time together at the holidays.

- **Consider trading off:** For instance, spend Thanksgiving this year with her family; Hanukkah or Christmas with yours; and then reverse the order the following year.
- **Share the holiday:** If everyone lives nearby, you can spend Christmas Eve with family and Christmas Day with your friends.
- **Move your celebration:** Some of us decide to celebrate our holiday on another day, a few days earlier or later, which can make it easier to be with others.
- **The eight days of Hanukkah:** If you're Jewish, you're in luck; you have more than a week to work with.
- **Invite everyone to your place:** Create your own new tradition.

Balancing Different Religious Beliefs or Traditions

When a same-sex couple doesn't share the same religious beliefs you'll likely need an extra serving of mutual respect and flexibility, because accepting your partner's religious beliefs or spiritual values is a central tenet of any healthy relationship. This doesn't mean that you need to abandon your own beliefs or adopt hers, just that you need to make room in your lives for both. Perhaps your partner generally attends religious services alone, but for more social events you join in.

As the holidays approach, discuss your respective preferences: Will your Methodist lover be fine celebrating Hanukkah with your family? How does your Muslim girlfriend feel about having a Christmas tree in the house (or reindeer on the roof)? What about those who are atheist or agnostic? Is there a way to blend your customs and create new rituals to make the holidays meaningful for both of you? Try your best not to be dogmatic about these matters; there's no reason to turn small differences into a holy war.

Much the same can be said for balancing differing beliefs with friends. Join in with them when you're comfortable, and ask them to do the same. In many cases, LGBT participation in churches and temples is as much about community and belonging as scripture and prayer.

Gift Giving

On the surface, giving and receiving gifts at the holidays seems pretty innocuous and cheery, but it can be cause for hurt and disappointment in many families, both in the ones we were born into and in the new ones we form with our friends and partners.

If you're in a relationship, talk with your partner about your expectations and budget. Some LGBT couples decide to do something jointly, such as getting a puppy, purchasing a necessary appliance, or putting down a deposit on a vacation. Others agree to a spending limit or to support a favorite charity.

Then there's the gift fuss itself: Many love the wrappings and tidings of holiday giving, while others disdain the commercialism. A lesbian therapist explained how she got her family to focus more on the sentiments and less on the materialism. "Instead of store-bought gifts, I suggested that we each make something for one person in the family. We chose lots and I picked my mom. I wrote her a heartfelt letter about how important she was to me. She loved it. My gay brother, who had picked my dad, compiled a CD of songs that he thought our father would appreciate. It went over really well."

When you do give a gift, take the time to personalize it. Giving generic presents suggests that the recipient isn't that important to you or that you couldn't be bothered to spend time on the effort. For a poetry lover, pick up a collection by W. H. Auden, Audre Lorde, or Mark Doty. If your best friend volunteers at a breast cancer action group, think about making a donation in her name. Does a good friend need something that she wouldn't (or can't) buy for herself? What about making or baking a gift—or giving the gift of time, perhaps in the form of babysitting or a long-overdue invitation to a one-on-one dinner?

STRAIGHT TALK

"How serious should my son and his boyfriend be before we include the newcomer in our holiday gift giving?"

Do the same as you would do with straight kids and their boyfriends or girlfriends: When it seems as though the couple is serious and becoming part of your family, be proactive and extend an invitation for two. If you have no precedent, why don't you just ask your son if he'd like you to invite both of them? But the entire responsibility doesn't rest with you. Your son could make your job easier by sending you an e-mail that says, "Hey Mom, I'm really hoping that James can join us in our family celebration this year." Bingo! Asking to bring home your significant other is a sign that the relationship is getting serious.

Then you're on to your next challenge: whether to gift the new boyfriend, too. The answer is yes—nothing too pricey, but a small gift that shows you gave it, and him, some consideration.

THE ESSENTIALS
Tipping Those Who Help Out

For the so-called service providers in your life, it can be a delicate matter to decide whether to give a present, and if so, exactly what, because you don't generally know their tastes. Fortunately, in our culture, thank-you gifts to those who take care of our homes, dogs, and bodies are often best expressed in dollars and cents. Beyond that, remember to actually express your gratitude and thanks in a short note or holiday card.

The following guidelines are a starting point. They will need adjustment depending on where you live, how long you've known the provider, the quality of the service, and whether you've tipped regularly during the year.

- **Housekeepers and dog walkers:** Give the equivalent of up to a week's pay if they come regularly.

- **Pet groomers:** Up to the cost of one service.

- **Personal trainers and massage therapists:** Up to the cost of a single session.

- **Teachers:** Gifts should be kept in line and shouldn't appear to be a bribe to raise your or your child's grade. Consumables are best: movie passes, a fruit basket, etc. No cash for teachers.

- **Haircutters:** Up to the cost of one haircut. Be sure to remember the salon staff, too. Your tip can be divided among your various attendants.

- **Newspaper delivery:** Between $10 and $30, depending on where you live.

- **Building superintendents:** Between $20 and $80, depending on the frequency of service.

- **Doormen:** About $15 per doorman. Check with your fellow residents to see what others give in your building, and be prepared to give considerably more in big cities.

- **Mail carriers:** Federal employees are not allowed to accept greenbacks and can only take gifts up to $20 in value (a gift card is a good idea). Alternatively, you could give a baked good or write a "letter of commendation" to your carrier's boss.

- **The boss:** This is the hardest one. First, consider the specifics of your work culture. Do others give to their bosses? If so, what kind of gifts? Stay in line. Think about your intention. Is this about being generous or currying favor? If it's the latter, don't do it. Finally, if you decide to give: Make it impersonal; don't overspend to impress.

"Bad" Gifts

Of course, there really aren't good and bad gifts, but there are those that you don't need, don't like, or already have. While faking it is generally not very good manners in other areas of life, holiday gift giving requires a slight modification of that rule. For instance, I've suggested to my three nieces that, when opening gifts, they put on their happy faces and keep them on. The same is true for adults; you don't need to say "I love it," but your expression does need to show appreciation for the effort and your lips need to say "thank you." Sometimes your initial horror of a gift gone wrong may fade.

If not, after a couple of days, try one of these options:

- If there's no gift receipt in the box, see if you can tell what store the gift came from. Call or check the website and ask for the exchange and return policies.

- Tell the gift giver some variant of the truth, such as "It doesn't really fit me" or "I realize I've got one just like that." Then ask for a gift receipt so that you can exchange it. Don't make your friend feel badly for getting it wrong.

- Create a regifting closet.

If you're a gift giver and have run into this problem before (and who hasn't?), here are some considerations for you:

- Enclose the gift receipt in the bottom of the box.

- Find out what's on your friend's "wish list" before choosing a gift.

- Give a gift card. Some cards are good for many stores, others for just one.

- Make a charitable donation in your friend's name instead.

Surprise Gifts

It's an all too common occurrence: You've made your list, checked it twice, and suddenly a new girlfriend or relative surprises you with a present. You don't have anything for this person. To avoid this potential gaffe, be prepared:

- **Buy small gift items ahead of time:** Bottles of wine, boxes of chocolates, cans of popcorn, and nice hand soaps will do just fine. Wrap them up and keep them on hand to dole out as needed. (Just make sure you don't give the wine to a friend in AA or the chocolate to a diabetic.)

- **Pick up some gift cards:** Bookstore or local department store gift cards work well at the holidays or anytime during the year. If you go this route, choose a card that doesn't expire or have fees associated with it.
- **Get crafty:** Make banana bread, frame a photo you took, or get out your glue gun and put together a winter wreath. A handmade gift will always be a hit.

Finally, if you get caught empty-handed, you can always buy time by saying, "I haven't finished my shopping, but you're on my list!" Or just say "Thank you very much." And while you're angsting about all this, don't forget that giving is a voluntary act that requires nothing in return.

The Art of Regifting

Not so very long ago, regifting was frowned upon by manners experts because it seemed, well, tacky *and* cheap. Fortunately, that's all changed now, as long as you do it correctly. Regifting is even seen by some as eco-friendly—because, after all, you're recycling.

This easiest regifting is to a favorite charity. Did you get a set of towels that you just don't like? Donate it to your local LGBT center. Were you the recipient of a signed photo of Susan Lucci or Fergie? Contribute her to your favorite HIV/AIDS organization's next silent auction.

If, however, you're planning to regift to someone else, here are some useful contemporary guidelines:

- **Be careful:** Make sure you never regift an item back to its original source. If your memory is short, keep a log of gifts and their givers so that you don't make this mistake.
- **Be smart:** If it was a coworker who gave you that distinctive purple sweater, better not to regift to anyone in your office for fear of exposure. Ditto for your or your partner's family.
- **Make sure it appears new:** Double-check that there are no personally identifying elements, such as an inscription to you in a book or a card left in the box.
- **Make sure it's suitable:** When regifting, consider if the particular item is an appropriate one for its intended recipient. Just as with a new gift, it should show evidence of premeditation.
- **No swapping of boxes:** Don't take a sweater from Walmart and put it in a Neiman Marcus box. Your friend won't be the only one embarrassed if he happens to try to return it to the wrong store.
- **Don't overgift:** Be careful not to recycle an item that your new recipient would think too expensive or grand for the occasion. Either she'll feel inadequate in the gift she has chosen for you—or you'll be busted.
- **If caught, confess:** Remember, it's always the cover-up that takes us down. There's nothing wrong with regifting; lying, however, is not a virtue.

The Importance of Volunteering

Community organizations almost always need extra hands in the weeks between Thanksgiving and New Year's (if not year-round). Most nonprofits have links on their sites explaining how to volunteer. You can also call the main phone line and ask how you can help. If you're planning to step up, bear in mind these recommendations:

- **Keep your commitments:** Whether agreeing to help on Thanksgiving Day with the slicing and dicing or to show up one afternoon a week to deliver meals on wheels, be dependable. That includes being on time. Just because you're not being paid doesn't mean anything less than professional behavior is acceptable.

- **Do what the nonprofit asks you to do:** Sure, it makes sense to let a group know that you happen to have an MBA or a stellar track record as a publicist, but be prepared for the more mundane, less glam tasks. That's often where nonprofits often need the most help, or where they start all new volunteers off.

- **Respect others' privacy:** If you come in contact with an organization's clients, keep what you learn in confidence. Don't gossip to others or post information on social media sites.

CHAPTER 13

Illness & Grieving

Manners for Life & Death

A generation of LGBT people took a premature page from the book of death and dying when HIV first struck during the 1980s and '90s. We adapted and reinvented long-held traditions for coping with serious illness and all manner of end-of-life issues. And we did this under the most challenging of circumstances, all too often facing widespread discrimination and personal rejection. In many ways, the epidemic's lessons continue to guide the way our community experiences illness and loss, even as new generations come of age.

Still, we have many questions when it comes to illness: When is the right time to tell your friends of a dire diagnosis? How should you tell them? What do you tell your employer? And how do you deal with family members who may not recognize our loving relationships at time of crisis? Even more difficult: How do you ask for help from those who care for you, who love you? Both offering assistance and asking for it can be challenging for people long habituated to living independent lives, and particularly so for those of us who are single. This reality poses special challenges as the first generation of openly gay seniors, often known as "Gen Silent," comes of age.

On the flip side of the coin, people whose loved ones have fallen ill have their own questions: What can I do? What should I do? What am I able to do? The answer is often quite simple: Be present. You don't have to be good with words or at expressing your feelings—*just listen,* whether seated on your lover's sickbed or Skyping with a friend in a hospital thousands of miles away.

Once death claims a loved one, the predictable rituals attending such a loss—whether it's telling others the news, planning a service, or writing a newspaper obituary—can provide an odd source of comfort. For those not quite so close to the deceased, the guiding hand of manners tells us what to do now: bring food, take care of children and pets, write notes of sympathy, continue to offer help and support.

Predictably, new times and new technologies have ushered in changes to these longstanding rituals. One example: We now sometimes convey the initial word of a death through e-mail, Facebook, or even a text message. And while there's always sadness and mourning surrounding any funeral or memorial, today's services are as likely as not to be celebrations of the deceased's life.

Many aspects of dealing with illness and death can't be anticipated. But it is possible to plan for the security and comfort of your partner, friends, and family members by making

plans, clarifying your personal preferences, and codifying your legal directives.

Note: The terms "friend," "partner," and "caregiver" are used fairly interchangeably in this chapter because of the variety of relationships involved.

IF YOU'RE SERIOUSLY ILL

Having a debilitating or life-threatening illness is frightening, what with concerns about health insurance and feelings of powerlessness, depression, often even anger. Adding insult to injury, you have to contend with modern medicine—being poked and prodded, imaged and cut. For your friends, family members, and colleagues, there's also bound to be much worry about your well-being, how to be helpful but not inappropriately solicitous, and how to safeguard your privacy, yet make sure you get the help you need.

Talking with Friends and Family

It's entirely up to you when and in what way to share the news of a serious or life-threatening illness with others. If you don't have a complete diagnosis, or your symptoms have you reeling, or you're just a private person, don't let your loved ones pressure you into a premature disclosure—no matter how concerned they are about your health. Curiously, choosing whether or not to talk about a serious condition may remind you of some of the conversations you had about coming out: whom to tell first, what exactly to say, whether the recipient will safeguard the information. And, How will your news be received? Similarly, the power you hold now is the ability—and right—to choose when to make your diagnosis known to others.

When you are ready to talk, start with those closest to you; choose a friend or family member whom you think will be supportive and can be trusted to keep your confidence (if that's important to you). Do your best to educate yourself enough in order to help explain your condition and the treatment options. Consider gathering some printed materials or make a short list of helpful websites. (Your doctor and other health care professionals can assist in these efforts.) Once you're together with this friend or relative (preferably in person), try not to be too dark, but make it clear that you have a serious topic to talk about. At the end of the conversation, be clear about whether you'd like this news kept private—or shared; for some, it's a help to have others spread the news so that they don't have to.

Breast cancer, which disproportionately affects lesbians, provides a useful example of how privacy and treatment concerns can complicate decision-making during a health crisis. Should you tell others about your illness when you've just been diagnosed? As you approach treatment? Or after it's started? Are there different answers for different people in your

QUEERY

"I'm not sure when to mention to a boyfriend that I had cancer."

Q **I was dating this guy for about two months and everything was going pretty well until I mentioned that I had had cancer a couple of years before. Even though I was considered cured, my boyfriend started acting more distant, until one day he explained that he was "freaked out" by my medical past. And then he broke up with me. I was really hurt by how abrupt—and rude—his actions were. What do you think?**

A As a cancer survivor myself, I have experienced this kind of rejection firsthand. I've also known others who panicked over a boyfriend's or girlfriend's illness but found it within themselves to stay. Some flee because they've lost other partners to similar diseases, and aren't prepared to experience loss again so soon. Others simply can't bear to see someone they care about go through a debilitating illness with the possibility of death.

It's easy to answer that your boyfriend was a creep—and good riddance. However, he may have done the best he could. Intention does matter, especially in how we treat each other (and it sounds as though his intentions were good). But consider this: You might have given him more information about your past history before becoming so attached, which might have mitigated the surprise. Although there are no rules about the best timing for medical disclosures, I'd suggest that in the future you get to it before you become "boyfriends," even if it's only mentioned in passing.

life? Could your job be in jeopardy? Will your friends support you? If you have a partner, how will she take this news?

There are no right or wrong answers to these questions, as long as you carefully weigh the pros and cons for yourself, ideally with the help of a close friend or family member. Also consider finding a support group or hotline for your specific ailment.

Dealing with Employers and Landlords

Although talking about your medical condition with everyone affected may seem the decent thing to do, think twice about revealing a serious illness to colleagues at work, your landlord, or anyone else who might be able to penalize you because of the situation.

It's not uncommon for HIV-positive people, among others, to face significant financial or social harm after making what seems at first to be a simple disclosure. People have been fired, thrown out of their apartments, and even faced child custody battles as a result of revealing they have HIV/AIDS, cancer, or another serious illness.

While such actions are usually illegal in Canada and the United States, they still occur. In the U.S., the Americans with Disabilities Act (ADA) protects you at work, in schools, and in most places where business is conducted or services are provided. For instance, an employer cannot legally refuse to hire someone known to have a specific medical condition; nor can you be fired for this reason. The ADA also requires employers to make what are called "reasonable accommodations" to people with illnesses regarding their workplace responsibilities, as long as they can still perform the "essential functions" of their job.

Still, having a strong case in court may not be your main concern. For one thing, it's stressful, especially when you are dealing with serious health issues. For another, it's expensive. You also may be more concerned about actually holding on to your job, your home, or your place in school and willing to keep mum in order to avoid a conflict (or to maintain your health insurance).

It's worth noting, however, that being discreet about a health condition—even HIV—is not always good for your health, for several reasons. Your coworkers may want to understand why you have frequent doctor visits or significant treatment side effects. Then, there are the benefits of being out for the sake of helping to fight the stigma attached to so many conditions, whether HIV, cancer, mental illness, or others.

Asking for Help

For many of us, asking for assistance when ill is among the toughest and most common challenges. Even if you have a Cadillac of a health plan and gobs of insurance, you'll likely find it necessary to reach out for help at some point, which may leave you feeling vulnerable and dependent at a time when you're already not yourself. Asking also raises the specter that someone will say no. These issues, certainly common, can be especially poignant and challenging for LGBT people, who may not have strong family support—perhaps you moved away from your birth family to come out, you don't have children, or you're estranged from your family for a reason that has nothing to do with sexual orientation or gender identity. Of course, many LGBT people have extremely supportive relationships with their parents, siblings, and other relatives, which can be called upon when you're ill.

There are ways to circumvent the need to ask others directly, however. If you have children, a garden, or pets, it may be easier to ask for assistance for those specific tasks rather than for yourself. Alternatively, ask one good friend to become "the organizer" or "angel" and to do your bidding, such as inviting others to bring meals on certain days, take you to the hospital for treatments, or just come and visit. In the age of social media, this process has become easier for everyone involved. Some of my own friends with life-threatening illnesses have created personal websites outlining what they need, complete with an easy-to-use online calendar for helpers to fill in when they have

"Hi. I'm from God's Love We Deliver. I've got your dinner . . ."

time. There are also several new sites where you can post condition updates—and calls for assistance. Two of the best known are CaringBridge.org and CarePages.com.

Whatever your approach to getting help, don't forget to express your gratitude. Even though you may not be in a position right now to reciprocate for any kindnesses shown you, it's definitely considerate to say "thank you"—repeatedly.

Visiting Hours

Some hospitals are more vigilant than others about making sure that patients have no visitors outside of designated hours and limiting the number of people who can show up at any one time. These rules can be annoying, but they are very helpful when you need to get rest as part of your recovery. Whether ill in a hospital or at home, if you've got a well-meaning friend or relative chatting away relentlessly at your bedside, your health—if not your sanity!—may be at stake.

To make sure you have the time and peace that you need, ask a caregiver—or a nurse—to help police others' comings and goings. When need be, this gatekeeper can take visitors aside and, while thanking them for coming, mention that it's time for you to take some meds or that you're just tired.

If you have no one to help you with this, don't be shy. Yawn dramatically, perhaps, or simply say it's your naptime. Express your thanks for the visit and any flowers or gifts, and let your visitor know you hope to see him again "but please call ahead of time." Most visitors will understand and take their leave.

GUIDELINES FOR VISITORS

Twenty minutes is usually about long enough for any visit. It's a good idea, upon arriving, to ask your friend how long a visit she is up to. You could even say, "Please let me know when you're tired or have had enough of me." Otherwise, look out for verbal and other cues that might indicate it's time to go. If other visitors come while you're there, consider leaving soon afterward, so that they may have a turn at a private visit.

Try to avoid asking, "Is there anything you need?" People don't usually like to feel as though they are in "need" (even if they are). Similarly, avoid the general statement "Is there anything I can do for you?" Be specific—for instance, ask whether the patient needs more reading material or the plants watered. Be proactive.

IF A FRIEND OR LOVED ONE IS SERIOUSLY ILL

Many of us have a deeply rooted fear of saying the "wrong" thing to a sick friend. You may find yourself tongue-tied, stammering, or endlessly blathering. For others, saying the right words comes instinctively. Another conundrum many of us face with friends who are ill is how to be a useful caregiver and when to supplement our best efforts with those of a professional.

What to Say

Although some of us become Florence Nightingale reincarnated, always knowing exactly what to do or say, others of us simply shut down upon learning that a friend is seriously ill. You may be afraid of putting your foot in your mouth, or you may be too upset and don't want to break down. As best you can, try not to let fear keep you away from your friend or loved one at this critical time. When words don't come easily, the wise thing to do is listen and attempt to understand as much as possible.

Here are some other ways to be available:

- **Let your friend guide the conversation:** She may tell you what's on her mind. She may ask your opinion about an upcoming decision. She may want you to tell others about her condition. Or she may not say much at all, leaving you to ask questions that indicate caring, such as "How are you feeling about your medical treatment?" or "Is there anyone else you'd like me to call?"
- **Remember to speak normally:** Just because someone has cancer or heart disease doesn't mean he's lost his mind or become deaf.
- **Don't become a Pollyanna:** Avoid saying things that negate the situation, like "Oh, I'm sure you'll be fine" (when that's highly unlikely) or "You look great" (even though you both know that's not the case). Also hold back on unsolicited advice, such as "Have you tried that new treatment I read about?" Finally, don't make statements that simply are not true, such as "I know just how you feel."
- **Talk about the same things you always have:** It can be a welcome break from health concerns

to chat about the news, mutual friends, or your pets or kids; more often than not, it isn't insensitive to turn the topic away from illness.

- **When in doubt, simply sit with your friend:** You may not need to talk at all.

Finding Out Secondhand

If you don't find out about a friend or colleague's illness directly but from a mutual friend or coworker, be sure to ask whether the illness is common knowledge. Also inquire whether the person who is ill knows that you're being told. If there's any question that the information is still private, wait to broach this topic with your ill friend, and don't tell others. If your friend's condition does seem to be public knowledge, go ahead and reach out. You may want to send a text or an e-mail first, saying something like "I am so sorry to hear that you're not feeling well." That sort of one-step-removed communication gives the person the necessary time to think about how to respond, rather than being put on the spot with a phone call or visit.

STRAIGHT TALK

"My gay friend's partner is ill. Is it okay for me to ask if it's HIV?"

It's really not okay to ask about anyone's medical diagnosis. Unless someone has a contagious disease, such as TB or the flu, you don't need to know his medical condition to be helpful and stay healthy yourself. Also, don't assume that someone who is gay and ill has HIV/AIDS.

Get-Well Wishes, Cards, and E-cards

If you have trouble knowing what to say or write to a sick friend or colleague, go ahead and buy a store-bought or e-card. But don't just sign your name; take a moment to write a few extra words before sending. Do your best to be genuine and natural; it's okay to express sadness and concern if that's how you feel. Also, try to personalize your message in some way, by mentioning that your mutual colleagues at work or your softball teammates "can't wait to have you back."

People who are normally wired 24/7 may be offline during an illness, so keep in mind that you may need to use old-fashioned communication methods like snail mail or a landline.

Taking Care of Yourself

Being a good caregiver also means eating well, sleeping enough, and getting exercise so that you can continue to do your job. If necessary, it even entails meeting with a therapist to deal with the stress of being so closely involved with a loved one's illness. Caregivers who don't take proper care of themselves are at high risk for depression, alcohol, drug, and tobacco abuse—not to mention burnout.

Likewise, friends and family members should beware of overlooking a loved one's partner or caregiver. From time to time, volunteer your time to help out the helper, whether that means making a meal, doing the marketing, or just taking a home shift so that the primary caregiver can take some time off. One caregiver who lost his partner to Lou Gehrig's disease after an eighteen-year relationship described

QUEERY

"Need some help taking care of Dad"

Q My sisters are both married with kids, and since I'm kid-free and single, I've been designated as my dad's caretaker (our mom passed away about five years ago). While the time I've spent with my father has been precious, I really wish I had a way to discuss my sisters' lack of involvement in his care. They always tell me I'm doing a great job and that they'll support any decision I make, but I still feel used. What can I do?

A First, you won't be surprised to learn that a recent study showed that more often than not gay men become their parents' primary caregivers. This seems to happen for precisely the reason you state: You don't "have a family of your own," so somehow it becomes your responsibility.

When possible, it's smart to start talking about these issues early on with our relatives and to bring in our parents' health care providers as information providers and allies. Family discussions of this kind are especially helpful in determining roles and responsibilities and set a precedent for later conversations.

Okay, so you missed that opportunity. Now what? Let your sisters know you want to talk about your father's care going forward. Be prepared both to ask for hands-on help beyond their generalized support and to lead a discussion about who will do what and when, including paying for "hands-on care." Make notes. Put it in writing. Agree to meet or talk on a regular basis, so that you can update one another and make any necessary adjustments. Don't let the gay card be played against you. And make sure your dad knows that he's covered—by all three of you.

how his "two best girlfriends" took care of him during his partner's illness: "Every Monday and Wednesday, whatever was being served in their homes was also served in mine. Tupperware containers would magically appear outside the front door. No demands, no intrusion."

Professional Caregivers

At some point it may become clear that an ill family member or partner would benefit from the expertise of a professional caregiver; perhaps the disease has become more serious or family or friends are simply exhausted. It may fall on you to call up an agency, hire a home care attendant directly, or make contact with

a government office such as the Veteran's Administration.

If you're not sure what services are available, contact your local LGBT center (or other social service agency) and request a referral, or ask your friend for permission to speak to his health care practitioner about available options. It could also fall on you to oversee the whole situation, first introducing the idea of bringing in a professional caregiver, then making sure the person hired gets up to speed quickly; finally, you may need to manage schedules and pay attention to the care being given.

If you have any concerns that a hired caregiver isn't LGBT-friendly, be sure to request an alternative. When seriously ill, the last thing an LGBT person needs is to be made uncomfortable about his or her sexual orientation or gender identity at home—or in a hospital room. (In fact, many LGBT seniors are returning to the closet as they become older and fall ill, finding themselves in assisted-living and hospice facilities that are not gay- or trans-tolerant.)

At the same time, don't take the services of a professional caregiver for granted. This is a low-paid industry that often involves very stressful work. Be courteous and warm, and make yourself available for any questions. Don't ask him to do other, menial tasks around the house; he is not a housekeeper. If you find yourself looking for a way to show your appreciation, a tip is generally not the way to go about it (health care professionals are not usually allowed to accept cash or gifts); a card of thanks is more appropriate.

Talking About Hospice Care

By definition, talking to your loved one about hospice care involves discussions about end-of-life issues, whether you address them directly or not. Even if the patient has accepted what seems to be the inevitable outcome, these conversations are about as emotional and challenging as they get. Indeed, if you haven't yet talked about such issues as a living will, a do-not-resuscitate order (DNR), and a power of attorney, there's no delaying those discussions at this point, either. The creation of a living will—or even raising the topic—often provides an opportunity to ponder and talk about the implications of such situations as "no tube feeding," "no artificial hydration," or

"no resuscitation." This kind of conversation can be especially helpful to flesh out what the implementation of a living will might mean in a practical sense.

Technically, hospice care starts to become an option when a doctor says a patient has six months or less to live. The idea is to provide pain relief and other comforts in lieu of aggressive medical treatment. Hospice care is given at home or in a hospital, a nursing home, or in a dedicated hospice facility. Wherever it takes place, the environment is by design less stressful and less medically oriented than a traditional hospital, and it always involves the close involvement of family and friends. In major cities across the country, you can find hospice facilities that have the experience and sensibility to tend to members of the LGBT community.

If this discussion falls to you, there are a number of ways to go about it:

- **Make a plan:** Set aside some uninterrupted time to start the conversation. You could start out by talking about hospice care in general—saying, for instance, "Do you know what hospice care is?" Alternatively, raise the subject during a talk about your friend's terminal diagnosis and see whether that leads to a discussion about quality of life in the weeks or months to come. It's not unusual to have to revisit the conversation several times.
- **Partner with your friend's doctor:** Often, it's helpful to involve your loved one's physician (or other medical professionals) in a discussion of his or her health status, likely prognosis, and, when considered terminal, the pros and cons of hospice care. Enlisting the doctor's help can relieve you of some of the burden of making decisions, at the same time

providing an unbiased medical perspective on this very difficult issue.

- **Be gentle:** You may find that your loved one deals with end-of-life issues in an unexpected manner; possible reactions can range from complete acceptance to total denial. Don't make the decision feel like a fait accompli. Both the illusion and the reality of choice are crucial for seriously ill patients. Let him or her know that, as one hospice worker stated, "starting with hospice care is not a commitment, but a way to get more support and have new choices. The patient can always change their mind."

- **Listen to your friend:** These are important conversations to have and it's especially crucial that your loved one ask questions, express fears, question decisions, and be as involved as medically possible. Don't shortchange this part of the process.

MEDICAL MANNERS AND THE LAW

LGBT people usually need to walk some extra distance to protect our legal, medical, and financial interests, whether because of discriminatory laws or because of the potential for strife with our families of origin. Ideally, it's wise to discuss all these issues before a serious illness; otherwise, you run the risk of allowing blood relatives (who in the eyes of the law may be next of kin) to take the decision-making away from you and yours or having to have "the talk" during a time of crisis. Not only will you want to talk about medical care, it's also important to discuss estate and funeral planning ahead of time. Try not to let denial or inertia prevent you from taking the necessary steps to safeguard your interests.

The Last Will and Testament

It's crucial for LGBT people, whether single or partnered, to have conversations about how our property will be distributed after our deaths and then to set down our wishes in a legal document as soon as we can. That means *now*—even if you're young and healthy. This process, often called estate planning, covers any property you own: home, artwork, a car, other valuables, even your pets. Not only is this kind of planning smart, it's also considerate to those closest to you.

The reason, of course, is that the default position of the law is disadvantageous to lesbian and gay couples. For instance, if you're partnered and you die without having drawn up a will, your spouse won't automatically become executor of your estate. The court will appoint somebody—likely your parents or a sibling—to distribute your assets however he or she sees fit. In the handful of states that recognize gay and lesbian couples—whether by marriage, civil unions, or domestic partnerships—same-sex partners can inherit property even if there is no proper will. But don't take that chance.

If you're single and gay, be sure to designate a relative or close friend as your executor and spell out who you want to be your beneficiary or beneficiaries.

"My lesbian sister is fighting cancer and trying to decide what kind of treatments are right for her. I feel very cut off from this process because she takes her longtime girlfriend's advice more seriously than mine. I'm her older brother and used to being leaned on. Don't I have the right to ask my sister to listen to me instead?"

It sounds like you're feeling left out at an important time in your sister's life. But since your sister has been with her girlfriend for a long time, she probably considers her to be a partner or spouse, so it's a good idea if you try to think of her that way as well. Even the federal government is beginning to catch up in the area of respecting LGBT partnerships on medical matters. There's now an executive order requiring hospitals and doctors to recognize LGBT partners' hospital visitation rights.

Therefore, don't fight the wrong fight. As a brother, there are many other ways you can help your sister. That includes trying to support her relationship and the couple's decisions, especially if they're getting flack from other family members. Or just being there as the caring brother it sounds like you are. Or even recognizing that your sister's partner—as a caregiver—could likely use a shoulder to lean on, if not some extra hands around the house.

SETTING UP A TRUST

Committed partners who are over forty, are ill at any age, or have assets of more than $100,000 should consider other estate planning tools, such as a trust. These tools, according to attorney Denis Clifford in *A Legal Guide for Lesbian & Gay Couples,* allow for "the least expensive and most efficient methods of transferring your property after death." Often, these conversations start when you make a significant joint purchase together, like a home; as part of the natural evolution of your financial life; or after you have the experience of witnessing what happens when someone else's partner isn't legally protected. A St. Louis salesman recalls what happened when he lost his partner to a sudden heart attack after they had been together ten years: "His parents came in and took everything that we had spent a lifetime accumulating together. It never crossed our minds to make a will or a trust, which would have protected my interest in our material things. We thought we had all the time in the world."

At some point, it's wise for one of you to say to the other, "We need to take care of each other." If your partner isn't ready to discuss such a seemingly macabre topic, let it go for the time being, but revisit it in six to twelve months. And then again, until you get on the same signed page.

Medical and Financial Matters

Whether you're partnered or not, if you're LGBT, you need to consider what will happen to you if you're seriously injured, face a medical emergency, or develop a life-threatening illness. Who will make health care decisions for you if you cannot? Whom do you want to act as "family," being able to visit and minister to you in a hospital or hospice? Who should have control of your finances and other personal affairs if you're unable to handle them yourself?

Start by pulling together and studying several key documents, easily found online and in books about LGBT family law. Whether in the United States or Canada, these papers include a health care proxy (also called a durable power of attorney for health care), which names the person you choose to make decisions on your behalf in the event you're unable; a living will; and a health care directive, which outlines the specific medical care you want and don't want if you're unable to articulate those decisions for yourself.

The person named in your health care proxy will be responsible—along with your physicians and the health care facility—for making sure your wishes are carried out. Again, this kind of planning is not only necessary to protect your interests, but so helpful and respectful of others who may be called upon to assist you.

Here's how to proceed:

If you're single: Make a short list of friends and family members you'd be comfortable having in these crucial roles. Explain that you're taking care of some personal business and that you'd like assistance. Then invite each person over—or out to lunch—and be prepared to explain why these legal protections are important to you, as well as exactly what his or her role would be. Don't pressure anyone into saying yes. If it appears that a friend isn't ready to take on this responsibility, either give the person more time or move on to another choice.

If you're in a couple: To avoid putting off this difficult discussion anymore, make an "appointment" with each other to discuss the range of documents you'll need. Conversations like these rarely just happen in the course of our regular lives. Better to be intentional with each other and say something like "Honey, why don't we spend next Saturday morning talking about the medical and financial paperwork we should have in place?" More often than not, each member of the couple will designate the other as his proxy, with one or two backup choices, such as a best friend or relative.

If a Hospital or Doctor Doesn't Afford Your Partner Rights

Until recently, hospitals were not legally required to recognize same-sex partners, whether for visiting or as the holders of medical power of attorney; this meant, in effect, that a lover could be banned by a blood relative or have no say in crucial medical decisions.

This kind of situation prompted President Obama to demand that federal law ensure all of a patient's advance directives, such as durable powers of attorney and health care proxies, are respected, and that any patient designee, regardless of sexual orientation or gender identity, can make informed decisions regarding a patient's care. This is a big step forward in protecting LGBT families.

Nevertheless, it remains crucial that, if one of you is hospitalized, copies of all such directives are given to hospital staff and that they are placed in the patient chart. Because you may find yourself with no legal standing as a same-sex couple in many states, lesbian and gay couples often travel with the necessary documentation in case they become ill away from home. Married same-sex Canadian couples are advised to do the same.

If a problem arises with the hospital staff and you're denied the opportunity to see your loved one, seek out a supervisor or ombudsman immediately. Keep your cool and explain the situation. If these actions don't resolve the issue at hand, get legal advice from a firm or nonprofit advocacy group well-versed in LGBT law.

Family Estrangements

One of the worst things that can happen when an LGBT person is seriously ill is a split between her partner and her birth family, whether about treatment options or about who can be allowed to visit. If you're partnered with someone who is seriously ill and you find yourself in this situation, try to keep heated conversations to a minimum, and do your best to have them out of earshot of your partner, so as not to further aggravate her condition or state of mind. If necessary, find someone to mediate, such as a hospital social worker, nurse, or psychologist.

If that fails and you are legally empowered by a health care proxy, ask a mediator or hospital staffer to explain the legal situation to the family. Obviously a health crisis or hospitalization is not the best time to rectify outstanding disagreements, but don't let propriety about "keeping the peace" stop you from make sure

that your rights are protected and, more important, that your partner's wishes and medical directives are followed.

Burial and Body Disposition

Here's another topic you (or you and your partner) might not embrace easily: making sure that the surviving partner (or someone else you designate) has the authority to make all decisions regarding burial and disposition of the body. If you don't specify this choice in a last will and testament, the authority will be granted to your next of kin, who could be an estranged or homophobic relative. The surest plan is to have taken care of these legal documents before death, so there will be no way for other family members to say, for instance, they would prefer a funeral to cremation or that they would like your partner buried in their home state rather than in the city where you have long lived. Try to have this conversation before any medical issues arise, so that it's still on the theoretical plane. Make sure you both create the necessary documents.

If, however, you and your partner are fortunate enough to live in Canada or in one of the states that provide for domestic partnerships, civil unions, or same-sex marriages, you automatically have the right to make decisions concerning disposition of the body of your deceased partner. Nevertheless, it's still considered good planning to draw up directives in case one of you dies elsewhere, especially in a jurisdiction that doesn't recognize our partnerships.

THE ESSENTIALS

Do-It-Yourself Burial Directives

Here are two examples of simple directives you can draw up yourself. Either can serve as a temporary measure before meeting with a lawyer to execute a more permanent document.

I have appointed my partner [fill in name] to make all decisions regarding arrangements upon my death and burial.

Or:

I have made the following arrangements upon my death:

1. It is my intention to donate my organs and body parts to [hospital or medical school of your choice].
2. It is my intention to be cremated and my ashes scattered at sea off the California coast. I have made arrangements with the Neptune Society.
3. My long-time friend [fill in name] is my executor and responsible for carrying out these wishes.

Print this out on personal letterhead (which is easy to create on the computer if need be), sign and date it, and make sure your partner, executor, or best friend knows where it is. Keep in mind that this is only a stopgap measure, until an attorney can draw up a directive that is tailor-made for your state of residence.

Also note that signing the Uniform Anatomical Gift Act card, which authorizes the donation of body parts, and carrying it in your wallet at all times, could help ensure that your wishes are followed in this regard.

WHEN SOMEONE DIES

Even when it isn't a partner, relative, or close friend, death manages to unsettle most of us. When it is a member of your inner circle or an untimely death, shock and grief can color every thought and action. Rely on the information that follows to help guide you through these troubled times, to make sure you do right by the deceased, and to take care of others, as well as yourself. Although certain aspects of mourning etiquette have evolved greatly in recent decades—notably the trend toward life celebrations and personalized services—when it comes to death and dying, tradition generally prevails.

Notifying Others

When someone dies, the first telephone calls traditionally go to "family." For LGBT people, since family is so often a hybrid of blood and nonblood ties, the right thing to do is to phone those closest to the deceased, even if that isn't his or her birth family. When a death has been anticipated, some of us activate a predetermined phone tree, which sets off a chain of calls and takes some of the pressure off the immediate survivor.

When making notification calls, it's important to try to maintain your composure and keep it simple, imparting just the necessary information about the death and any pending arrangements. However, few get through these calls completely dry-eyed. And while the phone is the medium of first choice, sending an e-mail is an acceptable alternative, especially if the deceased had a long, debilitating illness and the news will be sad but not shocking. If it's a sudden passing, definitely don't use e-mail (after all, imagine opening such an e-mail).

If you were posting regular updates on a social media page about your lover or friend's long illness—for instance, "Sheridan is back in the hospital yet again"—then it's okay to post a death announcement there *after* you've already told close family and friends directly.

STRAIGHT TALK

"I happen to know that our neighbor's gay daughter died after a long bout with cancer, but the family hasn't acknowledged the cause of death. Why not?"

It's the next of kin's decision as to whether to reveal the cause of death, be it in a death notice or in response to the question "What happened?" Some choose to address it directly by including it in the obituary. Others opt to stay mum, often because there's something sensitive about it, such as a death from drunk driving or suicide. That's their right, although what's "embarrassing" for one person is quite worth discussing for another. (Nevertheless, in this day and age, it's hard to keep information like that private, which is obviously true in your case since you already know.)

If a family makes such a decision, however, it's helpful for them to come up with an *honest* response to the "what happened" question. Being honest doesn't

mean telling all, however. They could say, for instance, "She died way too young" or "She fought so hard and we miss her terribly." And leave it at that.

Helping the Surviving Partner

One of the ways manners can provide comfort during the rites and rituals surrounding a death is to guide us in ways we can assist survivors. You can't exactly go on autopilot, but here's a list of options to consider:

- **Offer to help with specific things:** Avoid the cliché "Let me know if there's anything I can do." Instead, ask if you can do some food shopping, clean the house, or fix dinner.
- **Funeral matters:** Ask if you can assist with the funeral arrangements, let others know about the death, write the obituary, or help make any difficult decisions that require immediate attention.
- **Embrace your friend:** Hug or lightly touch the surviving partner or family members. Don't feel the need to fill in all silences with words.
- **Continue to be present in the survivor's life after the services:** Call and/or visit frequently. Try not to let the sadness or awkwardness of death get in your way. Tell your friend that you're open to talking day or night (if you are), even if she repeats the same anecdotes over and over.
- **Relate stories about loss in your own life:** Making the survivor aware she is not alone in this experience is helpful. However, don't assume any two losses are the same.
- **Use the deceased's name from time to time:** Recount happy times, wonder aloud how "Tim" or "Elena" might have enjoyed a new

movie or a winter's snowfall. Keeping the deceased in the conversation can bring comfort to both of you.

"Our daughter came out to us nearly a decade ago and because of our devout Catholic beliefs my husband and I didn't continue a relationship with her. Actually, this decision was more of my husband's doing. Now we hear that our daughter's partner has passed and there will be a memorial service. We understand that there will be many homosexuals there and that the minister will be from a gay church. I would actually like to go as a way to pay my respects to my daughter and perhaps to reopen our relationship. My husband is adamantly opposed, saying it would be hypocritical for us to attend a service that affirms their lifestyle. What do you suggest?"

Here's the short answer. You go. Your husband can stay home.

Here's the longer answer: Death is often a wake-up call in families, reminding us once again that life is precious and very short. You've already missed out on ten years of your daughter's life—and she on ten years of yours—so why not go for it? In order to reestablish a relationship with your daughter, you don't need to support LGBT rights or violate any of your beliefs. You may not be aware that the Catholic Church doesn't prohibit you from attending a gay funeral, and that your presence doesn't imply tacit support for LGBT issues

(unlike attending a same-sex wedding, which the Vatican condemns). When you go to a memorial service (or funeral), it means that you're showing that you care, and that you want to say good-bye. It also indicates that you want to give comfort to survivors, such as to your daughter.

In a sense you're fortunate that etiquette gives you a relatively easy pass card here. It's simply good manners to show up at a family memorial service, and in doing so you'll have wedged open the door without having had to initiate what would no doubt be a difficult conversation. In this case, actions speak louder than words. Then it's up to each of you to decide whether you want to go further. This includes your husband.

The Funeral Home

After notifying close friends and family members of a death, one of the very next steps is to be in contact with a funeral home. That task usually falls to the surviving partner or to someone considered in the "immediate family." If at all possible, look for an LGBT-friendly funeral home (now common in most bigger cities and towns) by asking friends for referrals, looking in your city's LGBT business directory, or doing an online search.

If there's any sort of dustup with blood family members about whether you have final authority in these matters, make sure that the funeral director understands the situation and has the right documentation from you. Unfortunately, there have been many instances of gay partners being turned away from their own partner's funeral. One lesbian who lost her lover recalls: "Her family took a picture of us, tore it in half, and gave her half to the mortician and my half to the funeral director to keep me out of the funeral."

The Death Certificate

Death certificates vary tremendously from place to place, but they always include information about the deceased and his or her cause of death. For LGBT people, what often matters most are the lines about "marital status" and "spouse's name." In Canada and in states where same-sex marriage, civil unions, or domestic partnerships are recognized, these forms are generally updated with inclusive language for gays and lesbians. In other states, surviving partners may find it difficult—if not impossible—to be memorialized on the death certificate. Inclusion of a surviving partner is, however, more than a sentimental or symbolic matter; it may be important for claiming insurance and other financial benefits.

Death Notices

Usually, the next of kin submits a paid death notice to the local newspaper, or the funeral home may provide this service on your behalf. These notices always include the name of the deceased, the date of death, and the names of immediate family members and relatives (if there are any). Death notices also may include information about the cause of death (although many consider that private), where and when you'll be receiving visitors, and any guidance about memorial contributions in lieu of flowers.

For some in our community, the death notice is the final coming out—helping others, both in the present and in the future, to see our relationships for what they were. Here's one such example:

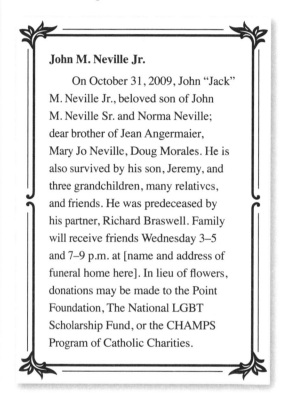

John M. Neville Jr.

On October 31, 2009, John "Jack" M. Neville Jr., beloved son of John M. Neville Sr. and Norma Neville; dear brother of Jean Angermaier, Mary Jo Neville, Doug Morales. He is also survived by his son, Jeremy, and three grandchildren, many relatives, and friends. He was predeceased by his partner, Richard Braswell. Family will receive friends Wednesday 3–5 and 7–9 p.m. at [name and address of funeral home here]. In lieu of flowers, donations may be made to the Point Foundation, The National LGBT Scholarship Fund, or the CHAMPS Program of Catholic Charities.

Sometimes, instead of this traditional sort of death notice, survivors pen a "death notice with personality," which might mention more idiosyncratic things about the deceased—his dog was named Diana Ross, for instance, or she loved motorcycles and embroidery. And it's not unheard of for the deceased to have written his or her own obituary while still alive, to be published at the appropriate time. (If you plan to do that, then be sure to give a copy to your executor, best friend, or partner.)

How to List LGBT Survivors

In a paid death notice, you may list and describe any and all survivors as you please. This also includes notices written for online sites such as Legacy.com and MemorialsOnline.com, as well as the virtual memorial pages many funeral homes now offer as part of their services. Generally, a spouse or partner is listed first as a survivor, followed by: the deceased's parents, children, siblings and other family members, as well as dear friends (although these are included less often in straight notices). In a paid death notice, most LGBT people refer to their deceased partner with the same term they used when he or she was living (i.e., spouse, companion, or partner).

Obituaries

Staff-reported obituaries are generally a phenomenon of urban North America. Considered part of the news budget, these obituaries are quite separate from paid notices, and they do not always reflect the precise sentiments of the survivors.

For many years, LGBT survivors were routinely left out of editorial obituaries because gay partners didn't have the same legal status (that is, marriage) as heterosexual couples. *The New York Times* first referred to a same-sex partner in an obituary in 1983, but it wasn't until the 1990s that the *Times* and other major dailies regularly listed gay and lesbian partners as survivors. These days, nearly all major U.S. and Canadian newspapers and news outlets include LGBT survivors—as long as it's brought to their attention. Depending on the couple's legal status, a surviving partner may be referred to as a "spouse" (legally married), "domestic partner" (legally partnered, but not married), or "partner" or "life partner" (no legal status).

QUEERY

"They left me out of my partner's obit."

Q I was in such a state of shock after my husband died that I had no idea his brother and sister were preparing an obit. It was bad enough that they didn't show it to me, but to make matters worse they didn't even include me as a survivor. What should I do now?

A Until you lose someone close to you, it's hard to see the importance of obituaries; the truth is that they carry a great deal of symbolism, so I understand why you're upset. Do this: Take aside the former in-law you are closest to and explain your point of view with as little rancor as you can. You could say, "After spending ten years as your brother's husband and best friend, I can't tell you how hurt I was not to be mentioned as his survivor." In the meantime, prepare your own notice and pay for its placement. Alternatively, if too much time has gone by, consider placing an "In Memoriam" notice on the anniversary of your partner's death, on his birthday, or on the date of your wedding anniversary.

"In lieu of flowers . . ."

Many death notices and obituaries contain the phrase "In lieu of flowers, please consider a donation to _____ ," and then mention a specific charity or instruct you to choose your own. While making such a gesture is optional, take the suggestion seriously as a way to honor the deceased.

If you decide to send a check to a charity, a good rule of thumb is to donate about the same amount you would have spent on flowers. Include with your check a short note indicating that your contribution is in memory of your late friend, and ask the charity to acknowledge your gift to the survivors. Don't forget to include your own address (even if it's on the check) so that you can get an official acknowledgment, which will also serve as your receipt for tax purposes. (At some services, you'll find preaddressed envelopes for giving to a charity of the deceased's choice. Feel free to take one and then follow the suggestions above.)

If you decide to give to a charity of your own choice, choose one that you think your friend would have supported. In the note of condolence that you write to the next of kin, include a line like "A contribution in George's name was made to the San Francisco AIDS Foundation."

On a related note, if a fund has been set up to help provide for the deceased's family—perhaps a partner and/or children—don't hesitate to send your contribution there. You might also take up a collection for the fund from fellow employees or any group to which you and the deceased belonged.

Funerals, Memorials, and Celebrations of Life

Whether you're the partner, best friend, or next of kin of someone who's just died, you'll have to decide what kind of service to arrange, whether a wake, shiva, funeral, or memorial (or none at all). Ideally, the deceased would have left a written directive outlining her wishes, but if there is none, do your best to remember your loved one in a way she would have appreciated. Regardless of the type of mourning ritual, and aside from any religious aspect, each of these services is a family and community event, with certain rules of etiquette.

As for the difference between a funeral and a memorial service, it's basic: The body is present at a funeral but not at a memorial (except perhaps for an urn of cremated remains). Funerals are generally scheduled to take place within days of the death, while memorial services may take place a month or more later.

CHRISTIAN SERVICES

A traditional Christian funeral often starts with a period of visitation or viewing of the deceased during the afternoon and/or evening of the day prior (sometimes called the wake). The funeral service itself then takes place either in the chapel of the funeral home or at a nearby church. The mourners proceed, if they wish, to join the family at the gravesite for burial—unless the death notice or obituary has specifically stated, "Committal services will be private." Generally, burial is followed by a lunch or reception of some kind.

JEWISH SERVICES

Jews believe in burying the body as soon as possible, often the next day, as a sign of respect. Following the funeral, the family may observe a seven-day period of mourning, known as sitting shiva. During this time friends and family gather to remember the deceased, pray, and provide support and sustenance for the survivors. Note that it is not Jewish custom to send flowers; donations to favorite charities are welcomed.

OTHER TRADITIONS

Muslims allow for a three-day period of mourning, except in the case of a spouse, where tradition extends that period to four months and ten days. Friends of family members usually bring food to the survivors; it is perfectly acceptable to send flowers after the funeral service.

Buddhist funerals generally take place within a week of death. Caskets are usually open and those in attendance are requested to view the body and make a small bow toward it. Sending flowers or making a donation is appropriate.

CELEBRATIONS OF LIFE

At the height of the HIV/AIDS epidemic in the 1980s and '90s, gay men and lesbians adapted more traditional memorial services into what are often billed as celebrations of life. The spirit of these celebratory memorials has continued for many LGBT services, regardless of the cause of death. Just as our community has redefined what a marriage ceremony looks like, memorial services have been reimagined to reflect our cultural and social preferences.

VOX POPULI

Should a funeral or memorial service for an LGBT person be different in any way?

"Do make it fabulous and fun if the deceased would have liked that. Madonna's 'Ray of Light' for the processional, for instance. Do not use it as a forum to bash homophobes, like the family of the deceased."

"Politics has a place only if the person had that ingrained in his/her life's work or passions."

"Absolutely not. There are no enemies in death, although people may choose to believe otherwise."

For instance, one gay baby boomer says he wants the theme song from *The Mary Tyler Moore Show* ("You're gonna make it after all . . .") to be played at his service. Whether in the choice of music, a video montage, or eulogies filled with humor, LGBT funerals often brim with poignant personality.

LENDING A HAND

At the time of a close friend's death, don't hesitate to ask whether you can help with the funeral or memorial since there are myriad tasks from choosing a casket or urn, to deciding how to conduct the service, to arranging food and drink for the reception. One gay widower wished he had had someone step up in that manner. "At the time I was overwhelmed from the caregiving and thinking that I didn't want to mourn publicly," he explained. "It would have been such a gift if someone had offered to help me with the arrangements."

"I'm headed to a memorial service for a gay man. Is there anything special I should know ahead of time about what to expect?"

There's nothing technically different about LGBT events marking someone's death. All such services are about remembering and honoring the deceased, fostering closure, and supporting the survivors. In practice, though, you may find that some LGBT memorials involve a greater sense of celebration of the deceased's life, and that the service may be more political than you're accustomed to. It wasn't uncommon during the height of the HIV/AIDS epidemic to hear angry references about government inaction or the high cost of treatment, for instance. Nowadays, you may hear about issues like hate crimes, the right to marry, and even bans on same-sex adoption. Not long ago, when I was at a service for a lesbian friend, her surviving partner talked movingly about the need for marriage equality and how such laws would have made a difference in their day-to-day lives.

Clothing for Burial

There's really no saying anymore how someone *should* be dressed if they are to be buried. Traditionally, conservative and dark clothes were considered most appropriate, but now any attire that reflects the spirit of the deceased will do, including sports clothes, athletic wear, full leather, a military uniform—even drag. Transgender men and women are usually buried in clothing indicative of their presenting gender, however they expressed that while alive.

Attire for a Funeral or Memorial Service

The traditional directive that mourners be dressed in black or dark gray from head to toe is passé. However, just as there are formal and informal weddings, the same can be said for funerals and memorial services. If the service is taking place in a church or other community institution, consider it more traditional and dress up. For men, that *usually* means a dark suit or a sports coat and slacks, dress shirt, and a tie. Choose solid or subdued colors or a low-key pattern. For women, a pants suit, dress, or well-put-together set of coordinates is appropriate. Avoid outfits that are too revealing, which may be considered disrespectful by some, and keep jewelry to a minimum. Be sure to follow any religious practices, such as wearing a yarmulke at a Jewish service.

If the service is beachside or at someone's home, dress to reflect those circumstances. The point is to be more casual but still respectful, however you decide to express that. If the deceased had a favorite color or gave you a particular item of clothing, anything from a tie to a brooch, go ahead and wear it in celebration of your friend's life—and take the time to explain its significance if asked.

When in doubt about what to wear, ask a close friend of the deceased or call the funeral home.

Giving a Eulogy

It's an honor to be asked by a surviving partner or family member to deliver a eulogy at a funeral or memorial service. Ask for some time to think about your decision before answering, as this is not a task to be taken on lightly. Will you be able to find a theme that sums up the importance of the deceased? Will you be able to get through it without breaking down completely? Did you know the person well enough? If, for whatever reason, the answer to any of these questions is no, it's best to respectfully decline the offer as soon as you can.

But if you've agreed to deliver such a speech, here are some steps toward writing a eulogy that will be well received:

- **Talk about the deceased's life with friends and family members:** This will help to jog your memory about important moments that you might want to include.
- **Think about the entirety of what you want to say:** Create a narrative or story arc. Perhaps the deceased lover was a devoted son, a devoted activist, or a devoted partner. Incorporate various stories and memories to support your particular theme.
- **Write your entire eulogy in advance:** It's not a good idea to wing it as you might a toast or less formal remarks. Once you have a draft you're satisfied with, practice reading it aloud, both to yourself and to others. Make revisions as needed, and then bring a printout (in a type size you'll be able to read) to the service.
- **Don't speak too long:** If you're one of many giving a prepared eulogy, stay under the five-minute mark. If you're the main speaker, there is no strict guideline. Talk long enough to show your respect but not long enough to make the audience restless. Generally, fifteen to twenty minutes is the outside limit—when in doubt, consult the officiant of the service.
- **Incorporate humor or levity when appropriate:** However, don't do this if the death was shocking or completely unexpected.
- **Show your emotions:** It's okay to tear up, even cry, but try to avoid completely breaking down. Many speakers choke up at one time or another, then collect themselves and go on.
- **Acknowledge the deceased's partner, if there is one:** Also mention close friends and family members who supported her in the final months and days.
- **Do not re-closet the deceased:** Pay homage to any LGBT institutions she may have volunteered with or supported and take note of her lesbian and gay friendships.
- **Do not use this opportunity to criticize others:** Even if the deceased's family refused to accept the person's homosexuality or gay lover, this is not the time to get into that.

Funeral Disputes

If there's a dispute at a straight funeral, more often than not it involves ex-spouses, ex-parents-in-law, or the like: whether to invite them and where to seat them. A more common problem at LGBT funerals is estrangement with the deceased's family of origin because of his or her sexual orientation. Specifically: What do you do if your lover's parents never acknowledged—or actively condemned—your relationship (or the deceased's sexual orientation or gender identity)?

Since most funerals and memorials are open to all, the surviving partner usually doesn't need to make a decision regarding whom to invite; in other words, explicitly disinviting an unsupportive family isn't much of an option—except in the most extreme situation. If the estranged family signals its desire to attend, a bit of grace may be called for, although the funeral should proceed exactly as the deceased would have wanted.

If, however, the deceased's family is orchestrating the funeral service, they should ideally treat the surviving partner as they would any other spouse, no matter what their views on homosexuality. Should this not be in the cards, you'll need to decide if you're willing to play a "supporting" role in the event, or not attend at all. As mentioned earlier, this is not a time to create a scene or teach anyone a lesson. You could, however, still plan a separate gathering in memory of your partner at home, in a park, or at a local LGBT center.

What About Exes?

Deciding how to include exes at a funeral or memorial service is not just a straight conundrum anymore. LGBT exes, whether straight or same-sex, may be interested in attending but not sure if that's appropriate. Two things are important in this calculation: What kind of relationship did the two share in recent months or years? And how does the surviving partner, if there is one, feel about the situation? If, since breaking up, the exes developed a cordial or even semifriendly relationship, it's acceptable for your former partner to attend the service. He or she can sit with other friends, but generally not with the immediate family. If, however, your relationship remained frayed or embittered, it's better for the ex to sit out the memorial or funeral, instead sending flowers or writing a condolence note.

EXPRESSING YOUR CONDOLENCES

Whether you buy a preprinted sympathy card or write a personal note—and even if your message feels awkward to you—the recipient can't help but appreciate the sentiment. If you're struggling to find the right words, keep in mind that your effort does actually help the grieving process, both for you and for those to whom you write. For example, if the deceased was estranged from her family for being a lesbian, it's especially important to recognize and support her surviving partner and acknowledge her close friends.

Sympathy Cards

Because it can be very difficult to find the right words when penning condolence notes, they remain among the greatest etiquette challenges for many of us. Will your note sound fatuous or awkward? Maudlin or macabre?

Here are some guidelines that can help you communicate your condolences (note that this is not a time to relay your sentiments via e-mail):

- **Letters and personal notes:** No matter how good or bad a writer you think you are, it's best to keep these notes simple and genuine. Do your best not to get hung up on the language. Just make it sound like you and avoid overblown clichés like "I'm sure he's in a better place now" or "I'm so glad her suffering has ended."
- **Store-bought cards:** If you decide to buy a card, take the time to choose one that feels right in tone and message. Add at least one original sentence yourself. Saying "I'm sorry for your loss" is sufficient, but if you can add a personal line or two, the card will have more meaning for the survivor.
- **Make note of the loss:** Begin by acknowledging the death, referring to the deceased by name. For instance, "I was so upset to learn of John's passing."
- **Mention any favorite memories of the deceased:** As you do so, weave in how the memory illustrates his or her best qualities. For instance, "I'll always remember that when I was coming out as a teen, Harry made sure to let me know that I'd be okay. I can't tell you how much I appreciated his support." Or "When Janie and I finally tied the knot, it meant so much to us that Loretta stood up for us at city hall, especially when my own parents wouldn't."
- **When to send:** Mail the card or note within two weeks of the person's death, if at all possible. Nonetheless, even if a fortnight

has passed, don't use that as an excuse not to write at all—it's better to be late than absent. Keep in mind that these notes often have another purpose beyond the immediate one: Many people save them, coming back to them at times to summon memories of their loved one, sort of like photographs.

Note: If you are writing to someone you have never met—such as the parents or partner of the deceased—make sure to mention how you knew the person, whether you were a friend, coworker, or a fellow student. They'll appreciate being able to "place" you in their loved one's world.

Whom to Address

In the straight world, it's generally pretty clear who receives a letter of condolence. If the deceased was married, it would be to the spouse; if not, the note generally goes to his parents, children, or siblings. In the LGBT world, the etiquette of all this can be a little more ambiguous, because our relationships can sometimes be that way, too. Here are some basic guidelines:

- If a friend's partner has died, send the note to your friend. Whether married or not, treat gay couples as though they were.
- If it's your friend who has passed away, send your note to his partner. However, if you're so inclined, consider sending a second note to the parents or to the deceased's children (if he had any).
- If your LGBT friend was single, find out the name and address of a best friend or close relative and send along your condolences.

"I'm headed to the funeral of a gay friend's partner and find myself very nervous about saying the wrong thing. Can you help?"

Everyone, straight or LGBT, may get dumbstruck around death. But while there's really no distinction between what you would say to a bereaved same-sex partner and a widowed heterosexual, I can understand that you might be apprehensive about it. Try not to be. What's most important is that you convey respect for the primacy of your friend's relationship and his loss; for instance, "I'm so sorry about Juan's death. It's hard to imagine you without each other."

Acknowledging Sympathy Cards

If you're the partner, next of kin, or best friend of the deceased, you'll likely have received many expressions of condolence after your loved one's death. It's good manners to send thank-you notes for sympathy cards, letters, and flowers sent to you, for any donations to a charity on behalf of the deceased, or for specific acts of kindness. Try to do this within a couple of weeks. You'll be glad you made the effort, because it will allow you another opportunity to contemplate and savor each letter or gesture and the memory of the deceased. By the way, despite their prevalence, it's considered bad form to use preprinted cards like the ones that say "We appreciate your expression of sympathy" without adding a personal note,

if only a sentence or two in your own hand. Again, it's about making an effort in response to an act of kindness.

To help your note writing go more quickly and less emotionally, especially if you have a lot of acknowledgments to write, jot down ten generic sentences on a notepad and then select a few to use for each note, rearranging and personalizing them as needed. Such sentences could include: "Thank you for remembering Jack," "Your flowers were so beautiful," or "Your gift of food [be specific] came at a time when it was most needed," and "Your friendship over the years has meant so much to us."

Others prefer to write completely original notes for each person. Here are two examples of personal thank-yous for this occasion:

Dear Laurence,
Thank you for taking the time to write me about how much Jay's work with Lambda Legal meant to you and how much his efforts helped others in the fight for marriage equality. It was so good to have you remind me about that part of his life.
Fondly, Chris

Debbie,
I truly appreciate your kind offer to help me with the dogs at this very confusing and difficult time. As you know, Heidi and I got married in Massachusetts only two years ago but we were so fortunate to have even that short period of time together. I'll call next week.
Love,
Juanita

After the Service

The end of a funeral or memorial service certainly does not mark the end of mourning; on the contrary, this is the period when survivors are making their first efforts to get used to life without the deceased. In the weeks and months following a loved one's death, continue to offer assistance with meals and other chores, with the assumption that your company alone will be helpful. Anyone who has lost a partner, friend, or family member may need long-term support.

Even years later, some people appreciate a mention of the deceased's name, as well as the telling of stories that help to keep our memories alive of those whom we miss. Explains one woman who lost her partner fifteen years ago, "I call her mother every year, specifically on Julia's birthday, which helps us both feel better." You might also remember the deceased on an anniversary (wedding or otherwise)—or by making a quiet toast or writing a card of remembrance.

Glossary

See also the list of commonly used abbreviations in personal ads on page 73.

Biphobia: A form of prejudice based on the fear, hatred, or dislike of bisexuals (see also **bisexual**).

Bisexual (also bi): Someone who is attracted sexually, physically, and/or emotionally to both men and women.

Civil union: A legal partnership available to same-sex couples in a handful of states; civil unions provide only some of the rights available to straight married couples, such as the ability to file state taxes jointly, medical benefits, and estate planning, but none of the federal rights, protections, and responsibilities of marriage. Civil unions are not recognized by the federal government. (See also **commitment ceremony; domestic partnership**.)

Closet; closeted: A word used to describe a state of not being "out" about your sexual orientation or gender identity. If you're "in the closet" or "closeted," you're being secretive about your LGBT identity. (See also **coming out**.)

Coming out: Being comfortable and open about one's sexual orientation or gender identity. Short for "coming out of the closet." (See also **closet**.)

Commitment ceremony: A marriagelike rite marking a couple's union, generally with a group of friends and family in attendance. Some religions recognize such ceremonies, but

they have no legal status. (See also **civil union; domestic partnership**.)

Cross-dresser: Someone who occasionally dresses as the other gender. This term is preferred over the word "transvestite," which is considered pejorative. Note that there's not necessarily a connection between cross-dressing and sexual orientation or gender identity. (See also **transgender; transsexual**.)

Domestic partnership: Another type of legal relationship for an unmarried couple. Domestic partnerships confer civil recognition and certain legal protections, but are secondary to a legal wedding. Increasing numbers of U.S. cities, states, and places of business afford domestic partners specific benefits, such as health and life insurance. Domestic partners can be same-sex or opposite-sex. (See also **civil union; commitment ceremony**.)

"Don't ask, don't tell": Shorthand for the U.S. military policy on gay men, lesbians, and bisexuals. Recently voted down by Congress, the policy prohibited service members from revealing their sexual orientation; at the same time it prohibited the military from asking or pursuing rumors about it. Considered discriminatory.

Down low: A term used to refer to men who secretly have sex with other men but don't identify as gay or bisexual, and may have concurrent relationships with women. Often abbreviated, as in the expression "being on the DL." (See also **MSM**.)

Drag: Dressing oneself as a member of the opposite sex, sometimes for performance or for humorous effect. Those "doing" drag often act in styles typically associated with the opposite sex. Men who dress as women are called drag queens; women who dress as men are drag kings.

Dyke: A slang word for lesbian. Can be used pejoratively or for offense by some, but also as friendly slang among lesbians. (See also **faggot**.)

Ex-gay: Someone who has supposedly "cured" him- or herself (or been cured) of homosexuality. Many of the organizations that claim to help people change their sexual attractions from same-sex to opposite-sex have ties to fundamentalist religious groups. This movement has been widely discredited by psychologists and LGBT civil-rights organizations.

Faggot: A pejorative word for a gay man, often shortened to "fag." Considered offensive when used by straight people, but sometimes understood as friendly slang among LGBT people, especially gay men. (See also **dyke**.)

FTM: An acronym for "female to male" (see also **transgender; transman**).

Gay: Someone who is sexually, physically, and/or emotionally attracted only to the same sex. Used as both an adjective and a noun, this word has largely replaced "homosexual" in referring to gay men. It also can refer to lesbians. (When referring only to women, "lesbian" is the preferred term.) (See also **homosexual; lesbian**.)

Gender expression: The outward manifestation of gender identity, as expressed through clothing, behavior, or physical characteristics (see also **gender identity**).

Gender identity: A person's emotional and psychological sense of being male, female, a combination of genders, or neither. Someone's gender identity is not necessarily the same as his or her biological gender. (See also **gender expression**.)

Heterosexism: An assumption that heterosexuality is universal. Also, a presumption that heterosexuality is superior to homosexuality.

Heterosexual: Someone who is attracted sexually, physically, and/or emotionally only to the opposite sex. Often referred to as "straight."

Homophobia: Fear, hatred, or dislike of lesbians and gay men (see also **biphobia; transphobia**).

Homosexual: Someone who is sexually, physically, and/or emotionally attracted only to the same sex. Used as both an adjective and a noun, the term is often considered outdated if not derogatory; nonetheless, some LGBT people are embracing or reclaiming it. (See also **gay; lesbian**.)

Intersex: Those born with sex chromosomes, external genitalia, or internal reproductive organs that are not considered standard for either male or female. Parents and doctors usually choose to alter the bodies of intersex infants surgically or by hormone treatment, to conform to one sex or the other; this practice is increasingly controversial. (See also **LGBT**.)

Lesbian: A woman who is sexually, physically, and/or emotionally attracted only to other women. Some women prefer to be called "gay" rather than "lesbian"; others feel "gay" refers more to men. Also used as an adjective. (See also **gay; homosexual**.)

LGBT: An acronym for "lesbian, gay, bisexual, and transgender." Occasionally rendered as GLBT. Sometimes the letters "Q" and/or "I" are appended to be even more inclusive: "Q" stands for "queer" or "questioning," referring to those who are examining their sexual/gender identities or curious about nonheterosexual life; "I" for those who are intersex.

MSM: An acronym for "men who have sex with men," used to describe men who don't identify themselves as gay or bisexual (see also **down low**).

MTF: An acronym for "male to female" (see also **transgender; transwoman**).

Outing: The public revelation of another person's sexual orientation or gender identity, generally when that person hoped to keep that information private. The word, used as both a noun and a verb, comes from the expression "out of the closet." The act of outing is usually considered inappropriate. (See also **closet; coming out**.)

Partner: One of the most common words for someone in a committed LGBT relationship. Other frequently used terms are "lover," "spouse," "girlfriend/boyfriend," and "husband/wife."

Queen: An effeminate gay man. While often considered pejorative, the word is sometimes regarded as affectionate slang among LGBT people.

Queer: Once a pejorative term for gay people, and sometimes still used that way, the word "queer" has been reclaimed by some LGBT people as an umbrella term.

Safe sex (also safer sex): Descriptive of sexual practices that attempt to reduce one's risk of transmitting STDs (or becoming infected), including HIV. The term "safer sex" is preferred by some HIV-prevention experts because it suggests that no sexual contact with others is 100 percent risk-free.

Sexual orientation: An innate sexual attraction. Gay, bisexual, and heterosexual are considered distinct sexual orientations. This is the preferred term, not "sexual preference"—the latter implies that sexuality is a result of choice, not biology.

Sexual preference: See **sexual orientation**.

Stealth: Transitioning between genders in secret, completely adopting a new identity, and generally leaving one's old life behind. (See also **transgender**.)

Stonewall Riots: The several nights of protest that occurred in New York City's Greenwich Village in June 1969 after the Stonewall Inn, a bar frequented by gay and transgender people, was raided by the police. The Stonewall Riots (also called the Stonewall Uprising or, simply, Stonewall) are regarded as marking the beginning of the modern LGBT civil rights movement.

Straight: See **heterosexual**.

Tranny: Short for transgender. It can be a friendly term when embraced by trans people, but is considered pejorative when used by others—those outside the transgender community should avoid it. (See also **transgender**.)

Transgender: Someone whose gender identity feels in conflict with the gender he or she was born with (or was assigned to) or with conventional male or female gender roles. Transgender is an umbrella term—the "T" in LGBT—and covers not only transsexuals, but cross-dressers, drag queens, and those who identify as bigender (both sexes) and genderqueer (neither sex, or a third sex). (See also **intersex; LGBT; transman; tranny; transsexual; transwoman**.)

Transman: A transgender person born with the biological identity of a female and the gender identity of a male. Also FTM, the acronym for "female to male," or F2M. Some transmen take measures to adopt more outwardly male characteristics, whether through surgery, hormone therapy, or behavior and mannerisms.

Transphobia: Fear, hatred, or dislike of transgender people or transsexuals (see also **biphobia; homophobia**).

Transsexual (TS): Someone who feels he or she was born into the wrong body and has generally given some thought to sexual reassignment surgery (SRS), through hormone replacement therapy and/or surgery. Many transsexuals prefer the term "transgender." (See also **transgender**.)

Transvestite: See **cross-dresser**.

Transwoman: A transgender person born with the biological identity of a male and the gender identity of a female. Also MTF, the acronym for "male to female," or M2F. Some transwomen take measures to adopt more outwardly female characteristics, whether through surgery, hormone therapy, or behavior and mannerisms.

Resources

ADDICTION AND RECOVERY

Crystal Meth Anonymous
www.crystalmeth.org
The twelve-step approach (set forth by Alcoholics Anonymous) is practiced in meetings throughout the country among crystal methamphetamine addicts—LGBT and not.

Gay and Lesbian Alcoholics
www.gayalcoholics.com
Resources for gay and lesbian alcoholics seeking recovery are collected on this website, ranging from gay-friendly Alcoholics Anonymous meetings to books about addiction.

The Pride Institute
http://pride-institute.com
This Minnesota-based nonprofit provides inpatient and outpatient treatment programs for the mental health and chemical dependency needs of the LGBT community.

Cruise Control: Understanding Sex Addiction in Gay Men, **by Robert Weiss (Alyson, 2005)**
Explores the difference between sexual compulsion and nonaddictive sexual behavior within the gay experience, along with resources for recovery.

The Politics of Crystal Meth: Gay Men Share Stories of Addiction and Recovery, **by Kenneth Cimino (Universal, 2005)**
Ten very personal tales of meth use and recovery are prefaced by an exploration of why so many gay men use methamphetamines, from homophobia to HIV.

Portrait of an Addict as a Young Man, **by Bill Clegg (Little, Brown, 2010)**
A powerful memoir of crystal meth addiction by a gay literary agent.

AGING

The Aging Initiative
www.thetaskforce.org/issues/aging
This National Gay and Lesbian Task Force project produced "Outing Age 2010," which makes recommendations for aging advocates, policy makers, and social service agencies.

The Elder Law Project
www.nclrights.org
This National Center for Lesbian Rights (NCLR) project advocates for policies to protect the medical and financial rights of LGBT elders, and also educates professionals.

The LGBT Aging Project

www.lgbtagingproject.org

A Boston-based nonprofit that works to make sure LGBT elders have equal access to life-prolonging benefits, protections, services, and institutions.

Services and Advocacy for Gay, Lesbian, Bisexual & Transgender Elders (SAGE)

www.sageusa.org

Works with LGBT elders to overcome the challenges of discrimination in senior service settings and help create informal caregiving support and new "family" networks.

Gen Silent

www.stumaddux.com

A 2010 documentary about the Stonewall generation of LGBT people who fought the first battles for equality but now face discrimination as elders and are in some cases returning to the closet.

CAREGIVER SERVICES

Family Caregiver Alliance: National Center on Caregiving

www.caregiver.org

A national clearinghouse that includes resources targeting LGBT caregivers such as moderated discussions and fact sheets.

Caregiving with Pride, edited by Karen I. Fredriksen-Goldsen (Routledge, 2007)

Practical information about informal caregiving between LGBT people, including frank talk about needing and receiving care.

CIVIL RIGHTS

Egale Canada

www.egale.ca

Fights homophobia in Canada by lobbying for more equitable laws, intervening in legal cases that have an impact on human rights and equality, and increasing public awareness.

The Equality Federation

www.equalityfederation.org

A national alliance of state-based LGBT advocacy organizations.

Family Equality Council

www.familyequality.org

Works at all levels of government to advance full social and legal equality for LGBT families.

The Gay & Lesbian Alliance Against Defamation (GLAAD)

www.glaad.org

Works to hold the media accountable for the words and images they present and to help grassroots LGBT organizations communicate effectively.

Human Rights Campaign (HRC)

www.hrc.org

Lobbies Congress and state and local officials for support of pro-LGBT bills, and mobilizes grassroots action among its members.

Lambda Legal

www.lambdalegal.org

Lambda lawyers fight for the rights of LGBT people and those with HIV through precedent-setting cases ranging from same-sex marriage to job discrimination.

National Center for Lesbian Rights (NCLR)

www.nclrights.org

Uses litigation, policy advocacy, and public education in pursuit of justice, fairness, and legal protections for all LGBT people.

National Gay and Lesbian Task Force (NGLTF)

www.thetaskforce.org

Helps equip activists and state and local organizations with the skills needed to organize broad-based campaigns to defeat anti-LGBT referenda and advance pro-LGBT laws.

Making Gay History: The Half-Century Fight for Lesbian and Gay Equal Rights, **by Eric Marcus (HarperCollins, 2002)**

Using the stories of more than sixty people, Marcus describes the battles of and the cultural changes brought about by the LGBT movement.

Stonewall, **by David Carter (St. Martin's Griffin, 2005)**

An hour-by-hour account of the 1969 riots outside the Stonewall Inn, viewed in the context of Greenwich Village life and the convergence of various social movements.

COMING OUT

BiNet USA

www.binetusa.org

Umbrella organization for bisexual, pansexual, fluid, and "somewhere in between" people as well as their friends and allies.

Children of Lesbians and Gays Everywhere (COLAGE)

www.colage.org

An organization of children, youth, and adults with one or more LGBT parent, focused on youth empowerment, leadership development, education, and advocacy.

Gay Canada

www.gaycanada.com

Online community for everything from personals to message board discussions and networking with LGBT professionals.

Gay, Lesbian and Straight Education Network (GLSEN)

www.glsen.org

Seeks to give LGBT youth a voice in the education community and the LGBT movement and addresses school climate issues such as bullying.

Straight Spouse Network

www.straightspouse.org

An international organization that provides support to heterosexual spouses/partners, current or former, of LGBT mates for constructively resolving coming-out problems.

How to Be a Happy Lesbian: A Coming Out Guide, **by Tracey Stevens and Katherine Wunder (Amazing Dreams, 2002)**

A humorous and helpful guide encouraging lesbians to love and accept themselves and live without fear or shame.

Outing Yourself: How to Come Out as Lesbian or Gay to Your Family, Friends, and Coworkers, **by Michelangelo Signorile (Simon & Schuster, 1996)**
The columnist and radio host presents a fourteen-step program for gay men and lesbians seeking to come to terms with their sexuality.

When I Knew, **by Robert Trachtenberg (Harper/It Books, 2005)**
A compilation of stories from eighty contributors about their first inklings that they might be interested in the same sex.

COMMUNITIES OF COLOR

Audre Lorde Project
http://alp.org
A New York City–based lesbian, gay, bisexual, two spirit, trans, and gender-nonconforming people of color community organizing center.

Human Rights Campaign (HRC)
www.hrc.org
Offers resource guides targeted specifically at LGBT African Americans, Latinos, and Asian Pacific Americans.

National Association of Black and White Men Together (NABWMT)
www.nabwmt.org
Focuses on fighting racism, sexism, homophobia, HIV/AIDS discrimination, and other inequities; it has chapters in thirty cities.

PFLAG Diversity Network
http://.community.pflag.org
Provides support and education nationwide to parents, friends, and coworkers of LGBT people. Also strives to make PFLAG members aware of cultural differences and issues in the LGBT community.

Drifting Toward Love: Black, Brown, Gay, and Coming of Age on the Streets of New York, **by Kai Wright (Beacon, 2008)**
Tracing the passage to gay identity for three young men of color, Wright touches on hate, violence, prostitution, drugs, HIV, and homelessness.

DEATH AND DYING

Gay Widowers: Life After the Death of a Partner, **by Michael Shernoff (Routledge, 1997)**
Explores the isolation, grief, and coping following the loss of a same-sex partner.

The Hurry-Up Song: A Memoir Of Losing My Brother, **by Clifford Chase (University of Wisconsin Press, 1999)**
The story of two gay brothers growing up in a suburban American family, one of whom dies of AIDS.

The Loss of a Life Partner, **by Carolyn Ambler Walter (Columbia University Press, 2003)**
Twenty-two stories of individuals whose partners have died, including a range of gay men and lesbians, against a backdrop of bereavement theories.

DOMESTIC VIOLENCE

Gay Men's Domestic Violence Project
http://gmdvp.org
Basic information about cycles of gay male relationship abuse and battery, plus a hotline (1-800-832-1901).

National Coalition of Anti-Violence Programs (NCAVP)
www.avp.org/ncavp.htm
A network of U.S. programs advocating for victims of anti-LGBT and anti-HIV/AIDS attacks, as well as victims of domestic violence (212-714-1141 or TTY: 212-714-1134).

The Network/La Red
www.thenetworklared.org
Bilingual hotline, shelter, and information on stopping partner abuse in lesbian, bisexual women's, and transgender communities (617-742-4911 or TTY: 617-227-4911).

FINANCES

Ameriprise
www.ameriprise.com
Helps locate LGBT-friendly financial advisors and offers advice on domestic partnerships and other binding arrangements.

Christopher Street Financial
www.christopherstreet.com
Financial and legal advisors to LGBT individuals and same-sex couples, on everything from tax issues to estate planning and investments.

Partnership Wealth Management
www.partnershipwealthmanagement.com
Baltimore-based group advises on investments and other financial decisions for a largely LGBT clientele.

Estate Planning for Same-Sex Couples, by Joan M. Burda (American Bar Association, 2004)
How same-sex couples can protect each other and their children, despite the tax and legal disadvantages of being in an LGBT family.

LEGAL ISSUES

See also Civil Rights

A Legal Guide for Lesbian & Gay Couples, by Denis Clifford, Frederick Hertz, and Emily Doskow (NOLO, 2010)
How to take the proper legal steps to define and protect your LGBT relationship in the eyes of the law, both in day-to-day life and to prepare yourself in the event of a crisis.

Making It Legal: A Guide to Same-Sex Marriage, Domestic Partnerships, & Civil Unions, by Frederick Hertz with Emily Doskow (NOLO, 2009)
Breaks down the legal and financial issues at stake when making decisions in the complex and ever-changing world of same-sex marriage.

Prenuptial Agreements: How to Write a Fair & Lasting Contract, 3rd ed., by Katherine E. Stoner and Shae Irving (NOLO, 2008)
How to decide whether a prenuptial agreement is right for you; assemble a draft; and negotiate a final contract.

MILITARY

OutServe
http://outserve.org
This underground network of actively serving LGBT soldiers (formerly known as Citizens for Repeal) was formed in 2010 to offer professional and social support to U.S. military personnel, and is now focused on the transition following the repeal of "Don't ask, don't tell."

Servicemembers Legal Defense Network (SLDN)
www.sldn.org
Originally dedicated to ending discrimination against and harassment of military personnel affected by "Don't ask, don't tell" and related forms of intolerance. Now focused on the implementation of the new "open service" regulations.

Ask & Tell: Gay and Lesbian Veterans Speak Out, by Steve Estes (University of North Carolina Press, 2008)
Interviews with more than fifty gay, lesbian, and bisexual veterans illustrate the harmful effects of the U.S. military's "Don't ask, don't tell" policy.

PARENTING

Circle Surrogacy
www.circlesurrogacy.com
Gay-focused agency that provides a full line of surrogacy and egg donation options through a network of supportive IVF clinics.

Growing Generations
www.growinggenerations.com
Los Angeles company with lots of LGBT clients helps build "families of choice" through sperm or egg donation and surrogacy.

Human Rights Campaign (HRC)
www.hrc.org/issues/parenting
This page on the HRC website tracks the relevant state laws on surrogacy, sperm donation, and LGBT adoption, along with related public policies.

Parents, Families, and Friends of Lesbians and Gays (PFLAG)
http://community.pflag.org (U.S.);
www.pflagcanada.ca (Canada)
Promotes the well-being of LGBT people, their families, and friends through direct support, advocacy, and efforts to enlighten the general public.

The Rainbow Babies
www.therainbowbabies.com
Resources and information for LGBT parents and those considering starting a family, including local meet-ups and online discussion groups.

The Complete Lesbian & Gay Parenting Guide, by Arlene Istar Lev (Berkley Trade, 2004)
A comprehensive manual for LGBT parenting that covers emotional, legal, even racial issues of building a family, and includes a range of personal stories as well.

The Gay Baby Boom: The Psychology of Gay Parenthood, by Suzanne M. Johnson and Elizabeth O'Connor (NYU Press, 2002)
Written by two developmental psychologists, this book reports the findings of the Gay and Lesbian Family Study, the largest national assessment of gay- and lesbian-headed families.

Heather Has Two Mommies, by Lesléa Newman (Alyson, 1989)
The groundbreaking children's book about a preschooler with two moms who discovers that some of her friends have very different sorts of families.

The Ultimate Guide to Pregnancy for Lesbians, 2nd ed., by Rachel Pepper (Cleis, 2005)
A friendly guide to insemination that takes lesbians right up through the first weeks after the baby's birth.

RELATIONSHIPS AND DATING

Curve Personals
http://curvepersonals.com
One of many small-scale lesbian-focused personals sites. (Note: Lots of gay and bisexual women also use such all-purpose dating sites as Nerve.com and Match.com.)

Gay.com
www.gay.com
A site that's great for sex dates with gay and bi men, but you'll also find many members seeking short-term or long-term relationships. (See also PlanetOut.com, Chemistry.com, and Yahoo! personals.)

Gay and Single . . . Forever? 10 Things Every Gay Guy Looking for Love (and Not Finding It) Needs to Know, by Steven Bereznai (Da Capo Press, 2006)
A look at the pressure to partner and what that means for a gay man who's never had a boyfriend.

Girl Meets Girl: A Dating Survival Guide, by Diana Cage (Alyson, 2007)
Colorful advice about meeting other women, making the first move, who picks up the tab, flirting, and surviving bad dates.

Lesbian Couples: A Guide to Creating Healthy Relationships, by D. Merilee Clunis and G. Dorsey Green (Seal Press, 2004)
Two therapists look at lesbian relationships by exploring everything from conflict-resolution to butch-femme issues, substance abuse, and more.

Love Between Men: Enhancing Intimacy and Resolving Conflicts in Gay Relationships, by Rik Isensee (Backinprint.com, 2005)
A look at male-male relationships in the context of challenges such as unsupportive families, AIDS, and various concepts of monogamy.

RELIGION

Dignity USA
www.dignityusa.org
Organization for Roman Catholics concerned about the church's sexual theology, particularly as it pertains to LGBT people; the group works with other Catholic organizations to reform the church's teachings.

Dignity Canada Dignité
www.dignitycanada.org
The Canadian equivalent of Dignity USA (see above).

Gay Buddhist Fellowship
http://gaybuddhist.org
San Francisco Bay area–based group for gay men that offers meditation, guest speakers, and spiritual teachings. See the website for other chapters.

Gay Church
www.gaychurch.org
A good site for finding gay or LGBT-friendly Christian churches throughout the United States and overseas.

Bulletproof Faith: A Spiritual Survival Guide for Gay and Lesbian Christians, **by Candace Chellew-Hodge (Jossey-Bass, 2008)**
Spiritual survival tips from a gay Christian searching for how to live with integrity while contending with sometimes hateful opposition.

A Jihad for Love, **directed by Parvez Sharma**
A 2007 documentary about being gay and Muslim that follows the stories of men and women trying to reconcile their sexuality with Islamic teachings.

Twice Blessed: On Being Lesbian or Gay and Jewish, **by Christie Balka and Andy Rose (Beacon Press, 1991)**
Essays addressing everything from growing up in a yeshiva to finding a new Judaism-based theology of gay sexuality.

What the Bible Really Says About Homosexuality, **by Daniel A. Helminiak (Alamo Square, 2000)**
An accessible analysis of biblical references commonly cited as denouncing homosexuality, which the author says meant something quite different in their own time.

SEXUAL HEALTH AND WELLNESS (INCLUDING HIV/AIDS)

Canadian AIDS Treatment Information Exchange (CATIE)
www.catie.ca
Extensive HIV resources, along with explanations of basic HIV science and research and practical thinking on prevention issues. In both English and French.

GMHC
www.gmhc.org
Among the largest providers of HIV/AIDS prevention, care, and advocacy in the country, GMHC serves HIV-positive clients in the New York area.

Latino Commission on AIDS
www.latinoaids.org
Works to educate the Latino community about HIV, develops model prevention programs for high-risk communities, and supports community organizations.

Project Inform
www.projectinform.org
Helps speed HIV medications to market, educates positive people about HIV care, and influences government support for public health.

The Good Vibrations Guide to Sex: The Most Complete Sex Manual Ever Written, **by Cathy Winks and Anne Semans (Cleis, 2004)**
Both educational and entertaining, this extensive volume covers everything from basic sexual anatomy to SM and "packing," with LGBT and straight sex on equal par.

The Joy of Gay Sex, **3rd ed., by Charles Silverstein and Felice Picano (HarperCollins, 2004)**
A sex guide, a resource on building self-esteem, and a trusted aid for coming out of the closet, this book covers gay male sex alphabetically from "anus" to "wrestling."

100 Questions & Answers About HIV and AIDS, **by Joel E. Gallant (Jones and Bartlett, 2007)**
An infectious disease specialist provides understandable explanations for the most common concerns about HIV/AIDS.

The Whole Lesbian Sex Book: A Passionate Guide for All of Us, **by Felice Newman (Cleis Press, 2004)**
A how-to guide for everything from basic oral sex to piercings and the SM hanky code, along with commentary on lesbian sexual politics.

TEENS/YOUTH/SCHOOL

Gender Spectrum
www.genderspectrum.org
Provides consultation, training, and events to families, educators, professionals, and organizations to create a more gender-sensitive and inclusive environment for all children and teens, at school and beyond.

The Point Foundation
www.pointfoundation.org
Provides scholarships, mentorship, and leadership training for students who have been marginalized due to sexual orientation, gender identity, or gender expression.

The Safe Schools Coalition
www.safeschoolscoalition.org
Resources for educators, parents/guardians, and youth dealing with or seeking to prevent anti-LGBT harassment and violence in schools.

The Trevor Project
www.thetrevorproject.org
Around-the-clock suicide-prevention helpline for gay and questioning youth. (Call 1-866-488-7386.)

The Gay and Lesbian Guide to College Life, **by John Baez, Jennifer Howd, and Rachel Pepper, and the Staff of the Princeton Review (Princeton Review, 2007)**
How to thrive on campus as an LGBT student, including advice from students and administrators at more than seventy of the nation's top colleges.

Gender, Bullying, and Harassment: Strategies to End Sexism and Homophobia in Schools, **by Elizabeth J. Meyer (Teachers College Press, 2009)**
An examination of bullying in schools that provides practical ideas for individuals and institutions interested in making schools safe.

GLBTQ: The Survival Guide for Queer and Questioning Teens, **by Kelly Huegel (Free Spirit, 2003)**
A practical guide for LGBT or questioning teens and their peers and parents, written in a non-judgmental voice and with young, modern style.

TRANSGENDER

Laura's Playground
www.lauras-playground.com
Support, resources, and tips about transitioning and other issues of transgender living.

National Center for Transgender Equality
www.transequality.org
A social justice organization dedicated to advancing the equality of transgender people through advocacy, collaboration, and empowerment.

Transgender Canada
www.transgendercanada.com
An active forum on trans issues, plus a list of resources coast-to-coast.

Her Name Was Steven
CNN documentary following Steve Stanton's journey to becoming Susan, after being fired when a newspaper revealed Steve was going to change his gender.

Original Plumbing
www.originalplumbing.com
A quarterly magazine that aims to document the diversity of trans male lifestyles through photographic portraits and essays, personal narratives, and interviews.

The Transgender Child, **by Stephanie Brill and Rachel Pepper (Cleis Press, 2008)**
A realistic but empowering guide to the medical and legal issues regarding the confusing social situations and the emotional challenges of raising a gender-variant child.

Transgender Law Center
http://transgenderlawcenter.org
California-based civil rights organization that connects transgender people and their families to technically sound and culturally competent legal services.

TRAVEL

Damron
http://damron.com
This company has been putting out gay guidebooks since 1964, lately supplementing them with a handy website.

GlobalGayz.com
www.globalgayz.com
A travel and culture website focused on LGBT life in nearly 200 countries that is based on actual visits.

Olivia
www.olivia.com
A travel service catering to lesbians, which features upscale resorts and a wide range of cruises. It emphasizes complete privacy for women.

Out Traveler
www.outtraveler.com
A full-service guide for LGBT travelers that is frequently updated with new tips about bars, hotels, and all the rest.

R Family Vacations

www.rfamilyvacations.com
Family-focused LGBT vacations, ranging from kid-friendly boat rides with Nickelodeon characters to adult-only cruises of the Greek islands.

The Travel Alternatives Group

www.tagapproved.com
Lists hotels that don't "discriminate on the basis of sexual orientation in their employment practices . . . and strive to create a gay-friendly experience for their guests."

WEDDINGS

Equally Wed

http://equallywed.com
An online "magazine" for couples planning a same-sex wedding or honeymoon, featuring news about the marriage debate and "real" wedding pictures.

GayRites

www.gayrites.net
A guide to planning a same-sex marriage, from researching your rights to finding vendors and choosing your vows.

Gayweddings.com

www.gayweddings.com
Advice, gifts, invitations, fashion guides, and everything else you need to plan a wedding—or keep up with the civil rights debates.

MyRegistry.com

www.myregistry.com
Gift registries for weddings and other events that allow users to request and deliver gifts from any store in the world, even those without websites.

Outvite

www.outvite.com
Custom-printed invitation site for LGBT people, which includes a "Commitment and Wedding" section.

Rainbow Wedding Network

www.rainbowweddingnetwork.com
Lists LGBT-friendly wedding vendors and other businesses in the United States and Canada and provides tools for organizing a ceremony, invitations, gifts, and more.

The Complete Guide to Gay and Lesbian Weddings, **by K. C. David and the Experts at GayWeddings.com (St. Martin's, 2005)**
A step-by-step wedding planner, including checklists and advice.

The New Essential Guide to Gay and Lesbian Weddings, **2nd ed., by Tess Ayers and Paul Brown (Alyson, 2009)**
An updated version of an indispensable guide, including real-world anecdotes and unexpected historical trivia, from the philosophical to the practical.

WORKPLACE

HRC Best Places to Work
www.hrc.org/issues/best-places-to-work-2011.htm
The Human Rights Campaign's annual guide to businesses that support equality for lesbian, gay, bisexual, and transgender employees.

Out & Equal Workplace Advocates
www.outandequal.org
A national organization dedicated to achieving workplace equality for lesbian, gay, bisexual, and transgender employees and professionals.

Pride at Work
www.prideatwork.org
Labor union (AFL-CIO) activists seeking equality for LGBT workers in workplaces and their unions.

Allies at Work: Creating a Lesbian, Gay, Bisexual and Transgender Inclusive Work Environment, **by Dr. David M. Hall (Out and Equal Workplace Advocates, 2009)**
Details the importance of LGBT allies in shaping workplace climates and the impact of living in the closet.

Lavender Road to Success: The Career Guide for the Gay Community, **by Kirk Snyder (Ten Speed Press, 2004)**
What it means to be gay in the workplace, why you will make more money out of the closet at work, and how to find an employer that's your perfect match.

Acknowledgments

This book has benefited from the kindnesses of strangers, friends, and colleagues. Indeed, a virtual *Who's Who* of dedicated professionals and layfolk gave their time and knowledge to help shape, deepen, and guide this book—parents, children, teenagers, couples, caterers, florists, lawyers and advocates, financial advisers, personal trainers and masseurs, wedding planners, travel agents, workplace specialists, hospice workers, photographers, DJs, undertakers, doctors, psychologists, activists, teachers and professors, fashion designers and haberdashers, hair stylists, publicists, politicians, producers, and many more.

———•———•———

Among all those who assisted me, however, I am most thankful for an esteemed group of advisers who read and edited chapters, challenged my thinking, broadened the scope of this book, and in every sense went beyond the call of duty. These good soldiers of etiquette include (in alphabetical order): Frank Andonoplas (Frank Event Design*), John Bartlett (menswear designer), Joel Baum (Gender Spectrum), Raymond Boney (Raymond Boney Event & Publicity Management), Vince Calcagno (restaurateur and Zuni Café cofounder), Lawrence Edwards, Psy.D. (private practice), Mark S. King

Institutional affiliations are for identification purposes only

(MyFabulousDisease.com), Joanne Laipson (Outvite.com), Jim May, LCSW (Duke Hospice), Richard McDonough (Van Horn-McDonough Funeral Home), Shannon Minter, Esq. (National Center for Lesbian Rights), Ian Palmquist (Equality NC), Maddy Petrow-Cohen, MSW (LGBT private practice), Terri Phoenix (University of North Carolina, Chapel Hill, LGBTQ Center), Ed Salvato (LGBT travel expert), Fred Silverman (Marin Community Foundation), Ron Stall, Ph.D., MPH (University of Pittsburgh Graduate School of Public Health), Peter Vincent (Time Inc.), and Bob Witeck (Witeck-Combs Communications).

At Workman Publishing, I was very fortunate to have both Peter Workman and Susan Bolotin take an early interest in this project, soon joined by Bob Miller. Their zeal and support for this project has made such a difference; and working with Suzie has shown me that editors in the twenty-first century still care about the art and craft of language! When I asked specifically for a gay editor, I could not have been more fortunate than to be placed in the generous and wise hands of Trent Duffy from Workman's sister imprint, Artisan (and Trent now gets to return to the beautiful cookbooks he's always produced for some of our best-known and loved chefs). And who could ask for a more talented creative director than David Matt; his reputation is legendary, his kindness and persistence so appreciated. And then there's the rest of the Workman team, whose professionalism is simply tops: Laura Andriani, Savannah Ashour, Marilyn Barnett, Tom Boyce, Jarrod Dyer, Page Edmunds, Avery Finch, Andrea Fleck-Nisbet, Joe Ginis, Sara High, Anne Kerman, Jenny Mandel, Selina Meere, Steven Pace, Barbara Peragine, Kristina Peterson, Michael Rockliff, David Schiller, Lidija Tomas, Janet Vicario, Beth Wareham, James Wehrle, Walter Weintz, Jodi Weiss, and Jessica Wiener. You guys really rock! Thanks to the very talented Paul Cox for the evocative illustrations throughout the book. (I'd be remiss in not praising the photographer and stylist who took such good care of me in doing my publicity shots: Bryan Regan and Shannon Hall. And thanks to the North Carolina Museum of Art for letting us in to shoot.)

———————

I always feel privileged to have Richard Pine at Inkwell Management as my literary agent. As both friend and adviser (and sometimes quasi-therapist) for more than fifteen years, Richard helps me to think about the arc of my literary life as well as the day-to-day minutiae of making a book. Gratitude also to the fabulous Elisa Petrini at Inkwell.

Then there are my friends at Everyday Health, Inc. (née Waterfront Media), where I've had another life as an editor during the three years I've worked on this book. Were it not for the support and friendship of Ben Wolin and Mike Keriakos, the book would simply not have lived to see the light of day. Thank you so much, guys! I've also learned a lot from our very talented Everyday Health authors, whom I gladly count as friends, too: Sari and Arthur Agatston, Denise Austin, Joy and Ian Bauer, Jillian Michaels, Suzanne Somers, Heidi (ms) and Erik (ss) Murkoff, and Jessica Wu.

Over the past years, fortune has smiled on me in the guise of residencies and fellowships at several esteemed writers' colonies, including the Virginia Center for the Creative Arts, the Vermont Studio Center, and The Porches Writing Retreat in rural Virginia. In this day and age, artists and writers are fortunate to have institutions such as these to provide both financial and creative support for our work. Special call-outs to Suny Monk, Carol O'Brien, Dana Jones, Bea Booker, and Gary Clark. At the Carrboro Creative Collective, where I worked on this book from my tiny closet of an office (but mine nonetheless), I appreciate the ribald support from my colleagues there, especially Michael Linnane, Brent Winter, and Brian Russell.

To this list, I must add my friend and former editor David Rakoff, who first saw the need for this kind of book, resulting in *The Essential Book of Gay Manners & Etiquette*, which we collaborated on many years ago. Thank you, David.

Since that book was published in the mid-1990s, much has changed in the world, not the least my expansion to the Internet, where I've had a first-rate group develop and maintain gaymanners.com, including: Ian Cook, Tony Brancato, Lisa Michurski, Jodi Paige-Lee (as always), Phoebe Reed, and Kristin Sladen. Jon Kimball: Thank you for the greatest steal of all time; you know what I mean.

To all my Facebook "fans" (Facebook.com/gaymanners) and Twitter followers (Twitter.com/gaymanners), a *huge* shout-out for responding to my various "Questions of the Day," participating in polls, and providing me with a constant pulse of real-world perspectives.

The well-connected troika at Media Masters Publicity (Ron Longe, Karen Wadsworth, and Tracy Daniels) has most certainly helped to pave the way for this book with their PR acumen. And Michael Taeckens at Algonquin, thank you for introducing us.

I'm also indebted to the many friends and colleagues who contributed to this project, whether reading parts of chapters, sitting for impromptu interviews, publishing early versions of this work, connecting me to others, or pouring glasses of wine (or even better, Manhattans): Chuck Adams, Ted Allen, Amy Barr, Jon Barrett, Amy and Peter Bernstein, Emma Bing, Jay Blotcher, Akilah Bolden-Monifa, Kathy Briccetti, Rich Cox, Allan Davis, Charlie Deal, Rick de Beauclair, Dory Devlin, Joe Dolce, Chris Duncan, Robin Epstein, Vince Errico, Julie Fenster, Laura Ann Freeman, Ina Turpen Fried, Michelle Garcia, John Habich, Kathryn Hamm, Mike Harrer, Katia Hetter, Susan Horowitz, Robert Huls, Denise Kessler, Jamie Lamkin, Jen Laskey, Marcia Lippman, Jonathan Louie, Susan Love, Lora Ma-Fukuda, Eric Marcus, Greg Mertl, Eleanor Meyer, Max Micozzi, Tom Musbach, Molly O'Neill, David Parker, Bruce Payne, Cynthia Perry, Cathy Renna, Margaret Rich, Steve Rothaus, Rhonda Scovill, Susan Seehusen, Bruce Shenitz, David and Roberto Shiver, Lisa Sorg, Ralph Spielman, Frank Stasio, Jeff Stephenson, Nathan Stephenson, Robin Stevens, Lindsay

Thomas, Vicki Threlfall, Amy Tornquist, Michael Tune, Ellen Ullman, Jennifer Vanasco, John Vasconcelles, Linda Villarosa, Ross von Metzke, Jim Walker, Jane Wampler, Brett Webb-Mitchell, Beth Weise, and Susan Schild Weiss.

I've also benefited from a great team that provided research and other crucial book assistance: Roseann Henry (especially for her contributions to the family chapters and her hilarious sense of humor), Cody Lallier (researcher extraordinaire), Ariel Levin, and Jen Christensen.

Then there's my cowriter and now friend, Sally Chew. Sally's contributions to this project cannot be overestimated and her imprint is on every page. Not to mention that she kept me on track, organized, and almost sane. Thank you so much, Sally Chew.

Finally, there's my family, who have been remarkably understanding about the solitary nature and seemingly endless arc of this work: My siblings and their spouses, Julie and Maddy Petrow-Cohen, Jay Petrow and Nancy Clarke (and my nieces and nephews, Jessica and Caroline, William and Anna), my parents, Richard and Margot Petrow, and my parents-in-law, Helen Bean and her late husband, Bill.

And last, but certainly not least, I am a lucky guy to have Jim Bean as my partner. Midway through the book, when I had disappeared yet again to work on chapters, he said, "I had no idea what it would be like for you to write a book as big as this one." Indeed, I didn't either, but I also had no idea what it would be like to have a friend, companion, and spouse like Jim. Now, I do. Thank you, honey.

Index

A Letter from Steven

Dear Readers,

After being asked question after question about how to live your best LGBT life (as Oprah would say), I began the first nationally syndicated gay manners column to answer friends' and strangers' queries alike. I still write it—I love that it's called "Queeries"—not only because it's so much fun for me, but also because I know it touches a large number of people, most of them young and LGBT. That sometimes overwhelming interest—and need—lies behind this big book of LGBT manners that you're holding in your hands. I just knew there had to be a resource for all the milestone events in our lives: **coming out, dating, starting a relationship, getting "gay-married," dealing with anti-gay bullying, starting a family (and raising the kids), and much more.**

In between the column and the book, I created the website GayManners.com, now a vibrant community of LGBTers seeking advice—and sharing their own experiences—or simply looking for a place to find the latest tips and up-to-date resources. The back-and-forth with my readers (you!) means that I'm able to provide quicker responses to your questions—and it keeps me in the know about what's on your mind too.

All my best,

Steven

Visit GayManners.com today and you can:

- Ask me your **personal questions**—about sex etiquette, dating, moving in together, using social media, raising a kid with two moms or two dads . . . whatever's on your mind.

- Take our **interactive poll** (known as the Q Poll) to find out how your views stack up.

- Sign up for our **free e-mail newsletter**, "Queeries," a timely digest of everything you need to know today about LGBT life and manners.

- Find late-breaking **information and advice** for living your LGBT life.

- **Meet and make friends** with other LGBT people like yourself, although there's also plenty of room for our straight allies–friends, colleagues, and family members.

 Facebook.com/gaymanners   Twitter.com/gaymanners   Gaymanners.com